Governance by Decree

The Impact of the Voting Rights Act in Dallas

Ruth P. Morgan

 University Press of Kansas

Published by the University Press of Kansas (Lawrence, Kansas 66049), which was organized by the Kansas Board of Regents and is operated and funded by Emporia State University, Fort Hays State University, Kansas State University, Pittsburg State University, the University of Kansas, and Wichita State University

Library of Congress Cataloging-in-Publication Data

Morgan, Ruth P., 1934–

  Governance by decree : the impact of the Voting Rights Act in Dallas / Ruth P. Morgan.

    p. cm.—(Studies in government and public policy)

Includes bibliographical references and index.

  ISBN 0-7006-1306-4 (cloth : alk. paper)—ISBN 0-7006-1307-2 (pbk. : alk. paper)

    1. Dallas (Tex.)—Politics and government.   2. Dallas (Tex.)—Race relations.   3. Dallas (Tex.)—Social conditions.   4. Election law—United States.   5. United States. Voting Rights Act of 1965.   I. Title. II. Series.

  JS803.2.M67   2004

  320.9764′2812—dc22   2003023964

British Library Cataloguing-in-Publication Data is available.

Governance by Decree

STUDIES IN GOVERNMENT
AND PUBLIC POLICY

Contents

List of Tables and Illustrations   vii

Acknowledgments   ix

List of Abbreviations   xi

Chronology   xiii

Introduction   1

PART I. POLITICAL PARTICIPATION AND THE LAW

1. The Voting Rights Act   9
    Evolution of Voting Rights Law   12
    The Voting Rights Act of 1965   15
    The Voting Rights Act Amendments   21
    Administrative Enforcement   29

2. Voting Rights Case Law   33
    Background   38
    Phases of Voting Rights Litigation   41
    The Voting Rights Act in Court   56

PART II. CONTEXT FOR POLITICAL PARTICIPATION IN DALLAS

3. History and Culture of the City   67
    Attitudes and Mythology   67
    Distinctive Historical Experiences   73
    Population and Economic Variables   79

4. Political Heritage   88
    Formal Rules: Charters and Election Laws   88
    Informal Rules: Parties and Slating Groups   102
    Opaque Rules: The Power Structure   113

5. Dallas in Court, 1967–1991   119
    The Goldblatt Case   121
    The Lipscomb Cases   124
    The Williams Case   140

PART III. THE LEGACY OF LEGISLATION AND LITIGATION

6. Electoral Effects of the VRA in Dallas   155
    Ballot Access   156
    Campaign Finance   166
    Redistricting   168
    Faces and Places   177

7. Governance Consequences   197
    Council-Manager Form of Government: Modified   197
    Relations Between Officials and Self-Appointed Policy Makers   225

8. Policy Results   229
    Setting the Agenda: Top Down   230
    Setting the Agenda: Bottom Up   247

Conclusions   268

Appendixes
    A. Candidates for the Dallas City Council by Race, Date of Candidacy,
        and Date of Election, 1967–1997   279
    B. Dallas City Council Members, 1967–2001   288

References   291

List of Cases   307

Index   311

Tables and Illustrations

Tables

Post-CCA *Dallas Morning News* Endorsements   161
Council Seats Held by Race   181
Comparison of Number of Council Seats Proportionate to Population with
    Actual Seats Held by Race/Ethnicity   183
Council Member Occupations by Election System   186
Election Success Rate of Candidacies by Race   190
Noncompetitive Election Comparisons   191

Figures

Vote in Majority Black Precincts Compared: 1971 City Council Election and
    1972 U.S. Presidential Election   160
1971 Dallas City Council Districts   170
1981 Dallas City Council Districts   171
1991 Dallas City Council Districts   172
2001 Dallas City Council Districts   173
Four 1991 Gerrymandered Dallas City Council Districts   175
Comparison of Dallas City Council District 2 in 1991 and 2001   177
Voter Turnout as Percentage of Registered Voters and Registered Voters as
    Percentage of Population, 1971–2001   194

Acknowledgments

As with all projects that span a number of years, I have accumulated many debts along the way. It would be impossible for me to acknowledge all those individuals with whom I have discussed some of the issues in this book, or who have assisted me in specific ways. A few deserve special mention.

Community leaders and public officials, listed elsewhere, generously granted interviews. Adlene Harrison and Mary Poss were notably liberal with their time. Many of the interviews I conducted could not find their way into the book, but they all added to my perspective.

Council member Lois Finkelman gave me the opportunity to work in the trenches as her appointee to the 2001 City of Dallas Redistricting Commission.

Karen Ferrell Lentz correlated census tract data with voting precinct boundaries to identify the majority black precincts.

Especially helpful at Dallas City Hall were Donald C. Walker, urban policy analyst; Jeff D. Watson, elections manager; J. Brooks Love, elections manager; and Cindy C. Smolovik, archivist.

Others who provided special assistance or information include Desmond Bond, Ruth Miller Fitzgibbons, Estevan T. Flores, Mark Gilman, Robin Gruner, Bonnie Harris, Gregory Ivy, Carolyn Jeter, Billie Stovall, Harriet Sullivan, and Billie Wood.

The final product was improved by the comments and suggestions of Anthony Champagne and an anonymous peer reviewer.

The professional staff at the University Press of Kansas was a pleasure to work with at every stage of production. I am particularly indebted to the director, Fred Woodward, for his vision and guidance.

Priceless friends allowed me to talk about the topic for years but had the good grace to quit asking when the book would finally be finished.

More broadly, my gratitude extends to Southern Methodist University for the supportive and collegial environment it afforded for teaching and research. My abiding professional debt is to the university's late president A. Kenneth Pye, not only for his confidence in me as provost but for his understanding when I wanted to leave office to pursue my scholarly interests, including this project.

Mainly, I am beholden to my son, Glenn Morgan, whose demanding and insightful critique, tempered by encouragement, produced a number of changes for the better. He challenged me to stay on topic and prodded this project to completion.

Deep appreciation extends to my family for their love and support through the years of research and writing. Glenn, Peg, Erin, and Zach received less of my undivided attention than I wished. My husband, Vernon, deferred many of his own plans to provide steady support of my commitment to this work. Foremost and always, I am indebted to him for his forbearance and encouragement.

Abbreviations

CCA	Citizens Charter Association
CDBG	Community Development Block Grant Program
CGS	Committee for Good Schools
CRD	Civil Rights Division
CRG	Citizens for Representative Government
DART	Dallas Area Rapid Transit
DCC	Dallas Citizens Council
DHA	Dallas Homeowners Association
DHL	Dallas Homeowners League
DISD	Dallas Independent School District
DOJ	Department of Justice
EPA	Environmental Protection Agency
HUD	U.S. Department of Housing and Urban Development
LEAD	League for Educational Advancement in Dallas
NAACP	National Association for the Advancement of Colored People
PAC	Political Action Committee
PR	proportional representation
PVL	Progressive Voters League
TI	Texas Instruments
VRA	Voting Rights Act
WPA	Work Projects Administration

Chronology

1841	First settlement in Dallas County.
1856	State of Texas issues papers of incorporation for Dallas.
1856–1907	Mayor-Alderman form of government, with aldermen elected from wards and mayor elected at large (except during Civil War and Reconstruction).
1902	Poll tax becomes a requirement for voting in Texas.
1907–1931	Mayor-Commission form of government, with mayor and four commissioners elected at large.
1912	Voters ratify home-rule amendment to the Texas Constitution; Dallas adopts its first home-rule charter in 1914.
1931	Citizens Charter Association is formed to spearhead drive for council-manager form of government.
	Charter election establishes council-manager form of government, with a city council of nine members, six elected at large from residence districts, three elected at large without a residence district requirement, and the mayor elected by the city council.
1949	Charter election approves direct election of the mayor.
1962	Supreme Court holds in *Baker* v. *Carr* that legislative apportionment is a matter subject to resolution by the courts.
1965	Voting Rights Act passes.
1966	Voters amend Texas Constitution to repeal poll tax as a requirement for voting.
1967	C. A. Galloway, the first black and the first non-white councilman, is appointed to fill an unexpired term.
	Max Goldblatt challenges the 6-3 at-large system.
1968	Three-judge federal court in a summary judgment holds that the Dallas 6-3 plan meets all the constitutional tests.
	Neighborhood association movement develops and Dallas Homeowners League is incorporated.
	Charter referendum enlarges city council from nine to eleven, with eight single-member districts and three at-large districts. City council appoints two new members, George Allen (black) and Henry Stuart (white).
	Charter referendum deletes "Segregation of the Races" section in the 1931 Dallas City Charter.
1969	First election under 8-3 plan, all elected at large, with eight residence districts. George Allen becomes the first council member of African descent to be elected to the Dallas City Council.

1971   Dallas Legal Services files suit on behalf of nineteen minority plaintiffs to challenge constitutionality of at-large method of electing council members.

1973   A proposed charter amendment to provide for an enlarged council with a mixed single-member/at-large district election system fails at the polls.

1975   U.S. District Judge Eldon Mahon rules the at-large system unconstitutional and approves the city's proposed mixed 8-3 election district plan.

    First election held under 8-3 single-member/at-large district election plan.

    Voting Rights Act amendment expands voting rights protection to Spanish-speaking minorities, bringing Texas under the Section 5 preclearance requirement, retroactive to November 1, 1972.

1976   Voters approve a charter amendment incorporating the 8-3 plan.

1978   In a 6-3 decision, Supreme Court upholds 8-3 plan but rules that the impact of the Voting Rights Act on the charter amendment approved by referendum would be open on remand.

1979   Three-judge federal court panel rules in February in favor of plaintiffs and halts city elections indefinitely.

    In August the U.S. Department of Justice (DOJ) agrees to accept the 8-3 plan, provided lines are redrawn to assure a majority of blacks or Hispanics in three of the single-member districts.

    In September, city council adopts a redistricting plan, which DOJ approves in November.

1980   After a ten-month delay, city election is held in January.

1982   Voting Rights Act is changed from requiring plaintiffs to prove an intent to discriminate, to requiring proof that an election plan results in racial discrimination. The "results" test makes it easier for minority plaintiffs to establish a violation of Section 2.

1986   Richard Knight becomes Dallas's first city manager of African descent.

1988   Two black plaintiffs file a lawsuit against the city challenging the 8-3 plan.

1989   City council–established charter review committee recommends a plan with ten council members elected from single-member districts, four from larger regional districts, and the mayor at large. A referendum election approves the 10-4-1 plan with 65 percent of the total vote, but with strong opposition from the black community.

1990   After an out-of-court settlement with plaintiffs in the redistricting suit, the city council places a 14-1 system before voters, who narrowly reject 14-1.

1991   In February Judge Buchmeyer orders a May 4 city council election under 14-1, approves a single-member-district plan designed to seat at least seven minorities, and dismisses the city's argument that the district lines split neighborhoods and are gerrymandered on a massive scale to guarantee council seats for minorities.

    In March city files appeal with 5th Circuit to provide a legal test of the voter-approved 10-4-1 system. DOJ rejects the 10-4-1 plan in May, saying it failed to provide fair representation for blacks and Hispanics.

The DOJ indicates that it may reject a 14-1 plan with four, rather than five, black districts.

On May 4, city holds first election under new districts drawn for 14-1.

1993   Dallas voters approve 14-1 in a city charter election in May.

1995   Dallas voters elect city's first black mayor to the only remaining at-large seat.

2001   Council approves new redistricting plan based on 2000 census, which DOJ approves.

2002   Council appoints charter review commission to consider a strong mayor form of government, but excludes 14-1 from consideration.

Introduction

You can't be universal anywhere save in your own backyard.
—Dietrich Bonhoeffer

Since the nation's infancy, issues of race have flowed as strong currents through American history, churning and changing features of the political and social landscape. The right to vote has had its own tortuous history. Continuing conflicts over competing claims for representation have marked efforts through the years to achieve the promise of political equality.

The setting for this book is the intersection of race and representation. The specific aim is to examine the issues raised by the Voting Rights Act of 1965 and voting rights case law for city government. Have the cumulative and long-term ripple effects of the voting changes advanced by Congress and the federal courts led to the desired results? If not, where have they failed? What are the lessons for future actions?

"Voting rights" and "fair representation" are notions that can neither be discussed intelligibly in a void, nor, as Dietrich Bonhoeffer observed, "be universal anywhere save in your own backyard." The City of Dallas provides a real-world laboratory to investigate the collision of race, representation, and public policy.

The initial Voting Rights Act (VRA) of 1965, and its subsequent amendments, includes both permanent and temporal provisions. All states are covered by the permanent provisions. One temporal provision, Section 5, will expire in 2007, unless renewed by Congress. Section 5 requires selected states, primarily in the South, to obtain preclearance from the U.S. Department of Justice or the U.S. District Court for the District of Columbia before any proposed changes affecting voting can take effect.

This study raises issues that have immediacy and importance for public discourse: the renewal of Section 5 of the VRA will be a divisive public policy issue; the decennial census of 2000 required a new round of redistricting by state and local governments, which will likely result in another decade of litigation; and evolving case law and U.S. Department of Justice VRA enforcement rulings have yet to provide a coherent message to state and local

1

governments on what is permissible in election law and in redistricting. Until resolved, these issues will continue to exacerbate racial divisiveness in American politics.

Several intellectual concerns motivate this study. One is the premise that theoretical political principles should guide political practice; social scientists should engage significant, real-world problems. Nearly four decades after Congress passed the Voting Rights Act, more citizens are enfranchised, but a smaller percentage of the electorate votes; racial gaps in voter turnout remain; minorities as groups continue to have less access to politically relevant resources; and the economic gap between classes widens, despite redistributive policies. These matters add a practical necessity to the moral urgency to identify the reasons voting rights legislation and litigation have failed to fulfill hopes and aspirations.

Dissatisfaction with analyses, which consider parts of a political system isolated from the whole, is an additional motivation. A plethora of studies measure the success of the Voting Rights Act primarily in terms of numbers—the increased number of minorities elected to legislative bodies—without attention to the consequences for the whole of the city's government and politics, or the wider interests of minorities, beyond a seat at the table. The argument that the government and politics in a city must be considered in a broader context is not new, but it bears regular repeating in an era that is ahistorical and excessively focused on that which can be measured.

An additional impetus for this research is to nudge the social sciences toward a mode of inquiry that values context, and historical and long-term perspectives. This is not to suggest de-emphasizing or devaluing the contributions of quantitative methods but, rather, to promote the research methods of the qualitative tradition. Aggregated data may bury information, because it mixes councils from cities of vastly different sizes, political cultures, patterns of elections, and city and state legal constraints. Disaggregating data to a finer pattern and a smaller scale permits the inclusion of ideas and human choices as important causes and consequences of political decisions, as well as the discovery of relationships and critical variables that might otherwise be overlooked or omitted.

This volume, as with many civil rights projects, has its origin in strong feelings: a passion for fairness, outrage at injustices, and objection to the reluctance of social scientists to report on controversial findings that might be construed as insensitive or racist. To ignore "politically incorrect" findings ill serves the cause of justice.

But why choose Dallas? The two principal reasons are that Dallas's experiences highlight (1) the tensions between the original Voting Rights Act (and the Fifteenth Amendment) and subsequent VRA Amendments (and the Fourteenth Amendment); and (2) the issues that surround attempts to ensure political equality through litigation.

Dallas is a tri-racial city of Hispanics, blacks, and whites. Dallas, while subject to the permanent provisions of the Voting Rights Act that are applicable to all cities, did not meet the "trigger formula" for discrimination of blacks that brought eleven southern states under the special provisions of the Voting Rights Act from the beginning. Texas was brought under the Section 5 pre-clearance requirement by the 1975 VRA Amendments, which established language minorities as a protected class.

Dallas also provides a classic opportunity to examine the limitations of the litigation model. Every four years, Dallas voters go to the polls to select their mayor. In 1995, in the regular rhythm of the city's electoral politics, neither the usual lineup of financial supporters, nor the predictable role of the city's sole major newspaper, were singular. Exceptional, however, was that a conservative, white-majority city elected a black to the only at-large seat on the Dallas City Council.

Five years earlier U.S. District Court Judge Jerry Buchmeyer forced Dallas to abandon its eighty-three-year-old system of at-large places in city council elections. Judge Buchmeyer instructed the city to hold an interim election to end all at-large places (mayor excepted), "as soon as possible," because "all of the fact witnesses for the plaintiffs and the intervenor testified that it was not possible for a black or Hispanic candidate to win . . . at-large seats."[1] Despite the Judge's categorical declaration, a black *did* win the mayoral at-large seat in Dallas in short order, and was reelected to a second term without serious opposition.

What can explain the outcome of the Dallas mayoral elections in 1995 and 1999? Did the courts subscribe to inappropriate social science theories? Can racial attitudes and voting patterns change that much in five years? Did an adversarial judicial system, by its nature, exclude key facts that bear on a city's politics? Were the courts in error in forcing their "preferred" election system choice on a city's electorate and governing body?

The answers to such questions go well beyond the experience of one city and have implications for political and social change more generally. Dallas's story seems to be instructive in several respects. The court's remedial strategy of single-member districts, after the city's long history with at-large elections, illustrates an event that altered the political landscape without affecting fundamental control of public policy by moneyed interests. Thus a court-forced change in an election system may restructure the "rules of the game" in a community and lead to unanticipated, and sometimes undesirable, consequences, yet fail to change the magnetic pull of political power toward certain economic interests. Hence substantive modification that is anticipated to result from an election change may be blunted.

Dallas also provides a setting for understanding how an attempt to "democratize" a basic political institution—in this case, by devising "safe"

1. *Williams* v. *City of Dallas*, 734 F.Supp. 1317 (1990).

seats for selected minority groups underrepresented on a city council—affects the institution itself, alters the general political processes, and produces unforeseen consequences. The many variables in a political system form patterns. A single change in rules or structure may create a new and distinctive political pattern. Americans, who have a propensity for tinkering with their political systems, often overlook the long-term price for making changes in reaction to particular election outcomes or to policies they have found to be objectionable.

For expository purposes, the present book has, in general, a chronological structure. Within that structure, each of the chapters addresses some aspect of the consequences that flow from viewing voting rights issues through the lenses of statutory and case law.

Part 1 begins with an outline of the complexities, successes, and shortcomings of the Voting Rights Act (chapter 1), followed by the mixed messages of voting rights case law (chapter 2).

Part 2 opens the case study of Dallas. Two chapters provide context for the voting rights suits in Dallas: chapter 3 contains the historical and cultural characteristics that molded Dallas politics and affected the city's responses to voting rights issues; and chapter 4 presents the way that city government functioned politically prior to court intervention, in order to provide a "before" perspective to the "after" analysis. Both chapters are a prelude to chapter 5, which covers the Dallas court cases and the political turmoil during the years of litigation.

The social sciences cannot "prove" a cause-and-effect relationship between a court-ordered change in one part of an electoral system and observed results in other parts of the system. In part 3, qualitative analysis, guided by theoretical principles in political science and participant-observation of events in Dallas over almost four decades, informs judgments as to the effects of court-ordered, single-member districting on elections (chapter 6), on governance (chapter 7), and on public policy (chapter 8).

The closing section offers conclusions as to how the concrete, particular experiences of Dallas might inform attempts by the federal government to ameliorate political inequalities. Can the judicial engineering of urban electoral systems, in general, be successful? Have the courts and Congress found the appropriate balance between group rights and constitutionally guaranteed individual rights? More specifically, do safe seats gerrymandered by race better serve the goal of fundamental fairness in urban government or is that goal more attainable by competitive elections and coalitions forged on the basis of values held in common?

The main thesis of the book is that the Voting Rights Act of 1965 achieved its intended consequence of protecting *individuals'* right to vote but that Congress and the federal courts veered off course into an entangling net of contradictions when they attempted to advance the political standing of discrete *groups.* U.S. Department of Justice preclearance rulings, and the federal court preference for single-member districts as the remedy for underrepresentation of statutorily protected minority groups, have had unintended and undesirable consequences.

Consideration of these consequences should prompt Congress to reassess the temporal provisions of the Voting Rights Act; federal judges to restrain from prescribing remedies that should be debated instead in constitutional conventions or legislative assemblies; and citizens to move beyond litigation to find ways to further the goal of fair representation in American political institutions through healthy, competitive, political processes.

PART I
Political Participation and the Law

1
The Voting Rights Act

This Act flows from a clear and simple wrong. Its only purpose is to right that wrong. Millions of Americans are denied the right to vote because of their color. This law will ensure them the right to vote.
—President Lyndon B. Johnson on signing the Voting Rights Act, August 6, 1965

Race and law have been inextricably linked since the founding of the nation. The Voting Rights Act of 1965[1] is the twentieth century manifestation of the ongoing, episodic attempts to fulfill the promise of the Declaration of Independence in 1776, that "all men are created equal" and that governments derive "their just powers from the consent of the governed." The framers of the U.S. Constitution made clear in 1787 that the form of government for achieving "the consent of the governed" would be a representative one. This was guaranteed to the states in Article IV.[2] What the term *representative* may mean, however, has puzzled and preoccupied political philosophers and practitioners from the Middle Ages to the present.[3] It should not be surprising, therefore, that neither the U.S. courts nor Congress have been able to define a workable gauge for enforcing "fair representation."

Proponents and scholars hail the Voting Rights Act (VRA) of 1965 as "the single most effective piece of legislation drafted in the last two decades,"[4] even

1. Pub. L. No. 89-110, 79 Stat. 437 (1965).
2. Article IV, Section 4: "The United States shall guarantee to every State in this Union a Republican Form of Government, and shall protect each of them against Invasion, and on Application of the Legislature, or of the Executive (when the Legislature cannot be convened) against domestic Violence."
3. See Hanna F. Pitkin, ed., *Representation* (New York: Atherton, 1969), for analyses of various concepts of representation; see also idem, *The Concept of Representation* (Berkeley: University of California Press, 1967).
4. Statement by Benjamin L. Hooks, executive director of the National Association for the Advancement of Colored People and chairman of the Leadership Conference on Civil Rights, in U.S. Congress, House, Committee on the Judiciary, Subcommittee on Civil and Constitutional Rights, *Hearings on Extension of the Voting Rights Act,* May–July 1981. 97th Cong. 1st sess., part 1, 60. Hereafter cited as *1981 House Hearings.*

as "perhaps the single most successful civil rights bill ever passed."[5] Critics characterize the Act as having brought affirmative action into the polling booth,[6] and as having so distorted "our constitutional structure of government as to render any distinction drawn in the Constitution between state and federal power almost meaningless."[7]

These divergent opinions stem, in part, from honest philosophical and political disagreements. They also arise from a failure to distinguish between markedly different provisions of the VRA itself, as well as between original provisions and the significant transformations in the law that were created by the VRA Amendments of 1970, 1975, and 1982.[8] In the minds of many, the VRA is synonymous only with original provisions that resulted in a dramatic increase in registration and voting in the jurisdictions covered by the legislation.[9] The immediate, positive impact on voter registration that resulted from those original provisions is undeniable. The effects of other provisions added later, however, are problematic.

The argument that follows is not in opposition to any voting rights legislation or even to the principles of the VRA of 1965. Rather, it is a challenge to recognize the limitations of legislation to effect complex political change. The federal government must intervene when states and localities pass discriminatory voting laws or when they delay or fail to prosecute election irregularities. The disgraceful record of racial and ethnic discrimination in many jurisdictions is amply documented, so it need not be retold here. That shameful history reinforces Madison's observation, in *The Federalist*, no. 51, that government itself is the greatest of all reflections on human nature: "If men were angels, no government would be necessary." And one might add that no laws would be needed.

Starting from the premise that laws *are* necessary, the appropriate range

5. Chandler Davidson and Bernard Grofman, eds., *Quiet Revolution in the South: The Impact of the Voting Rights Act, 1965–1990* (Princeton, N.J.: Princeton University Press, 1994), 386.

6. Abigail M. Thernstrom, *Whose Votes Count? Affirmative Action and Minority Voting Rights* (Cambridge, Mass.: Harvard University Press, 1987), ix.

7. Justice Hugo Black, concurring and dissenting, *South Carolina* v. *Katzenbach*, 383 U.S. 301 (1966), 358.

8. Pub. L. No. 91-285, 84 Stat. 314 (1970); Pub. L. No. 94-73, 89 Stat. 402 (1975); Pub. L. No. 97-205, 96 Stat. 131 (1982).

9. See Davidson and Grofman, *Quiet Revolution,* for comments on an extensive project to measure the impact of the VRA on increasing black registration, and the holding of office by blacks and Mexican-Americans, in eight southern states. For a differing view, see Richard J. Timpone, "Mass Mobilization or Government Intervention? The Growth of Black Registration in the South," *Journal of Politics* (May 1995), 57:425–442. Timpone finds that the increase in the aggregate level of southern black registration began before the VRA, because of such factors as the Voter Education Project and voter interest in the 1964 election. He does concur that the VRA was the impetus for change in the three states of greatest resistance—Alabama, Louisiana, and Mississippi.

of the law, and what can and cannot be achieved through law, become the foci. A complex issue, such as "representation," requires legislators to consider the systemic effects of any change contemplated by law, and not just an accommodation of the aggrieved at a moment in history.

A legislated change, which may not seem to be momentous, may entirely alter the pattern of politics in a political system. President John F. Kennedy cautioned against tampering with one part of a political system without considering the prospects of unbalancing "a whole solar system of governmental power."[10] For instance, the new rules for delegate selection adopted in the aftermath of the 1968 Chicago Convention was a well-meaning attempt to open the processes of the Democratic Party to all groups. An unintended consequence was that attempts by states to accommodate the new convention rules started the slide from party politics to candidate-centered politics. Similarly the well-intentioned Voting Rights Act of 1965 began with new rules, which protected the right to vote but which also initiated a transformation that restructured local governments, destabilized political systems, and, in some cases, exacerbated race relations.

The Fifteenth Amendment to the U.S. Constitution provides that "the right of citizens of the United States to Vote shall not be denied or abridged by the United States or by any State on account of race, color, or previous condition of servitude." Section 2 of the Voting Rights Act, which strengthened provisions for enforcement of the Fifteenth Amendment, applied a nationwide prohibition of state discriminatory practices or procedures that, in practice, applied only to blacks.

A major difficulty with the legislation is that the assumptions, applicable to blacks, that underlie the Fifteenth Amendment and the original VRA were not applicable to the Fourteenth Amendment, which became the focus of enforcement through subsequent VRA amendments. The Fourteenth Amendment, which stipulates, inter alia, that "no State shall . . . deny to any person within its jurisdiction the equal protection of the laws" became the basis for requiring equal treatment of minority groups.

Among the assumptions applicable to blacks as a protected group, and not necessarily to other minority groups in our society, are a history of official political discrimination, residence in geographically defined areas as a result of segregated housing, and political cohesiveness. When language minorities subsequently were added as a protected group under the VRA, some of the assumptions were inapplicable. Among Spanish-language minorities, for example, there is more geographic dispersal and less political cohesiveness among nationalities. Nevertheless, the preferred remedies that had been identi-

10. 102 *Congressional Record* 5150 (1956), as cited in Ward E. Y. Elliott, *The Rise of Guardian Democracy: The Supreme Court's Role in Voting Rights Disputes, 1845–1969* (Cambridge, Mass.: Harvard University Press, 1974), 212.

fied, based on those earlier assumptions applicable to blacks, had become fixed as the only choices. Political scientist Mark Rush is correct in his argument that "a systemic theory of representation cannot be grounded on advocacy of discrete groups' fortunes."[11]

EVOLUTION OF VOTING RIGHTS LAW

A brief review of the evolution of voting rights law provides a context for analyzing the VRA of 1965. Statutory law regarding voting rights has had a bright, and a dark, history.[12] Law has been used to protect minorities from discriminatory treatment. Undeniably law has also been used to legitimate and to perpetuate racial injustice. Thus "the tension between an acknowledged ideology of equal political rights and a deep and common desire to exclude and reject large groups of human beings from citizenship" has marked each stage of the history of American democracy.[13]

When the U.S. Constitution was drafted only propertied white males had the privilege of being allowed to vote. Slaves were neither viewed as citizens nor counted as whole persons.[14] The original U.S. Constitution did not include a "right to vote" per se; indeed, no *individual* legal rights were included. The document was framed as a source of authority, and as a source of constraint on the power of *governments*. The qualifications for voting were left to the states. The only requirement was that voters in a state meet the same qualifications to vote for national offices as to vote for members of the most numerous branch of the state legislature.

One path in the development of voting rights law has been the judicial interpretation of constitutional provisions. Under the principle of judicial review, established in *Marbury* v. *Madison* in 1803, the Court has responsibility to void any federal or state law not squaring with its reading of the Constitution.[15] Prior to the 1960s most such cases nullified, as contrary to the Constitution, state actions based on voter exclusion schemes, such as literacy requirements, poll tax payments, and property ownership.

Another path in the evolution of political rights has been the gradual

11. Mark Rush, "The Beginning of the End or the End of the Beginning? Voting Rights after *Shaw* v. *Reno* and *Miller* v. *Johnson*," paper prepared for the annual meeting of the American Political Science Association, 1995.

12. For a succinct history of black enfranchisement and the VRA of 1965, see Armand Derfner, "Racial Discrimination and the Right to Vote," *Vanderbilt Law Review* (1973), 26:523–584.

13. Judith N. Shklar, *American Citizenship: The Quest for Inclusion* (Cambridge, Mass.: Harvard University Press, 1995), 28.

14. The existence of "servitude" is acknowledged in the U.S. Constitution by counting slaves as three-fifths of a person for purposes of population count and taxes.

15. *Marbury* v. *Madison*, 1 Cranch 137 (1803).

nationalization of voter qualifications through constitutional amendments. These changes include limitations on the states in setting voter qualifications in terms of race in the Fifteenth Amendment (1870), gender in the Nineteenth Amendment (1920), payment of poll taxes or other taxes in the Twenty-fourth Amendment (1964), and age in the Twenty-sixth Amendment (1971). These amendments are negative, "thou shalt nots." An affirmative constitutional right to vote was not protected until the Supreme Court ruling in *Wesberry* v. *Sanders* (1964).[16]

Two of the three Civil War Amendments, the Fourteenth and the Fifteenth, provide the constitutional foundation for statutory law to end voter discrimination. Attempts to enforce these amendments by legislation surged in two periods—the post-1860s and the post-1960s. The Fifteenth Amendment was used as the basis for statutory law in the first period; the Fourteenth emerged in importance after 1965.

Following the Civil War the former slave states enacted laws, known as black codes, to relegate blacks to inferior status. These codes, coupled with incidents of violence against the newly freed blacks, pressured Congress to enact a series of laws designed to enforce the Civil War Amendments.

Two of four major civil rights laws passed during the Reconstruction era to enforce the Fifteenth Amendment are relevant to voting rights. The First Enforcement Act (May 31, 1870) made it a federal crime for state officials to deny qualified blacks the right to vote.[17] Under this Act, any person who hindered or obstructed qualified voters in the exercise of their franchise was subject to fines and imprisonment. The Second Enforcement Act (February 28, 1871) granted federal courts jurisdiction over supervisors of elections; interference with the work of the supervisors was made a federal crime.[18]

This wave of action protective of the vote was followed by a backwash era of disenfranchisement. After about 1890, the chief means for keeping blacks from voting in the South, in addition to literacy tests, was the so-called white primary. Since the Democratic Party primary was tantamount to election in most southern states, limiting participation in primaries to whites in effect excluded blacks from the political process.

In 1894 Congress repealed the sections of Reconstruction legislation that dealt specifically with elections.[19] The era of darkness, insofar as voting rights were concerned, extended over the entire nation—de jure disenfranchisement

16. *Wesberry* v. *Sanders,* 376 U.S. 1 (1964).

17. First Enforcement Act, 16 Stat. 140 (1870).

18. Second Enforcement Act, 16 Stat. 433 (1871). See Abraham L. Davis and Barbara Luck Graham, *The Supreme Court, Race, and Civil Rights* (Thousand Oaks, Calif.: Sage, 1995), 13 et seq. for an argument that "the civil rights acts that were passed between 1866 and 1875 were no more than cosmetic legal symbols not taken seriously by the populace or by the Supreme Court."

19. 28 Stat. 144 (1894).

largely in the south and de facto disenfranchisement in the rest of the nation. From the 1880s until World War I the national government officially abandoned blacks to the caprice of state governments. State after state in the South and in border areas, including Texas, instituted constitutional and statutory measures, which were designed to prevent blacks from political participation. The only recourse was in federal courts, where litigation on a case-by-case basis was slow, costly, and frustrating.

Black protest began to develop after World War I. Leaders such as W.E.B. Du Bois challenged the accommodationist approach epitomized by leaders such as Booker T. Washington. Washington believed that "the Reconstruction experiment in racial democracy failed because it began at the wrong end, emphasizing political means and civil rights acts rather than economic means and self-determination."[20] What Eliot Rudwick called the "unbridgeable differences that thus appeared between Washington's accommodating stance and Du Bois's advocacy of militant protest"[21] continue to characterize divergent leadership strategies in Dallas.[22]

The protest movement surged nationally in the 1950s. In the 1960s it broke through the barriers that historically had blocked the aspirations of blacks. In response to a swelling tide of anger and pressure, U.S. presidents, and then Congress, responded to what became known as the Civil Rights movement of the 1960s.[23] Congress passed four significant pieces of legislation between 1957 and 1968, the first congressional legislation on civil rights since 1875. Voting rights provisions were included in all four—the Civil Rights Acts of 1957, 1960, and 1964, and the Voting Rights Act of 1965.

The Civil Rights Acts of 1957 and 1960 contained provisions that protected voters in federal elections from intimidation and interference, that authorized the Attorney General to seek injunctions on their behalf, and that required state election officials to preserve federal election records. After the enactment of statutes that prevented barring blacks from voting, the next strategy of resistance by state officials was to deny voter registration, either by violence, harassment, the use of literacy tests, or other screening methods. Civil

20. Louis R. Harlan, "Booker T. Washington and the Politics of Accommodation," in John Hope Franklin and August Meier, eds., *Black Leaders of the Twentieth Century* (Urbana: University of Illinois Press, 1982), 2.

21. Eliott Rudwick, "W.E.B. Du Bois: Protagonist of the Afro-American Protest," in Franklin and Meier, *Black Leaders,* 66.

22. In general, the educated middle- and upper-class black leadership in Dallas have followed Booker T. Washington's approach, whereas the less educated and economically disadvantaged have pursued political power through litigation and protest strategies.

23. On the use of presidential executive orders to combat segregation in the military and on discrimination in housing and in employment prior to the enactment of civil rights legislation, see Ruth P. Morgan, *The President and Civil Rights: Policy-Making by Executive Order* (New York: St. Martin's, 1970).

rights groups and the U.S. Department of Justice challenged those barriers repeatedly in the courts, while simultaneously pursuing a strategy for legislation.

The Civil Rights Act of 1964 included provisions requiring that blacks be registered under the same standards applicable to whites, and prohibited the use of immaterial errors to disqualify individuals. The statutes also established a complex process to enroll black voters.

Enforcement of these statutory provisions, however, was judicial. The government had the burden of proof. Massive efforts were required to document discrimination in each case. After seven years of court battles, which began after the passage of the 1957 Civil Rights Act, only 37,146, of some half a million blacks of voting age, were registered in forty-six counties in which suits had been brought.[24]

In 1965 the brutal beatings of civil rights demonstrators attempting to march from Selma to Montgomery, Alabama, spurred national outrage. President Lyndon Johnson seized the moment and forged a bipartisan coalition, which passed the Voting Rights Act of 1965, containing strong measures to enforce the Fifteenth Amendment of the U.S. Constitution.[25]

THE VOTING RIGHTS ACT OF 1965

Until the 1960s the history of voting rights in the United States had followed dual paths: (1) successive enfranchisement of classes of citizens through the nationalization of voting qualifications; and (2) federal protection of the right to vote against specified forms of discrimination and abuse. The Voting Rights Act of 1965 marked the first diversion from those approaches.[26] The new course used two methods: (1) it sustained the tradition of protecting the right to vote, by banning literacy tests, authorizing federal registrars and election observers, and providing criminal penalties for intimidating voters; and (2) it departed radically from prior practice by authorizing review by the U.S. Attorney General (or the U.S. District Court for the District of Columbia) of planned

24. Jack Bass, "Election Laws and Their Manipulation to Exclude Minority Voters," quoted in *1981 House Hearings,* part 1, 17.

25. Extensive literature is available on obstacles that blacks face in voting. An eloquent account can be found in Taylor Branch, *Parting the Waters: America in the King Years, 1954–1963* (New York: Simon & Schuster, 1988). See, esp., 485–491, 503–515, 633–639.

26. Considerable discussion focuses on subsequent extensions and amendments to the VRA. Thus it is important to emphasize that the VRA of 1965 itself is a permanent statute, not needing periodic extension. Extensions, however, do pertain to temporal provisions in the statute, which apply special requirements to jurisdictions identified by formula.

changes in election processes in jurisdictions identified by the application of a formula.[27]

By prohibiting the literacy test in the covered jurisdictions, the VRA of 1965 removed the major means used to keep blacks from registering. Federal observers collected evidence of incidents of harassment, intimidation, or violence, and federal examiners registered voters. This meant that uncooperative local registrars could no longer thwart voter registration drives.[28] These steps led to a dramatic increase in the registration of blacks.[29] Between 1965 and 1972 more than one million black citizens were added to voting rolls.[30] These early positive figures caused many Americans to view the Act as synonymous with achieving minority registration.

The two approaches in the statute, federal protection of the right to vote and requirements for approval of proposed changes in election rules before implementation, are contained in Sections 2 and 5, respectively, of the 1965 VRA. Section 4 includes the formula, or the "trigger" mechanism, as it came to be called, that determines which jurisdictions are covered by the provisions in Section 5.

Section 2 of the Voting Rights Act

Section 2 tracks the Fifteenth Amendment of the U.S. Constitution, but with some notable modifications. Like the Fifteenth Amendment, it applies to the entire nation. The Fifteenth Amendment provides that "the right of citizens of the United States to vote shall not be denied or abridged by the United States or by any State on account of race, color, or previous condition of servitude." Section 2 of the VRA provides that "no voting qualification or prerequisite to

27. Section 4(b) of the VRA provides: "The provisions of subsection (2) [preclearance] shall apply in any State or in any political subdivision of a state which (1) the Attorney General determines maintained on November 1, 1964, any test or device, and with respect to which (2) the Director of the Census determines that less than 50 percentum of the persons of voting age residing therein were registered on November 1, 1964, or that less than 50 percentum of such persons voted in the presidential election of November 1964."

28. David Hunter, *Federal Review of Voting Change: How to Use Section 5 of the Voting Rights Act,* 2nd ed. (Washington, D.C.: Joint Center for Political Studies, 1975), 9.

29. "On the first supervised registration day under the new statute, 1,144 Negroes were enrolled in nine counties with a history of rampant discrimination in Alabama, Louisiana, and Mississippi—an increase of 65 per cent!" Henry J. Abraham, *Freedom and the Court: Civil Rights and Liberties in the United States,* 2nd ed. (New York: Oxford University Press, 1972), 340–341.

30. "Voting Rights Act Extension," U.S. Congress, Senate, Committee on the Judiciary, 97th Cong., 2nd Sess., 1982, S. Rept. 97-417, 6. Hereafter cited as *1982 Senate Report.*

voting, or standard, practice, or procedure shall be imposed or applied by any State or political subdivision to deny or abridge the right of any citizen of the United States to vote on account of race or color." The added terms *qualification or prerequisite, standard, practice,* and *procedure,* are not defined in the statute. Supreme Court justices disagree as to whether these terms apply only to access to the ballot or also to schemes that might affect the "weight" given to a ballot.[31] The terms *vote* and *voting* are defined in the statute as including:

> all action necessary to make a vote effective in any primary, special, or general election, including, but not limited to, registration, listing pursuant to this Act, or other action required by law prerequisite to voting, casting a ballot, and having such ballot counted properly and included in the appropriate totals of votes cast with respect to candidates for public or party office and propositions for which votes are received in an election.[32]

Two important points in the definition of a vote are, first, that the law applies to political party primaries and offices, as well as to state elections and offices; and, second, that the term *effective* is used to mean that the vote is cast and counted.

The recommendation of the Civil Rights Commission to include the word *party* was built on the history of the "white primary" cases, by recognizing that the vitality of black votes could be impaired as much by restrictive political party rules, which prevented candidates sympathetic to the group from seeking office, as by denying blacks the right to vote.[33] This was a key issue in Dallas court cases in which slating groups were viewed as analogous to political parties.

The term *effective,* in addition to meaning that a vote is cast and counted, later came to be understood to mean ensuring political results for blacks, especially in terms of holding seats in proportion to their numbers in the population.

Another significant difference between the Fifteenth Amendment of the U.S. Constitution and Section 2 of the 1965 VRA is the addition of the term *political subdivision,* defined in the statute to mean any "subdivision of a State which conducts registration for voting." Texas officials questioned the applica-

31. See, for example, *Holder* v. *Hall,* 114 S. Ct. 2581, 2583 (1994), in which Justices Thomas and Scalia, in dissent, adhere to the restrictive interpretation.

32. Section 14(c)(1).

33. Richard Claude, *The Supreme Court and the Electoral Process* (Baltimore: The Johns Hopkins Press, 1970), 114–115. Texas passed its white primary law in 1924. The Court banned the white primary, if required by the state, in a Texas case, *Nixon* v. *Herndon,* 273 U.S. 536 (1927). Other ruses were tried in Texas until finally, in the Texas case *Smith* v. *Allwright,* 321 U.S. 649 (1944), the Court held exclusion by a political party to be invalid, even if parties are private voluntary associations under state law.

bility of "political subdivision" to municipalities in Texas, as voter registration is a county responsibility, but the Supreme Court rejected that interpretation.[34]

Section 4 of the Voting Rights Act

Section 4 of the VRA establishes the formula to determine which states or political subdivisions are covered by special provisions of the statute.[35] This section prohibits the use of "tests or devices" in the covered jurisdictions in any federal, state, or local election.[36] Exceptions are made in a declaratory judgment, if the U.S. District Court for the District of Columbia determines that no test or device has been used during the preceding five years "for the purpose or with the effect of denying or abridging the right to vote on account of race or color."

The provisions in this section, as in Section 5, apply to any state or political subdivision of a state which the Attorney General determined had maintained on November 1, 1964, any test or device, and the Director of the Census determined that less than 50 percent of the persons of voting age were registered on November 1, 1964, or voted in the presidential election of November 1964. These determinations were not reviewable in any court, and were effective on their publication in the *Federal Register.*[37]

This automatic coverage formula, or so-called trigger mechanism, initially brought seven states (Alaska, Alabama, Georgia, Louisiana, Mississippi, South Carolina, and Virginia) and parts of four states (North Carolina, Arizona, Hawaii, and Idaho) under the special provisions of the VRA.[38] In addition, if

34. In Texas Secretary of State Mark White and Attorney General John Hill maintained that they did not believe the DOJ's interpretation, in applying the law to *all* governmental units in Texas, to be correct. In 1978 the Supreme Court held that Section 5 applied to political subdivisions within a covered jurisdiction, which have any influence over any aspect of the electoral process, whether or not they conduct voter registration (*United States* v. *Board of Commissioners of Sheffield*, 435 U.S. 110 [1978]).

35. See note 27 above.

36. The phrase "test or device" was defined to mean any requirement that a person, as a prerequisite for voting or registration for voting, "demonstrate the ability to read, write, understand, or interpret any matter, demonstrate any educational achievement or his knowledge of any particular subject, possess good moral character, or prove his qualifications by the voucher of registered voters or members of any other class."

37. After Texas came under the purview of the special provisions of the VRA on September 23, 1975, a suit was filed to challenge the Act's applicability to Texas. The Court ruled, in *Briscoe* v. *Bell,* 432 U.S. 404 (1977), that the determinations of the Attorney General and the Director of the Census are final; the only recourse for Texas to escape coverage would be through a "bailout" suit.

38. Jurisdictions covered as of 1996 are listed in 28 CFR, Ch. 1, Pt. 51, App. (1996). What may seem to be a discrepancy between jurisdictions listed in the CFR and those that are listed as initially covered is because of the VRA's provision that a jurisdiction may exempt itself from special coverage if it can persuade the District Court for the District of Columbia that it has not used a test or device in a discriminatory manner for a specified

discrimination could be shown to have taken place under the general prohibition of discriminatory practices nationwide, the Attorney General was authorized to ask the Court to impose the same remedies that apply automatically to areas covered by the Section 4 trigger. These include the ban on tests or devices, as well as examiners, observers, and preclearance of new laws.

Congress believed this combination of a literacy test and low voter registration or turnout was evidence of discrimination. Senator James B. Allen of Alabama maintained that the trigger formula was manipulated. According to Allen, "it was first determined which states the law should be made applicable to, and then they proceeded to find the formula that would end up with those states being covered."[39] Had they used only the 50 percent voting factor, Allen suggested, Texas would have been included. But with President Johnson from Texas, a second factor, the literacy test, was added, since Texas did not have one.[40]

Had the focus in 1965 been on outcomes, as it came to be later, rather than solely on discriminatory voting laws, it would have become evident that black voters were not represented in proportion to the black population in the legislatures and city councils of northern states. There, the black franchise had been unimpeded by law for at least a hundred years. After passage of the Civil Rights Act of 1964, Harlem Congressman Adam Clayton Powell Jr. privately commented that "the 'Southern phase,' which emphasized 'middle-class matters,' of the 'black revolution' was ending, but that the 'Northern,' 'proletarian,' 'rough' phase was at hand." Powell added that the New York or Chicago Negro had long been able to sit where he pleased; now he was heading into the "gut issue of who gets the money."[41] One is reminded of the views of Booker T. Washington and Wendell Phillips, who argued that blacks needed to build a foundation of economic rights on which to exercise political rights. Emory Professor of Law Andrew Kull contends similarly that because "voting rights were demonstrably not the problem, voting rights alone could not be the answer."[42]

---

period (five years in the original legislation; ten years, later). Alaska, for example, successfully sued in 1972, and was exempted, but was brought back under coverage by the 1975 Amendments. In extensions of the Act in 1970 and 1975, the so-called trigger formula of Section 4 came to include jurisdictions which, on November 1 in 1968 or 1972, had a literacy test or similar device, and which had less than half the electorate registered or voting in the presidential elections of those years.

39. Cited in Joseph F. Zimmerman, "Election Systems and Representative Democracy," *National Civic Review* (fall–winter 1995):285.

40. Ibid.

41. Quoted in Eric F. Goldman, *The Tragedy of Lyndon Johnson* (New York: Knopf, 1969), 204–205.

42. Andrew Kull, *The Color-Blind Constitution* (Cambridge, Mass.: Harvard University Press, 1992), 211.

Section 5 of the Voting Rights Act

Section 5 provides that any jurisdiction that came under the special provisions of Section 4 could not "enact or seek to administer any voting qualification or prerequisite to voting, or standard, practice, or procedure with respect to voting, different from that in force or effect on November 1, 1964" without centralized federal review. The state or subdivision has two choices—either to institute an action for a declaratory judgment in the U. S. District Court for the District of Columbia or to submit the change to the Attorney General, who has sixty days to interpose an objection. Even if neither objects, subsequent action to enjoin enforcement of a change is not barred.

This section, which did not become important until after 1969, marked a dramatic turn from the then existing voting rights laws, by shifting attention from access to the ballot to the complex and difficult matters of fair and effective representation. The burden of proof shifted from the federal government, which can invalidate official actions determined to be discriminatory, to the covered jurisdictions, which have to obtain a finding that a proposed voting practice or policy is *not* discriminatory, before it can be instituted.

Section 2 receded in importance as barriers to accessing the ballot fell, and Section 5 emerged as the most important and frequently used section of the VRA.[43] The new prominence for Section 5 came in 1969, when the Supreme Court gave it broad interpretations in a case discussed in chapter 2, *Allen* v. *State Board of Elections* (393 U.S. 544). This decision resulted in vast increases in the number of changes submitted for Section 5 preclearance: one in 1965, 255 in 1970, 7,340 in 1980, 17,832 in 1990, and 16,558 in 2000.[44]

As Section 5 moved to the foreground, enforcement of the VRA became increasingly controversial. It had accorded extraordinary power to the federal government over state and local laws on two counts: first, by requiring states and localities to preclear any change in law; second, by shifting the burden of proof to states and localities to prove that their proposed changes were *not* discriminatory.

One of the most controversial aspects of the VRA was its inclusion of only some states under its preclearance provisions. Because this was designed to address de jure discrimination, an unintended consequence was that early literature regarding the impact of the VRA necessarily focused on those states that had discriminatory laws. As a result, data comparisons tended to be confined to "before" and "after" conditions in southern states. By not using national data comparisons, the de facto discriminatory patterns in other parts of the nation were largely ignored. Furthermore, the law only applied to changes per

43. Subsequently Section 2 did reemerge prominently, when Congress amended it in 1982 to prohibit vote dilution without requiring proof of discriminatory purpose.

44. Figures provided to the author by U.S. Department of Justice, Civil Rights Division, Voting Section.

se. Therefore, even in states that were covered by VRA special provisions, some discriminatory practices continued to prevail until changes were proposed.

THE VOTING RIGHTS ACT AMENDMENTS

A brief review of the VRA Amendments of 1970, 1975, and 1982 illustrates the drawbacks if officials develop statutory law additively, with each new provision considered independently of its effect on the extant body of law. The statutory bases for voting rights moved from protecting the right of blacks to vote, to federal preapproval of prospective actions on voting by certain states and localities, to including other minority groups under the umbrella of remedies designed for blacks, to protecting the right to representation, and then, to attempting to protect minority officeholders.

Initially the target may have seemed clear, but when blacks could register and vote, and their political situation did not seem to change, further remedial experiments were tried. Each change in law, or in enforcement priorities, upset the equilibrium that had accommodated the preceding change.

President John F. Kennedy cautioned against the American propensity to tinker with the political system whenever results are deemed to be unsatisfactory. His words seem applicable here: "If it is proposed to change the balance of power of one of the elements of the solar system [of governmental power], it is necessary to consider all the others."[45]

The Voting Rights Act Amendments of 1970

The VRA Amendments of 1970 were the first to tinker with the 1965 law. They extended prohibitions on the use of tests or devices an additional five years and updated the trigger dates to November 1, 1986, for voter registration, and to the 1986 presidential election for voting percentage. In retaining the same formula for coverage, yet changing the dates, Congress included several areas outside the South.[46]

In this development a numerical rule of thumb became the criterion for determining which states and political subdivisions would be subject to preclearance requirements. Although the test had been designed to single out particular states in the South with histories of discrimination,[47] the criterion of

45. 102 *Congressional Record* 5150 (1956), as cited in Elliott, *Guardian Democracy,* 212.

46. These areas included election districts in Arizona, California, New York, and Wyoming, and towns in Connecticut, New Hampshire, Maine, and Massachusetts. *Congressional Digest* (June–July 1975), 54:167.

47. Thernstrom, *Whose Votes Count?* 17.

voter turnout in presidential elections was a moving target. The benchmark of 50 percent turnout, applied to the 1968 figures, brought an assortment of counties, with no history of black disenfranchisement, under special provisions specifically intended to enfranchise southern blacks.[48]

In addition, the ban on literacy tests and on similar barriers to registration were extended to the entire country on a trial basis. This legislation brought the Fourteenth Amendment into the VRA by abolishing residency requirements; by requiring nationwide, uniform standards regarding absentee registration and absentee balloting in presidential elections; and by prohibiting denial of the right to vote to citizens of the United States eighteen years of age or over.[49]

The Voting Rights Act Amendments of 1975

The VRA Amendments of 1975 extended the temporal provisions of the 1965 legislation for seven years, made permanent the nationwide ban on literacy tests, which it had imposed on a temporary basis in 1970, and brought language minorities, nationwide, under the Section 2 general prohibition against voting discrimination. Moreover, English-only elections were prohibited for ten years in states or political subdivisions where the Director of the Census determined that more than 5 percent of citizens of voting age were members of a single-language minority and that the illiteracy rate of such persons as a group was higher than the national illiteracy rate. "Illiteracy" was defined as failure to complete the fifth primary grade.[50]

New jurisdictions came under the special provisions, which included preclearance, if they had used a "test or device" as of November 1, 1972, and had registration or voter turnout rates of less than 50 percent. The use of English-only election materials in jurisdictions where a single-language minority group comprised more than 5 percent of the voting-age population met the expanded definition of "test or device." The term *language minorities* or *language minority group* was defined as meaning persons of American Indian, Asian American, Alaskan Native, or Spanish heritage.[51]

48. Ibid., 38–39. The same was true when the trigger dates were changed in the 1975 Amendments; in the 1982 Amendment, for the first time, the trigger dates were not revised.

49. Later the Supreme Court, in *Oregon* v. *Mitchell,* 400 U.S. 112 (1970), struck down as unconstitutional the eighteen-year-old-vote provisions insofar as they pertained to state and local elections, rather than to federal elections. Ratification of the Twenty-sixth Amendment to the U.S. Constitution in 1971 superseded the Court's decision in *Oregon* v. *Mitchell.*

50. These jurisdictions included all of Texas, and all or portions of New Mexico, Arizona, California, Colorado, and Oklahoma (*1982 Senate Report,* 9 n. 17).

51. Texas did not have a literacy test, and so it did not become one of the "covered" jurisdictions at the time the Voting Rights Act was adopted in 1965. But Texas did meet

These changes created a tense relationship between the Fourteenth Amendment and the VRA. Congress dealt with the problem simplistically and amended the Act by substituting "Fourteenth or Fifteenth Amendment" for "Fifteenth Amendment." But fair representation for all groups under the "equal protection of the laws" clause of the Fourteenth Amendment cannot just be predicated on the VRA's protection of specified minorities according to the Fifteenth Amendment. Specifically the VRA was passed to protect blacks, based on the underlying assumptions of previous official disenfranchisement, segregated residential patterns, low voter turnout, and bloc voting. These assumptions did not apply in the same way to language minority groups brought under Section 2 and Section 5 coverage in 1975.

Because Hispanics have experienced political subjugation, especially in southwestern states, including Texas, extending Section 5 coverage to language minorities proved to be a potent weapon in eradicating barriers to Hispanic participation in the electoral process. As was the case for blacks, the number of registered Hispanic voters increased substantially immediately after the 1975 Amendments passed. Between 1975 and 1980 the Southwest Voter Registration Project, a nonpartisan project working in Texas, as well as Arizona, California, Colorado, New Mexico, and Utah, conducted 336 voter registration campaigns. These efforts increased Hispanics registered to vote from 488,000 to 798,000, a 64 percent increase in four years.[52]

The Voting Rights Act Amendments of 1982

The VRA Amendments of 1982 renewed Section 5 for twenty-five years; provided a new standard, which went into effect in 1985, on how jurisdictions could terminate (or "bail out" from) coverage under the special provisions of Section 4; and codified in Section 2 of the VRA the "results" test, first enunciated by the Supreme Court in *White* v. *Regester* (1973)[53] and subsequently followed in numerous lower federal court decisions.

Later the plurality opinion in *City of Mobile* v. *Bolden* (1980) held that the Fifteenth Amendment (and therefore Section 2 of the VRA) only barred direct

---

the 1975 expanded definition of "test or device." In addition to Texas, this trigger caught the states of Alaska and Arizona, counties in California, Colorado, Florida, North Carolina, and South Dakota, and two townships in Michigan (*1982 Senate Report,* 9 n. 16).

52. *1981 House Hearings,* part 1, 30, 32, Statement by William Velasquez, founder and executive director, Southwest Voter Registration Education Project.

The president of the AFL-CIO put a human face on these statistics when he said, "Statistics, of course, are only a lifeless summary of a living reality. Numbers cannot gauge the depth and range of emotion—the will for power, the fear of those who are different, the racial class and cultural antagonism—expressed in laws restricting the right to participate in political life" (Statement of Lane Kirkland, *1981 House Hearings,* part 1, 21).

53. *White* v. *Regester,* 412 U.S. 755 (1973). See chapter 5 for a discussion of this Texas case.

interference with the right to vote and did not reach voting dilution claims based on a "results" test.[54]

A proposed electoral change based on measurable electoral outcomes, rather than on the intent to discriminate, is more easily proved. The House Judiciary Committee heard testimony in 1981 that "it becomes extremely difficult and in some cases nearly impossible to prove subjective intent to discriminate, even where the facts fairly and clearly indicate that intentional discrimination might have been in the minds of the officials in charge of voting practices."[55]

After extensive hearings, Congress amended Section 2 in 1982 to prohibit vote dilution, without a requirement of proof of discriminatory purpose, according to essentially the same factors employed in the leading pre-*Bolden* vote dilution case, *White* v. *Regester*. Despite the Senate Judiciary Committee's protestations that the amended Section 2 "is not an effort to overrule a Supreme Court interpretation of the Constitution," it was, and it did.[56]

The new Section 2 provisions delineated the legal standards under the results test:

A violation . . . is established if, based on the totality of circumstances, it is shown that the political processes leading to nomination or election in the State or political subdivision are not equally open to participation by members of a class of citizens protected by subsection (a) in that its members have less opportunity than other members of the electorate to participate in the political process and to elect representatives of their choice. The extent to which members of a protected class have been elected to office in the State or political subdivision is one circumstance which may be considered: *Provided,* That nothing in this section establishes a right to have members of a protected class elected in numbers equal to their proportion in the population.[57]

This new provision includes a number of ambiguous phrases defined neither in the legislation nor by the courts. For example, how does a candidate qualify as a "representative of choice"? Must a minority-preferred candidate be a minority? Lani Guinier points out that the House Report, which accompanies the 1982 Amendments, defines representatives of choice as "minority candidates or candidates identified with the interests of a racial or language minority."[58]

54. *City of Mobile* v. *Bolden,* 446 U.S. 55 (1980).
55. *1981 House Hearings,* part 2, 906, A Statement of William H. White, attorney and visiting professor of law, The University of Texas at Austin.
56. *1982 Senate Report,* 16–17.
57. 96 Stat. 131, 134.
58. House Report No. 227, 97th Congress, 1st Session (1981), 30, cited in Lani Guinier, "The Triumph of Tokenism: The Voting Rights Act and the Theory of Black Electoral Success," *Michigan Law Review* (March 1991), 89:1078 n. 2.

1982 Voting Rights Act Amendments: Legislative History

A disturbing factor regarding the congressional consideration of the 1982 VRA Amendments was the lack of a deliberative atmosphere. Various pressures channeled the debate such that anyone diverging from the mainstream momentum risked being called a racist. Senator Orrin Hatch noted: "Great principles of constitutional law, and public policy, are not normally decided by 389-24 vote margins unless such [exceptional political] circumstances exist."[59]

Representative Henry Hyde testified before the Senate subcommittee:

> The Voting Rights Act is a very complex piece of legislation which has been merchandised in extraordinarily complex terms. By the time it reached the floor, suggestions that alternate views should be considered were quickly met with harsh charges that any deviation whatsoever from what was pushed through the full Judiciary Committee merely reflected "code words for not extending the Act." This intimidating style of lobbying had the ironic effect, although clearly intended, of limiting serious debate. . . . No one wishes to be the target of racist characterizations and the final House vote reflected more of an overwhelming statement of support for the principle represented by the Act than it did concurrence with each and every sentence or concept it contains.[60]

The hearings before the House Judiciary Committee were skewed and witnesses were intimidated. During eighteen days of Judiciary Committee hearings, only 13 of 156 witnesses expressed reservations about the House measure. Perhaps even more remarkable, given the significance of the results test amendment to Section 2, is that only one of the eighteen days was devoted to this issue, with only three witnesses testifying regarding it. All three gave their full support.[61] As to intimidation, particularly, a black attorney from Mississippi was asked if he had been subjected to pressure not to testify. He responded:

> It stopped being pressure and started being intimidation at some point. Apparently someone called most of my colleagues in Mississippi and I found my friends, my black friends in the Republican Party, calling me up asking if I was coming up here to testify against the Voting Rights Act. . . . [M]y father who's co-chairman of the Democratic Party in one county said that he had never heard such vicious things about his son.[62]

59. *1982 Senate Report,* 103–104.

60. Ibid., 126 n. 61, citing statement by U.S. Representative Henry Hyde, Senate Hearings, January 28, 1982.

61. Ibid., 126 n. 62, citing statements by James Blacksher, David Walbert, and Armand Derfner, in *1981 House Hearings.*

62. Quoted in *1982 Senate Report,* 125. Similar allegations were made about other potential witnesses, who might have opposed the House bill. The following references are

In the Senate, consideration of the proposed 1982 Amendments fared better: witnesses with diverse viewpoints were invited to testify. The Senate Subcommittee on the Constitution voted to recommend a simple ten-year extension of the Act. The full Judiciary Committee rejected these recommendations, and subsequently the House-passed measure, which extended the preclearance requirement for an additional twenty-five years to 2007, passed the Senate by a vote of 85 to 8 and was signed by President Reagan on June 18, 1982.

Concept of Vote Dilution

The incorporation of the concept of vote dilution in Section 2 of the VRA was significant, with profound implications.[63] The issue of dilution might not have arisen had cultural pluralism not supplanted the melting pot as the metaphor of social policy, and had the U.S. Bureau of the Census, and other entities, not classified by race. According to one scholar, "as recently as 1950 an American academic who voiced a phrase like 'the Jewish vote' or 'the Negro vote' would have put himself beyond the pale, for in relation to federal elections, American citizens were expected to act as individuals in an ethnically undifferentiated population." Furthermore, Peterson maintains, even the American Civil Liberties Union tried to have race deleted from the 1960 census schedule.[64] Consequently the "brief period [at mid-century] during which it was thought wrong to identify by race, gender, or national origins . . . was swept away by the emergence of affirmative action and statistical parity in the 1970s."[65] One analyst's view is that "if statistical information has not caused, it has certainly abetted the emergence of demographically defined groups as a category in public policy."[66]

The "anti-dilution" concept was developed in the first generation of congressional district apportionment cases in the mid-1960s. It derived from the "one person, one vote" reapportionment case of *Reynolds* v. *Sims* in 1964.[67] But when Congress embedded the concept of dilution into the VRA, it was not

---

cited in the *1982 Senate Report* at 126 n. 61: "Senate Hearings," January 28, 1982, U.S. Representative Henry Hyde; Bunzel, "Voting Rights Hardball," *Wall Street Journal,* March 19, 1982; and Brimelow, "Uncivil Act," *Barron's,* January 25, 1982.

63. For a comprehensive treatment of the evolution of the vote dilution standard, see Bernard Grofman, Lisa Handley, and Richard G. Niemi, *Minority Representation and the Quest for Voting Equality* (Cambridge: Cambridge University Press, 1992), esp. chapters 2 and 3.

64. William Petersen, "Politics and the Measurement of Ethnicity," in William Alonso and Paul Starr, eds., *The Politics of Numbers* (New York: Russell Sage Foundation, 1987), 195.

65. Kenneth Prewitt, "Public Statistics and Democratic Politics," in Alonso and Starr, *Politics of Numbers,* 272.

66. Ibid., 273.

67. *Reynolds* v. *Sims,* 377 U.S. 533 (1964).

defined—no doubt because scholars and practitioners have also been unable to develop a workable definition. In 1984 Chandler Davidson, a leading scholar on voting issues, wrote that "in spite of two decades of vote dilution litigation and a number of articles on the subject in law reviews and other scholarly journals, no concise and comprehensive definition has emerged."[68] The matter was left to the federal courts and the Department of Justice to develop a checklist of structural forms and practices to be considered as evidence of dilution. But how could one evaluate the diluting impact of structural forms and practices without knowledge of the full strength standard by which to measure dilution? In a dissenting opinion in 1991, Justice Antonin Scalia noted the conceptual weakness at the heart of enforcing politically fair objectives on an unruly electoral system. He asked how one can, ultimately, measure the dilution of voting influence in the absence of a comprehensible baseline definition of proper outcome.[69]

Prominent among structural forms and practices identified as ones that might be used for discriminatory purposes are the gerrymander, at-large elections, and majority votes. The theme in court litigation, and later in congressional hearings and debates, was based on a simplistic assumption that these structural forms and practices were instituted for discriminatory reasons to offset the gains made at the ballot box under the VRA.[70] This supposition fails to address the issue of the at-large elections that were instituted before the VRA passed, for they, too, fell under the large net cast over at-large electoral systems.

Typically the remedy on findings of vote dilution is to require creation of single-member districts. A prominent civil rights litigator, who had testified as expert witness in a number of voting rights cases, told the Senate Judiciary Committee, in 1975, that "we might want to put in permanent bans that bar at-large elections not only in the covered states but perhaps in the rest of the country as well."[71]

68. Chandler Davidson, ed., *Minority Vote Dilution* (Washington, D.C.: Howard University Press, 1984), 4.

69. Samuel Issacharoff, "Supreme Court Destabilization of Single-Member Districts," *The University of Chicago Legal Forum* (1995), 228. The case referenced is *Chisom* v. *Roemer*, 501 U.S. 380, 414–416 (1991).

70. *1982 Senate Report*, for example, notes at page 6: "Following the dramatic rise in registration, a broad array of dilution schemes were employed to cancel the impact of the new black vote. Elective posts were made appointive; election boundaries were gerrymandered; majority runoffs were instituted to prevent victories under a prior plurality system; at-large elections were substituted for election by single-member districts, or combined with other sophisticated rules to prevent an effective minority vote. The ingenuity of such schemes seems endless. Their common purpose and effect has been to offset the gains made at the ballot box under the Act."

71. *1982 Senate Report*, 109–110 n. 4; quoting Armand Derfner. See also Davidson, *Minority Vote Dilution*, esp. chapter 4 by George Korbel and Chandler Davidson, "At-Large Elections and Minority Group Representation," and chapter 11 by Edward Still, "Alternatives to Single-Member Districts."

No doubt some jurisdictions did change to at-large elections for discriminatory purposes. J. Morgan Kousser has argued persuasively that at-large elections were used from 1868 on to deny black political power.[72] Others have argued, equally forcefully, that at-large elections and council-manager government were the products of the "good government" movement early in the last century.[73] This view suggests that the reforms had more to do with business interests, and the economy and efficiency movement, than with racial concerns. In 1972 approximately 12,000, or two-thirds of the 18,000 municipalities in the nation, had at-large systems of election.[74] Likely a number of reasons caused municipalities to adopt them. But the Justice Department routinely objected to at-large voting systems submitted for Section 5 preclearance. "Objective factors of discrimination," such as the at-large system of voting, have even been attacked in cities in which racial minorities represent population majorities within a community.[75]

Without a defined baseline for determining proper outcomes, Congress followed a course set by court decisions, thus moving toward a standard of proportional representation.[76] The only "circumstance" that Congress specifically identified to consider as dilution was "the extent to which members of a protected class have been elected to office." This seems to contradict the proviso that Section 2 does not establish "a right to have members of a protected class elected in numbers equal to their proportion in the population." Opponents of the results test argued that it would lead, inevitably, to a requirement of proportional representation for minority groups on elected bodies, a divisive factor in local communities because of the emphasis on the role of race in politics. On this latter point, others posited that it was the "intent test" that would lead to divisiveness in the community, because racist public officials would have to be identified.[77]

72. J. Morgan Kousser, "The Undermining of the First Reconstruction: Lessons for the Second," in Davidson, *Minority Vote Dilution,* 27–46.

73. For an explanation of the change in Dallas, see Robert B. Fairbanks, *For the City as a Whole: Planning, Politics, and the Public Interest in Dallas, Texas, 1900–1965* (Columbus: Ohio State University Press, 1998), 56–59.

74. International City Managers Association, *Municipal Yearbook 1972,* cited in *1982 Senate Report,* 110.

75. For example, in San Antonio, Texas (*1982 Senate Report,* 143, citing statement by Vilma Martinez, Executive Director, Mexican-American Legal Defense and Education Fund, in Senate Hearings, January 27, 1982).

76. Traditionally "proportional representation" refers to a category of electoral systems designed to translate voters' preferences, proportionally, into representatives' seats in multi-member representative bodies. The most common form is to award seats proportionate to the number of votes received by a political party. Extensive literature exists on proportional representation; a concise treatment is by Arend Lijphart, "Proportional Representation," *The Encyclopedia of Democracy* (Washington, D.C.: Congressional Quarterly, 1995), 3:1010–1016. See also a summary of varieties of electoral systems in Douglas J. Amy, *Real Choices/New Voices: The Case for Proportional Representation Elections in the United States* (New York: Columbia University Press, 1993), Appendix A.

77. *1982 Senate Report,* 31.

Given a finding of underrepresentation, which has to be defined in proportion to the total population, and the existence of any one of a countless number of so-called objective factors of discrimination, it is difficult to see how a finding of discrimination could not be established. Congress provided no guidance as to which electoral structure and arrangements would be valid or invalid.

ADMINISTRATIVE ENFORCEMENT

As noted, one of the main goals of the VRA was to develop administrative remedies to address the difficulties endured by disadvantaged classes, which are resource poor, in conducting litigation, which is costly and time-consuming. To ensure speedy handling of preclearance submissions, the VRA provides that the Attorney General, if objecting to a proposed change, must do so within sixty days of receiving the submission. The sixty-day clock does not start, however, until the Attorney General has received all the information considered to be necessary for making a determination as to discriminatory effect. Some jurisdictions are not timely in responding to a request for additional information about a proposed voting change, and hence the clock may not be started for months or, in some instances, years.[78]

More serious than delays in responding to the Department of Justice (DOJ), however, is that some jurisdictions proceed with changes without completing the preclearance process. In an investigation of election practices in Georgia, The *Atlanta Constitution* found that many communities had failed to submit voting changes to Washington as required by the VRA. In the case of an election change in Rome, Georgia, the DOJ did not learn of changes until eight years after they had been made, and then only when they had become the subject of litigation.[79]

In 1975, during congressional testimony, Senator William L. Scott noted that of 2,200 changes (according to figures provided by the DOJ and the Attorney General of the Commonwealth of Virginia) submitted under the Act, objection was raised only to eight.[80] Gerald Jones, Chief of the Voting Section of the Civil Rights Division (CRD) of DOJ from its inception, told Dale Krane, in 1977, that more than 90 percent of all electoral changes are reported to the Attorney General.[81] Krane attributed this remarkable compliance to the cooper-

78. Dale Krane, "Implementation of the Voting Rights Act Enforcement by the Department of Justice," in Lorn S. Foster, ed., *The Voting Rights Act: Consequences and Implications* (New York: Praeger, 1985), 131. Also see Howard Ball, Dale Krane, and Thomas P. Lauth, *Compromised Compliance: Implementation of the 1965 Voting Rights Act* (Westport, Conn.: Greenwood, 1982), for an analysis of the Section 5 implementation process.

79. *Atlanta Constitution,* December 11, 1980, cited in *1981 House Hearings,* part 1, 299.

80. Senate Judiciary Committee, Subcommittee on Constitutional Rights, May 1, 1975. Testimony reprinted in *Congressional Digest* (June/July 1975), 54:177–179.

81. Krane, "Implementation of the Voting Rights Act Enforcement," 132.

ative and consultative procedures developed between local attorneys and the attorneys in the CRD, particularly since the CRD has no enforcement penalties, such as withholding federal funds.[82]

During hearings on the 1982 Amendments, Congressman Bob Krueger observed that, in Texas, the majority of instances in which the DOJ raised objections to proposed changes during the preclearance process occurred when interested parties raised objections. He suggested that the number of submissions could be greatly reduced, if the DOJ simply noted the proposed changes to interested parties, such as the Mexican American Legal Defense and Educational Fund League of United Latin American Citizens (MALDEF), the League of United Latin American Citizens (LULAC), and the National Association for the Advancement of Colored People (NAACP). If such relevant groups had no objections, the full documentation to support review would not have to be submitted.[83] The complaints of state officials about the administration of preclearance by the CRD had concerned, primarily, the paperwork and expense required to make submissions.

Justice Department statistics show that, from 1965 through 1980, state and local governments submitted 34,798 proposed election law changes. Of those, the DOJ objected to 815, or about 2.3 percent. Most of these objections were to proposed changes in local election procedures (337), annexations (244), and redistricting (103). During the first five years that Texas came under preclearance coverage, it submitted 16,208 proposed election law changes and had 130 (about 0.8 percent) DOJ objections.

Texas had far more submissions than any other state but had fewer than average DOJ objections.[84] But as the former Attorney General of the State of Texas cautioned on the hazards of comparative statistics, "Texas has more political subdivisions and more voting entities than all the Old South put together."[85]

That the DOJ objected to 815 proposed changes in Texas can be interpreted in several ways. If the number were to be viewed as small, one might argue that the legislation had put a damper on further attempts to develop ingenious devices to exclude minority voters from political participation. One might also argue that, among the 815 objections, many could have been interpreted, inadvertently or incorrectly, to be discriminatory, so that real instances of errant behavior would be reduced to an even smaller number.[86] One might argue,

82. Ibid., 134–135.

83. *1981 House Hearings,* part 2, 904–905.

84. *Congressional Quarterly Weekly Report,* April 11, 1981, 635–636.

85. Mark White, *1981 House Hearings,* part 2, 1268. Texas has 254 counties, far more than any other state.

86. When Texas was brought under the VRA in 1975, federal lawyers met with Texas officials to explain the impact of the legislation on Texas. The DOJ deputy voting rights chief Barry Weinberg is reported to have said that "darn near everything you can think of

alternatively, that the number is large and is evidence that, in some quarters, a determination to block minorities unfairly from political participation must persist. But, according to Justice Department attorney David Hunter, if the attorney general is unable to decide during the allotted period whether a new practice is discriminatory, he will enter an objection to it.[87]

The Justice Department has been both praised and condemned for its enforcement efforts. As in any complex enforcement situation, among jurisdictions there has been unevenness over time and in interpretation.[88] Voting Rights Act enforcement issues for the DOJ, whether through internal departmental initiatives or external pressures, have come in successive waves. The first initiatives are to protect minority voters, then to ensure opportunities for minorities to be elected, and finally to attempt to protect minority officeholders once elected. During a six-month investigation in eleven states, investigative reporters Susan Feeney and Steve McGonigle, of the Washington Bureau of the *Dallas Morning News,* found that some minority officeholders were denied official powers, equipment, information, and other governmental courtesies afforded to their white predecessors.[89] This has not been a voiced complaint in Dallas.

CONCLUSIONS

The future impact of the Voting Rights Act, now in its fourth decade, seems uncertain, unless congressional action can clarify its ambiguities. But with the

---

is covered." He noted that the DOJ routinely approves most changes in election procedures and concentrates on "big issues," such as the rejection of Texas voter registration laws (Sam Kinch Jr., "Vote rights law jolts local election officials," *Dallas Morning News,* December 21, 1975).

87. David H. Hunter, *Federal Review of Voting Changes: How to Use Section 5 of the Voting Rights Act,* 2nd ed. (Washington, D.C.: Joint Center for Political Studies, 1975), 35–36.

88. For sources with an "inside" view, see Drew S. Days III and Lani Guinier, "Enforcement of Section 5 of the Voting Rights Act"; and Howard Ball, Dale Krane, and Thomas P. Lauth, "The View from Georgia and Mississippi: Local Attorneys' Appraisal of the 1965 Voting Rights Act," in Davidson, *Minority Vote Dilution,* 181–202. Drew Days was assistant attorney general for civil rights from March 1977 to December 1980; Lani Guinier was his special assistant. For an early history of the Civil Rights Section in the DOJ, see Robert K. Carr, *Federal Protection of Civil Rights: Quest for a Sword* (Ithaca, N.Y.: Cornell University Press, 1947). For an overview of the development of the civil rights enforcement role of the Department of Justice, see Brian K. Landsberg, *Enforcing Civil Rights: Race Discrimination and the Department of Justice* (Lawrence: University Press of Kansas, 1997).

89. *Dallas Morning News,* August 14, 1994. During their investigation, the reporters also found that the Justice Department stays on the sidelines when minority officeholders complain that their authority has been transferred. This practice stems from a 1992 U.S. Supreme Court decision that limited the DOJ's role when the powers of minority officeholders are reallocated: *Presley* v. *Etowah County Commission,* 478 U.S. 109 (1986). The Court ruled that the Justice Department could not intervene in transfer-of-authority cases.

decline in public and political support for advancing race-conscious public policies, such action is problematic.[90] A generation after the development of a national consensus, which supported the initial enactment of the VRA, race relations remain troubled. Minorities are still faced with barriers to full and effective political participation. The theories and assumptions, which underlie the legal rights approach to ensuring fairness in electoral politics, are open to question.

The VRA has had its successes. It effectively ended de jure voting discrimination, a landmark in the history of U.S. civil rights. The VRA sensitizes local officials to the need to consider the impact on minorities of changes in electoral structures and rules. The requirement to submit changes for preclearance and approval is an electoral equivalent to an environmental impact statement—both of which force a rise in awareness levels. Some advantage has been realized in applying the VRA special provisions to states in the South, which had a history of de jure discrimination.

But congressional attempts to devise standards for subtle de facto discrimination have failed. The target was unclear and even kept changing. How to measure, and to remedy, discrimination once the issues moved beyond the ballot were not obvious. Public support declined as Congress muddled through complex questions. A national consensus cannot be built on shifting goals, nor can law remediate all the problems a society must deal with.

"Popular governments," as John Jay, the first Chief Justice of the United States, once wrote, "must be influenced by popular opinion and popular opinion must be *created* not commanded. It is a kind of *creation* too which can proceed but slowly, because often opposed by Prejudices, Ignorances, clashing Interests, and . . . illfounded [*sic*] Jealousies."[91]

---

90. See Thomas Byrne Edsall and Mary D. Edsall, *Chain Reaction: The Impact of Race, Rights, and Taxes on American Politics* (New York: W.W. Norton, 1991), for an exploration of the race-driven conflicts that have structured much of the nation's politics since 1965.

91. John Jay to Reverend D. Price, unpublished letter, August 24, 1775, in *Statutory History of the United States: Civil Rights,* ed. Bernard Schwartz (New York: Chelsea House, 1970), 1:13.

2
Voting Rights Case Law

It is not unfair to say that the mid-twentieth century revolution in the field of
civil rights has been the rarest of all political animals—a judge-led
revolution.
—Bernard Schwartz, *Statutory History of the United States*

After more than thirty years navigating fogbound in voting rights issues, the
courts have yet to provide state and local governments with a coherent message
on the standards for complying with the developing body of voting rights law.
An appreciation for the clutter on the guidance radar because of undefined
terms, ambiguous concepts, and amorphous theories provides an important
context for understanding the impact of the Voting Rights Act at the micro
level.

Voting rights cases may be brought either under the U.S. Constitution,
especially the Fourteenth and Fifteenth Amendments, or under the Voting
Rights Act of 1965. Thus two streams of decisions, which sometimes converge
and occasionally conflict, flow from the federal courts on voting rights. An
important difference is the more favorable standards of proof available to litigants claiming discrimination under the VRA than in a traditional constitutional suit.[1] Furthermore, an action may be ruled unconstitutional under
provisions in the U.S. Constitution and yet be found constitutional under statutory provisions, provided that Congress has acted within its constitutional
authority.

While the idea of rights may not be explicit in the U.S. Constitution, an
underlying premise is to protect the individual from arbitrary acts of government. The framers, recognizing that self-restraint by officials may not have
been sufficient protection, divided power into three branches. This implicitly
established the fundamental principles of separation of powers and checks and

---

1. In a suit under the VRA, the state or subdivision must prove that its new procedure
does not unconstitutionally burden the right of a minority to vote; in a constitutional suit,
plaintiff has to assume an inverse burden, with the state able to justify its procedure merely
by showing it as rationally related to a permissible governmental interest (27 ALR
Fed. 29).

balances. Despite the theoretical neatness of vesting "all legislative powers herein granted" in a Congress, "the executive power" in a president, and "the judicial Power . . . in one supreme Court, and in such inferior Courts as the Congress may . . . ordain and establish," in practice, throughout U.S. history, the boundaries have been a sieve through which these powers have flowed and intermingled among the three branches in various ratios.

The principle of federalism is an additional constitutional constraint on the encroachment of central government into the lives of individuals. The Tenth Amendment specifies that, "the powers not delegated to the United States by the Constitution, nor prohibited by it to the States, are reserved to the States respectively, or to the people." Reflecting the enduring philosophical tension between the will of the people and rule by the wise, the other two branches, being coequal to the legislative branch, were designed as additional curbs, by providing for an indirectly elected president and an appointed Supreme Court. The judiciary was viewed by the framers as "the least dangerous" branch of government, and therefore the best guarantor to protect these constitutional principles against tyranny of the majority by the elected representative body.[2] Thus the protection of a minority from a majority of the moment is implicit in the concept of rights. These fundamental constitutional principles— federalism, separation of powers, and majority rule tempered by protection of the minority—are the standards against which actions by the federal courts in voting rights cases are measured.

Because the rights the Constitution protects are essentially "negative," that is, freedoms and immunities *from* government interference, the courts infrequently have had to consider providing benefits *to* individuals. Only in special circumstances have courts had to develop affirmative remedies, moving beyond *proscriptive* adjudication to *prescriptive* law.[3] The extraordinarily complicated issue of fair representation is one of those instances.[4] But in over-simplifying the problem of "fairness," and by prescribing simplistic solutions, the courts have short-circuited states and localities from serving as the nation's laboratories for innovation. In so doing, the courts have devalued and under-mined the democratic processes in which bargaining and persuasion can build consensus. Issues most dependent on political compromise, because of their complexity and subtlety, are least conforming with the legal model, in which plaintiffs frame the questions and "rules" frame the answers. In such instances

2. Hamilton, *The Federalist,* no. 78.

3. For differentiation between the two periods of sustained judicial activism, "proscriptive judicial activity" (the era between 1889 and 1937) and "prescriptive activism" (the period since 1954), see Gary L. McDowell, *Curbing the Courts: The Constitution and the Limits of Judicial Power* (Baton Rouge: Louisiana State University Press, 1988), 3–4, 9, 151, 198, 205.

4. Other areas in which remedial decrees have been used to enforce constitutional standards on institutions include prisons, housing, and schools.

the legal model is inadequate, because it limits the scope of relevant factors to be examined as well as the range of remedies that might be considered.[5]

The judicial process channels complex problems through the narrow bounds of legal concepts and remedies, and then reformulates them as concrete issues in controversy between parties so that they might be susceptible to proof by discrete items of evidence. This process fundamentally alters the problem by reductionism. Or, stated somewhat differently, "framing a social problem as a legal issue produces a transformation of the issue itself—a reconceptualization of the problem, yielding unique questions and concerns that first become the focus of the legal debate and subsequently tend to dominate public discussion."[6]

Doctrines that channel judicial review include the requirement that constitutional issues be raised by persons with a proper interest, or "standing," in a specific "case or controversy" on a concrete issue that is ready for adjudication between parties. This means that the Court does not issue advisory opinions, the case cannot be moot, and it has to be filed by an interested party. Another doctrine that clearly channels decisions is the binding force of precedent, referred to as *stare decisis*.[7] Litigation, then, is constrained by its own internal dynamics.

As voting rights litigation has evolved, courts have become mired in making policy choices among competing theories of representation, conflicting testimony of expert witnesses, and inconclusive debates on empirical and methodological questions. To enforce nondiscrimination, or negative remedies, is clearly within the jurisdiction of the courts. But they have neither expertise nor tools to determine affirmative remedies for resolving racial issues. Neither a reduction in concern or attention to minority political participation, nor the abandonment of a legal strategy, is suggested here but, rather, recognition that the judicial process has internal constraints. This recognition frees a society to

5. Much of the criticism of litigation strategy focuses on the allocation of resources to techniques of political mobilization, which might be more effective. Stuart Scheingold argues that "The myth of rights is . . . premised on a direct linking of litigation, rights, and remedies with social change," which is "an approach that grossly exaggerates the role that lawyers and litigation can play in a strategy for change" (*The Politics of Rights: Lawyers, Public Policy, and Political Change* [New Haven, Conn.: Yale University Press, 1974], 4). Scheingold's work is a superior volume on the political approach to the problem of law and change. See also Judith N. Shklar, *Legalism* (Cambridge, Mass.: Harvard University Press, 1964), for an essay on the relation of law to morality and politics. Also see Mary Ann Glendon, *Rights Talk: The Impoverishment of Political Discourse* (New York: Free Press, 1991).

6. Stephen C. Halpern, *On the Limits of the Law: The Ironic Legacy of Title VI of the 1964 Civil Rights Act* (Baltimore: The Johns Hopkins University Press, 1995), ix.

7. For a study of the reasons justices vote as they do when overturning cases and to what extent *stare decisis* plays a role, see Saul Brenner and Harold J. Spaeth, *Stare Decisis: The Alteration of Precedent on the Supreme Court, 1946–1992* (New York: Cambridge University Press, 1995).

think outside narrow channels so as to develop holistic strategies for resolving complex, multifaceted racial issues.

The increase in plurality opinions is indicative of the difficulty the Supreme Court has in designing remedies regarding complex public policy issues. From 1801 until 1955 there were forty-five plurality decisions; during the Warren Court, forty-two; and from 1970 to 1980 there were eighty-eight, according to a 1981 analysis in the *Harvard Law Review*.[8] "Plurality decisions" are rulings in which no single opinion draws the support of a majority of the justices. One of the areas in which plurality rulings, which represent "a failure to fulfill the Court's obligations," have occurred most frequently is voting rights.[9] The editors do acknowledge weakness in the social consensus being a contributing factor, but they believe that a base reason for the increase in "useless" Supreme Court rulings is the tendency for justices to reach outside the law to try to settle questions presented to them in a narrow legal context. The result is the "inevitably arbitrary choice of underlying values."[10]

Since 1954, with the Supreme Court's unanimous decision in the *Public School Desegregation Case*,[11] the courts have "reached outside the law" and have become more prescriptively active than at any other time in the nation's history. That milestone case introduced a new approach in court litigation, which extended through the 1990s. After *Brown*, the "equal protection of the laws" clause emerged into predominance, and courts began to affirm that positive outcomes should result from prescribed remedies in several policy areas, including voting rights. With the expansion of affirmative action concepts of civil rights after *Brown*, judges have been called on to "navigate a statistical quagmire." They must choose between conflicting testimony of expert witnesses and their proposed methodologies to establish results-oriented evidence to satisfy constitutional and statutory civil rights requirements.[12]

8. "Plurality Decisions and Judicial Decisionmaking," *Harvard Law Review* (1981), 94:1127 n. 1.

9. Plurality opinions in voting rights cases include *Oregon* v. *Mitchell*, 400 U.S. 112 (1970); *Whitcomb* v. *Chavis*, 403 U.S. 124 (1971); *United Jewish Organizations* v. *Carey*, 430 U.S. 144 (1977); *Wise* v. *Lipscomb*, 437 U.S. 535 (1978); and *City of Mobile* v. *Bolden*, 446 U.S. 55 (1980) ("Plurality Decisions," *Harvard Law Review* [1981], 94:1128; Appendix, 1147).

10. Ibid., 1128.

11. *Brown* v. *Board of Education*, 347 U.S. 483 (1954).

12. Kimi Lynn King, Jennifer Marie Morbitt, and John Francis Ryan, "Voting Rights and Wrongs: Federal District Court Decision-Making, 1965–1993," paper prepared for the annual meeting of the American Political Science Association, 1996. See this paper for problems regarding the increasing use of statistical methodology to provide evidence of disparate treatment in vote dilution cases. Also see Nicholas Eberstadt, *The Tyranny of Numbers: Mismeasurement and Misrule* (Washington, D.C.: AEI Press, 1995), for a sobering view by a demographer on our statistics-oriented, meliorative state, and the direct and injurious consequences for citizens. For an engaging debate among social scientists

Brown and subsequent civil rights cases, as one might expect, produced a spate of literature on the overextension of the Supreme Court in its attempt to establish a social agenda. More fundamental, though, is that the very nature of the judicial process itself precludes the necessary decisions to ensure majority-minority equity in the political process.[13]

A plausible argument may be made that the right to vote is a special circumstance that may require affirmative judicial intervention in the political system. The unresponsiveness of political institutions was a primary factor for disadvantaged groups having to resort to the judiciary to achieve their objectives. If the disenfranchised cannot use conventional methods to bring pressure on legislators and executives to respond to their interests, they may have to turn to nonelective forums. As Justice Clark pointed out in his concurring opinion in *Baker* v. *Carr,* the majority of the people of Tennessee had no "practical opportunities for exerting their political weight at the polls" to correct existing "invidious discrimination," since Tennessee had no initiative and referendum.[14]

After a century of using the courts to try to achieve full political participation of minorities in American society, and despite good intentions of lawmakers and law enforcers, that goal has not been realized. In part, this unfulfilled hope is owing to reliance on the law to achieve what the law alone cannot provide.[15] An expectation was that if legal remedies could assist minorities in overcoming the effects of discrimination, then these minorities would be able to use their political power to achieve their ends. This reflected a misplaced

---

on the disparities among the experts deriving from differing normative views and disputes on difficult empirical and methodological questions, see "Minisymposium, Political Gerrymandering: Badham v. Eu, Political Science Goes to Court," *PS: Political Science and Politics* (summer 1985), 18:537–581.

13. This is not a new argument. Halpern, in *On the Limits of the Law,* presents a similar argument in his analysis of the 1964 Civil Rights Act litigation.

14. *Baker* v. *Carr,* 369 U.S. 186 (1962), 258–259. The standard used by Justice Douglas was the "traditional test under the Equal Protection Clause [of] . . . whether a State has made 'an invidious discrimination,' as it does when it selects 'a particular race or nationality for oppressive treatment'" (*Baker* v. *Carr,* 369 U.S. 186 [1962], 244).

15. On the shortcomings of the litigation strategy, see Gerald N. Rosenberg, *The Hollow Hope: Can Courts Bring about Social Change?* (Chicago: University of Chicago Press, 1991); Stuart A. Scheingold, *The Politics of Rights: Lawyers, Public Policy, and Political Change* (New Haven, Conn.: Yale University Press, 1974); and Donald L. Horowitz, *The Courts and Social Policy* (Washington, D.C.: The Brookings Institution, 1977). One of the criticisms is the diversion of resources to costly litigation. For example, to win *City of Mobile* on remand required expenditure of "tens of thousands of dollars, at least 6,000 hours of lawyers' time, 800 hours of paralegals' time, 4,400 hours of expert witnesses and research assistants' time, and eleven and a half days of trial," according to the *Annual Report for 1981/1982* of the NAACP Legal Defense Fund, cited in Stephen L. Wasby, *Race Relations Litigation in an Age of Complexity* (Charlottesville: University Press of Virginia, 1995), 42 n. 57.

faith in the ability of the courts to function "primarily as the last refuge for the correction of all inequality or injustice, no matter what its nature or source."[16]

BACKGROUND

Significantly the decisions of the courts regarding voting rights cases are marked by inconsistencies, seesaw reversals, and an absence of a clear body of law. One result of the blurred focus of the legal lens on voting rights issues is the inevitable, continuing stream of cases searching for guidelines, as the courts muddle through ill-defined issues and contradicting claims.

Many voting rights rulings stem from district and appellate court decisions, which may not be challenged or, if challenged, may not be reviewed by the Supreme Court. Consequently a judicial decision reached in one locale may not resemble one in another locale. In the early period of judicial review of the Voting Rights Act, this situation prevailed, particularly when cases were brought under the special provisions that did not apply nationwide. Furthermore, circuit courts developed different patterns in adjudicating voting rights cases. For example, a majority in *Thornburg* v. *Gingles* (1986) failed to agree on a definition of "minority-preferred candidates": the Fifth and Seventh Circuits adopted Justice White's race-conscious rule that only minority candidates could be the minority-preferred candidates; the Eleventh Circuit applied Justice Brennan's race-neutral rule that the race of a candidate is irrelevant to an analysis of bloc voting; and the Third and Tenth Circuits have applied Justice O'Connor's test of taking race into account as one of several factors in making the determination.[17]

Nevertheless, a number of issues do thread through most of the cases. Two important ones here are the "political question" doctrine, and the matter of apportionment and districting.

"Political Question" Doctrine

Article IV, Section 1, of the U.S. Constitution provides that "the United States shall guarantee to every State in this Union a Republican Form of Government." This provision would appear to be an avenue for protection against state and local interference with the right to vote. The pioneer case of *Luther* v. *Borden*[18] established that questions which arise under this section are political, not judicial, in character, and that it rests with Congress as to whether a

---

16. Justice Harlan, concurring, *Baker* v. *Carr,* 369 U.S. 186, 339.

17. Scott Yut, "Using Candidate Race to Define Minority-Preferred Candidates Under Section 2 of the Voting Rights Act," *The University of Chicago Legal Forum* (1995), 1995:571–599, at 583. *Thornburg* v. *Gingles,* 478 U.S. 30 (1986).

18. 7 Howard 1 (1849).

"republican form of government has been guaranteed to [a] State."[19] But this constitutional provision has not yet emerged into prominence in voting rights controversies.[20]

The concept of a "political question" actually predates *Luther* v. *Borden*. In *Marbury* v. *Madison,* in 1803, Chief Justice Marshall stated that courts have no authority "to inquire into and control political matters left by law to executive discretion . . . or matters left to legislative discretion."[21] In its origin, then, the issue involved separation of powers. In practice, the doctrine is a "rule of expediency," rather than a definable principle, because it is undermined by prospective inability to shape or enforce a remedy."[22] Since 1803 issues have steadily migrated from the nonjusticiable political question realm into the justiciable realm. The Supreme Court has held that the "dominant considerations" in determining whether a question falls within the political question category are "the appropriateness . . . of attributing finality to the action of the political departments and also the lack of satisfactory criteria for a judicial determination."[23]

That "political questions" should be solved in the political rather than the judicial arena is one of the major philosophical differences leading to a divergence of opinion as to the role of courts in bringing about social change. Controversies over where a line should be drawn between judicial and political jurisdictions persist. Distinctly different views on social policy making have not subsided, even after four decades of court decisions on voting rights issues.

Apportionment and Districting

The controversies of apportionment and districting arise from congressional authority under the original constitution. Article I, Sections 2 and 3, stipulate that "representatives . . . shall be apportioned among the several States . . . according to their respective Numbers," that is, according to population; and the Senate "shall be composed of two Senators from each State," that is, according to geography. The former requirement gave rise to the practice of reapportioning representatives to states after each decennial census.

19. *Luther* v. *Borden,* 7 Howard 1, 2 (1849).

20. For a more detailed discussion of justiciability, see Terry B. O'Rourke, *Reapportionment: Law, Politics, Computers* (Washington, D.C.: American Enterprise Institute for Public Policy Research, 1972). O'Rourke reviews the "political question" doctrine developed in *Luther* v. *Borden,* and the application of that doctrine by Justice Frankfurter in 1946 to reapportionment in *Colegrove* v. *Green.* O'Rourke's discussion concludes with a reevaluation of the *Colegrove* position in the case of *Baker* v. *Carr.*

21. *Marbury* v. *Madison,* 1 Cranch 137, 143, 145 (1803).

22. Robert G. Dixon Jr., *Democratic Representation: Reapportionment in Law and Politics* (New York: Oxford University Press, 1968), 101.

23. *Coleman* v. *Miller,* 307 U.S. 433, 454–455 (1939).

Congressional legislation that established districts in states for the purpose of electing U.S. Representatives derives from Article I, Section 4. This provision stipulates that "the Times, Places and Manner of holding Elections for Senators and Representatives, shall be prescribed in each State by the Legislature thereof; but the Congress may at any time by Law make or alter such Regulations, except as to the Places of chusing [sic] Senators." Congress was thus given the power to legislate to protect the right to vote for U.S. Representatives and Senators, though states were vested with the discretion to prescribe voter qualifications and delineate House districts.

Districts have not always been required for the election of representatives. Congress first exercised the power to regulate the "Times, Places and Manner of holding Elections" for members of Congress in 1842, when it passed a law requiring the election of representatives by districts.[24] This requirement was dropped in 1850[25] but was readopted in 1862.[26] In subsequent years Congress expanded on its requirements, successively adding contiguity, compactness, and substantial equality of population to districting requirements. These requirements were omitted in 1929, when Congress set the permanent size of the House of Representatives at 435. This legislation meant that the size of districts had to be increased in order to reflect population increases rather than the size of the House.[27] In 1967 Congress first mandated the use of single-member districts from which to elect members of the U.S. House of Representatives.[28] Article I, Section 4, of the Constitution had opened the door through which Congress and the courts could enter the fray of state reapportionment and redistricting.

Undeniably apportioning population to districts and drawing district lines are political exercises in balancing multiple interests. In an early case, *Colegrove* v. *Green,* the Supreme Court, citing nonjusticiability, dismissed the complaint that the Illinois apportionment law created districts glaringly unequal in population.[29] In *Colegrove,* Justice Felix Frankfurter coined the term *a political thicket* to describe the "matters that bring courts into immediate and active relations with party contests."[30] Justice Frankfurter announced the judgment of the court in a 4–3 plurality opinion: "It is hostile to a democratic system to involve the judiciary in the politics of the people . . . [even if] judicial intervention in an essentially political contest be dressed up in the abstract phrases of the law."[31] Justice Hugo Black, joined by Justices William

24. 5 Stat. 491 (1842).
25. 9 Stat. 428 (1850).
26. 12 Stat. 572 (1862).
27. 46 Stat. 13 (1929).
28. 81 Stat. 581, 2 U.S.C. § 2c.
29. *Colegrove* v. *Green,* 328 U.S. 549 (1946).
30. Ibid., 553, 556.
31. Ibid., 553–554.

O. Douglas and Frank Murphy, dissented emphatically, stating that the right to vote implies that districts "should be designed to give approximately equal weight to each vote cast" under the equal protection clause.[32]

The views of the dissenters ultimately prevailed. The Court ruled, in *Wesberry* v. *Sanders* (1964), that state laws, which established congressional districts grossly unequal in population, presented a justiciable, rather than a political, question under Article I.[33] Thus ended the era of judicial nonintervention in controversies as to the malapportionment of congressional districts.

The first allegation of racial gerrymandering of congressional districts, again under Article I, also arose in 1964, in the case of *Wright* v. *Rockefeller.*[34] In this first instance, the Court ruled that the minority voters had not proved that the New York apportionment statute, which created irregularly shaped racially concentrated districts, was motivated by race.

PHASES OF VOTING RIGHTS LITIGATION

Voting rights cases over the years have moved through different, increasingly complicated phases. The four phases in which voting rights have been viewed by the courts to date are as follows:[35]

1. The right to vote;
2. The right to an effective vote, as measured by a numerically equal vote;
3. The right to an effective vote, as measured by representation equity; and
4. The right to an effective voice once elected.

Phase 1: The Right to Vote

During this first phase of court litigation, voting was viewed as an individual right; the protection provided by government was to ensure formal participation, including registration and access to the ballot and to the polling booth. In this phase the courts sought to remove direct legal impediments to racial and ethnic minorities' right to vote. The thrust of most cases prior to the 1960s was to nullify, as contrary to the Constitution, state actions based on voter exclusion schemes, such as literacy requirements and character qualifications, and poll tax payments and property ownership, as well as preventing participation in primaries and other political party activities. The issues raised by the party primary cases in Texas are reviewed here.

32. Ibid., 570.
33. *Wesberry* v. *Sanders,* 376 U.S. 1 (1964).
34. *Wright* v. *Rockefeller,* 376 U.S. 52 (1964).
35. For discussion of a generational metaphor as a way of organizing the history of VRA enforcement, see Lani Guinier, *The Tyranny of the Majority: Fundamental Fairness in Representative Democracy* (New York: Free Press, 1994), 7–9. Guinier combines the first and second phases as the "first generation" of voting rights cases.

State action and overt discriminatory purpose were critical to decisions based on Fourteenth Amendment violation, which invalidated Texas laws that excluded blacks from primary elections. First, in a unanimous decision, the Court struck down a 1923 Texas state law that established all-white primaries.[36] The Texas legislature countered with a law to permit the central committees of state political parties to proscribe voting qualifications for political parties in primary elections, thus enabling political parties to exclude blacks. In a 5–4 decision, this law was ruled unconstitutional under the Fourteenth Amendment.[37] Next, at its state convention, the Democratic Party restricted voting in its primary to whites. This time, in a unanimous decision, the Court held that neither the Fourteenth nor the Fifteenth Amendment prohibited actions by political parties not acting under state law.[38]

Then, in 1941, in a 5–3 decision, the Court ruled that Congress had the authority to regulate primary elections for representatives in Congress according to Article I, Section 4, of the Constitution.[39] Subsequently the Court held that, where political parties are entrusted by statute to select candidates for public office, a political party may not, under the Fifteenth Amendment, exclude blacks from such elections.[40] In an 8–1 plurality decision, nine years later, the Court invalidated a "slating" practice.[41]

Terry v. *Adams* is an important case because it addresses slating, a significant issue in the litigation involving the governmental structure in the city of Dallas. The Court invalidated the discrimination against blacks practiced by the Jaybird Democratic Association, a club consisting only of white voters in a Texas county. This association, although independent both of state laws and of the use of state election machinery or funds, selected candidates for county offices to run for the party's nomination in the official Democratic primary. With one exception, in more than sixty years, the association's candidates ran unopposed in the Democratic primary, without identification as Jaybirds, invariably winning election to office. The Court opinion held that the Jaybird primary was the only effective part of the elective process in the county and was tantamount to election; participation of county election officials in the Jaybird primary thus amounted to state action prohibited by the Fifteenth Amendment; and a state is precluded from constructing its electoral apparatus so that a discriminatory association, whether as an auxiliary of the Democratic Party or as a separate organization, becomes the decisive power in the electoral proc-

36. *Nixon* v. *Herndon,* 273 U.S. 536 (1927).
37. *Nixon* v. *Condon,* 286 U.S. 73 (1932).
38. *Grovey* v. *Townsend,* 295 U.S. 45 (1935).
39. *United States* v. *Classic,* 313 U.S. 299 (1944).
40. *Smith* v. *Allwright,* 321 U.S. 649 (1944).
41. *Terry* v. *Adams,* 345 U.S. 461 (1953). For a detailed accounting of the Texas white primary and relevant cases, see Abraham L. Davis and Barbara Luck Graham, *The Supreme Court, Race, and Civil Rights* (Thousand Oaks, Calif.: Sage, 1995), chap. 2.

ess. Justice Sherman Minton dissented on the grounds that no state action was involved.

Phase 2: Vote Equality

After the first apportionment cases, the courts departed from the principle of federal protection of the right to vote against specific forms of discrimination and abuse, and developed the "dilution" concept. This recognized that although a person's right to vote might be secured, the "effectiveness" might be diminished or "diluted" if that person resided in a district with a low number of representatives-per-population compared to districts in other parts of the state.[42]

The justiciability of apportionment cases moved sequentially from the election of representatives to Congress to the election of representatives and senators to state legislatures from geographically based districts. This change followed *Brown* v. *Board of Education* (1954), when the "equal protection of the laws" clause of the Fourteenth Amendment emerged into predominance. In the later landmark case of *Baker* v. *Carr* (1962), the Court held in a plurality opinion that malapportionment of seats in a state legislature, as distinguished from seats in the House of Representatives, does not present a political question, when its validity is challenged on the basis of the Fourteenth Amendment, which applies to states, rather than on the basis of Article I, which applies to Congress.[43]

Justice William J. Brennan delivered the opinion of the Court, which decided only the issue of justiciability and remanded the case for decision.[44] Concerned by the Court's failure to muster a majority to decide the case on its merits, Justice Tom C. Clark asserted that the practice of judicial self-restraint and discipline are well and good, but "never in its history have those principles received sanction where the national rights of so many have been so clearly infringed for so long a time."[45] In this case the minorities were not racial minorities but urban communities in a state where rural sections of the state

42. This problem may seem simple to solve, but it is both a practical and a theoretical challenge. See H. Peyton Young, *Equity: In Theory and Practice* (Princeton, N.J.: Princeton University Press, 1994), esp. chap. 3. For a comprehensive treatment of the history and mathematics of legislative apportionment, see Michel L. Balinski and H. Peyton Young, *Fair Representation: Meeting the Ideal of One Man, One Vote* (New Haven, Conn.: Yale University Press, 1982).

43. Within nine months of the decision in *Baker,* litigation to challenge the constitutionality of state legislative apportionment schemes had been instituted in some thirty-four states. See Robert B. McKay, "Political Thickets and Crazy Quilts: Reapportionment and Equal Protection," *Michigan Law Review* (February 1963) 61:645, 706–710, cited by Justice Warren in *Reynolds* v. *Sims,* 377 U.S. 533, 556 (1964).

44. In 1986 urban/rural representation inequities were invalidated (*infra,* n. 64).

45. *Baker* v. *Carr,* 369 U.S. 186, 262 (1962). Justice Clark, concurring.

were favored in legislative representation, which Justice Douglas found to be "invidious discrimination."[46]

Justices Frankfurter and Harlan filed vigorous dissents, contending that the inability to formulate judicial standards in this area underscored the nonjusticiability of malapportionment complaints. According to Frankfurter:

> Apportionment, by its character, is a subject of extraordinary complexity, involving—even after the fundamental theoretical issues concerning what is to be represented in a representative legislature have been fought out or compromised—considerations of geography, demography, electoral convenience, economic and social cohesion or divergences among particular local groups, communications, the practical effects of political institutions like the lobby and the city machine, ancient traditions and ties of settled usage, respect for proven incumbents of long experience and senior status, mathematical mechanics, censuses compiling relevant data, and a host of others.[47]

In view of this extraordinary complexity, Justice Frankfurter predicted that if the federal judiciary permitted itself to become embroiled in apportionment battles, which are "overwhelmingly party or intra-party contests," it would "embroil the federal judiciary" in "a virulent source of friction and tension in federal-state relations."[48]

The Court ignored Frankfurter's warnings and went on to devise, and impose, a theory of representation—*namely,* "one man, one vote"—which required that districts be drawn as nearly equal in population as possible. The requirement that state legislatures should be apportioned so that every qualified resident has "the right to a ballot for election of state legislators of equal weight to the vote of every other resident" was established in *Reynolds* v. *Sims.*[49]

In this second phase of voting rights litigation, then, the concept of dilution meant districts comprised of equal numbers of voters, which is an objective standard. Hence any permissible divergence from the standard of absolute equality becomes a matter for judgment.

Even a presumably objective standard, such as "one man, one vote," generated vigorous dissent. Justice Harlan argued that the rule "possesses the simplistic defects inherent in any judicially imposed solution of a complex social problem."[50] In his *Reynolds* dissent he had set forth his views at length, specifically that the Court should not engage in adventures into the realm of political science beyond its constitutional powers.[51]

46. Ibid., 244–245.
47. Ibid., 323.
48. Ibid., 324.
49. *Reynolds* v. *Sims,* 377 U.S. 533 (1964).
50. *Avery* v. *Midland County,* 390 U.S. 474, 494 (1968).
51. *Reynolds* v. *Sims,* 377 U.S. 533, 589 et seq. (1964).

Scholars also voiced their concerns. A long-time student of representation issues argued that a focus "on equalizing legislative district population as the guide to fair and effective political representation puts 'one man-one vote' on too narrow a base," which ignores that "what is represented is never merely the individual, but always certain purposes common to groups of individuals."[52] Another scholar was even more blunt: "The 'one man, one vote' slogan, in equating the whole of democracy with majority-rule elections, represents naive political philosophy, bad political theory, and no political science."[53]

Chief Justice Warren delivered the opinion of the Court in *Reynolds*, which rejected interest group representation: "Legislators represent people, not trees or acres. Legislators are elected by voters, not farms or cities or economic interests."[54] The *Reynolds* opinion also rejected the proposition that a bicameral state legislature is analogous to the U.S. Congress, on the basis that political subdivisions of states are not sovereign entities. Therefore the Court ruled that seats in both houses of state legislatures must be apportioned substantially on a population base under the "equal protection" clause.[55]

Another equal protection argument was raised in *Fortson* v. *Dorsey*. Plaintiffs alleged that countywide voting in multi-member district counties denied those residents a vote "approximately equal in weight to that of voters resident in the single-member constituencies."[56] This argument was not accepted. Justice Brennan made a point relevant to municipal at-large elections. He suggested that because districts are only for candidate residence and not election in multi-member elections, the person elected "must be vigilant to serve the interests of all the people in the county, and not merely those of people in his home district."[57] This view became prominent in the arguments of proponents of at-large election systems for municipalities.

In 1968 the "one person, one vote" state apportionment rule from *Reynolds* was extended to local governments in a decision Justice Harlan deemed "both unjustifiable and ill-advised," as it affected "an estimated 80,000 units of local government throughout the land."[58] *Avery* v. *Midland* generated three dissenting opinions, by Justices Harlan, Fortas, and Stewart. Justice Harlan vehemently disagreed with the decision, which he said "wholly disregards statutory limitations upon the appellate jurisdiction of this Court in state cases and

52. Dixon, *Democratic Representation*, viii.

53. Martin Shapiro, *Law and Politics in the Supreme Court* (New York: Free Press, 1964), 250, as cited in Gary J. Jacobsohn, "The 'Pragmatic Dogma' of the Political Thicket: The Jurisprudential Paradox of 'One Man, One Vote,'" *Polity* (spring 1977), 9:295.

54. *Reynolds* v. *Sims,* 377 U.S. 533, 562 (1964).

55. Ibid., 568–576.

56. *Fortson* v. *Dorsey,* 379 U.S. 433, 436–437 (1964).

57. Ibid., 438.

58. *Avery* v. *Midland County, Texas,* 390 U.S. 474, 487 (1967).

again betrays such insensitivity to the appropriate dividing lines between the judicial and political functions under our constitutional system."[59] The case involved a county judge, elected at large from the entire county, and four commissioners, one elected from each of the four districts (precincts) into which the county was divided. The standard for redistricting, set by the Texas Supreme Court, included the number of qualified voters, land areas, geography, miles of county roads, and taxable values.[60]

Districting. The issue of districting is equally as complicated as that of apportionment. The practice of gerrymandering dates back to at least 1812, when the term was applied to a redistricting plan in Massachusetts, designed to give Republicans control. Gerrymandering, simply defined, is the drawing of district lines to achieve either partisan or some other advantage. All districting, really, is gerrymandering, since "whether or not there is a gerrymander in *design,* there normally will be some gerrymander in *result.*"[61]

Anti-dilution concepts were not, at first, applied to gerrymandering. This situation changed with the 1960 decision in *Gomillion* v. *Lightfoot,*[62] which recognized that political differentiation made along racial lines can "lift [a] . . . controversy out of the so-called 'political' arena and into the conventional sphere of constitutional litigation."[63] Federal courts adhered for several years thereafter to a distinction between "political" gerrymandering, engaged in for political party advantage, and "racial" gerrymandering. Until 1986 the former remained nonjusticiable.[64]

In the first congressional district racial gerrymandering case, *Wright* v. *Rockefeller,*[65] Justice Douglas's dissenting opinion appears to be prophetic. He probed the issue of "segregated" voting districts and concluded: "The fact that Negro political leaders find advantage in this nearly solid Negro and Puerto Rican district is irrelevant to our problem." "Rotten boroughs," he continued, "were long a curse of democratic processes [and] [r]acial boroughs are also at war with democratic standards."[66] His dissent was premised on the equality of the individual voter, not his race, his creed, or his color:

> The racial electoral register system weights votes along one racial line more heavily than it does other votes. That system, by whatever name it is called, is a divisive force in a community, emphasizing differences

59. Ibid., 486.
60. Ibid., 495, as cited by Justice Fortas.
61. Dixon, *Democratic Representation,* 462.
62. 364 U.S. 339 (1960).
63. Ibid., 346–347.
64. Political gerrymandering was held justiciable under the Fourteenth Amendment in *Davis* v. *Bandemer,* 478 U.S. 109 (1986).
65. 376 U.S. 52 (1964).
66. Ibid., 62.

between candidates and votes that are irrelevant in the constitutional sense. Of course race, like religion, plays an important role in the choices which individual voters make from among various candidates. But government has no business designing electoral districts along racial or religious lines.[67]

Douglas raised the point that even if "polarized voting," as it later came to be tagged, were to occur, violation of the Fourteenth Amendment by segregating people by race into voting districts is not justified.

Phase 3: Representation Equity

The third phase of voting rights litigation emphasized a concept of representational equity that recognizes how a person can have a mathematically equal vote yet have little chance of being represented in the governing body. These third phase cases recognized that adherence to the principle of "one person, one vote" does not, necessarily, guarantee equity of representation. The "submergence" of a minority group within a jurisdiction may still occur. Federal courts have examined whether the equal protection clause of the Fourteenth Amendment is violated by districting schemes that perhaps provide unequal representation opportunities by canceling out the votes of minorities. This phase reflected a shift in the dominant focus from viewing the voting right as an individual right to seeing it as a group right.

Early ideas of how to detect unconstitutional dilution developed in cases involving multi-member election schemes with at-large voting, which became the subject of most of this litigation.[68] To deal with claims of dilution, a general rule developed that multi-member districts are not unconstitutional per se; they can be struck down, on a case-by-case basis, if plaintiffs can show that a district operates to "minimize or cancel out the racial or political elements of the voting population."[69]

In defining *dilution,* the Court settled on single-member districts as the remedy. Then, after settling on single-member districts, the next step was to create districts in which racial minority groups would be in the majority in order to be assured of seats. Such districts, which I refer to as "minority-dominant" districts, are commonly referred to as "majority-minority" districts.

The concept of "dilution" raised serious methodological problems for courts, as they attempted to identify evidentiary standards for dilution. This

67. Ibid., 66.
68. For the first major study on the complicated issues surrounding dilution, see Chandler Davidson, ed., *Minority Vote Dilution* (Washington, D.C.: Howard University Press, 1984).
69. *Fortson* v. *Dorsey,* 379 U.S. 433, 439 (1965); *Burns* v. *Richardson,* 384 U.S. 73, 88 (1966).

involved, inter alia, the increasing use of data on precinct voting patterns in order to decide if electoral practices of jurisdictions were discriminatory against racial minorities. Statistical methodologies frequently generate heated debate in the scholarly community, and no less so than in voting rights cases, where controversy focused on the application of a technique known as double regression. An early and leading expert witness, Bernard Grofman, used this technique, and the courts came to rely on it to such an extent that the Supreme Court noted that Grofman's use of "two complementary methods of analysis—extreme case analysis and bivariate ecological regression analysis—in order to determine whether blacks and whites in these districts differed in their voting behavior" yielded data by methods found to be "standard in the literature."[70]

Even parties less disposed to attack Grofman's method believe that the Supreme Court "made a supreme mistake in endorsing that method."[71] As one scholar pointed out, the "controversy distills to the old ecological fallacy question: can the individual-level relationship between race and vote be reliably inferred from aggregate-level election results?"[72]

In the mid-1960s and early 1970s multi-member districts came under scrutiny by the federal courts. A rash of court cases, as well as scholarly and public attention, focused on the use of certain voting processes in multi-member legislative districts, which might be viewed as enhancing a finding of "dilution." As the case law on the use of multi-member districts in state legislatures developed, judges presumed it to be applicable to city councils elected at large. Chief Justice Rehnquist observed in 1978 that "while this court has found that the use of multimember districts in a state legislative apportionment plan may be invalid if 'used invidiously to cancel out or minimize the voting strength of racial groups,' . . . we have never had occasion to consider whether an analogue of this highly amorphous theory may be applied to municipal governments."[73]

Regarding municipal elections, malapportionment cannot occur in at-large systems, as the numerical equality of votes is inherent in the system. Litigation

70. *Thornburg* v. *Gingles,* 478 U.S. 30, 52–53 (1986).

71. Glenn Firebaugh, "Are Bad Estimates Good Enough for the Courts?" *Social Science Quarterly* (September 1993), 74:488.

72. Ibid. See also Kenneth C. Land, "Discriminatory Electoral Practices, Contextual Effects, and a New Double Regression Method for the Courts," and John K. Wildgen, "Social Alchemy in the Courtroom: The 'Double Regression' Hoax," both in *Social Science Quarterly* (September 1993), 74:469–470, 471–479, respectively. A current work on this problem is Gary King's *A Solution to the Ecological Inference Problem: Reconstructing Individual Behavior from Aggregate Data* (Princeton, N.J.: Princeton University Press, 1997).

73. *Wise* v. *Lipscomb,* 437 U.S. 535, 550 (1978). Rehnquist noted that whether relevant constitutional distinctions between a state legislature and a municipal government might be drawn had not been considered in this case, and would not be, because the issue had not been preserved on appeal.

over the at-large election system in municipalities involves Phase 3 litigation on issues of representation equity.

In *Fortson* v. *Dorsey*, in 1965, the Supreme Court held that use of multi-member districts was not unconstitutional per se, but warned that either by design, "or otherwise," a multi-member constituency might operate to minimize or cancel out the voting strength of racial or political elements of a voting population.[74] In *Burns* v. *Richardson* the following year, the Court made it even clearer that a plaintiff could prevail by proving an "invidious result."[75] These cases established that a claim of vote dilution could rest on either discriminatory purpose or effect. Then, in 1971, the Supreme Court established the guideline that single-member districts are preferable to large multi-member districts when district courts fashion apportionment plans.[76]

Also in 1971, in *Whitcomb* v. *Chavis*, the Justices could not agree in a plurality opinion whether the plaintiffs had met the *Fortson/Burns* intent or result test.[77] The Supreme Court ruled in *Whitcomb* that "the fact that the number of ghetto residents who were legislators was not in proportion to ghetto population" did not prove "invidious discrimination," unless the ghetto residents had "less opportunity" than did other residents "to participate in the political processes and to elect legislators of their choice."[78]

The evidence showed that the ghetto area had voted Democrat, that the Republicans had won four of the five elections from 1960 to 1968, and that in 1964, when the Democrats had won, a ghetto area senator and representative had been elected. The majority concluded that "the failure of the ghetto to have legislative seats in proportion to its population emerges more as a function of losing elections than of built-in bias against poor Negroes."[79] The *Whitcomb* decision held that no dilution could be claimed if a minority were afforded the opportunity to participate in the slating of candidates, if the representatives slated and elected were responsive to minority's needs, and if the multi-member districting scheme were rooted in a strong state policy divorced from the maintenance of racial discrimination.

The Court struggled to provide a "simple" standard for Phase 3 litigation, such as "one man, one vote" used in the Phase 2 litigation. In the leading case of *White* v. *Regester* a "totality of circumstances" standard was offered.[80] This was not a workable standard against which to measure a challenged electoral system. How to measure "vote dilution" was still undefined by social scientists.

74. 379 U.S. 433 (1965).
75. 384 U.S. 73 (1966).
76. *Connor* v. *Johnson*, 402 U.S. 690 (1971).
77. *Whitcomb* v. *Chavis*, 403 U.S. 124 (1971).
78. Ibid., 149.
79. Ibid., 153.
80. 412 U.S. 755 (1973).

In *White,* the Supreme Court for the first time struck down multi-member districts as a violation of equal access, based on results, with no consideration of discriminatory intent. Justice White, writing for the majority, noted that multi-member districts were not in themselves unconstitutional but were invalid if, under "the totality of circumstances," minority members have "less opportunity than did other residents in the district to participate in the political processes and to elect legislators of their choice."[81] The Court held that multi-member districts for Mexican-Americans in Bexar County, Texas, and for blacks in Dallas County, Texas, "operated to dilute the voting strength of racial and ethnic minorities" because they invidiously discriminated against these groups, in violation of the equal protection clause."[82]

The *White* decision held that plaintiffs in Dallas County (blacks) and Bexar County (Mexican-Americans) had established their denial of voting rights based on the following findings:

1. A history of official racial discrimination that, at times, touched the right to register and vote and to participate in the democratic processes;
2. A majority vote requirement for party primaries;
3. A requirement for a "place" or post that limited candidates to a specified "place" on the ballot, which was not in itself "improper nor invidious," [but which] enhanced the opportunity for racial discrimination;
4. No sub-district residency requirement for candidates, that is, "all candidates may be selected from outside the Negro residential area";
5. Correlation between election and endorsement by a white-dominated slating group;
6. Slating group electoral success independent of support of the black community;
7. Lack of good-faith concern for the needs and aspirations of the black community; and
8. Use of racial campaign tactics in white precincts to defeat candidates with overwhelming support of the black community.

In the case of Mexican-Americans in Bexar County, additional factors were cited:

1. A history of "invidious discrimination and treatment" in the fields of education, employment, economics, health, politics, and others;
2. Cultural and language barriers making participation in community processes extremely difficult;
3. A history of a discriminatory poll tax and restrictive voter registration procedures, which continued to have a residual impact reflected in disproportionately low voter registration levels;

81. Ibid., 766.
82. Ibid.

4. Underrepresentation in the Texas Legislature; and
5. Lack of responsiveness by the legislative delegation in the State House to Mexican-American interests.

In neither *Whitcomb* nor *White* did the Supreme Court examine intent in designing the electoral districts at issue. Thus plaintiffs in dilution cases could prevail only by showing discriminatory results. In approximately two dozen subsequent decisions, the federal courts, particularly the Fifth Circuit Court of Appeals, followed *White* in the results test, and also in holding that at-large elections were vulnerable to attack if, in the context of the "total circumstances," they denied minority voters an equal chance to participate in the electoral system. How one might calculate the "total" circumstances was left ambiguous.

The seminal Court of Appeals decision was *Zimmer* v. *McKeithen*,[83] a ruling, affirmed by the Supreme Court in *East Carroll Parish School Board* v. *Marshall*,[84] that at-large elections diminished the black voting strength of East Carroll Parish in Louisiana. The *Zimmer* decision held that normal preference for single-member districts may yield in two situations: if significant interest would be advanced by use of multi-member districts, provided they are not rooted in racial discrimination and do not jeopardize constitutional requirements; and if multi-member districts afford minorities a greater opportunity for participation in the political process than do single-member districts.[85]

The *Zimmer* decision also elaborated the factors the Supreme Court had employed in *White* to establish a finding of dilution in multi-member districts. *Zimmer* held that dilution could be established upon proof of the existence of an aggregate of the following factors:

1. A lack of access to the process of slating candidates;
2. Unresponsiveness of legislators to the particularized interests of minorities;
3. A tenuous state policy underlying a preference for multi-member or at-large districting; and
4. Existence of past discrimination in general, precluding effective participation in the election system.

Such proof is enhanced by the existence of the following features:

5. Large districts;
6. Majority vote requirements;
7. Anti–single shot voting provisions, that is, a requirement to vote for all positions shown for the ballot to be counted; and

83. 485 F.2d 1297 (5th Cir. 1973). This case was decided in the Fifth Circuit, where district courts have been most involved in apportionment plans.
84. 424 U.S. 636 (1976).
85. *Zimmer* v. *McKeithen*, 485 F.2d 1297 (5th Cir. 1973).

8. No provision for at-large candidates running from particular geographical sub-districts.

The courts have not established the *White/Zimmer* factors in a hierarchical order of importance. The lists did not register other factors, which could be just as significant as those listed, such as the effect of partisan versus nonpartisan elections, or control of the media and the impact of media endorsements.

In changing from multi-member districts to single-member districts, gerrymandering in the drawing of district lines is inevitably introduced. Racial gerrymandering may be "affirmative racial gerrymandering" (the creation by design of minority-dominant districts) or "negative racial gerrymandering" (intentionally packing or cracking districts). "Packing" refers to a racial minority group that has been concentrated into one district, so as to dilute opportunities to "influence" the outcome in several districts. "Cracking" refers to a homogeneous minority community that has been split among several voting districts to dilute their strength. Blacks, as well as social scientists, cannot agree among themselves whether "safe" districts or "influence" districts are optimal for maximizing participation. Yet courts have accepted the challenge to choose among alternative proposed districting plans, and thus to follow, again, a path to wall in choices.[86]

The preferred remedy that courts developed, and that dominated enforcement in the 1980s, was to create minority-dominant districts (districts in which the black population was in a majority) to ensure election of a "minority-preferred" candidate.[87] The minority-dominant district remedy to dilution reduced representation to a judicially manageable standard, a requirement in litigation. Again, this illustrates the limitations of the legal model, with its need for a uniform standard; preferable, as Lani Guinier suggests, would be "a model which reflects a preference of experimentation and innovation in government . . . with positive-sum solutions in which everyone stands to benefit from the infusion of alternative viewpoints and from consensus solutions."[88]

But what size must a black majority be to avoid an allegation of packing and yet to ensure a "safe" seat? Should it be a simple majority or an extraordi-

---

86. In *Voinovich* v. *Quilter,* 113 S.Ct. 1149 (1993), the Court had an opportunity to choose between an "influence" district plan and a "safe" district plan but refused to resolve the issue on the basis that the Court had not yet ruled on whether "influence-dilution" claims were viable under Section 2 of the VRA.

87.   The remedy of single-member, racially gerrymandered districts was forced on Norfolk, Viginia, even though its black population in 1980 accounted for 35 percent of the total population; it had achieved nearly proportional minority office holding since 1984, using an at-large electoral system; and the vast majority of Norfolk's black leaders wanted to retain the at-large system (Michele A. Davis, "The Evolution of the Voting Rights Act and Its Impact on Virginia Localities," M.A. thesis, University of Virginia, 2000).

88. Lani Guinier, "No Two Seats: The Elusive Quest for Political Equality," *Virginia Law Review* (November 1991), 77:1461.

nary majority? A rule of thumb developed, namely, that a district should be 65 percent minority dominant for it to be "safe." This 65 percent rule, which became the standard in subsequent cases, had its beginning in the case of *United Jewish Organizations* v. *Carey* in 1977.[89]

In their choice of the minority-dominant district as a remedy for dilution of minority groups, courts followed civil rights activists and scholars who were proponents of racial redistricting. They argued that the only way racial minorities could have a political voice was through creation of districts in which the minority could cast a majority of the votes.[90] This view suggested that race consciousness was so pervasive in American politics that whenever black candidates ran against white candidates, racial bloc voting occurred. Thus black and Latino candidates could win elections only by running in districts in which minorities constituted a voting majority.[91]

Other scholars were equally prolific in their opposition to racial redistricting, but their concerns did not surface until after the courts had laid out a path. Guinier asserted that black electoral prospects are thwarted by majority rule whether in single-member districts or multi-member districts. She advocated interest representation, a form of proportional representation.[92] In an influential study entitled *Whose Votes Count?* Abigail Thernstrom argued that creating black-majority districts mandated a form of proportional representation contrary to the American majoritarian political tradition.[93] These competing assertions were based on different underlying premises regarding fairness in representation, but they have in common a rejection of the simplistic solution of the courts.

By the close of the 1996 term, the Supreme Court had demonstrated that it still had not settled on a standard for the use of race in drawing district lines. In a pair of 5–4 decisions, the majority had made clear that the Court was retreating from using race as a dominant factor in drawing district lines. The Court declared unconstitutional four congressional districts designed by legislators after the 1990 census, which were to give minority voters more electoral influence in Texas and North Carolina.[94] This issue is considered in more detail in the context of the Voting Rights Act in the next major section below.

89. 430 U.S. 144 (1977). The rule arose from a telephone call from a staff member, identity unknown, at the Voting Rights Section of the Department of Justice to attorneys representing the State of New York in that case (*1982 Senate Report,* 121, citing testimony of Professor George C. Cochran, Senate Hearings, February 25, 1982).

90. See Bernard Grofman and Chandler Davidson, eds., *Controversies in Minority Voting: The Voting Rights Act in Perspective* (Washington, D.C.: The Brookings Institution, 1992); and Bernard Grofman, Lisa Handley, and Richard G. Niemi, *Minority Representation and the Quest for Voting Equality* (New York: Cambridge University Press, 1994).

91. Paul E. Peterson, *Classifying by Race* (Princeton, N.J.: Princeton University Press, 1995), 9.

92. Guinier, *Tyranny of the Majority.*

93. Abigail M. Thernstrom, *Whose Votes Count? Affirmative Action and Minority Voting Rights* (Cambridge, Mass.: Harvard University Press, 1987).

94. *Bush* v. *Vera,* 517 U.S. 952 (1996); and *Shaw* v. *Hunt,* 517 U.S. 899 (1996).

Phase 4: The Right to an Effective Voice

Disappointed by the results of the earlier phases of voting rights litigation, attention turned to the right of minorities to a meaningful voice after elected. Most concerns over a meaningful voice can be grouped into two areas: once elected, minorities could be frozen out of decision making; or, the electoral process itself could produce representatives who may not promote the tangible interests of minorities.

The former issue is that the rules and practices of the legislative body might preclude minority representatives, once they are elected, from having an effect on the decision-making process. The right to a meaningful vote, in Guinier's words, means "a chance of winning a fair number of contested policy decisions."[95] Until 1992 the Justice Department's Voting Section addressed this issue by routinely reviewing reallocations of authority for violation of the Voting Rights Act."[96] Then, in *Presley* v. *Etowah County Commission*,[97] the Court ruled that the preclearance provisions of Section 5 of the VRA did not cover shifts in power on local governmental bodies unless such changes resulted in disenfranchisement of a protected class. In narrowly construing Section 5 of the VRA, Justice Kennedy, writing for a six-justice majority, said that changes that "affect only the distribution of power among officials" are not subject to the VRA, because "such changes have no direct relation to or impact on voting."[98] The three dissenters, led by Justice Stevens, argued that the reallocation of decision-making authority in an elective office "had the same potential for discrimination as gerrymandering district boundaries and changing from district voting to at-large voting."[99]

Another way to view the fourth phase of voting rights litigation is that the courts, to date, have focused on *descriptive* representation rather than *substantive* representation.[100] While a seat at the table has its own benefits,[101] the prem-

95. Lani Guinier, "No Two Seats," 77:1461. Guinier views the "right to vote" essentially as three different rights: the right to cast a ballot, the right to cast a ballot that "counts," and the right to cast a ballot that embodies a fair chance to influence legislative policy making (*Tyranny of the Majority*, 1–20).

96. Susan Feeney and Steve McGonigle, "Voting Rights: The Next Generation," *Dallas Morning News*, August 14, 1994.

97. 502 U.S. 491 (1992).

98. Ibid., 506.

99. Ibid., 525.

100. "Descriptive representation," as defined by Hannah Pitkin, means a "descriptive likeness between representatives and those for whom they stand" (*Representation* [New York: Atherton, 1969], 10). In voting rights literature, "descriptive representation" refers to representatives mirroring the social characteristics of their constituencies, such as race, ethnicity, or gender. "Substantive representation" refers to representatives mirroring the policy preferences or ideologies of their constituents. The two are not mutually exclusive.

101. See, particularly, Anne Phillips, *The Politics of Presence: Democracy and Group Representation* (University Park: Pennsylvania State University Press, 1993).

ise of the entire votes-seats controversy was that if minorities could elect "their own," they could achieve substantive representation, or desired outcomes in the policy-making process. But after more than three decades of voting rights litigation focusing on descriptive representation, disappointment with the substantive results have caused scholars and activists to turn to other considerations. One remedy, subject to considerable recent scholarly attention, is the assortment of voting systems, which could replace plurality voting or majority voting.

Two vocal proponents of substantive representation, Carol Swain and Lani Guinier, both criticized the Court's solution of "safe seats" for minority representatives in single-member districts as insufficient. Swain, basing her view on a study of the House of Representatives, found that white Democrats offered substantive representation to non-white voters.[102] Substantive representation, in other words, might be more important than descriptive representation.

Guinier approached the issue from the perspective of "authentic representation," that is, that the creation of single-member districts did not sustain the electoral participation of blacks. This effect reduced the accountability of black representatives to the policy concerns of the black community.[103] She also believed that districting "uses a delegated model of representation but fails to ensure substantive accountability to constituents' policy preferences, not just service needs."[104]

Political scientist Iris Marion Young, along with Guinier, proposes changing the electoral system itself to provide formal representation for a variety of groups and interests.[105] This change might be to some form of proportional representation, which attracted considerable attention, particularly in the aftermath of the redistricting controversies following the 1990 census.[106] A much broader and more fundamental approach, persuasively argued by David K. Ryden, is to "embrace political parties as the institutional means of integrating

102. Carol M. Swain, *Black Faces, Black Interests: The Representation of African-Americans in Congress* (Cambridge, Mass.: Harvard University Press, 1993). Using a dataset obtained through a nationwide survey of 1,467 city council members from two hundred cities in 1995, a Stanford political scientist found that the data verified neither the Guinier "unresponsive representatives" theory nor the Swain proposition of white liberal/non-white council member agenda convergence (Bari E. Anhalt, "Minority Representation and the Substantive Representation of Interests," paper prepared for the annual meeting of the American Political Science Association, 1996).

103. Guinier, "No Two Seats," 77:1433–1434.

104. Ibid., 1433.

105. Iris Marion Young, *Justice and the Politics of Difference* (Princeton, N.J.: Princeton University Press, 1990).

106. For an analysis of various forms of proportional representation, see Douglas J. Amy, *Real Choices/New Voices: The Case for Proportional Representation Elections in the United States* (New York: Columbia University Press, 1993).

individual and group voices and facilitating their access to the public square, thus ensuring effective participation for all."[107]

Thus the failure of the legal approach has generated strong renewed interest in the art of negotiation and compromise, characteristic of party politics.

THE VOTING RIGHTS ACT IN COURT

That the original purpose of the VRA was to remedy disenfranchisement and increase the number of black registered voters is incontrovertible. But the congressional objective was substantially transformed, owing, in part, to a number of judicial decisions regarding the constitutionality and interpretation of the Act.

Within one year of its passage, the constitutionality of major sections of the VRA of 1965 were tested in *South Carolina* v. *Katzenbach,* on the grounds that they amounted to an unconstitutional encroachment on jurisdiction reserved for the states.[108] In declaring the Act constitutional, the Court, in an 8–1 opinion, determined that Congress had the power to pass it under Section 2 of the Fifteenth Amendment, which authorizes Congress to "use any rational means to effectuate the constitutional prohibition of racial discrimination in voting" by appropriate legislation.[109]

Chief Justice Warren, speaking for the Court, acknowledged that the preclearance provisions of Section 5 of the VRA "may have been an uncommon exercise of congressional power," but that the "Court has recognized that exceptional conditions can justify legislative measures not otherwise appropriate."[110] Although Section 5 applied to the specified covered states, a federal court may impose the preclearance requirement on any other jurisdiction where there has been a finding of discrimination.

While Justice Black agreed with the suspension of literacy tests, and other devices, to deny voting rights, he dissented on the constitutionality of Section 5, as violating fundamental principles of U.S. federalism. In his view, "Section 5 . . . so distorts our constitutional structure of government as to render any distinction drawn in the Constitution between State and federal power almost meaningless."[111] Black viewed the Section 5 preclearance provision as contrary in three respects: to the Article IV Republican Form of Government guarantee, to the Tenth Amendment State Reserved Powers clause, and to the role

107. David K. Ryden, *Representation in Crisis: The Constitution, Interest Groups, and Political Parties* (Albany: State University of New York Press, 1996).

108. 383 U.S. 301 (1966).

109. Ibid., 324.

110. Ibid., 334.

111. Ibid., 358.

of judicial power to invalidate a law *after* it had become effective, rather than to prevent a state from passing a law.[112]

Three years later the Court gave an extraordinarily broad construction to Section 5 in *Allen* v. *State Board of Elections.*[113] The Court opinion, again by Chief Justice Warren, held that not only new laws, which might deny blacks their right to register and vote, but "any state enactment which altered the election law of a covered state in even a minor way" came under the umbrella of Section 5.[114] In Justice Harlan's view, this decision effected a substantial change in the VRA by requiring "a revolutionary innovation in American government that goes far beyond . . . permitting the Negro people to gain access to the voting booths of the South once and for all." He continued: "In moving against 'tests and devices' . . . Congress moved only against those techniques that prevented Negroes from voting at all. Congress did not attempt to restructure state governments."[115] Justice Black continued to maintain, as he had in *South Carolina* v. *Katzenbach,* that the preclearance provisions violated the U.S. Constitution: "I doubt that any of the 13 colonies would have agreed to our Constitution if they had dreamed that a time might come when they would have to go to a United States Attorney General or a District of Columbia court with hat in hand begging for permission to change their laws."[116]

In 1980, in *City of Rome* v. *United States,* the Court confirmed the transformation, broadly interpreted, that had taken place in Section 5.[117] The Court held that although electoral changes in Rome, Georgia, were enacted without discriminatory purpose, they were nevertheless prohibited under Section 5 of the Act because of their discriminatory effect.

Thus, the Court affirmed that the effects of a change could be the exclusive measure of the standard of conduct in covered jurisdictions seeking preclearance pursuant to Section 5. The evolution of Section 5, therefore, was fundamentally complete. It had been transformed from a provision that focused on voter access to registration and the ballot to one focused on the electoral process itself. Under Section 5 litigation, then, the "effects," or "results," test was constitutional.

This redirection of Section 5 would likely have occurred as well in the context of Section 2 of the VRA, but for the case of *City of Mobile* v. *Bolden* (1980).[118] As noted, prior to the passage of the VRA, the Supreme Court had

112. Ibid., 359, 361.
113. 393 U.S. 544 (1969).
114. Ibid., 566.
115. Ibid., 585. For a history of the enforcement of Section 5, see *Perkins* v. *Matthews,* 400 U.S. 379 (1971), which expanded the interpretation of the coverage of Section 5 even further.
116. Ibid., 595–596.
117. 446 U.S. 156 (1980).
118. *City of Mobile* v. *Bolden,* 446 U.S. 55 (1980).

indicated that a finding of unconstitutional vote dilution could rest on proof of *either* discriminatory purpose *or* discriminatory results.[119] In a major break with precedent, the Supreme Court held in a plurality opinion that an unconstitutional vote dilution case required proof of discriminatory purpose. *Bolden* involved a class action on behalf of all black citizens of Mobile, Alabama, alleging that the city's practice of electing commissioners through an at-large system unfairly "diluted" minority voting strength in violation of the Fourteenth and Fifteenth Amendments.

In upholding the city's at-large elections as constitutional, absent proof that the system was intended to discriminate, the Court overruled the lower court's order that the city of Mobile totally revamp its municipal system because it had not achieved representation of minorities in proportion to their population. The Court found that the evidence in the case fell "far short" of showing that the at-large system was "conceived or operated" as a purposeful device to further racial discrimination. Significantly the Court held that the *Zimmer* criteria, on which the lower courts relied, were "most assuredly insufficient to prove an unconstitutionally discriminatory purpose in the present case."[120]

In *Bolden* the Court adhered to a strict constructionist interpretation of the Fifteenth Amendment, as offering protection for the right to register and vote, but no protection against vote dilution. This decision reaffirmed the original understandings of Section 2 of the VRA, that it was designed to codify the Fifteenth Amendment. Moreover, the Court concluded that while the Fourteenth Amendment did prohibit vote dilution, it did so only in cases where it could be proved that an electoral procedure had been established for racially discriminatory purposes.

Two years later the Court invalidated an at-large election system used in Burke County, Georgia, but the system met the discriminatory intent test required for a finding of unconstitutional vote dilution under the Fourteenth Amendment.[121]

When Congress added a new subsection to Section 2 in the Voting Rights Act Amendments of 1982, it did so to overrule the *Bolden* case, and to reestablish the results test by codifying *White* v. *Regester.* This meant that the effects of electoral rules, once again, were sufficient to sustain a vote-dilution claim. The amended VRA opened the floodgate to claims of dilution, again, and applied pressure on redistricting to optimize prospects for minority seats. According to one legal scholar, this "in effect has turned the courts into a secondary forum for political jockeying over the spoils of redistricting."[122]

119. *Fortson* v. *Dorsey,* reaffirmed in *Burns* v. *Richardson,* supra.
120. Ibid., 66, 73.
121. *Rogers* v. *Lodge,* 458 U.S. 613 (1982).
122. Samuel Issacharoff, "Supreme Court Destabilization of Single-Member Districts," *The University of Chicago Legal Forum* (1995), 1995:233. For "compelling accounts of how hazily cast legal commands turn federal courts into alternative forums

The first case to reach the U.S. Supreme Court involving allegations of a Section 2 violation of the VRA Amendments of 1982 was *Thornburg* v. *Gingles* (1986).[123] *Gingles* established a three-prong test for vote dilution in multi-member, at-large districts under Section 2: (1) the minority must be "sufficiently large and geographically compact" for there to be a potential for remedy based on the drawing of a single-member district plan; (2) the minority must be "politically cohesive"; and (3) the majority must, when voting as a bloc, customarily defeat "the minority's preferred candidate."[124] This three-part test signaled "the emergence of polarized voting as the real measure of vote dilution."[125] When polarized voting became the center of attention, judges were pushed farther into the unsatisfactorily charted terrain of statistical analyses of voting patterns, requiring choices between expert witnesses as to their credibility.

To illustrate the ambiguities, and hence the bases for further litigation, Scott Yut pointed out that there were no less than three definitions in *Gingles* itself of "the minority's preferred candidate." Justice White stated that only minority candidates could be minority-preferred candidates. Justice O'Connor believed a candidate's race is one of several factors for the courts to consider when determining a minority-preferred candidate. Justice Brennan viewed a candidate's race as being irrelevant.[126]

This controversial case spawned a cottage industry of articles and books, and so it is not analyzed here in detail. What is of interest, however, is that the Court addressed the question of whether bivariate or multivariate analysis should be utilized to prove vote dilution, as lower courts had employed both methods.[127] The Court rejected the requirement of multivariate analysis, or the consideration of multiple factors in proving differential racial voting patterns, indicating that the proper question to ask is *whether* voters have divergent voting patterns on the basis of race, not *why* they vote differently.[128]

---

for political battles over representational advantage," see Pamela S. Karlan, "The Rights to Vote: Some Pessimism about Formalism," *Texas Law Review* (June 1993), 71:1705–1740; see also Pamela S. Karlan, "All Over The Map: The Supreme Court's Voting Rights Trilogy," *Supreme Court Review* (1993), 245, as cited by Issacharoff, "Supreme Court Destabilization of Single-Member Districts," 224 n. 92.

123. *Thornburg* v. *Gingles,* 478 U.S. 30 (1986).

124. For a thorough discussion of *Gingles,* the problems of its interpretation, and how it relates to earlier vote dilution case law, see Grofman, Handley, and Niemi, *Minority Representation,* esp. chaps. 3, 4.

125. Samuel Issacharoff, "Polarized Voting and the Political Process: The Transformation of Voting Rights Jurisprudence," *Michigan Law Review* (June 1992), 90:1852, 1854–1856.

126. Scott Yut, "Using Candidate Race," 583.

127. Olethia Davis, "Tenuous Interpretation: Sections 2 and 5 of the Voting Rights Act," *National Civic Review* (fall–winter 1995), 84:321 n. 37.

128. Ibid., 314–315. One of the ironies of a subsequent case, *Shaw* v. *Reno* (1993), is that plaintiffs' representatives had to switch positions, and argue for the use of multivariate techniques, to avoid charges that districts are drawn solely for racial reasons. See Susan

Justices White and O'Connor both endorsed the concept that, when differing political or socioeconomic characteristics of whites and minorities explain racially polarized voting, Section 2 does not protect that cause of minority voter electoral failure—what Justice White called "interest group politics."[129] For example, where minorities usually vote Democratic and whites usually vote Republican, and where Republicans generally win elections, a court should determine whether racial discrimination or "interest group politics" cause the candidate for whom the minorities vote to lose.[130]

The controversy over *Gingles* had not abated when the Court stirred another onslaught of commentary with its ruling in *Shaw* v. *Reno,* in which the Court established that white voters could challenge a majority black congressional district.[131] In *Shaw,* the North Carolina legislature had created a second minority-dominant congressional district to comply with the DOJ's objection to a reapportionment plan with only one minority district. White voters had then challenged the district that it was a racial gerrymander, in violation of the Fourteenth Amendment, which treats race as a suspect classification. The Supreme Court, in a 5–4 decision, held that it is permissible to violate equal protection if redistricting legislation "is so extremely irregular on its face that it rationally can be viewed only as an effort to segregate the races for purposes of voting, without regard for traditional districting principles[132] and without sufficiently compelling state justification."[133] Yet again the Supreme Court majority failed to establish clear and objective guidelines to define which district shapes violate this new constitutional standard. The Court remanded *Shaw* back to district court for a rehearing based on this new legal test.

Immediately afterward, however, in *Shaw* v. *Hunt,* another sharply divided court upheld the North Carolina black congressional district at issue in *Shaw* v. *Reno,* as having survived the "strict scrutiny" standard. The district was saved because it was narrowly tailored to further the state's compelling interests in complying with Sections 2 and 5 of the Voting Rights Act.[134]

In a related case, *Miller* v. *Johnson,* the Court held that racial gerrymandering is permissible to remedy past discrimination, and possibly where neces-

A. MacManus, "The Appropriateness of Biracial Approaches to Measuring Fairness of Representation in a Multicultural World," *PS: Political Science and Politics* (March 1995), 28:45 n. 2.

129. *Thornburg* v. *Gingles,* 478 U.S. 30, 83 (1986).

130. Ibid.

131. *Shaw* v. *Reno,* 509 U.S. 630 (1993).

132. Traditional districting principles have historically been compactness, contiguity, communities of interest, and political subdivision boundaries. For a helpful discussion of issues in the boundary-drawing process introduced by recent federal cases, see Richard L. Engstom, "Shaw, Miller, and the Districting Thicket," *National Civic Review* (fall–winter 1995), 84:323–336.

133. *Shaw* v. *Reno,* 509 U.S. 630 (1993).

134. *Shaw* v. *Hunt,* 517 U.S. 899 (1996).

sary under the VRA, but is not permissible to promote greater minority representation.[135]

Since many jurisdictions had devised minority-dominant, single-member districts in response to litigation under the VRA, they were open to challenge under the equal protection clause of the Fourteenth Amendment after *Shaw*. The Court now had to balance the protections set out in Section 2 of the VRA against protections provided by the Fourteenth Amendment. States and their political subdivisions were subjected to conflicting obligations. A law professor pointed out: "If a state wants to make a good-faith effort to comply with the Voting Rights Act—or minorities threaten litigation because a plan does not create enough majority-black and majority-Hispanic districts—and the state carves out more such districts, states then run the risk of expensive white countersuits charging that the new districts are not sufficiently compact."[136]

Although the *Shaw* majority denied it, a plausible argument can be made that this decision contradicts the precedent established in *United Jewish Organizations* v. *Carey* in 1977.[137] That case was an early example of the conflict between the Fourteenth Amendment's "equal protection of the laws" clause and the VRA and its judicial and administrative enforcement.[138] The Attorney General rejected a 1972 legislative redistricting by New York, as it applied to Brooklyn, a covered jurisdiction under the Act. The Attorney General objected that there were an insufficient number of election districts in which minority candidates might prevail, and that a minority population of 65 percent was necessary to create a safe minority seat.

In meeting the objections of the Attorney General, the New York Legislature divided a community of Hasidic Jews, which had previously resided in a single district. They filed, claiming they were victims of discrimination. The Supreme Court rejected their claim.[139] This case was forerunner to the untenable position taken by the Court in making one group "more equal than others"—to borrow from the lesson learned in George Orwell's *Animal Farm*.

In the Court's retreat from an expansive interpretation of the VRA, Justice Thomas moved back to the interpretation of the right to vote, as embodied in the Act, as only "to register and to vote."[140] Justice Thomas articulated his voting rights philosophy in a lengthy concurring opinion, joined by Justice Scalia, in *Holder* v. *Hall* (1994). Thomas proclaimed that he could "no longer

135. *Miller* v. *Johnson*, 515 U.S. 900 (1995).

136. Frank R. Parker, "Shaw v. Reno: A Constitutional Setback for Minority Representation," *PS: Political Science and Politics* (March 1995), 28:49.

137. Ibid.

138. *United Jewish Organizations* v. *Carey*, 430 U.S. 144 (1977).

139. See Davis, "Tenuous Interpretation," 84:310–322, for commentary on the continuing line of cases after *Shaw* that make it difficult for jurisdictions to meet the requirements of the VRA without violating the Fourteenth Amendment.

140. *Holder* v. *Hall*, 114 S.Ct. 2581, 2592 (1994).

adhere to a reading of the Act that . . . has produced such a disastrous misadventure in judicial policy-making."[141]

In Justice Thomas's view, not only had the courts immersed themselves in "a hopeless project of weighing questions of political theory," but they also had "devised a remedial mechanism that encourages federal courts to segregate votes into racially designated districts to ensure minority electoral success."[142] "In construing the Act to cover claims of vote dilution," he continued, "we have converted the Act into a device for regulating, rationing, and apportioning political power among racial and ethnic groups."[143] In a separate opinion, Justice Stevens, joined by Justices Blackmun, Souter, and Ginsburg, criticized Justice Thomas's "narrow interpretation" as "radical," one that would require the Court to overrule a "sizable number of this Court's precedents," as well as congressional enactments.[144]

CONCLUSIONS

Case law concerning voting rights mainly falls into two categories—whether voting rights are considered as an individual right or as a group right. In the former the courts did develop manageable standards. In the latter, however, the Court has not been able to develop a coherent theory of representation to guide federal court decisions.

Professor Joseph Goldstein of the Yale Law School wrote that it is the Justices' duty not simply to write a coherent opinion by itself but to "fine-tune the opinions so that, whether read separately or together, they constitute a comprehensible . . . message about the Constitution."[145] After more than thirty years of litigation, coherent communication is still lacking in the voting rights body of law. Instead, the Court has restructured state and local governments, introduced remedies that have satisfied few, created confusion in public discourse, and caused tensions between the national government and the states, and between the federal courts, Congress, and the Department of Justice. Except for increases in voter registration and in minorities elected to office, both susceptible to the legal model, the results of voting rights litigation appear disappointing.

A plausible explanation for the disenchanting results is that the law narrowly channels elements of representation, focusing on those that can be quan-

141. Ibid.
142. Ibid.
143. Ibid.
144. Ibid., 2628, 2629.
145. Joseph Goldstein, *The Intelligible Constitution: The Supreme Court's Obligation to Maintain the Constitution as Something We the People Can Understand* (New York: Oxford University Press, 1992), 110, 126.

tified, and thus made to seem manageable. Statistical analyses have relied on the size of the minority population, the proportionate number of seats, and past voting patterns. But political scientist Bruce Cain is correct to argue that "attempts to use fairness formulae are fundamentally flawed and impractical [because they] underestimate the complex factors that determine the outcome of an election and overestimate the capacity of social scientists to predict future outcomes."[146] Remedies based on limited ranges of considerations are necessarily flawed.

When the prescribed legal solution to representational inequities failed to fulfill the hopes of even the protected class of minority voters, then scholars, legislators, and even the courts in a few instances began to explore alternative remedies. Most of these studies and recommendations have examined either formal voting requirements or ways to foster a healthy political environment. Alternative voting systems, as a way to help minorities gain direct representation, include several forms of proportional and semi-proportional systems for counting votes, such as the single transferable vote and cumulative voting.[147] On the other hand, some scholars have renewed interest in the role of political party politics as a means to represent multiple groups in society.[148]

Justice Felix Frankfurter's view may yet gain dominance in matters of representation: "It is hostile to a democratic system to involve the judiciary in the politics of the people . . . [even if] judicial intervention in an essentially political contest be dressed up in the abstract phrases of the law."

146. Bruce Cain, "Excerpts from Declaration of Bruce Cain in Badham v. Eu," *PS: Political Science and Politics* (summer 1985), 18:562.

147. See Kenneth Benoit and Kenneth A. Shepsle, "Electoral Systems and Minority Representation," in Paul E. Peterson, ed., *Classifying by Race* (Princeton, N.J.: Princeton University Press, 1995), 50–84. They propound that alternative voting systems, such as limited or cumulative voting are likely to increase the number of minority legislators. Also see Lani Guinier, "More Democracy"; and Richard H. Pildes and Kristen A. Donoghue, "Cumulative Voting in the United States," *The University of Chicago Legal Forum* (1995), 1995:1–22, 241–302, respectively.

148. See, for example, David K. Ryden, *Representation in Crisis: The Constitution, Interest Groups, and Political Parties* (Albany: State University of New York Press, 1996).

PART II
Context for Political Participation in Dallas

3
History and Culture of the City

The great enemy of truth is very often not the lie . . . but the myth.
—John F. Kennedy

Evaluating the impact of the Voting Rights Act at the micro level permits a mode of inquiry that values context. Macro studies that measure the success of the Voting Rights Act primarily in terms of the number of minorities elected to legislative bodies need not take into account the distinctive characteristics of cities. Aggregated data, therefore, often mix councils from cities of vastly different sizes, political cultures, patterns of elections, and city and state legal constraints. These differences are important in identifying the consequences of the Voting Rights Act, since particular VRA provisions may yield different results when planted in different soils. Factors that provide a context for understanding the causes and consequences of Dallas's experiences with the Voting Rights Act include the city's cultural attitudes, ideas, and mythology; the geographic location and founding era; and the evolution of its population and economy.

ATTITUDES AND MYTHOLOGY

Local communities tend to share distinct sets of beliefs and ideas that characterize a given locale. As D. H. Lawrence expressed it, following years of foreign travel, "spirit of place is a great reality."[1] Without intending to imply that a city is an anthropomorphic entity, what follows are attitudes that have dominated in Dallas. Some have been consistent over time, while others have prevailed only during specific periods. Nor is a citywide, all-inclusiveness suggested, since multiple communities and groups hold contrary views in such a large and complex urban environment.

Three prevalent and enduring patterns have been perpetuated from the

1. Douglas C. D. Pocock, "Place and the Novelist," in *Re-Reading Cultural Geography,* ed. Kenneth E. Foote (Austin: University of Texas Press, 1994), 364.

1930s that are directly relevant to the way that Dallas has dealt with minorities and with the transition to single-member election districts:

1. A myth persists that Dallas's success is attributable to the aggressive business "can-do" spirit of its leadership, absent the benefits of the geographical attributes of other cities. In reality, the "can-do" spirit has created a fusion of public and private interests in support of economic return, to the concomitant diminution of social, cultural, and educational issues. This reality fueled the race- and class-based problems that Dallas has faced since at least the 1960s.
2. City leaders, who have exhibited an undue concern over image and the economic effects of bad publicity, have been held hostage to the demands of the most vocal members of minority communities. This in turn undermined the prospects for long-term substantive change.
3. An insistence on conformity with the "party line" of the business elite insidiously and effectively has silenced the other voices that make a community intellectually and culturally vital.

The Exceptionalism Myth

The exceptionalism myth is important to an understanding of Dallas, because it serves as a basis for claiming that the city is the creation of men who willed it into existence with their vision and "can-do" spirit. In this claim to exceptionalism, city leaders discovered a means to justify their decisions and conduct as being "for the good of Dallas," a view that sustained their commitment to at-large elections and the council-manager form of government.

This foundational and enduring myth is based on the view that the city has no physical or geographical reason for being, because of its lack of natural resources and absence of mountains, forests, and oceans. Such a situation, of course, is true of hundreds of other cities across the nation that came into being because a stake was planted for one reason or another.

As with most mythologies, the Dallas myth does not coincide with reality. The site for Dallas was a natural one. Furthermore, this same location is now viewed as an asset in attracting relocations to the city. The city's location is touted to be in the geographical center of the United States, on a north-south axis between Canada and Mexico, and midway between the East and West Coasts in the central time zone, an asset in an age of telecommunications. In addition, its mild winter climate has become an attractive feature, especially since air conditioning has made the summer heat tolerable, which resulted in Dallas benefiting from the migration to the "Sun Belt."

Important to this narrative is that the myth, which emerged from the Texas Centennial celebration in 1936, served as the justification for a noblesse oblige oligarchic leadership by Dallas's businessmen. This ethos was reflected in Dallas's inhospitable atmosphere for minorities and for anyone but the like-minded.

Enduring myths derive their strength from a basis in reality. Political scientist James David Barber has claimed that U.S. presidents pursue in office the style that gained them their first political success.[2] Dallas leaders appear to have followed suit. In obtaining two railroad lines for Dallas in the early 1870s, the leadership initiated a pattern of providing generous public inducements to private enterprise. This method for securing trophy projects continues into the twenty-first century.

In the 1930s Mayor Robert L. Thornton outmaneuvered other cities to win the 1936 Texas Centennial for Dallas. Inducements, again, rather than a historical claim, won for Dallas the opportunity to be the Centennial host city. Dallas had not even been on the map when Texas won its independence in 1836. Out of the Centennial experience, Mayor Robert L. Thornton created the Dallas Citizens Council, which has played a major role in Dallas since the 1930s.

The Citizens Council was initially composed of only CEOs of major companies, who would make the final decisions on whether to commit funds to projects. Among them, Thornton enlisted the economically powerful presidents of the two largest banks in Dallas, First National Bank and Republic Bank. As a complement to his bank, Fred F. Florence of Republic Bank became official treasurer for the City of Dallas in 1931, a position he held for two and a half decades.[3] This early role for Dallas business leaders proved to be a continuing one in which public and private interests are commingled, even fused.

The Centennial State Fair experience demonstrated another pattern, one of less admirable quality, which was to prevail: what is good for the city's economy trumps social and cultural values. The Centennial exhibits were predominantly educational, historical, futuristic, and cultural. So Fort Worth, in contrast, developed a competitive Frontier Centennial Exposition that stressed entertainment. After a traffic study revealed that a large number of automobiles were traveling to Fort Worth, an unofficial city council meeting was called in a downtown office to review the situation. As a result, "the decision was made to loosen enforcement to permit bookies to operate, to stop closing bars for illegal liquor sales, and to keep the whores as safe as possible . . . in the houses and off the streets."[4]

For years thereafter Dallas allowed a gambling industry to exist, with only

2. James David Barber, *The Presidential Character: Predicting Performance in the White House* (Englewood Cliffs, N.J.: Prentice Hall, 1972).

3. Darwin Payne, *Big D: Triumphs and Troubles of an American Supercity in the 20th Century* (Dallas: Three Forks, 1994), 168.

4. Ibid., 169–171. Payne bases the details of this account largely on Kenneth B. Ragsdale, *The Year America Discovered Texas: Centennial '36* (College Station: Texas A&M University Press, 1987).

token arrests. At blame for the hands-off policy were the city's churchmen, Chamber of Commerce officers, bankers, and "leading people," all of whom agreed that it was good for the city's economic health.[5]

The pattern continued. In the late 1990s the yeoman efforts of community leaders in poorer sections of south Dallas to clean up the blocks of liquor stores, especially the ones across the street from schools, met with delay, indifference, and opposition, despite minority representatives on the city council.

Likewise, a once thriving residential and restaurant area near Bachman Lake in the northern sector is declining steadily, while topless clubs circumvent zoning and sexually oriented business ordinances. For more than fifteen years the liquor stores and topless clubs simply have factored citations and litigation into the cost of doing business.

Similarly code enforcement and environmental concerns have taken back seats to economic development and private profits. Because the majority of code violations occur in modest and lower-income neighborhoods, the backing off from aggressive code enforcement has had a disproportionate effect on those local residents.[6]

Environmental pollution also has been glossed over. For years the pattern in Dallas has been to push for change in federal standards, rather than to cause businesses to assume added expense or responsibility for pollution abatement. Not surprisingly environmental concerns were skirted in the campaigns for two trophy projects in Dallas in the late 1990s: the downtown arena, approved by the voters in a special election in 1998, and the Trinity River Development Plan, approved by the voters in a bond referendum in May 1998. Both projects were pushed by the city's business leaders, the mayor and city manager, and Dallas's only local daily newspaper.

Dallas's Image

With the dominance of developer interests in local affairs, city leaders have been preoccupied with Dallas's image and its effects on business interests. This concern has continued from the time Dallas burst on the national stage in the 1930s with the Centennial to the present.

In the late 1940s, following World War II, the thousands of blacks who moved to Dallas to seek a better life were greeted with bombings, as they began to buy houses in previously white blocks in south Dallas. Concerned by the ensuing national publicity at a time when companies were beginning to be attracted to Dallas, the leadership of the Dallas Citizens Council persuaded the district attorney to empanel a special grand jury to investigate the bombings. When the investigations began to point to certain prominent white citizens, the

5. Payne, *Big D,* 235.
6. Lori Palmer, *Dallas Morning News,* May 16, 1988.

grand jury adjourned without indicting any major players, convinced that they would not be convicted in a courtroom.

Similarly, for most of Dallas's business elite, "the reality of black housing could be ignored just as long as it did not tarnish the city's bright image of progressive commercial prosperity."[7] A group of white civic leaders, however, took the initiative to try to mute the problem of blacks seeking better housing in white neighborhoods. Hamilton Park, which opened in 1954, was designed and built as a middle-class black residential neighborhood in what was then empty land in Far North Dallas, and today is near the intersection of two Dallas arteries, Central Expressway (Highway 75) and LBJ Freeway (Highway 635).

Between the adoption of the council-manager form of government, with at-large elections, and the 1990s, Dallas took pride in its clean government. Since 1997 Dallas's "Clean City" image has been besmirched by the convictions of two sitting city council members, as well as a superintendent of public schools. Council member Paul Fielding pleaded guilty to mail fraud and conspiracy to commit extortion, and was sentenced to forty-one months in prison. Council member Al Lipscomb was found guilty on sixty-five counts of conspiracy and bribery for trading his influence at City Hall for money. He was also sentenced to forty-one months in prison.[8] The city's only daily newspaper responded to this failure in civic leadership with concern for Dallas's image in a bold four-column headline: "Corruption may not blemish city's image."

Intolerance of Dissent in Dallas

Historically business interests have trumped efforts to listen to voices that can make a community intellectually and culturally vital. Many business leaders in Dallas have not seemed to want to be with, or to listen to, anyone not considered a peer. This selectivity was evident in Bob Thornton's desire that only CEOs comprise his Citizens Council; it was also apparent when a leading civic leader and member of the current Citizen's Council privately said that no one should be in the Citizens Council who could not make a decision for his com-

7. William H. Wilson, *Hamilton Park: A Planned Black Community in Dallas* (Baltimore: The Johns Hopkins University Press, 1998), 10.

8. On July 12, 2002, a three-judge panel of the Fifth U.S. Circuit Court of Appeals, while making it clear that it did not dispute the evidence against Lipscomb, reversed the case and ordered a retrial on the basis that the presiding judge had inappropriately moved the case to Amarillo. U.S. Attorney Jane Boyle did not seek a retrial, although she described the decision as "a very close call" and cautioned that her move "should not be viewed as an exoneration of Lipscomb's conduct," because there was "overwhelming evidence presented at trial that Mr. Lipscomb engaged in corruption while he served on the Council." In a press release from her office, she cited one of the factors that had led to her decision, namely, that Lipscomb had already served two-thirds of his forty-one-month sentence (U.S. Department of Justice, United States Attorney, Northern District of Texas, Press Release, August 30, 2002).

pany. He also said that he did not want to have to talk to someone he did not know.

Sam Bloom, the advertising executive who implemented many Citizens Council policies, thought that the leaders of Dallas, like other people, sought out their own kind, with the result that the Council was successful in accomplishing the things it could see and understand.[9] The city's trouble areas, he suggested, "exist because the city has been asking wisdom and enlightenment and a kind of moral vision not to be found, as a rule, in a businessmen's organization oriented toward the practical use of cash."[10]

Conforming with prevailing ideology has a long history in Dallas, as "stepping out of line" carries with it the fear of economic repercussions. In the 1920s Dallas, with its recognized propensity to do everything on a grand scale, had the largest local Klan in the nation. Ku Klux Klan members "were expected to support one another by showing preference to fellow Klansmen in their business dealings." The Dallas Klan, organized in late 1920, swelled to an estimated 13,000 members within four years.[11]

Glenn Pricer of the *Dallas Dispatch* later recalled: "People were afraid to belong to it and afraid not to. One of the main reasons for its growth was fear of boycott on the part of little businesses. And large firms encouraged their employees to join—they also feared boycott."[12] Hortense Sanger, descendant of early mercantile families in Dallas, recalls that many respectable people joined because they were afraid of economic reprisals if they did not join. She credits George B. Dealey and the *Dallas Morning News* as having been the strongest influence in driving the Klan out of Dallas, because few others had the courage, or inclination, to speak out.[13]

Clearly the members of the Citizens Council have left an indelible imprint on the City of Dallas—a legacy that has had negative implications, even though many of their contributions were positive and made, in most instances, with what they considered to be good intentions. What is suggested here is that the dedicated efforts of members of the Citizens Council would have been more constructive for the community in the long run, and would have developed a greater level of trust rather than resentment among various minorities, had they taken seriously voices other than their own. Instead, they reinforced their own viewpoint within their tight circle of peers, that "what is good for business is good for the city."

A political climate in Dallas intolerant to dissent has not been limited to the business community. Two examples support this point. When Stanley Mar-

9. Warren Leslie, *Dallas Public and Private: Aspects of an American City,* rev. ed. (Dallas: Southern Methodist University Press, 1998), 83.

10. Ibid., 80.

11. Payne, *Big D,* 75–76.

12. Ibid., 76.

13. Hortense Sanger, Remarks to Charter 100 of Dallas, April 9, 1985.

cus announced, in 1960, in favor of candidate John F. Kennedy, he was shocked by a deluge of letters from customers who closed their Neiman-Marcus accounts in protest.[14] In the 1980s Taylor Publishing in Dallas canceled the contract to publish local writer Jim Schutze's book, *The Accommodation: The Politics of Race in an American City,* as the book is an account of Dallas politics devoid of the booster spin customary in the city. The *New York Times* quoted the editor of the publishing company as saying, "It's so image-conscious here, you can't say anything negative."[15]

DISTINCTIVE HISTORICAL EXPERIENCES

In addition to shared attitudes, beliefs, ideas, and myths in a given locale, local communities also have historical experiences in common that influence their development and their politics.

Dallas may look like many other major cities in the United States, indeed, in many parts of the world, with its dominant skyscrapers, highway loops, and shopping malls. It may even face problems similar to those confronting other major cities, such as crime, education, environmental pollution, and lack of affordable housing. Further, it may have characteristics common to other major cities, such as population density, organizational complexity, dependence on commerce and industry, and a variety of heroes, celebrities, and colorful characters.

Nevertheless, although such features may be universal elements of major cities, the local manifestation of each of these elements is distinctive. Apparent similarities often obscure the physical, cultural, economic, and political variety of American cities. This variety causes similar policies and strategies to yield dissimilar results in different urban environments. Yet while Dallas's responses to its challenges surely contain idiosyncrasies, its choices and conduct have been neither unprecedented nor unique, and its experiences can be instructive and modified for other urban environments, as theirs can be for Dallas.

The development of a major city is not as inevitable as it may seem in retrospect. The accident of geographic location, and the historical era in which a city may be founded, influence the direction of its development. Furthermore, at every point the cumulative decisions and nondecisions of individuals help determine the course of a city's history.

Since a rich literature on the history of Texas and of Dallas exists, I intend to identify only the major influences in the development of Dallas that contribute to an understanding of voting rights issues as they relate to Dallas. These

14. Payne, *Big D,* 321.
15. Ruth Miller Fitzgibbons, *D* magazine (March 1987), 14:91. Citadel Press subsequently published *The Accommodation* in 1986.

influences include the state's colonial history and its Spanish heritage, and Dallas's location in space and time during its early development.

Spanish Heritage

Distinctively different types of communities developed in the Spanish border-lands of the Southwest than on the Atlantic seaboard. Each of the five impor-tant urban centers that existed in the Atlantic seaboard colonies by the early eighteenth century—Boston, Newport, New York, Philadelphia, and Charles-ton—dominated its coastal region. They had closer ties to London than to one another.[16] Similarly the chain of towns and villages, from Texas to California, that were settled between the founding of Santa Fe in 1610 and San Francisco in 1776 were tied to Mexico City, the dominant metropolis in the hemisphere.[17] These communities developed in even greater isolation from one another than did the Atlantic coastal cities.

The colonial era lasted nearly two centuries on the Atlantic seaboard and three centuries in the Southwest. Freed from their ruling authorities during this time by distance and official neglect, the colonists had an opportunity to put individual stamps on their societies. Different value orientations, colonial experiences, and economic bases led to distinctive types of communities that continued to develop along divergent paths, contributing to the variety of cul-tures found from coast to coast.

Because the 1975 Amendment, which covered language minorities, brought Texas under the special preclearance provisions of the Voting Rights Act, and because Hispanics are now the largest population group in the city, the state's Spanish heritage is directly relevant to its politics.

Significant differences in the historical experience of cities in the East and those in the Southwest have roots in their respective colonial eras. In 1776 the Atlantic seaboard colonies declared their independence and freed themselves from the British. Statues and buildings, from New England to Virginia, memo-rialize the heroes of the American Revolution and of the Constitutional Con-vention.

The Southwest, on the other hand, has no direct ties to the American Revo-lution, since the Spanish and mestizos settled this region. The Spanish ruled from 1540 until 1821, the year Mexico gained its independence from Spain. The Republic of Mexico ruled the region from 1821, until the United States gained the territory of the Southwest, except for Texas, by force of arms in the Mexican War (1846–1848). Texas gained its independence from Mexico in

16. Eric H. Monkkonen, *America Becomes Urban: The Development of U.S. Cities & Towns, 1780–1980* (Berkeley: University of California Press, 1988), 43.
17. David J. Weber, *Foreigners in Their Native Land: Historical Roots of the Mexican Americans* (Albuquerque: University of New Mexico Press, 1973), 16.

1836, voted to enter the Union in 1845, and commemorates its own revolutionary heritage. The state celebrates Texas Independence Day on March 2; its monuments are to heroes of the Texas Revolution; and its revered battleground sites are at San Jacinto, Goliad, and San Antonio. These experiences have contributed to an attitude of exceptionalism and independence, as well as to a kind of self-confidence, bordering on arrogance, that characterizes the stereotypical Texan.

After Mexico's independence from Spain in 1821, foreigners were permitted, for the first time, to live and work in Mexico. Most of those who settled on Mexico's northern frontier were North Americans. The development of Texas, however, was distinctive from that of the other states now bordering on Mexico. Texas, from the outset, attracted colonists, whereas California and New Mexico attracted mainly foreign merchants at the start. The subsequent Colonization Law of 1824 opened Texas to a flood of foreign settlers who were assigned land through empresario grants. A foreigner who settled in Texas could receive a liberal grant of land in exchange for developing it, becoming a Mexican citizen and a Roman Catholic, and obeying the law. By the time of the Texas Revolution in 1836, Texas was already overwhelmingly Anglo American.[18]

Mexico opposed slavery, but beginning in 1821 granted the colonists permission to bring in their slaves. Most of the colonists arriving in Texas between 1821 and 1836 were from slave-holding, southern states; they settled in East Texas to produce cotton. Because these colonists dominated politics at that time, the 1836 Constitution of the Republic of Texas recognized slavery. In 1845 Texas was annexed into the United States as a slave state.

After 1836, when Mexico lost Texas, Texas Mexicans (Tejanos) felt themselves to be "foreigners in their own land."[19] Not only did they lose political power quickly during the decade that Texas was an independent nation, but gradually land ownership shifted from Hispano to Anglo.[20] Furthermore, the years of bloodshed in the Texas Revolution and later in the Mexican War "intensified existing prejudices into deep hatreds which lingered long after the fighting was forgotten."[21]

The Treaty of Guadalupe-Hidalgo, signed in February 1848, ended the Mexican War. This treaty promised that Mexicans who stayed in Texas and the rest of the Southwest would receive "all the rights of citizens of the United States." However, as borderlands historian David J. Weber has written, "it seems clear in retrospect that this promise was not fulfilled. At best, Mexican Americans became second-class citizens. At worst, they became victims of

18. Ibid., 52, 57–58.
19. Pablo de la Guerra, Speech to California Senate, 1856, in Weber, *Foreigners,* vi.
20. Weber, *Foreigners,* 156.
21. Ibid., 88.

overt racial and ethnic prejudices."[22] This situation occurred, in part, because there were insufficient numbers of Americans of Mexican descent, except in New Mexico, to control politics at the state level in order to protect their rights as citizens.[23]

One outcome of this scenario is that Americans of Mexican descent in Texas believe, justifiably, that they have as great a claim to economic and political affirmative action programs as do Americans of African descent. Conflict between the two groups, which has become a significant political factor in Dallas, is discussed in later chapters.

Another result of the state having been a part of Mexico is its diversity and size, along with its former status as an independent nation, all of which fostered a sense of self-sufficiency, independence, and a pioneer spirit. These qualities help to explain the state's political conservatism and its historical rejection of what it views as federal government intrusion.

Its size has direct political implications; Texas has 254 counties, more than any other state. According to the 1992 Census of Governments, Texas had a total of 4,792 government units, more than the combined total of the five southern states of Alabama, Georgia, Louisiana, Mississippi, and South Carolina. Thus the VRA preclearance requirements place a heavier burden on Texas than they do on most states subject to Section 5. Furthermore, the trigger mechanism that brought Texas under the Section 5 preclearance provisions of the Act, the 1975 Spanish language amendment, raises special issues, addressed in chapter 5.

Dallas's Location in Space and Time

Dallas's geographical location and the particular era in which its development began have both contributed to making the city distinctive, even within the context of Texas. Just as Texas had no role in the American Revolution, Dallas had no role in either the Texas Revolution or the Mexican War. In 1845 Dallas had a mere thirty-two residents to vote on whether Texas should join the United States.[24] Texas would be the only state to enter the Union as an independent republic.

Because Texas, unlike any other state, retained ownership of all its public lands when it entered the Union in 1845, it was able to continue to dispose of land freely to foster settlement. As a result, from the time of the first empresario grants in 1821, Texans have equated growth with progress, and "this became a fixation that never died."[25]

22. Ibid., 143.
23. Ibid.
24. Michael V. Hazel, *Dallas: A History of Big "D"* (Austin: Texas State Historical Association, 1997), 6.
25. T. R. Fehrenbach, *Lone Star: A History of Texas and the Texans* (New York: American Legacy, 1983), 281.

In 1841 Dallas began as a one-man venture by a frontiersman named John Neely Bryan. A city's origin is often influenced by the nature of its physical environment. The particular site chosen for Dallas does not appear to differ greatly from other possible sites in the vicinity. Furthermore, the geographical characteristics seem relatively unimportant, especially when compared to later developments that resulted from actions taken and opportunities missed, during the city's formative years. In spite of the river frontage, the absence of physical attributes such as mountains or seashore or forests provided sufficient basis for the myth of exceptionalism, mentioned earlier, that was to become so important to Dallas in later years.

Accidents of history may fuel a perception of exceptionalism, if they are deemed to impose hardships more extreme than those experienced by others. Dallas's early experiences may have differed slightly in degree, but certainly not in kind, from the experiences of many other U.S. cities. The examples that follow, although important in the development of Dallas, hardly justify the claim of the exceptionalism myth that Dallas has the distinction of having been willed into existence by men of extraordinary vision and "can-do" spirits.

The first milestone in the development of Dallas was the victory, by a margin of only 28 out of 460 votes, to make the city the county seat. This event was the catalyst for Dallas's development into a commercial center. Anyone with legal business had to come to Dallas, and, of course, while in town, had to patronize its businesses. Had Dallas developed earlier, and become the state capital, it would have developed differently. But when Austin was named the permanent capital of Texas in 1839, Dallas had not yet been founded.

Circumstantial factors can strongly affect a city in its formative years. In the case of Dallas, the establishment of La Reunion Colony on the west side of town in 1855, and the disastrous downtown fire in 1860, are examples.

In reaction to the grim industrial towns spawned by the Industrial Revolution, a number of utopian experiments in community living captured the imagination in several countries in the mid-nineteenth century. One of these attempts was La Reunion, a colony established just to the west of Dallas in 1855 by French writer Charles Fourier's disciple, Victor Prosper Considérant. As with other utopian experiments, the Dallas colony failed; it was extinct by 1867. Many of the community members returned to France, but a sufficient number stayed and moved into Dallas. The city became more of a cultural center than would be expected on the frontier because of the intellectual and artistic awareness brought by La Reunion community members.[26] Their contributions established a pattern early on in the development of the city that continues to earn Dallas the reputation as the most cosmopolitan city in the state.

Dallas had the good fortune to inherit fine craftsmen, tradesmen, artists,

26. A. C. Greene, *The Deciding Years: A Historical Portrait* (Austin: Encino, 1973), 14–15.

and naturalists from Considérant's decision to found a colony near the city. But a misfortune, just a few years later, might have ended the development of Dallas to major city status. On July 8, 1860, a fire broke out and destroyed much of the downtown district—about twenty-five businesses and some residences. The cause of the fire is unknown. Of the various possibilities, blame was assigned to blacks and Abolitionists. As a result, within a few weeks of the disastrous fire three slaves were hanged, an action spawned, apparently, by hysteria.[27]

The timing of the fire proved unpropitious, as recovery from the disaster was halted by the outbreak of the Civil War. However, offsetting the negative economic effects of the fire, Dallas was selected to be the general quartermaster and commissary headquarters for the collection of food and supplies during the Civil War. This action stimulated the town's commercial development as a regional distribution center.

The location of Dallas and Texas, both in time and space, was crucial for both during the Civil War. Although the people of Texas voted 3 to 1 to secede from the union, the campaign was marked by intimidation, intolerance, and violence. According to historian Claude Elliott, "it is extremely doubtful whether more than one-third of the people of Texas actively supported the Confederacy."[28] Eight counties north and east of Dallas County, and ten counties around Austin, voted against secession. Ten other counties in those two areas voted, by more than 40 percent, against secession.[29] Certain leaders, such as Sam Houston, were so opposed to secession that they withdrew from political participation altogether during the war, while the secessionists held power.

The fighting did not ravage the state of Texas. Although prior to the Civil War the main stream of immigration to Texas had been from southern states, Texas was still a frontier state and Dallas a frontier town. Only 152 of the 254 counties in Texas had been established and organized by the time of the Civil War. Frontier settlements did not extend beyond, approximately, a line from Wichita Falls on the Red River to Eagle Pass on the Rio Grande, a north to south line not far to the west of Dallas and Austin.

Consequently a majority of Texans in military service during the Civil War were engaged in frontier defense against the Indians of the Great Plains.[30] By 1860 no other American state still faced such a frontier, with a line of fixed settlement exposed to continual threats of violence.

27. Randolph Campbell, *An Empire for Slavery: The Peculiar Institution in Texas, 1821–1865* (Baton Rouge: Louisiana State University Press, 1989), 224–228. See also Robert Prince, *A History of Dallas from a Different Perspective* ([Dallas]: Nortex, 1993), 17–20; and Karen Ray, "The Untold Story," *Dallas Life Magazine,* June 8, 1990, 10–11.

28. Claude Elliott, quoted in William C. Pool, *A Historical Atlas of Texas* (Austin: Encino, 1975), 110.

29. Pool, *Historical Atlas,* 109.

30. Ibid., 110.

On September 28, 1874, at Palo Duro Canyon in the Texas Panhandle, the last important Indian engagement in Texas occurred, nine years after the end of the Civil War.[31]

Because of its particular development, Texas does not fit consistently into any one region. Combining characteristics from the plantation South, the Spanish Southwest, and the frontier West, the state is a reflection of all these regions. Moreover, the state's vast size encompasses several areas in which different heritages dominate. This is an important consideration with regard to voting rights as it poses a special problem regarding macro-level studies of voting rights that, for statistical analyses, place Texas in a particular region.

POPULATION AND ECONOMIC VARIABLES

The composition of a city's population and the diversity and strength of its economy are particularly relevant to its politics. These two variables have an important relationship to each other and to Dallas's experiences under the Voting Rights Act.

On the one hand, the minorities who migrated to Dallas came with their own historical memories, especially those who migrated from the southern states via East Texas. Subsequently they developed shared memories from their common experiences in Dallas. And those shared experiences in Dallas often fueled grievances and anger, as minorities suffered shortages of affordable housing, the loss of their neighborhoods to development, and inattention to their educational and social needs.

On the other hand, for Dallas business leaders, a self-image of having made grand accomplishments in the economic sphere created an aura of progress and well-being that obscured the need for the development of political, social, and cultural capital. Like two ships passing unseen in the night, these divergent perspectives seemed to pose an unbridgeable racial and class divide, one in which litigation seemed the only recourse enabling minorities to gain access to the political system.

Population Composition and Migrations

Dallas County was in an early stage of economic development prior to the Civil War, producing grains rather than cotton. Thus the 1850 census revealed a low number of slaves (207).

Black Migrations. The blacks flooding into Dallas County during and immediately following the Civil War were from states heavily engaged in fighting.

31. For a brief account of the last Indian uprising and the attack at Adobe Walls in June 1874, see Fehrenbach, *Lone Star,* 545–547.

Although a large number of blacks were brought to the area at this time, they were hired out to farm families to cultivate wheat, corn, and oats.[32]

Several settlements of former slaves were established in the county, including one called "Freedman Town"—now a gentrified area called "State-Thomas" or "Uptown." The Deep Ellum–Central Track area, just to the east of Dallas's main business district, was apparently the "downtown" for minorities.[33] According to a local black physician, this area was "the gathering place of blacks from all over the country, for Mexicans fleeing oppression in Mexico, for Jews who established businesses, and for poor whites looking for 'action.'"[34]

For nearly a century after the close of the Civil War the blacks of Texas lived mainly on the small farms of East Texas. There they either worked for wages or were tenants; few owned land. The migration of blacks to cities was a result of the depression of the 1930s, when blacks were forced to leave rural areas in search of employment. This migration placed considerable pressure on available housing. In 1940 blacks in Dallas found few places to go outside the confines of the invisible walls of their segregated residential areas. A series of bombings, fires, hangings in effigy, and throwing of stones and bricks in late 1940 and early 1941 reinforced the separation. Little was done to alleviate the housing shortage for black families. Construction of the Central Expressway in the late 1940s destroyed blocks of black houses, and also covered graves in Freedman's Cemetery, a black cemetery from 1861 to 1925.[35]

History repeated itself in 1950; another large migration of blacks, seeking a better life, came to Dallas from small towns and rural areas.[36] Again bombings began. Middle-class blacks, those who could afford to buy homes in fringe areas, began pushing the boundaries of overcrowded black neighborhoods and were met with resistance. This time the bombings continued over a two-year period and received national attention. Mayor J. B. Adoue Jr. observed that the publicity was "blackening the name of Dallas."[37]

32. John H. Cochran, *Dallas County: A Record of Its Pioneers and Progress* (Dallas: Service Publishing, 1928), 87.

33. For years local historians perpetuated the view that Deep Ellum was the most famous of the "freedman towns." The authors of a recent book on Deep Ellum could find no documentation that it was ever a freedman town; they found, instead, that it was the "black downtown" of Dallas. See Alan B. Govenar and Jay F. Brakefield, *Deep Ellum and Central Track: Where the Black and White Worlds of Dallas Converged* (Denton: University of North Texas Press, 1998), ix–x, xiv.

34. Prince, *History of Dallas,* 68.

35. This occurrence was not the first. A portion of the cemetery had been used for the Houston & Texas Central Railroad in 1872 (Prince, *History of Dallas,* 30).

36. For an account of the desperate housing situation, the violence, and the city leadership's response, see Jim Schutze, *The Accommodation: The Politics of Race in an American City* (Secaucus, N.J.: Citadel, 1986), esp. chaps. 1–5.

37. Quoted in ibid., 20.

Because the city's focus was on controlling and dampening racial tension, rather than on resolving the desperate housing shortage, the fuse to reignite the violence remained lit. In his observations on the turn that slavery took in Texas, Frederick Law Olmsted wrote: "There seemed to be the consciousness of a wrong relationship and a determination to face conscience down, and continue it."[38] This pattern of "facing conscience down," doing just enough to pacify blacks so as not to disrupt business, has continued into the twenty-first century.

Hispanic Migrations. In comparison with the black migrations into Dallas, the rapid growth of the city's Hispanic population is relatively recent. Although their culture and their traditions extend back to 1519,[39] until after 1900 the Mexican population in Texas largely remained in south Texas and border areas, extending not much beyond San Antonio.

The need for unskilled laborers to build the railroads in the 1870s brought the first influx of Hispanic settlers to Dallas. This provided opportunities to establish businesses to serve the small but growing community, and by the turn of the century Mexican restaurants had opened. Further, Americans who were of Mexican descent were working as tailors, printers, candy manufacturers, cotton buyers, grocers, and tamale vendors.[40]

Not until refugees from the Mexican Revolution of 1910 immigrated to Dallas did the city's first sizable Mexican community form. By 1915 there were at least four definable barrios. Most of this population lived in deplorable conditions, in a congested, slum-like area just north of downtown, known as "Little Mexico."[41] The local Mexican population was far from homogeneous; even by the 1930s the barrios were broken into smaller communities, dissected by lines of class and culture.[42]

As in the case of Freedman Town in the State-Thomas area, Little Mexico fell victim to highway construction. Most of the area disappeared because of construction of the Dallas North Tollway in the 1960s and the Woodall Rodgers Freeway in the 1970s. Residents dispersed into other neighborhoods. Except for Pike Park, a few homes, and a former school (St. Ann's), little remains of the barrio that was the center of Hispanic community activities in Dallas.

Other Immigrant Groups. Because Dallas is a relative newcomer to the urban scene in America, the city missed most of the early waves of European immi-

---

38. Ibid., 35.

39. Pool, *Historical Atlas,* 146.

40. Hazel, *Dallas: A History,* 22, based on Nina Nixon-Mendez interview, February 12, 1989; "Hispanic Beginnings of Dallas" exhibition, Old City Park, 1989; and Gwendolyn Rice, "Little Mexico and the Barrios of Dallas," *Legacies* (fall 1992), 4:21–27.

41. Gwendolyn Rice, "Little Mexico and the Barrios of Dallas," *Dallas Reconsidered: Essays in Local History,* ed. Michael V. Hazel (Dallas: Three Forks, 1995), 159, 161.

42. Ibid., 161.

grants that pressed their interests on cities such as New York (Jews), Boston (Irish), Chicago (Irish and Polish), Baltimore (Italians), and Milwaukee (Germans). Beginning in the 1830s there were German, Norwegian, Swedish, Czech, and Polish migrations to Texas. But most of these European immigrants settled in rural areas, so they did not become a factor as population groups in the politics of Dallas.

During the periods of rapid population growth in Dallas, Congress was restricting immigration with quotas. As recently as 1940, about 5 percent of Dallas's population was foreign-born.[43] Dallas did participate, however, in the wave of migration that followed the 1965 change in U.S. immigration laws, which led to an increase in immigration from Asia and the Middle East, as well as from Latin America. The sizable Asian population, as well as the growing middle-class and professional community of Indian and Pakistani immigrants, have settled primarily in the suburban cities surrounding Dallas.

Within Dallas, the pockets of immigrant communities are small and scattered, and have not become major components in city politics. Leaders in Dallas who are of Asian descent, for example, attribute the lack of political involvement by Asians to language barriers, cultural differences, and not understanding the system. Most are recent immigrants.[44]

Population Shares. In addition to the size of immigrant and minority groups, the population share is relevant in politics. For example, Los Angeles, which attracted 2 million legal Mexican immigrants in the 1920s, surpassed San Antonio as the American city with the largest Mexican population in 1930. The proportional influence of the group was small in Los Angeles, however, where Mexicans accounted for only 8 percent of the total population. In contrast, Mexicans dominated San Antonio, where they accounted for 36 percent of the total population.[45] In the case of blacks, in the 1990s the nation counted 33.6 million people of African descent, or 13 percent of the population. Most of the ninety-nine majority-black counties were rural, but three communities— New York City (2.3 million blacks), Chicago (1.4 million), and Los Angeles (1 million)—had more Americans who were of African descent than all of Mississippi, the state with the highest share (36 percent).[46]

In the 1990 census Dallas showed a tri-racial population, with 29.5 percent black, 20.9 percent Hispanic, and 55.3 percent Anglo, as well as a growing

43. *The WPA Dallas Guide and History* (Dallas: Dallas Public Library and University of North Texas Press, 1992), 105.

44. Esther Wu, *Dallas Morning News,* March 9, 2000.

45. Daniel D. Arreola, "The Mexican American Cultural Capital," in *Re-Reading Cultural Geography,* ed. Kenneth E. Foote (Austin: University of Texas Press, 1994), 39–40.

46. The 1996 estimate based on 1994 U.S. census data, *U.S. News & World Report,* October 7, 1996, 26.

population of Asian descent.[47] According to the 2000 census, the pattern changed to 25.6 percent black, 35.6 percent Hispanic, and 34.6 percent white.[48]

The existence of two minority groups, each with a large share of the total population of the city, distinguishes Dallas from most major cities. In Dallas the Hispanic population is growing more rapidly than the black, and this change in the relative size of these two minority populations has created conflict in the city. This situation is not unique. Indeed, it mirrors patterns that occur when any community in the nation experiences rapid changes in the composition of its ethnic populations. Blacks, who had waged a long battle for power, resented seeing their gains limited by the more rapidly increasing population shares of Hispanics and Asians.

Economic Development and Diversity

The economic vitality of a city depends, to some extent, on its economic resources within the context of state and national events. For Dallas the railroads, as well as the city's selection as an administrative and distribution center during the Civil War, stimulated commercial development. The Federal Reserve Bank, established in Dallas in 1914, stimulated the growth of Dallas banks and lent the city credibility as a financial center. The discovery of oil in Texas ushered in a new era for both the state and the city. World War II signaled the beginning of major corporate relocations to Dallas. Dallas leaders capitalized on some opportunities and missed out on others. But it was the economic development launched by Dallas business leaders through the Citizens Council and the Chamber of Commerce that fueled the city's myth of exceptionalism.

The mode of transportation during the initial development of a city plays a key role in its growth patterns. Dallas did not fully begin to emerge until the era of rail transportation. Still Dallas was late, because the first railroads in Texas, even before the Civil War, radiated from Houston.

Nevertheless, the efforts of Dallas business leaders were successful in securing for the region an early leadership role in air transport. Early in 1917 the War Department announced that it wanted a place in the Dallas area for training pilots. The Dallas Chamber of Commerce bought and leased land south of Bachman Lake as a way to benefit from the prospective federal investment. The War Department leased the site, and the Air Service of the Army Signal Corps constructed a $1.5 million training facility on the land, which became known as Love Field.

47. Unless otherwise indicated, 1990 census figures are used throughout for comparative consistency, rather than projections developed later in the decade.

48. Because of differences between 1990 and 2000 census tabulation methods, the 2000 Hispanic origin results may not be directly comparable to those of 1990.

In the fall of 1927 the city of Dallas bought Love Field from the Chamber and developed it as a municipally owned airport.[49] This won dominance in aviation for Dallas over Fort Worth. Talk of a single, super airport equally distant between the two cities emerged as early as 1940. The controversy simmered for more than three decades, causing enmity between the two cities that continued to the end of the century, even after a regional airport had become successful.[50]

Noting the many years of conflict, the Civil Aeronautics Board issued an ultimatum in 1964. Dallas and Fort Worth were given six months to agree on a site for a regional airport, or the board would designate one. Mayor Erik Jonsson then initiated discussions with Fort Worth officials. By 1965 both city councils had agreed to create a regional airport authority to build and operate a facility at a site midway between the two cities.[51] Dallas–Fort Worth International Airport, which opened in 1974, soon became one of the busiest in the nation.

In other economic developments the Dallas Fed opened for business on November 16, 1914. This immediately boosted the city's banking capital and assured its rise to financial dominance in the region. The Texas oil boom years began in 1896, with a find at Corsicana, south of Dallas. By 1930 Texas had become the nation's leading oil-producing state. Although no oil was ever pumped in Dallas County, the city became the service center to the oil industry.[52]

The World War II years signaled the beginning of a pattern of major corporate relocations to Dallas. Important factors in relocation, such as a favorable public attitude toward free private enterprise, low taxes, and a largely nonunion labor force, became icons of the city's policy, bearing with them significant implications for city politics, such as a low priority on spending for social services.

At the same time that Dallas was attracting relocations, homegrown businesses were becoming major national firms. One example is Texas Instruments (TI). In 1941 J. Erik Jonsson, Eugene McDermott, Cecil H. Green, and Henry Bates Peacock bought Geophysical Service, which provided seismic services for the oil industry. The new owners branched out to produce submarine detection devices as part of the World War II effort. After the war, with a huge line of credit from Dallas's Republic National Bank, the company became TI and broadened into the electronics industry. In the early 1950s TI was the first

49. Payne, *Big D,* 116–117. According to A. C. Greene, Love Field was given to the city and became a municipal airport in 1927. See Greene, *Deciding Years,* 43.

50. For an account of the early controversies, see Payne, *Big D,* 207–211, 269–272.

51. Interviews by Michael Hazel of J. Erik Jonsson, November 18, 1993, and Najeeb Hallaby, January 13, 1994 (Hazel, *Dallas,* 56–57).

52. Pool, *Historical Atlas,* 160, 162. In contrast, Houston became the center of the Texas petroleum-refining industry.

company to produce commercial silicon transistors, and Jack Kilby invented the integrated circuit (1958). Kilby's invention catapulted Texas Instruments into the forefront of the digital revolution.

The CEOs of the banks dominated Dallas politics from the 1930s to the mid-1980s. The dominance of bank leadership had both negative and positive effects. As in the case of TI, mentioned above, access to capital could determine the fate of institutions, but individual enterprise could be affected, too. Many groups and individuals in Dallas remember their inability to gain access to credit. They were forced to the sidelines, while others prospered from loans and paybacks from large civic projects supported by the banks. A major goal for minorities who have sought a seat at the council table has been to participate in the decision of "who gets the money."

Heady with the success of the boom years in the 1970s and early 1980s, the crash of the mid-1980s was a seismic shock to the city. Dallas lost its three major commercial banks as a result of the oil and real estate crash.[53] According to an insider, the most critical loss was the institutional base that produced many notable business and civic leaders. "Indeed," in the words of the former CEO of Texas American Bancshares, Inc., of Fort Worth, "the executive training and community outreach programs of these major banks served as incubators for leaders, and the executive offices and boardrooms of major banks were seats of power where many of the most critical decisions affecting their communities were made."[54] Minority leaders were fully aware of this reality and their exclusion from the club.

After the crash the control of the city's major banking resources passed into out-of-state hands. The executives of failed banks, Savings and Loans, and real estate companies, with their confidence shattered, retreated from civic participation. Most of the CEOs of international corporations headquartered in greater Dallas viewed a commitment to shareholders as their primary responsibility, rather than the growth and development of Dallas. In its January 1997 issue, *D* magazine named Caltex, CompuCom, CompUSA, Halliburton, and Quaker State as Dallas's worst corporate citizens: "Every cultural and civic organization has heard their excuses—that is, when they even bother to return phone calls. 'Our customers are spread all over the globe.' 'We don't have that many employees here.' 'Our commitment has to be to shareholders first.'"[55]

Similarly most of the offspring of the founders of the homegrown businesses did not take up the slack and contribute to the city, except to protect their own financial interests. This may have been part of a national trend in

53. These banking organizations were RepublicBank Corporation, MCorp, and Inter-First Corporation, the nation's eighteenth, twentieth, and twenty-fifth largest.

54. Joseph M. Grant, *The Great Texas Banking Crash: An Insider's Account* (Austin: University of Texas Press, 1996), 3.

55. *D* magazine (January 1997), 24:94.

which money itself became more important than meaningful contribution, and the pressures of economic changes took precedence over community and quality of life. Or it may have been that the vision and motivation characteristic of the entrepreneur were lost in the second generation of leaders.

CONCLUSIONS

Like other municipalities, the distinctiveness of Dallas derives from its own particular combination of influences that form strands in the warp and woof of the cultural, sociopolitical, and economic fabric of the city. The effects of some of these strands will be evident in later chapters.

Although Dallas was founded only four years before Texas entered the Union in 1845, it inherited the characteristics of a state whose unique heritage contributed to an attitude of exceptionalism, independence, and self-confidence. Dallas's own formative years as a frontier town also contributed to a sense of self-sufficiency and a pioneer spirit, qualities that help to explain its political conservatism, and its historical rejection of what it viewed as federal government intrusion.

Neither Texas nor Dallas has a proud record in the treatment of minority populations. This is important to the narrative, because the existence of past discrimination in general, precluding effective participation in the election system, was an important criterion for the courts in voting rights cases. Although there was an influx of freedmen to Dallas during and after the Civil War, and of Hispanics during the building of the railroads in the 1870s, the large migrations of both blacks and Hispanics to Dallas occurred in the twentieth century. The first large migration of blacks arrived in Dallas from East Texas during the depression of the 1930s, and the second came from small towns and rural areas in the 1950s. The first sizable Mexican community in Dallas was made up of refugees from the Mexican Revolution of 1910. There was also a wave of migration from Latin America following the 1965 revision of U.S. immigration laws.

In the 2000 census racial and ethnic minorities, for the first time, became the majority in the city, with population shares of 25.6 percent black and 35.6 percent Hispanic origin. This distinguishes Dallas from most major cities and has given it experience in matters, such as redistricting, that highlight the problems that result from internal conflicts in current voting rights law. Each of these minority groups brings its own historical memories and legitimate grievances to bear on its claims to full political participation. While Americans of Mexican descent and blacks were both treated as second-class citizens and were victims of overt prejudice in Texas, blacks were subjected to de jure discrimination and Hispanics to de facto discrimination. As a result, voting rights law applies to each group differently.

An unresolved question is whether the myth of the city's exceptionalism has been beneficial or harmful to Dallas. On the positive side, the sense of exceptionalism has, at times, served the community well by increasing its capacity to achieve its goals. In the ever-present tension between Dallas's public and private interests, such self-confidence by civic leaders has goaded the community to remarkable achievements in collective action.

On the negative side, since the myth of exceptionalism distorts reality, it can cause harm. As a source of self-delusion, the myth undercuts critical and rational analysis of current or emerging problems and leads to contempt of views dissenting from a prevailing orthodoxy. More significantly a false sense of exceptionalism among leaders and their followers can create a psychological climate that leads to the disregard of internal grievances, and of experiences of other cities. A city and its leaders, who perceive themselves or their situation as exceptional, seldom seek to draw lessons or to establish a rational process for learning from the experiences of others. Such overconfidence permits an ethical regression that can stem from the concept that "superior" people are entitled to follow their own standards of behavior.

As suggested, Dallas's self-image of grand accomplishment in the economic sphere fogged lenses, which obscured the need for the development of political, social, and cultural capital. This result was partially responsible for the inadequate treatment of minorities and the poor that left the route of litigation as the only recourse for the dispossessed. This, in turn, led to a long and costly experience for the city, in both human and financial terms, that resulted in the court-ordered changes in city government.

4
Political Heritage

The study of politics is the study of influence and the influential.
—Harold D. Lasswell

Washing one's hands of the conflict between the powerful and the powerless
means to side with the powerful, not to be neutral.
—Paulo Freire

Continuity of rule by an economically conservative elite, imbued by a myth of exceptionalism, characterizes the political history of Dallas. The periodic surges of populism have been short-lived. Participants either did not have the staying power of the economic elite or were submerged in the dominating business culture or were co-opted by moneyed interests.

My intent in this chapter is to examine the city's political heritage, and the evolution of its political system, as a prologue to court intervention, the subject of the next chapter. The legal constraints, the extra-legal rules that evolved, and the community power structure, each discussed, are interrelated. The experiences of Dallas citizens with their governmental institutions, and the exercise of political power before the Voting Rights Act, provide a baseline for evaluating effects of voting rights law after 1965.

FORMAL RULES: CHARTERS AND ELECTION LAWS

The starting point for any discussion of governmental structure in the United States begins with the fundamental document: the constitution or charter that delineates institutions and distributes powers. While the scholarly literature supports the proposition that institutions *do* matter, no consensus exists on *the degree* to which they matter or *the ways* in which they matter.

Without question, different structures of government have different biases. Seldom does consensus exist on the identification of the bias, on who benefits most from the bias, or on the likely systemic effects of a particular structural bias. Nor do political actors have an optimal strategy to use in order to gain advantage from an identifiable bias. For these reasons, a vast literature exists on the pros and cons of the commission, mayor-council, and council-manager forms of government, as well as on the advantages and disadvantages of various election features, such as election from at-large or from single-member districts.

Conflicting interpretations on these issues raise sober concerns over a court's decision to enter the fog, to choose among structural forms, and to assign them to cities. Such debatable matters as election features should be resolved in the processes of negotiation and compromise that characterize legislative bodies, rather than in the adversarial process of win-lose characteristic of the judicial process.

Institutional changes do not occur in a city in isolation from external forces. Cities adapt, and modify to their own needs, political institutions that are popular in a nation or in a region at a particular time. For example, the new idea of the commission form of government, introduced in 1901 in Galveston, Texas, shattered the near monopoly that the aldermanic system had held on nineteenth-century city charters nationwide. Then, as the commission movement lost its momentum, and academicians and reformers began to attack it as misguided, the manager plan began to acquire its own momentum, after about 1914.[1] New governmental forms such as these provide choices for cities, rather than one-size-fits-all "preferred" solutions.

Responding to national trends, Dallas adopted the aldermanic form in 1871, when it was incorporated as a city,[2] then the commission form in 1907, and finally the council-manager form in 1931. The circumstances that dictated each change are described below.

National Context

Even though local governments are not mentioned in the U.S. Constitution, all cities in this country are legal entities that operate within the constraints of the U.S. Constitution and federal laws. In the federal structure of government, some powers are allocated to the national government and others are reserved for the states. Cities are organized as entities of the states. Arguments over the appropriate balance between "nation's rights" and "states' rights" began early in the country's history. These continuing arguments reflect the enduring tension between forces favoring centralized power and those favoring decentralized power.

The individualism and conservatism that has marked Texas political culture for most of the state's history has traditionally favored states' rights. At

1. Bradley Robert Rice, *Progressive Cities: The Commission Government Movement in America, 1901–1920* (Austin: University of Texas Press, 1977), 100, 105–107.
2. Dallas had earlier been incorporated as a town in 1856.

times, both the state government and the Dallas city government have refused federal aid programs so as to avoid federal "meddling."[3] For example, Dallas was one of four major cities in the country to refuse participation in the federal school lunch program. Business leadership feared that participation might threaten capital investment projects, by forcing the city to contribute its own funds to projects outside the mainstream interests of business.[4] For many citizens, this aversion to federal intrusion heightened their frustration with federal court interventions that altered their local governance structures. Especially offensive were the court orders on council districting that contravened the results of voter referenda.

A major concern of the framers of the U.S. Constitution, relevant to this analysis, was whether political representation should be based on population or on geography (states). The populated states preferred the former; the small states urged the latter, fearing they would be dominated by the large states. To secure the fundamental document, the framers worked diligently to seek compromise. The resulting constitution ameliorated the major concerns of most interests, a necessity for securing ratification by the required number of states.

Democracy, always difficult and time-consuming at best, requires a commitment to negotiation, compromise, coalition building, and respect for opinions different from one's own. Leadership by key players is of crucial importance in arriving at decisions that are at least acceptable to multiple parties, even if they are not their preferences. In the political struggle in Dallas over the structure of government, both business leaders and minority leaders missed opportunities over the years to reconcile differences in viewpoints and interests. Wasted chances bred mistrust and hardened positions that continue to have lingering effects.

This predicament is not unique to Dallas. In recent years denigration of compromise has had dysfunctional consequences for the American polity. As an outcome, citizens and their representatives have staked out intractable positions on issues, and then, if they have not been able to win, have either disrupted or bailed out of the system. Alternatively they have resorted to the win-lose arena of the federal courts for resolution. This state of affairs is important contextually for interpreting Dallas's route to the courts, as well as for assess-

3. This was true even for urban renewal and redevelopment programs. In 1964 W. T. Overton, president of a major development company, stated: "We think it's the responsibility of businessmen to solve the redevelopment problems of our cities here. If the businessman doesn't assume this responsibility, the federal government will" (Martin V. Melosi, "Dallas–Fort Worth: Marketing the Metroplex," in *Sunbelt Cities: Politics and Growth since World War II,* ed. Richard M. Bernard and Bradley R. Rice [Austin: University of Texas Press, 1983], 173).

4. Melosi, "Dallas–Fort Worth," 184.

ing the use of the courts in lieu of the negotiation and compromise characteristic of political processes.

In drafting a constitution for the United States, the framers reached a compromise on the appropriate basis for representation by establishing a bicameral legislature, with numerical representation based on population in the House of Representatives, and geographical representation based on states in the Senate. As presidential selection became more directly citizen participatory, presidents began to be viewed as the only representative of *all* the people. Since a bill must pass in both houses and be signed by the president to become law, three differently configured constituencies—district, state, and nation—are active in public policy making at the national level. This achieved the checks-and-balances system intended by the framers to temper popular passions, and to slow a rush to judgment, allowing time for reflection and due deliberation.

In cities, in contrast, the mayor, more often than not, is a member of the legislative body, a significant departure from the system of separated power between the president and Congress at the national level.[5] Mayors have a veto similar to the president's in less than one-third of cities.[6] In the case of council-manager governments, administrative authority is vested in a council-appointed executive.

A common characteristic in elections in the United States, at most governmental levels, is winner-take-all single-member constituencies, and plurality/majority voting systems. Only one winner emerges from a voting district, whether it is for a seat in a legislative body or as chief executive; the winner is that candidate who receives either a plurality or a majority of votes, depending on the voting jurisdiction's requirement.

Most Western democracies, however, use proportional representation (PR) voting systems and multi-member constituencies. Candidates gain office by winning a defined percentage, or a numerical threshold of the total vote, in a voting district with multiple seats. Some scholars believe that PR is the best means for ensuring representation of numerical minorities.[7] PR for city elec-

5. Of the jurisdictions responding to the International City/County Management Association's 1996 Municipal Form of Government survey, 65 percent reported that their mayor is a member of the legislative body. Mayors are members of the legislative body in more than one-third of the mayor-council jurisdictions (*Municipal Year Book 1998* [Chicago: International City Manager's Association, 1998], 35).

6. Ibid., 36. The International City/County Management Association conducts a "Municipal Form of Government" survey every five years.

7. For an analysis of fairer representation of minorities, as well as other claims in support of proportional representation, see, especially, Kathleen Barber, *A Right to Representation: Proportional Election Systems for the Twenty-first Century* (Columbus: Ohio State University Press, 2000); Lani Guinier, *The Tyranny of the Majority: Fundamental Fairness in Representative Democracy* (New York: Free Press, 1994); and Douglas J. Amy, *Real Choices/New Voices: The Case for Proportional Representation Elections in the United States* (New York: Columbia University Press, 1993).

tions has yet to gain significant popular attention or favor in the United States.[8] Rather than focusing on the pros and cons of alternative voting systems, proponents of greater access to council seats have focused on whether a council member's constituency should be a single-member district or a citywide (at-large) district.

A form of city government analogous in principle to the checks-and-balances system at the national level would be a mixed-representation system. Such a mixed system might include some council members elected from districts, some elected at large, or at least from differently configured districts, and the mayor elected citywide. Since the 1960s, however, single-member districts have been the preferred choice by Congress and the courts, and by minorities, for use in state and local elections.

Besides conflicting interpretations of the advantages and disadvantages of certain forms, political experiences create preferences for particular structures. In addition to diverse political, economic, and intellectual viewpoints regarding single-member versus at-large districts, the issue carries emotional baggage. For racial and other minorities in Dallas, the fight against at-large seats on the city council was a moral crusade to right the wrongs of the past. For the business and professional community that had supported council-manager government and at-large elections, single-member districts were emblematic of all that had gone wrong under the commission form of government, abandoned in 1931. The civic-business community took pride in having run a "clean" city for more than five decades; the concept of "ward politics" conjured images of corruption similar to what the business community believed to be the case in Chicago, Los Angeles, or Philadelphia.

For the black plaintiffs and the intervenors of Mexican descent in the Dallas litigation, at-large districts represented the forces of evil written into a governmental structure that had kept them out of office. The plaintiffs were confident that the judicial bias for single-member districts provided their frontline attack strategy for more political and economic power, as well as their rearguard action, if eliminating at-large districts failed either in a negotiated settlement or at the ballot box. Having this backstop available affected both litigation strategies and political strategies. The black plaintiffs staked out an intractable position and assigned it to all racial minorities, but especially to blacks. The plaintiffs viewed a system with all single-member districts as the only solution for their political empowerment and, after 1975, vowed to settle for nothing less.

Other Dallas citizens, however, including a majority of the voters in three

---

8. During the first half of the twentieth century Cincinnati, Cleveland, New York, and a few other cities used proportional representation systems for a while. With renewed, contemporary interest in PR, movements have developed in some states, and in cities such as Cincinnati and San Francisco, to adopt PR voting systems.

referenda on the issue, wanted to retain a mixed system, with some single-member districts and some seats with a citywide constituency.[9] Legitimate interests of minority groups other than blacks, dissenting views in the black community itself, and the preferences of a majority of voters were either excluded from consideration in court or were voided by the very nature of the legal process.

Given the trajectory of the developing case law and the U.S. Department of Justice guidelines under the Voting Rights Act, the black plaintiffs and their constituents in Dallas had little incentive to work toward a compromise. The judicial bias for single-member districts, therefore, sabotaged the efforts of the citizens of all races to find a political accommodation to the new realities of federal law and to rapidly changing demographic patterns.

The controversies, which have surrounded at-large elections since the 1960s, might lead one to conclude that there has been a significant decline in their use in municipalities. While federal courts may have required single-member districts in some cities in which suits were filed, such as Dallas, aggregate nationwide data indicate that, from 1981 to 1996, the use of at-large elections in municipalities remained at about 60 percent, mixed systems at about 20 percent, and district systems at less than 20 percent.[10]

State Context

In addition to the U.S. Constitution and federal laws, local governments are constrained by state constitutions and laws, and exist solely as entities of the states. The current Texas constitution was adopted in 1876, after military rule ended and the Democratic Party regained control of state government. Texas government still retains structural features, such as biennial legislative sessions, that reflect a general distrust of government generated by experiences under Reconstruction governments.

On the other hand, the suffrage provisions in the Constitution of 1876 were liberal for the times. The Constitutional Convention defeated a proposal for a poll tax and made aliens who indicated an intention to become citizens eligible to vote. Not until after the turn of the century did Texas become more restrictive than the norm with regard to voting rights.

9. Dallas voters approved the 8-3 plan in April 1976, defeated the 14-1 plan in December 1990, and approved the 10-4-1 plan in August 1989. In 1973 the electorate indicated a preference for the at-large system by defeating a plan to elect eight council members from districts and five at large.

10. Tari Renner, "Minority Election Processes: the Impact on Minority Representation," *Municipal Year Book 1988*, 55:13–22; Tari Renner and Victor S. DeSantis, "Contemporary Patterns and Trends in Municipal Government Structures," *Municipal Year Book 1993*, 60:67; Tari Renner and Victor S. DeSantis, "Municipal Form of Government: Issues and Trends," *Municipal Year Book 1998*, 65:30–41.

In 1902 Texas instituted the poll tax as a requirement for voting and to serve as a statewide voter registration system. In 1904 the State Democratic Executive Committee approved use of the white primary by counties.[11] In 1903 and 1905 the state legislature passed a series of election reforms, known collectively as the Terrell Election Law, which codified the poll-tax measure, established a statewide direct primary system, and allowed local party officials to exclude blacks from voting in primaries. Although advertised as Progressive measures, these devices severely restricted voter participation by the poor, and by racial and ethnic minorities.[12] Thus racism became intertwined with Progressive reform in Texas.[13] Each of these voting restrictions was abandoned only after federal intervention by legislation or by court decision.

Texas was liberal in adopting, in 1912, a home rule amendment to the constitution, which granted cities the right to choose their own form of government. Cities with a population of more than 5,000 are authorized to adopt self-governing charters, subject only to limitation by the constitution and general laws of the state.[14] Of the 290 home rule charters in existence in May 1994, 251 provided for the council-manager form of government, 39 for the mayor-council form, and none for the commission form.[15]

Forms of City of Dallas Government

As mentioned, the City of Dallas has been governed under three different forms of city government: mayor-alderman from 1871, commission from 1907 to 1931; and council-manager from 1931 to the present.[16] Each time, the business community initiated the changes to the new form of government, as well as the other major changes to the city charter, until the 1960s, when the disaffected began seeking redress through the courts.

11. The name "white primary" was given to primary elections from which blacks were excluded by party rules.

12. For a thorough treatment of the impact of race on Texas politics, see Chandler Davidson, *Race and Class in Texas Politics* (Princeton, N.J.: Princeton University Press, 1990).

13. Progressivism in U.S. history was a broadly based reform movement in the early twentieth century that developed in response to vast changes brought by the industrial revolution.

14. Cities with a population of less than 5,000 are incorporated as "general law" cities, governed by state law.

15. Terrell Blodgett, "Home Rule Charters," *The New Handbook of Texas,* 6 vols. (Austin: Texas State Historical Association, 1966), 2:116. Also see Terrell Blodgett, *Texas Home Rule Charters* (Austin: Texas Municipal League, 1994).

16. From 1846, when Dallas County was organized by the state legislature, until 1856, the City of Dallas came under county administrative authority. No records have been located to indicate government of any form from the founding of the settlement in 1841 to 1846. For details on persons and events during these earlier years, see Darwin Payne, *Big D: Triumphs and Troubles of an American Supercity in the 20th Century* (Dallas: Three Forks, 1994).

Beginning in 1876, during the aldermanic period, election of aldermen other than the mayor was by wards. The Dallas City Charter of 1899 provided for eight wards and four at-large districts, establishing a precedent for a mixed system of council members to represent different constituencies.[17]

After the hurricane of 1900 the commission form of government was devised by Galveston in 1901 as a temporary expedient, but it became popular as the first wave of Progressive reform of municipal government after the turn of the century. In Dallas, and in other cities in Texas that adopted the commission plan during the first decade of the century, support for and opposition to the changes in government were similar. The organized business community or the daily press or both initiated and supported the commission plan, while the working-class, especially organized labor, led the opposition. In Dallas the Trades Assembly tried to prevent adoption of the plan, with its at-large elections, but failed. Later, no union-related candidate was included on the business-oriented Citizens Association slate. The Association's campaign literature appealed to "those who have to depend upon their labor for their support," but went on to stress that their candidates were "men who have made a success of their private affairs" and that such businessmen could provide "an honest, efficient, and progressive administration."[18]

The commission charter adopted in Dallas provided for a mayor and four commissioners, elected citywide, for terms of two years each. The mayor exercised general supervisory authority over all departments of the city government, while each of the commissioners separately administered one of the major departments: fire and police, water and sewage, streets and public property, and finance and revenue. Citizens charged that commission government was unrepresentative, because ward representation had been replaced by citywide elections. Other serious problems included the lack of centralized leadership to coordinate government work and poor fiscal control.[19]

By 1931 there was no doubt that the city had serious difficulties.[20] The

17. For more detail, see John H. Cochran, *Dallas County: A Record of Its Pioneers and Progress* (Dallas: Service Publishing, 1928), 217; *Charter: City of Dallas* (1991), iii; Robert B. Fairbanks, *For the City as a Whole: Planning, Politics, and the Public Interest in Dallas, Texas, 1900–1965* (Columbus: Ohio State University Press, 1998), 15–16.

18. Rice, *Progressive Cities,* 28. See chapter 2, in idem, *Progressive Cities,* for a history of the spread of the commission form of government in Texas. See chapter 1 in Fairbanks, *City as a Whole,* for the efforts to adopt the commission form of government in Dallas.

19. According to a 1937–1938 study of Dallas government, the commission's "major political trouble was not spectacular graft or patronage but the disintegration produced by the private political ambitions of five administrative heads who, after being independently elected, managed their departments separately rather than collectively" (Harold A. Stone, Don K. Price, and Kathryn H. Stone, *City Manager Government in Nine Cities* [Chicago: Public Administration Service, 1940], 275).

20. Ibid., 280.

commission form of city government had not led to businesslike and efficient government, as its proponents had espoused. Rather, commissioners became too closely associated with their departments, which led to the collusion of city officials and interest groups, the courting of constituent interests, and patronage employment.[21] For many citizens, commission government came to symbolize cronyism, corruption, inefficiency, and indebtedness. This attitude is important to recall later, in the discussion of governance consequences of court-ordered single-member districts.

Progressivism early in the twentieth century brought a set of changes that have had lasting influence on the structure and operations of national, state, and local governments. Reformers at the municipal level reacted to the way that political party machines had run the older cities in the Northeast and the Midwest, and to the cronyism and mismanagement that had developed in the ward-based election system in the younger cities of the Southwest, such as Dallas.[22]

In fact, the municipal reform movement had its greatest triumphs in the Southwest, where it did not have to overcome the opposition of entrenched political parties.[23] Since that time citywide nonpartisan elections and commission and council-manager governments have been the rule, not only for small cities, as in other regions of the nation, but also for large cities. Dallas remains one of the largest cities in the nation with a council-manager form of government.[24]

Richard S. Childs, whose crusade for council-manager governance earned him the title of the "father of the council-manager plan," worked through national organizations, such as the National Municipal League, to make the manager plan, rather than the commission plan, the Progressive idea of choice for business-minded reformers. Childs, and others, pointed out that the specific departmental interests of commissioners often caused internal confusion and

21. Reform crusader Richard S. Childs predicted these outcomes. New York City in the 1850s experienced similar results from its charter revisions. Eager machine building by each of the city's administrators immediately followed adoption of the new form of government. Commissioners competed for budget shares and wrestled over the boundaries of departments. Elections hardly secured competent administrators, as voters were unable to judge managerial ability.

22. For an account of alternative interpretations of the support for reform institutions, see David R. Berman and Bruce D. Merrill, "Citizen Attitudes Toward Municipal Reform Institutions: A Testing of Some Assumptions," *Western Political Quarterly* (June 1976), 29:274–283.

23. For an account of reform politics and government in large southwestern cities since 1901, see Amy Bridges, *Morning Glories: Municipal Reform in the Southwest* (Princeton, N.J.: Princeton University Press, 1997).

24. Eight additional cities among the top thirty in population operate under the council-manager plan: San Diego, Phoenix, San Antonio, San Jose, Austin, Fort Worth, Oklahoma City, and Kansas City.

inefficiency, and that the absence of a chief executive resulted in a lack of central direction. Childs argued that manager charters could retain beneficial aspects of the commission system, such as the short ballot, at-large voting, nonpartisanship, and the merit system, as well as direct democracy features, such as the initiative, referendum, and recall. At the same time the reform plan could replace leaderless bickering with a professional city manager, thus establishing businesslike management akin to the corporate model. Originally the concept was to place policy responsibility in a part-time elected body, and management of the city's business in a professional city manager.[25]

Of considerable importance is that the National Municipal League's Model City Charter, as adopted in 1915, recommended nonpartisan at-large elections. Indeed, for years, most textbooks applauded the virtues of at-large elections for city councils. Conventional wisdom supported at-large elections as sound public policy, and the council-manager form quickly gained acceptance among cities of all sizes.[26]

The original features of the council-manager plan included a mayor elected from among the city council members. The council was nearly always elected at large, received no pay, and spent little time at city hall. Part-time council service was attractive to the business-civic elite, whose members did not have time to serve as full-time city commissioners.

Dallas was not in the vanguard of those adopting the council-manager plan; the city stayed with the commission form for more than two decades, until 1931.[27] The News began its campaign for the council-manager form in 1916 but was distracted in the early 1920s by the Ku Klux Klan movement. The Klan controlled both city and county governments in 1923. After moderate business leaders regained control of the city commission in 1927, Mayor R. E. Burt appointed a Charter Committee to draft a new charter. On March 5, 1929, the committee issued its report, in which it recommended that the city adopt a council-manager form of government. The report also favored at-large elections for council seats, in order "to eliminate the possibility of sectional jealousies and so-called log-rolling."[28]

25. Richard J. Stillman II, *The Rise of the City Manager: A Public Professional in Local Government* (Albuquerque: University of New Mexico Press, 1974), 3, 15–19.

26. According to data collected by the International City-County Management Association, the council-manager form continues to be the most popular form in American cities (*Municipal Year Book 1998*, 30–32). In Texas this form is even more dominant, with 251 of the 290 home-rule cities under council-manager governments. Only four cities in Texas with a population of more than 40,000 are governed under the mayor-council form: Houston, El Paso, Pasadena, and Texas City.

27. Newspaperman G. B. Dealey of the *Dallas Morning News* viewed commission government as a transitional form; as early as 1911 he predicted that Dallas would adopt the more progressive city manager form some day (Carolyn Jenkins Barta, "The Dallas *News* and Council-Manager Government" [M.A. thesis, University of Texas at Austin, 1970], 4).

28. *Dallas Morning News*, March 6, 1929, cited in Fairbanks, *City as a Whole*, 61.

Opposition to council-manager government was even more vitriolic than the resistance had been to the commission form. Opponents feared "big business in the saddle" and the undemocratic character of an appointed executive.[29]

In 1930 some of the veterans of the campaign for the city's commission plan joined with a younger generation of businessmen to organize the Citizens Charter Association (CCA) to promote the council-manager plan of government. The businessmen stressed ways in which the new governmental structure would bring greater efficiency, as well as more responsiveness to the public, by having a majority of the members reside in city districts.[30]

When the incumbent commission officials refused to submit the charter amendments to the voters, a charter election was forced by popular petition. The voters approved the change in 1930, and the city held its first election under the new structure on April 7, 1931.

In adopting the council-manager plan, Dallas followed the norm of non-partisan, at-large elections; a mayor elected by the council from among its members; and token pay, which in the Dallas charter was $20 per diem for each regular meeting, with a cap of $1,040 per annum. Another feature of the Dallas charter was that it specifically excluded primary elections for selecting nominees to stand for election to the council.

The charter provided that candidates could secure a place on the ballot by a petition, signed by no fewer than 300 qualified voters, and filed with the city secretary not less than thirty days prior to the election. Because of easy access to the ballot and no nominating primary, a runoff election would be held if no candidate received a majority vote in the general election for a council seat.

Since the first election in 1931 under the council-manager plan, Dallas has been divided into city council districts. Under the at-large plan, all nine council members were elected at large. Six of the nine represented specific districts, however, and had to be residents of those districts, designated Districts A–F; three could live anywhere in the city; the council selected the mayor.

The new charter also specified that "the City Council shall, by ordinance, rearrange said districts so as to make them as nearly equal in population as practicable." Although "equal in population" was not important insofar as voting was citywide, this provision preceded the Supreme Court's "one man, one vote" rulings in 1964.[31]

Council size can be a significant factor, with trade-offs between more representatives on large councils and greater efficiency on small councils. In Dal-

29. Amy Bridges, "Boss Tweed and V. O. Key in Texas," in *Urban Texas: Politics and Development,* ed. Char Miller and Heywood T. Sanders (College Station: Texas A&M University Press, 1990), 62.

30. Executive Committee of the CCA, *Report,* May–November 1931, in Carol Callaway Collection, Dallas Public Library, cited in Fairbanks, *City as a Whole,* 68.

31. *Reynolds* v. *Sims,* 377 U.S. 533 (1964); and *Wesberry* v. *Sanders,* 376 U.S. 1 (1964).

las the size of the council was not changed for almost four decades from the nine members of the original council-manager charter. The subsequent changes in size have been to increase representation for minorities, rather than to respond to organizational concerns.

In a special election on October 22, 1968, Dallas voters approved creating two new districts, which increased the council seats from nine to eleven. The purpose of increasing the size of the council was to reserve one of the new seats for a black. One new district was created in northeast Dallas to respond to population growth, and the other in south Dallas and part of south Oak Cliff, an area with a large black population. Under this plan, eight on the council were required to live in home districts, and three could live anywhere in the city. All citizens of Dallas would still vote on all council members. Districts were designated Districts 1–8, and the three at-large seats, 9–11, with the mayoral seat designated Place 11. The first election under the new "8-3 plan" was on April 1, 1969.

Opposition to the change in the charter was directed less at the change in council size than at the continuation of citywide voting. Former council candidate Max Goldblatt mounted a strong campaign in Pleasant Grove for council members to be elected by districts. Later, Goldblatt filed a single-member district suit under the Fourteenth Amendment in 1967, claiming that the at-large election system was a scheme to perpetuate control of the city by "powerful millionaires."

The next attempt to change the size of the council was in 1973. Proposition 3 in that charter election provided for a thirteen-member council, with eight elected in districts and five elected at large. The "8-5 plan" was defeated by 73.6 percent of the vote. Again, the defeat was due more to proposed election from single-member districts than to council size.[32]

The last increase in the size of the council was the 1991 court-ordered, and subsequently voter-adopted, "14-1 plan," with only the mayor elected citywide. After the 2000 census, however, when blacks in Dallas realized that their proportionate share of the total population was declining and they might lose one of their "safe" seats, some began to press, once again, to enlarge the city council, this time to sixteen.[33]

At-Large Challenge

The feature of the Model City Charter most relevant to this study is at-large elections. Beginning in 1963, and coincident with the Civil Rights movement,

32. In 1975 the "8-3 plan," ordered by U.S. District Court Judge Mahon, provided for election from eight single-member districts, with three at-large positions. Subsequently, on April 3, 1976, voters passed this 8-3 plan in a special election referendum.

33. For example, statement of Roy Williams, litigant in *Williams* v. *City of Dallas*, at a public hearing on redistricting, May 19, 2001, at the Dallas Public Library.

scholars and politicians began to challenge conventional political wisdom. They advanced the view that at-large elections reduce opportunities for anyone outside leadership circles to conduct successful campaigns, and they identified the factors that made it difficult to win at-large elections: financial costs, organizational demands, the need for name recognition, and, in the case of minority candidates, negative attitudes toward minority groups. This argument was first advanced by Harvard professors Edward C. Banfield and James Q. Wilson.[34]

By the time the first Dallas racially based single-member district case was filed in 1971, no evidence in the scholarly literature existed to definitively conclude that cities with at-large elections elected fewer blacks to city councils than cities with single-member district elections. To argue the theoretical issues involved is easy, but to obtain conclusive evidence of the linkage between one element of governmental structure—namely, at-large elections— and underrepresentation of minorities is problematic.

During the ensuing decade, a number of scholars, using a variety of databases and varied methodologies, tested the Banfield/Wilson thesis, with both confirming and contradicting results.[35] A review of thirteen studies between 1969 and 1981 of the effects of at-large elections on minority representation found that ten confirmed the conventional hypothesis that the election of minority candidates is much more difficult under at-large elections.[36] A dissenting view held that electoral structures vary in impact according to the demographic and socioeconomic environments in which they operate.[37] Another study concluded that "there is no inevitable causality between election type and black council penetration . . . [but] the evidence is persuasive that, for the most part, district races promote and at-large races impede black council representation."[38]

By 1988, when Dallas was challenged in court regarding its mixed system (eight council members elected by single-member districts and three elected at

34. Edward C. Banfield and James Q. Wilson, *City Politics* (Cambridge, Mass.: Harvard University Press, 1963), 307, cited by Thomas R. Dye, letter to N. Alex Bickley, City Attorney of Dallas, March 7, 1974.

35. For an overview of this early literature, see Richard L. Engstrom and Michael D. McDonald, "The Effect of At-Large Versus District Elections on Racial Representation in U.S. Municipalities," in Bernard Grofman and Arend Lijphart, eds., *Electoral Laws and Their Political Consequences* (New York: Agathon, 1986). Also see Peggy Heilig and Roger J. Mundt, *Your Voice at City Hall: The Politics, Procedures, and Policies of District Representation* (Albany: State University of New York Press, 1984).

36. Chandler Davidson and George Korbel, "At-Large Elections and Minority-Group Representation: A Re-Examination of Historical and Contemporary Evidence," *Journal of Politics* (November 1981), 43:982–1005.

37. Susan A. MacManus, "City Council Election Procedures and Minority Representation: Are They Related?" *Social Science Quarterly* (June 1978), 59:153–161.

38. Albert K. Karnig and Susan Welch, *Black Representation and Urban Policy* (Chicago: University of Chicago Press, 1980), 147.

large), the move to single-member districts had by no means become universal. Of thirty-three cities surveyed by the International City Managers Association, fifteen were elected totally at large, five were elected totally by single-member districts, and thirteen were elected by some combination of the two.[39] Austin, one of the five largest cities in the state, and the most liberal, continues to elect all council members at large, having rejected single-member districts four times in the last twenty years, most recently in 1994.

Prior to 1971, when the first racially based single-member district case was filed, scattered opposition to at-large elections had occasionally arisen in Dallas. In the 1930s the Catfish Club proposed a district-elected council. A slating group in the 1949 city election, Change the Charter Association, supported district elections. Since then, other opposition groups have acted similarly from time to time.

Gene G. Freeland, secretary-treasurer of AFL-CIO's Dallas Council, proposed election by single-member districts at the 1966 Goals for Dallas conference. Although the conferees rejected Freeland's single-member district proposal, Mayor Erik Jonsson agreed to place the proposal on the agenda for the "town hall" meetings to be held for citizen response to the Goals for Dallas report.[40] These meetings generated little enthusiasm for changing to election by single-member districts.

The following year, in 1967, the city council scheduled a charter amendment election to enlarge the council from nine to eleven positions. At that time members of the steering committee of the Citizens for Representative Government (CRG), a candidate endorsement group opposed to the Citizens Charter Association, unsuccessfully pressed the council to add an election-by-district proposition. The CRG steering committee included representatives of four groups historically in the minority in Dallas politics: Republicans, labor, blacks, and liberals.[41]

Other cities, including some not under the jurisdiction of the Voting Rights Act, had similar experiences of minority interests pressing for single-member districts. For example, in another council-manager city, San Diego, a coalition of environmentalists, Progressives, neighborhood groups, and racial minorities

39. Among those included in the survey that were elected totally at large were San Diego, Boston, Phoenix, San Francisco, Seattle, Pittsburgh, El Paso, Fort Worth, Austin, Miami, and Tucson. At the time, Houston had a system of nine district and six at-large members, Atlanta had twelve district and six at-large members, and Washington, D.C., had eight district and five at-large members (Rena Pederson, *Dallas Morning News*, April 15, 1987).

40. Dorothie Erwin, *Dallas Morning News*, June 20, 1966.

41. These representatives included Hughes Brown, former Republican state legislator from Dallas County; Gene Freeland, AFL-CIO Council executive secretary; C. B. Bunkley Jr., black attorney; and Don Fielding, then one of the community's few outspoken liberals.

were defeated four times before securing voter approval of single-member districts in 1988.

The main opposition to at-large elections by minority interests in Dallas was twofold: first, the inability to raise sufficient funds to run viable citywide campaigns against the dominant Citizens Charter Association and, second, an inability to elect "a candidate of one's own choice." These were to become major issues in litigation.

INFORMAL RULES: PARTIES AND SLATING GROUPS

The electoral success of the Citizens Charter Association under at-large elections was a major issue in the litigation in Dallas. Slating groups, such as the CCA, perform functions similar to the traditional functions of political parties. They organize individuals of similar values to recruit candidates, to support campaigns, and to mobilize voters to win elections, and thereby to control governmental policy making. The advantage to the voter is that these slates simplify choices and also give clues to candidates' policy preferences.

Context

Political parties are not mentioned in the U.S. Constitution; they developed extra-constitutionally. Similarly nonpartisan slating groups are not mentioned in Dallas's city charter. Slating groups and political parties both developed in addition to—not contrary to—these fundamental documents in order to fill a political need for organizations that could recruit candidates and conduct campaigns.

In U.S. history one political party or the other has occasionally dominated for long periods in the presidency or in Congress. Similarly, at state and local levels, one party, or one slating group, has controlled legislative bodies over a number of years. Despite this historical record, the courts deemed a lengthy period of dominance by one slating group in Dallas to be prima facie evidence of a structural defect in municipal government, one having a discriminatory effect on racial minorities.

Dallas, however, is located in a state in which one-party dominance has been a regular characteristic of state politics. Except during Reconstruction, the Democratic Party was the leading political party until the 1960s. The Democratic primary was tantamount to election, since primary nominees normally ran without opposition in the general election. The Democratic primary did not cease to be seen as the important election by voters until 1982, when only sixteen Texas counties had higher turnouts in the primaries than in the general election.[42]

42. Glenn A. Robinson, "The Electorate in Texas," in *Texas at the Crossroads: People, Politics, and Policy,* ed. Anthony Champagne and Edward J. Harpham (College Station: Texas A&M University Press, 1987), 71, 79.

The New Deal period stimulated a pronounced factionalism on a conservative-liberal axis within the Democratic Party in Texas. Although the liberal-conservative battle was fought on many fronts, it usually centered on the issue of civil rights, especially during the late 1950s and 1960s, when racial integration overshadowed almost all else in Texas. Texas moved into the Republican presidential column in 1952 to support Dwight D. Eisenhower's election.[43] Subsequently the Civil Rights movement permanently rearranged the U.S. and state party systems, and racial attitudes that had once cut across party lines became polarized along partisan lines.[44]

No Democrat won the White House after Texas entered the Union in 1845 without carrying Texas, until President Clinton's election in 1992. Dallasite Ross Perot's third-party candidacy in the 1992 presidential election helped to split Democratic support in Texas, and George Bush carried the state. While Texans supported Republican presidential candidates, starting with Eisenhower in 1952, Texans voted in Democratic primaries and for Democratic candidates for state office until the 1980s.

Nevertheless, the Republican movement had been active for some time. The phrase "first since Reconstruction" entered the Texas political lexicon in 1954, when Republican Bruce Alger of Dallas was elected to Congress. In 1961 John G. Tower became the first Republican U.S. Senator since Reconstruction; in 1978 Dallas's William P. Clements was elected as the first Republican governor since Reconstruction. In fact, all the Republican electoral "firsts" in Texas have been from Dallas. So it should not be surprising that conservative Democrats and Republicans long dominated politics in Dallas's city elections.

Republican strength in the state continued to grow in the 1980s and 1990s. In 1980 the Republican Party achieved a breakthrough in Dallas County, heavily assisted by voting the straight ticket, by winning twelve of fourteen judgeships. By 1994 Republicans held both U.S. Senatorial seats, a record eleven of Texas's thirty U.S. congressional seats, the state governorship, and a majority on the Texas Supreme Court. Also for the first time since Reconstruction, in 1996 Republicans won a majority in the state Senate and, in 2002, won control of the Texas House.[45]

---

43. Texas had broken Democratic dominance by moving into Herbert Hoover's column in 1928, but that change was more a function of anti-Catholic sentiment than party sentiment.

44. For an insightful analysis, see Edward G. Carmines and James A Stimson, *Issue Evolution: Race and the Transformation of American Politics* (Princeton, N.J.: Princeton University Press, 1989).

45. Two individuals were instrumental in breaking the lock held by the Democratic Party in Texas. Governor Allan Shivers has been acknowledged as having helped to dissolve Democratic loyalties by encouraging voting for Eisenhower across party lines in 1952. Dallas investor Peter O'Donnell Jr. was the organizational genius in the development of the Republican Party in Texas. See Robert Allyn, "How Dallas Switched Parties:

Urban areas led the way for the development of the Republican Party in Texas in the 1980s and 1990s; Dallas became the most Republican of the major cities. In twenty-two presidential, senatorial, and gubernatorial elections from 1968 to 1990, Dallas County voted Republican in eighteen of them.[46]

Dallas Nonpartisan Slating

Dallas has had a seventy-year history, from 1907 to 1977, with a dominant slating group effectively in control of city government. The Citizens Association, formed in 1907 to secure the commission form of government, for the most part ruled city politics until the 1923 election. The Citizens Charter Association, organized in 1930 to promote council-manager government, largely dominated Dallas elections until 1977. Opposition groups, which periodically emerged to challenge both these business-dominated slating groups, were occasionally successful at the polls, but none had staying power.

The political history of Dallas directly relevant to the single-member district litigation is the period of dominance by the Citizens Charter Association. The CCA held one of the most remarkable records of any municipal political organization in the country, maintaining control of the council from 1939 to its demise in 1977, when it failed to slate candidates for the first time since 1931.

Dallas's experience with a dominant slating group has not been unique. In the 1920s and 1930s the battles to win adoption of new city charters that established council-manager plans were hard-fought. As a result, leaders of successful campaigns to establish city-manager governments typically organized nonpartisan slating groups to ensure that supporters of the new charter were in control of local government. San Antonio formed the Good Government League; Phoenix elites formed the Charter Government Committee; and citizens in Cincinnati, the Cincinnati City Charter Committee.[47] The chairman of the charter campaign in Dallas observed: "We cannot permit the work we have done to be wasted by turning the government over to the politicians."[48]

Peter O'Donnell and the Dallas Republicans: 1950–1972" (M.A. thesis, Southern Methodist University, 1983). Also see Roger Olien, *From Token to Triumph: The Texas Republicans since 1920* (Dallas: Southern Methodist University Press, 1982).

46. The four elections that the Republicans lost included the gubernatorial elections of 1974 and 1990, and the senatorial elections of 1982 and 1988.

47. For details, see Bridges, *Morning Glories,* 118–124. In Houston the "Suite 8F Crowd," a group of powerful corporate executives, was a particularly significant force from the late 1930s through the 1960s. Except for five years in the early years, they preferred the strong-mayor form, with mayors dependent on them (Robert E. Parker and Joe R. Feagin, "Houston: Administration by Economic Elites," in *Big City Politics in Transition,* ed. H. V. Savitch and John Clayton Thomas [Newbury Park, Calif.: Sage, 1991], 175).

48. *Dallas Morning News,* January 28, 1931, cited in Barta, "Council-Manager Government," 40.

Although slating groups had functions similar to those of political parties, the former differed in that they met in private, renewed their own ranks, and avoided candidates who put themselves forward. A Dallas CCA leader stated a common policy: "Anyone who asks for a place on the council is never considered."[49] Further, these nonpartisan slating groups, unlike candidate-endorsement groups, provided their candidates with financial and logistical support.

After successfully promoting the 1931 council-manager form of government, the CCA established rigid principles, which the organization followed until its demise in 1977:

1. Candidates for the council would not seek the job—C.C.A. would "draft" them.
2. [Candidates] . . . must be pledged to protect the council-manager form of government and to fight any trace of scandal, personal selfishness, and political bias.
3. After each election in the spring, the C.C.A. would disband until the next city election in order to avoid any charge of political pressure.
4. Candidates must be nonpartisan, devoted to running the city on a business-like basis as a board of directors runs a corporation. Day-to-day operation of City Hall would be in the hands of a city manager and appointed department heads.
5. Although councilmen were chosen from certain areas, they were to put the interest of this city as a whole before those of any particular district.
6. Each C.C.A. councilman was to serve only two terms, then let a new crop take over.[50]

The CCA had established this last principle, a two-term tradition, half a century before term limits at all levels of government, including municipalities, became popular in the United States in the mid-1980s. However, term limits were not included in the Dallas city charter until 1981, when a three-term limit was adopted.

Nonpartisan elections in Dallas, together with the Citizens Charter Association serving as the dominant slating group in city politics from 1931 to 1975, meant, in reality, de facto control of city government by conservative Democrats. However, when the frankly partisan Dallas County Democratic Association ran an opposition slate in 1949, the CCA won all nine seats in that election.[51]

During the period of Democratic Party dominance in Texas, Republican

49. Lorin Peterson, *The Day of the Mugwump* (New York: Random House, 1961), 116; cited in Bridges, *Morning Glories,* 122.

50. Dick West, "CCA Points to Remarkable Record," *Dallas Morning News,* March 16, 1975.

51. Richard S. Childs, *The First 50 Years of the Council-Manager Plan of Municipal Government* (New York: National Municipal League, 1965), 89.

stalwarts were highly critical of CCA policies. Some charged that CCA candidates and appointment to city boards always seemed to go to persons who voted in the Democratic primary. The charge held true to an extent, because the same conservative Democratic businessmen, who dominated local partisan affairs, also dominated city politics.

Until 1975, and the first single-member districts, former mayor Erik Jonsson and former councilman Fred Zeder, who lost to Gary Weber in a bitter 1973 election battle, were the only identifiable Republicans. The single-member district decision gave city politics in Dallas a decided shove in the Democrat-Republican partisan direction. Since then, precinct chairs, both Democrat and Republican, have won council seats.

Nonpartisan slating groups, such as the ones in Dallas and comparable groups elsewhere, governed without effective challenge until the mid-1960s. Then the underpinnings of big-city reform began to give way to opposition slates that denounced local government as unrepresentative and undemocratic.[52]

In Dallas, without the CCA in existence to motivate opposition groups to organize and slate candidates, campaign organizations are candidate-run and considerably less transparent. Endorsement by the *News* is a cue to support by the Dallas Citizens Council and its quasi-political arm, the Breakfast Group. Numerous other groups and individuals publicly endorse candidates, which brings volunteers and money to campaigns, but there are no publicly advertised organized slates.

Dallas Election Patterns

A brief account of key moments in Dallas election politics brings into relief the struggle that groups outside the ruling elite experience in order to have their voices heard.

Between 1931 and 1939 the transition to the new council-manager form of government was a tussle, while alliances and memories of life under the commission form were still strong. In spite of opposition candidates, the CCA carried the first two elections in 1931 and 1933. Then organized opposition developed, and the Citizens' Civic Association ("Catfish Club") and Forward Dallas slates defeated the CCA slates in 1935 and 1937, respectively. Until the CCA failed to slate candidates in 1977, these occasions were the only ones in which a rival group won a majority of places on the Dallas City Council.

Blacks played a key role in the 1937 defeat of the CCA slate. Black leaders in Dallas, such as Antonio Maceo Smith and The Reverend Maynard H. Jackson, organized a political base in 1934, which led to the formation of the Progressive Voters League (PVL) in 1936. The League, whose key objectives

52. Bridges, *Morning Glories,* 149, 176.

emphasized paying the poll tax and voting, coordinated the efforts of some 100 black organizations in Dallas in 1936 in a campaign that registered almost 7,000 voters.[53] This large black voting bloc carried the balance of power in both the 1937 and the 1939 Dallas City Council elections.

The League's 1937 support for the Forward Dallas Association's slate of candidates, in opposition to the Citizens Charter Association slate, assisted Forward Dallas in winning a majority of the seats on the council. The rewards for this support included a new black high school, more jobs for blacks in city government, and consideration of blacks for police jobs in the city. But in 1939 the League shifted its support to the CCA, according to the black newspaper, the *Dallas Express*, because the CCA gave the League's agenda the strongest support.[54]

Ironically, a year before the 1939 election, CCA opponent George Owens had promoted district elections, rather than citywide elections, because he feared that blacks as the swing vote, under the leadership of the PVL, might have too much say in citywide elections.[55] The next year the CCA regained a majority on the council, aided by the black vote. After the Voting Rights Act passed, minorities in Dallas apparently have not seen advantages in pursuing a swing vote strategy by supporting "influence" districts, rather than "safe" districts.

With its successes in 1937 and 1939, the League continued to register and organize black voters in the city, to endorse candidates in local elections, and to encourage black participation in the political process. In 1944, in *Smith* v. *Allwright*, the court held that blacks were entitled, under the Fifteenth Amendment, to participate in primary elections. But the League's leaders then split over whether they should align with, and accept funding from, the Democratic Party or remain nonpartisan. The majority opted for the former; the League chartered itself in 1948 in Dallas County as the Democratic Progressive Voters League. Since then, the League primarily has interviewed and endorsed candidates for local and state elections. Although it has maintained some influence in local elections, the League has not been the mass organization that it was from the 1930s to 1950.

Losing control of the 1937 City Council stirred the city's leading businessmen to action, and helped to push the organization of the Dallas Citizens Council (DCC). In his prescient keynote address to the first meeting of the full membership of the Dallas Citizens Council on March 1, 1938, theater owner Karl Hoblitzelle called for "fairness to the Negro population." He asked the

53. W. Marvin Dulaney, "Democratic Progressive Voters League," *The New Handbook of Texas*, 2:590–591.

54. *Daily Express*, March 12 and April 8, 1939; cited in Fairbanks, *City as a Whole*, 122.

55. *Dallas Morning News*, April 10, 1938, and March 12, 1939; cited in Fairbanks, *City as a Whole*, 122.

city to participate in the federal government's slum clearance and public housing program, and pleaded with the leaders to help "protect those sections
where Negroes live" and to "help them to help themselves." Hoblitzelle cautioned that results under the new government structure "depend upon bringing
in around the council table representatives of those classes not ordinarily found
at such meetings." "It is the only way the democratic form of government can
survive," he added.[56] Had Hoblitzelle's advice been followed, the political history of Dallas might have evolved differently.

The CCA, revived by the Citizens Council, came back strongly in 1939.
Between 1939 and 1959 the CCA lost only one seat, and that in 1947. After
1959 the CCA faced formidable opposition from independents. The CCA's
mayoral candidates, Joe Geary and Avery Mays, lost, respectively, to Earle
Cabell in 1961 and Wes Wise in 1971. In 1961, in addition to Cabell as mayor,
two other independents, Elizabeth Blessing and Joe Moody, were elected to the
1961 council, giving the CCA its worst setback since 1937.

In light of longtime complaints about business dominance in Dallas, the
experiences of two of the independents warrant noting. On March 6, 1939, one
hour before Earle Cabell was scheduled to open his campaign headquarters,
one of the city's "Big Banker Bosses," as Cabell later described him,
approached him with an offer. If Cabell would postpone his race until the next
city election, the CCA would agree to nominate him for mayor, place a large
sum of money in escrow for his campaign, and obtain fifty sworn pledges of
support from prominent businessmen.

This manipulative maneuver infuriated Cabell; he refused the offer,
launched a hard-hitting campaign, and articulated grievances that had been
building against the arrogant dominance by the Citizens Council and the CCA.
Cabell, who had been a member of both the Dallas Citizens Council and the
Citizens Charter Association, campaigned on the themes of machine politics,
of "windfall profits" from municipal projects made by members of the CCA
or their friends, and of special favors, such as zoning exemptions. The vote
was sufficiently close that the CCA mayoral candidate, Robert L. Thornton,
was forced into a runoff, which he later won.[57]

The Cabell experience was not an anomaly. Elizabeth Blessing had run a
strong race as an independent in 1959 and forced her CCA opponent into a
runoff, which she lost. She then won in 1961 and was reelected in 1963. In
1965 Blessing, who was the first female independent to win a council seat, led
the Charter League ticket against incumbent Mayor Erik Jonsson, who led the

56. *Dallas Morning News,* March 2, 1938; cited in Fairbanks, *City as a Whole,* 117.
    57. This account is based largely on the papers in the Earle Cabell Collection at DeGol-
yer Library Special Collections, Southern Methodist University, Dallas; recounted in
Payne, *Big D,* 286–294.

CCA ticket.[58] Blessing was quoted in the *Dallas Morning News* as saying, "I have no dedication to the status quo, to closed meetings, closed doors, and closed minds. The 'father knows best' approach is not good enough for a city on the thrust."[59] Mayor Jonsson dismissed her candidacy, remarking to the downtown Dallas Rotary Club that he was going to send her back to her kitchen.[60]

This experience may have been more damaging to her than Cabell's was to him. When she entered the race, she did not believe she could be hurt politically if she ran for mayor, as she had won over 60 percent of the vote in her election to the council for a second term. Then she was offered money not to run, by a person who was "high-powered" in town, who said, "we'll set you up in business." Some pressure was made through her husband, William Blessing, who was told: "You can't turn this down. It's a big deal." She refused the inducement; she ran; she lost. In this election, her vote in the black precincts in south Dallas dropped to 15 percent, from over 90 percent in the previous election. "There was a payoff, I am almost sure," she said. Furthermore, she and her husband, in their real estate ventures, depended on the banks for credit. They learned the day after her political demise that the banks had called in their notes.[61]

The Charter League was unable to enter a slate of candidates in 1967, which a spokesman for the League attributed to public apathy: "Everyone figures this one group (the CCA) is so big and powerful, what can you do?"[62] Then an attorney, Joseph A. Devany, and a liberal activist, Don Fielding, spearheaded the organization of a new opposition group, the Citizens for Representative Government (CRG). The CRG opposed CCA slates in 1969, 1971, 1973, and 1975.

Another group, the Dallas Homeowners League (DHL), was spawned in 1968 to oppose the CCA, because the city council habitually overruled the zoning recommendations of the City Plan Commission, granting multifamily or business zoning opposed by homeowners. In 1967 fifteen out of a total of twenty-eight zoning cases were overruled.[63] The DHL was incorporated in April 1968 as a nonprofit organization, with Clay McFarland as president. By

58. Calvert Collins, who ran as Mrs. Carr P. Collins Jr., was the first woman nominated to run on a CCA slate, and the first woman to serve on the council when she was elected in 1957. Following tradition, Elizabeth Blessing ran as Mrs. William Blessing, until Judge Sarah T. Hughes told her that she would not support her unless she ran under her own name (Elizabeth Blessing, author interview, May 15, 2001).

59. *Dallas Morning News,* February 12, 1965; cited in Barta, "Council-Manager Government," 112–113.

60. Blessing, author interview, May 15, 2001.

61. Ibid.

62. *Dallas Morning News,* January 6, 1967.

63. Larry Howell, *Dallas Morning News,* April 28, 1968.

April 1969 eighteen neighborhood organizations (including two groups of black homeowners) with an estimated membership of 25,000 had joined the DHL. The Dallas Homeowners Association (DHA), a political action organization created by the DHL, announced three candidates for the 1969 council election. The DHA had tried, first, to work through the Citizens Charter Association district meetings by nominating five candidates. But none of its nominees had been placed on the CCA slate.[64]

For the Citizens Charter Association and for Dallas politics, 1972 was a watershed year. After 1959 the CCA had faced formidable opposition from independents on twelve occasions, but it was the staggering 1971 defeat of its mayoral candidate, Avery Mays, by Wes Wise that led CCA President John Schoellkopf to a radical departure from the way the forty-two-year-old organization had been run. On August 12, 1972, he announced the formation of a broad-based executive committee, to include not only business and professional persons but representatives of organized labor, minorities, women, young and old leaders, Republicans as well as Democrats, liberals as well as conservatives, and experienced CCA members, as well as some members new to the organization.[65]

Schoellkopf announced a shift from the selection of people to run for the city council to endorsement, and from a closed organization to one involving more people in the candidate selection process. Throughout its history the CCA had abhorred any candidate who had "volunteered" to run, for fear she or he may have been motivated by personal political gain. Candidates "drafted" by a highly select group of CCA leaders had been businessmen with strong civic records and close ties to the city's business-oriented power structure. Under the new policy, volunteers from all walks of life were encouraged to offer themselves as candidates.[66]

What might have happened had Schoellkopf not broadened the base is speculation. It may have been a matter of too little, too late, for damage control. But what is clear now is that his broadening of the base was not a viable strategy for reconstructing the slating group. It did not even produce a candidate for mayor to challenge incumbent Wes Wise in 1973. Schoellkopf claimed that more than 500 letters had been sent out but that no one wanted to try to unseat the mayor.[67]

The CCA also ran into difficulty attempting to broaden the representation of minorities on its slate in 1973, the first election in which the slate included two blacks, two women, and one Hispanic. The choices were not without problems. One group of black leaders forwarded a name to the CCA selection com-

64. Carolyn Barta, *Dallas Morning News,* March 3, 1969.
65. Ibid., August 13, 1972.
66. Ibid.
67. Henry Tatum, *Dallas Morning News,* February 18, 1973.

mittee for Place 8 only to have the name opposed by several other black leaders.[68] Members of the Dallas Coalition of Mexican-American Organizations and of the La Raza Unida coalition charged that the CCA had rejected all their suggested council candidates.[69]

Whether broadening the base of the CCA was necessary to give it viability in a changing Dallas environment is debatable. The diversity of the 1973 Dallas City Council can be attributed to the reorganization of the CCA. But the attempt to be a more open organization, which meant that it did not stand for its old principles, may have contributed to its demise. One council member elected with CCA support, Charles Terrell, reportedly told friends that he was deeply disturbed by the partisan politics that the CCA had injected into its selection of candidates under the new single-member district plans.[70]

In the April 1975 elections the CCA suffered its worst setback in thirty years: it was still in debt, and it had less than a technical majority on the eleven-member council, with only five members seated with CCA endorsement.[71] The 1975 election resulted in confusion as to why the CCA existed, if it was going to depart from its traditional principles. When the CCA had tried to broaden its base in 1973 to become all things to all people, it had become less attractive to the business leadership.

The CCA leadership was faced with several alternatives: disband altogether; reorganize into a full-time organization with an executive director, an office, and a staff; sponsor candidates for the at-large positions only; or structure an organization to include a mini-CCA in each district, with those units part of an overall CCA council to include district leaders and at-large leaders. It tried to regroup but, as it turned out, 1975 was to be the last election for the CCA.

Slating Group Demise

Although some accommodations were made to dissatisfied groups during the CCA era, the 1965 Voting Rights Act initiated a series of challenges that altered the legal environment, and shifted the course of city government in those cities impacted by litigation. Two cases gave some attention to slating groups: *Lipscomb* v. *Jonsson* in 1972 and *Thornberg* v. *Gingles* in 1986.[72] At

68. The name forwarded was The Reverend Robert Wilson, pastor of St. John's Missionary Baptist Church and board chairman of the Southern Christian Leadership Conference.

69. Henry Tatum, *Dallas Morning News,* February 13, 1973.

70. Ibid., February 18, 1975.

71. The CCA-endorsed members of the council included Bill Nicol, John Leedom, Richard Smith, L. A. Murr, and Lucy Patterson. Even some of these members did not follow CCA leadership during council tenure.

72. *Lipscomb* v. *Jonsson,* 459 F.2d 335 (5th Cir. 1972); and *Thornburg* v. *Gingles,* 478 U.S. 30 (1986). See also the discussion of *Terry* v. *Adams,* 345 U.S. 461 (1953) in chapter 2.

that time, and even now, little research exists on the extent of the influence of slating groups in nonpartisan systems, their ability to replace parties as effective nominating groups, and the power of slating groups vis-à-vis other legitimate groups that simply endorse individual candidates. No census of slating groups in U.S. cities exists, and many of the formerly strong slating organizations have now "demobilized" or faded, although some do still operate.[73]

What caused the demise of the slating group that dominated Dallas politics for almost four decades? Far more was responsible than single-member districts. The crumbling of the CCA began before court-ordered single-member districts were instituted in Dallas. The decline was part of the national and state political trend of turning away from leadership and organized political groups—including, at the national level, from the two major political parties. The decline was partly the result of the anti-establishment mood of the late 1960s, and the changing demographics and political context in Dallas. Support from a group that was essential for victory from the 1930s through the 1950s became the kiss of defeat in the 1970s.

For much of the first half of the twentieth century, Dallas civic leaders and government officials held that leadership carried with it a responsibility to act for the good of the whole community, not for one segment of it. That earlier tradition was founded on consent. Voters could have withdrawn their consent from their leaders in elections during the CCA era and, in general, they did not. The situation changed in the 1960s, however. Faith in leaders suffered a breakdown, and demands were made for participatory, rather than representative, democracy. Power became fragmented and special interest groups multiplied throughout the political arena nationwide. No particular leadership organization, at any level, could satisfy all the varied claims made on governments.

Likewise, the spirit of community and of shared values broke down. The centrifugal forces of fragmentation elicited increasingly smaller arenas, in which lesser groups could dominate and exact concessions.

Groups similar to the CCA also died. The Committee for Good Schools (CGS), for example, a conservative organization that had slated candidates for the Dallas School Board since 1950, endorsed no candidates in 1977 and thereafter. The CGS had been the only political group to endorse candidates, until the League for Educational Advancement in Dallas (LEAD) rose to offer a challenge in 1967.

The final balance sheet that weighs the good against the bad during the CCA rule has yet to be written. But Tom Unis, former head of the CCA, believed that the organization had been the most successful slating group in

73. Renee Bukovchik Van Vechten, "Nonpartisan Elections in the United States," paper prepared for the annual meeting of the American Political Science Association, 1996.

Dallas because "we worked harder than anybody else, we organized better than anybody else, we raised more money than anybody else and we had better candidates than anybody else."[74] What is clear is that, with the demise of the CCA as a slating group, occasional opposition groups, organized to address specific concerns, also died. The impact that this development has had on elections in Dallas is the subject of chapter 6.

OPAQUE RULES: THE POWER STRUCTURE

An understanding of the legal bases and the extra-legal rules of government and politics is necessary, but insufficient, for explaining how an urban political system functions. The community power structure is neither monolithic in a particular period nor unchanging throughout the history of a particular city, and includes key leaders who can alter the course of events. The question, "Who has the power?" extends the analysis of governments beyond formal structures and informal rules to "shadow government." These are the persons or groups who may not have legal authority to make decisions but assume an influential, if not predominant, role in deciding public policy.

Much has been published on this subject. A few of these works are particularly relevant to an understanding of Dallas and warrant a brief discussion. As an analysis of power and manipulation by ruling elites and counter-elites, Harold Lasswell's classic *Politics: Who Gets What, When, How,* published in 1936, was the forerunner of inquiries into power relationships in American politics.[75] Twenty years later C. Wright Mills coined the phrase "the power elite" in a book by that title.[76] He argued that "overlapping cliques," who head major political, economic, and military institutions, serve their common interests through the policy decisions for which they are responsible and which in turn have national consequences. President Dwight D. Eisenhower popularized this elitist theory of power by expressing his concern over the influence on public policies of the "military-industrial" complex, a phrase coined in his Farewell Address at the end of his second term in 1960.

Not surprisingly the "power elite" national climate of opinion in the 1950s found expression in community power studies of cities, triggering a debate between urban elitists and pluralists that continued for at least another twenty years.[77]

74. Ruth Eyre, *Dallas Times Herald,* December 16, 1974.
75. Harold D. Lasswell, *Politics: Who Gets What, When, How* (New York: McGraw-Hill, 1936).
76. C. Wright Mills, *The Power Elite* (New York: Oxford University Press, 1956).
77. See Floyd Hunter, *Community Power Structure* (Chapel Hill: University of North Carolina Press, 1953). This study of Atlanta was the first to apply elite theory to a study of urban politics directly.

In a study of Dallas, Carol Estes Thometz tried, through interviews, to determine who by reputation were the powerful, as Floyd Hunter had done in a study of Atlanta ten years earlier.[78] Hunter had found that little, if anything, in Atlanta government happened without approval of the business-dominated elite. Thometz found that, in Dallas, recognizable leaders within the general structure of decision making formed a pyramid, with the seven "Key Leaders" at the top, supported by a somewhat larger group of "Top Level" leaders, with a broad base of "Second Echelon" leaders, numbering from 150 to 200. Of the seven top decision makers she identified, three were from banks, two from utilities, one from trade, and one from industry.[79] Thometz concluded that at the time of her original fieldwork in 1961, Dallas was "a city characterized by men of power rather than by organizations of power." Notably she observed that no one among the sixty-seven leaders she interviewed mentioned the city council when discussing how decisions were made regarding the city's main problems.[80]

Journalist and business executive Warren Leslie also found that Dallas in the 1960s was not run by a power elite of 200 but, rather, was "strongly led" by a group of at most 10 men, and at the fewest 3.[81] "The bankers are present not only because of the personal influence of the men but because in any civic project the bank 'clearing house,' an organization of all Dallas banks, must approve; if it doesn't, the utilities will not go along either," according to Leslie. "Without the banks and the utilities the project is dead, unless—as almost never happens—somebody wants to finance it himself."

Leslie continued:

> If these nine men agree on something, and if at the same time the newspapers, led by Joe Dealey of the *News* and James Chambers of the *Times-*

78. Carol Estes Thometz, *The Decision-Makers: The Power Structure of Dallas* (Dallas: Southern Methodist University Press, 1963).

79. Rather than naming them, Thometz gave them code names. Her profiles of these leaders seem to indicate that they included Karl Hoblitzelle, Robert L. Thornton, and James Aston, representing the banks; Les Potter and C. A. Tatum Jr., representing utilities; Stanley Marcus, trade; and J. Erik Jonsson, industry.

80. Thometz, *Decision-Makers,* 40, 41.

81. In addition to Jonsson, Leslie concluded that these included Robert Cullum, head of a food store chain and of the chamber of commerce; C. A. Tatum, president of the power company and chief leader of the successful integration action; James Aston, head of the Republic National Bank; Robert Stewart, president of the First National Bank; and Les Potter, head of the gas company. In addition, Stanley Marcus, the president of Neiman-Marcus, and Karl Hoblitzelle, who built the Interstate Theater chain and at the time was board chairman of the Republic Bank, were players, but the former was a liberal and the latter was elderly and less involved (Warren Leslie, *Dallas Public and Private: Aspects of an American City,* rev. ed. [Dallas: Southern Methodist University Press, 1998]). The quotations from Leslie's book in the following account may be found at 64, 75–77, and 79–82.

Herald, also agree, this automatically means that the two Dallas television stations will agree, since they are both owned by the newspapers. In the end, it means that the rest of the Citizens Council will agree and so, eventually, will the rest of the city.

This condition, Leslie cautioned, did not imply that accord was reached without argument and dissension. Furthermore, what made the system work was the common selfish interest in the growth and economic betterment of Dallas, not individual selfish interest. One member told Leslie, "We know each other pretty well and we know the city pretty well. If there's a private buck involved, most of us can smell it at twenty feet."

Both the Thometz and Leslie studies of Dallas were published near the time that President John F. Kennedy was assassinated. In the intensive media coverage of Dallas that followed, the popular press fastened onto the oligarchic nature of power in the Citizens Council at the time. According to Leslie, the repetitious use of the term *oligarchy* irritated Erik Jonsson, a former president of the Citizens Council and former chairman of Texas Instruments: "You know damned well it's a benevolent organization," Jonsson said. "Time and again I've seen men do things that were contrary to their best interest for the good of the city. This is a competitive city and these fellows will fight like hell all day long against each other, but then they'll sit down at dinner and try to figure out a way to bring a new business here, or build an auditorium, or whatever."

Warren Leslie, who had observed Dallas as a reporter for the *Dallas Morning News,* concurred that, in the case of the business-civic leadership in Dallas, the implication that Dallas was run by the selfish few, for the selfish few, was simply not factual. These leaders "understand power structures, they are intelligent, they are devoted to their city, they check and balance each other adroitly and they are superb salesmen." The major point to be made about the Citizens Council's failures, according to Leslie, "is that it has done its material city-building so well that it has been expected to do everything else just as well, including a lot of things it is totally unequipped to do."

Two of the strongest leaders in Dallas history, R. L. (Bob) Thornton, who served nine years as mayor, and Erik Jonsson, who served eight years as mayor, both adhered to an elitist view. In 1981, when he was nearing the age of eighty, Jonsson observed that a city should grow deliberately and that "its direction should be charted by wise and humane leaders who have proven themselves in business and civic pursuits, and thereby, earn the respect and confidence of voters." He was acutely nervous about political opportunists, and about Dallas returning to the corruption of ward politics, losing the benevolence of noblesse oblige.[82]

The counterargument by the urban pluralists to elitist theory began with

82. Leslie, *Dallas Public and Private,* 64.

Robert Dahl's study of New Haven, in which he challenged the view that urban political power is highly stratified.[83] Dahl found that, in New Haven, a diversity of groups existed that had a bearing on the making of public policy and thus power was dispersed.

In the 1970s both pluralist and elite theorists started to consider the wider political economy within which local decision makers had to operate. This body of work includes refinements and broadening of elite theory (the growth machine literature) and of pluralism (the regime theory literature). Harvey Molotch's "growth machine" concept defines modern cities as engines of economic development for business interests, with individuals and institutions in the growth machine profiting from the intensification of land use.[84] Molotch's seminal article in 1976 set in motion a new research agenda that addressed basic issues of growth, local economic development, and the individuals who promote them. Two decades later he still asserted that virtually every city (and state) government was a growth machine and long had been.[85]

In the mid-1980s regime theory, most closely associated with Clarence N. Stone, extended the body of pluralist literature. Stone analyzed "the informal arrangements through which public bodies and private interests function together to make and carry out governing decisions" in Atlanta. His work delineates those who comprise effective governing coalitions, as distinguished from electoral coalitions, how they come together, and with what consequences.[86]

Another pioneer in regime studies, Stephen L. Elkin, found that Dallas, in the 1980s, was a particularly useful case study "because the defining characteristics of the entrepreneurial political economy are strikingly evident, especially the natural alliance between local businessmen and public officials."[87] Elkin's major contribution to an understanding of a changing Dallas is his analysis of the distinction between the Dallas "pure" entrepreneurial political economy, which characterized the politics of the city from the late 1930s until approximately the mid-1970s, and the subsequent "complex" entrepreneurial political economy. Some of his factual observations were true when he con-

83. Robert A. Dahl, *Who Governs? Democracy and Power in an American City* (New Haven, Conn.: Yale University Press, 1961).

84. Harvey Molotch, "The City as a Growth Machine: Toward a Political Economy of Place," *American Journal of Sociology* (1976), 82:309–332.

85. Harvey Molotch, "Growth Machine Links: Up, Down, and Across," in *The Urban Growth Machine: Critical Perspectives Two Decades Later,* ed. Andrew E. G. Jonas and David Wilson (Albany: State University of New York Press, 1999), 249.

86. Clarence N. Stone, *Regime Politics: Governing Atlanta, 1946–1988* (Lawrence: University Press of Kansas, 1989). For a discussion of these and other theories of urban politics, see David Judge, Gerry Stoker, and Harold Wolman, eds., *Theories of Urban Politics* (Thousand Oaks, Calif.: Sage, 1995).

87. Stephen L. Elkin, *City and Regime in the American Republic* (Chicago: University of Chicago Press, 1987), 61. Chapter 4 of *City and Regime* provides a case study of Dallas.

ducted his fieldwork in 1982, but these are no longer valid. His conclusion, however, remains applicable to Dallas: in entrepreneurial political economies, citizens are drawn into politics either to speak for their neighborhood, ethnic group, or some other interest or as a bureaucratic client, but not to offer reasoned versions of the best way to make a city vital.

CONCLUSIONS

The applicability of a particular theory of political power to a specific city is time-contingent and, perhaps even more important, depends on the perspective of the beholder. Most of the extant literature on Dallas covers the period between the 1930s and the 1970s. In that period Dallas business leaders appeared to have amassed unprecedented political power and civic influence because of their successes at the polls with their slating group, the Citizens Charter Association.

Social scientist Patricia Evridge Hill's study of Dallas in the years from 1880 to 1940 challenged the view that business interests have always run Dallas. She contended that between 1880 and 1920 many groups competed for and, to a significant extent, shared power. These groups included labor organizations, women's groups, radical political parties, and progressive reformers.[88] Similarly the first history of the city that was based on a variety of documentary and oral sources, *The Dallas Guide,* provided a perspective of Dallas from the vantage point of 1940 and did not support the commercial-civic elite theory. The *Guide* included a full chapter on the organization and struggles of labor.[89]

Also plausible, however, is the argument that, before the 1930s, the business community was dominant and the city only seemed to be more pluralistic because the business and civic leadership was often fragmented. This interpretation places even greater historical importance on the business leaders who organized to take control of civic affairs in the 1930s, and the culture these leaders created.

Beginning in the 1930s Dallas entered an era dominated by an alliance of "city builders," who established a pattern of strong alliances with public officials. This development, in retrospect, may seem to have been inevitable, but it was not a given. Not all cities, even in the Southwest where certain commonalities in historical growth were shared, developed a cooperative, official alliance between business interests and public officials. In San Antonio, for example, the booster community was divided and, since the late nineteenth

88. Patricia Evridge Hill, *Dallas: The Making of a Modern City* (Austin: University of Texas Press, 1996).

89. See *The WPA Dallas Guide and History,* researched and written under the auspices of the Federal Writer's Project, Work Projects Administration (WPA).

century, its business people had been antagonistic to government as a viable partner in economic development. Only with the establishment of the Good Government League in the 1950s did a sense of collaboration emerge.

Furthermore, given the propensity to see clearer patterns in history in retrospect than seems to be the case at the time, the stereotype of business-elite indifference to the need to accommodate neighborhood interests, the civil rights movement, and other public concerns during the era of the Citizens Charter Association may be overdrawn, as historian Robert Fairbanks suggested.[90]

The timing of the founding of Dallas, as discussed in chapter 3, was a factor in business dominance. By missing the age of the traditional party-based political machines that dispensed specific benefits in exchange for the votes of immigrants, Dallas never had to accommodate mass demands for services. Similarly, by missing the era of industrialization, strong labor unions did not develop, which might have challenged the business sector's control over city affairs.

Without sustained opposition by organized parties or by labor, the political terrain was much less contested for than in cities that had developed earlier. This absence of a balance of power left the Dallas business community, when organized, in an advantageous position.

Locally and nationally the dominant political trends of the past twenty years show the diffusion of power and the proliferation of actors demanding to play leading roles. In Dallas some key players may have changed, such as corporate leaders and bank presidents who today focus internationally, rather than locally, but the view that a cooperative business elite/public official alliance died with the demise of the Citizens Charter Association is a premature obituary.

Because of single-member districts, new constituencies are represented at the council table and demand to be accommodated. However, as late as 1999, former Mayor Steve Bartlett told social scientist Royce Hanson that the civic decision-making process in Dallas is a two-meeting system. "A small group decides what needs to be done, and then they invite in other people and tell them about it so they can ratify it," Hanson said. "All you need to do is say yes—say yes to Dallas."[91]

Whether court-ordered single-member districts trumped the city's political heritage, and altered the functioning of the community's political organization as an adjunct to the business community, is a subject of chapters 7 and 8. Before examining the evidence to answer those questions, the city's experiences in federal courts are examined next.

90. Robert B. Fairbanks, "The Good Government Machine: The Citizens Charter Association and Dallas Politics, 1936–1960," in *Essays on Sunbelt Cities and Recent Urban America,* ed. Robert B. Fairbanks and Kathleen Underwood (College Station: Texas A&M University Press, 1990), 125–150.

91. Quoted by Randy Lee Loftis, *Dallas Morning News,* April 25, 1999.

5
Dallas in Court, 1967–1991

The great generalities of the Constitution have a content and a significance
that vary from age to age. The method of free decision sees through the
transitory particulars and reaches what is permanent behind them.
—Benjamin Cardozo

Some play the game to lose. Some play the game to win. The winners walk
out laughing. The losers cry, deal again.
—Larry Gatlin

The convoluted journey of the federal courts through Justice Frankfurter's
"political thicket," described in chapter 2, should not imply that case law
evolves in a straight line over time. Pathways can also zig and zag and retreat.
The process by which the Supreme Court develops constitutional doctrine both
is—and should be—a continuing one, in which Justices "grapple with a new
problem" and "deal with it over and over again, as its dimensions change."[1]

Nevertheless, the linear paradigm of court processes does create constraints on solving complex social issues that are not found in the give-and-
take of legislative politics. The nature of the judicial process is adversarial: the
plaintiffs frame the questions, and rules frame the answers.

These constraints on solving complex social issues in the courts need to
be identified, not only in the abstract but also in application. What are the costs
in personal and political terms to a major city caught in those "zigs and zags"
of case law?

A primary point of contention in Dallas was its at-large electoral system,
which had been used continuously since 1907, first under special charter
granted by the Texas legislature, and later under the city's home rule charter,

1. Joseph Goldstein, *The Intelligible Constitution: The Supreme Court's Obligation to
Maintain the Constitution as Something We the People Can Understand* (New York:
Oxford University Press, 1992), 118; citing W. Rostow, "American Legal Realism and the
Sense of the Profession," *Rocky Mountain Law Review* (1962), 34:123, 142.

adopted in 1931.[2] The at-large system involved the city in voting rights litigation from 1967 to 1991. The conflicting interests of two sizable minority
groups, one with a dispersed population (the Hispanics) and the other with segregated residential concentrations (the blacks), complicated the protracted
legal battle.

The majority of Dallas voters favored the traditional at-large system,
whereas political minorities, both racial and ideological, favored a system with
single-member districts. The mixed-system compromise, adopted by Dallas
voters, was not ruled unconstitutional, although it wound its way back and
forth through federal courts for a decade. The mixed plan, however, was unac-
ceptable to minority litigants.

Whatever their legitimate reasons for subscribing to single-member districts, the plaintiffs were confident that the judicial bias toward single-member
districts would provide their front-line attack strategy for increased political
and economic power, as well as their rear-guard action, if they failed to eliminate at-large districts at the ballot box or in a negotiated settlement. Furthermore, for minorities to win legal challenges, the 1982 VRA Amendment
required only that they show that the effects of a plan were discriminatory.
Nationally, as a result, minorities won, for example, twelve of the fourteen
cases fought in federal courts in 1988.[3]

In hindsight, the time and effort spent by large numbers of Dallas citizens—citizens of all races—to find a political solution to issues of fair representation in the context of the VRA was, in effect, fruitless. Political turmoil
consumed the time and energies of the Dallas City Council throughout the
1980s. The nightly news on TV and the newspapers fanned racial tensions with
angry images and inflammatory statements. The practice of democracy, which
is always difficult and time-consuming, requires commitment to negotiation,
compromise, coalition building, and respect for opinions different from one's
own. When one of the parties plays by different rules, the democratic process
fails.

Was Dallas caught in the web of evolving case law that dealt with Justice
Benjamin Cardozo's "transitory particulars"? Did judicial decisions subvert
democratic processes? Might the city have avoided the litigation route altogether, had leaders, willing to seek compromises, emerged to participate in
facilitating a political resolution?

Dallas remained exempt from the Section 5 preclearance special provisions of the VRA until 1975, when Congress amended the Act to expand vot-

2. "Charter of the City of Dallas," Texas Laws 1907, chap. 71, art. III, sec. 1, p. 596;
"Charter of the City of Dallas," 1931, chap. III, sec. 9; "Charter of the City of Dallas,"
1931, as amended 1968, chap. IV, sec. 4.
3. Brenda Wright, a voting rights analyst for the Washington-based Lawyers Committee on Civil Rights Under the Law, quoted in *Dallas Morning News,* September 4, 1989.

ing rights protection to additional minority groups, which included Spanish-speaking minorities. Prior to 1975 voting rights cases in Dallas were filed under the Fourteenth and Fifteenth Amendments to the U.S. Constitution, rather than under Section 5 of the VRA.

Those who filed the lead cases on the election system in Dallas were Max Goldblatt in 1967, Al Lipscomb in 1971, and Roy Williams in 1990. Because plaintiffs frame the questions in litigation, the rationale of lead plaintiffs are relevant for any findings that the at-large election system used in Dallas was racially discriminatory. The trail through the court decisions below illustrates the toll that can be exacted when a city attempts to govern in the shifting sands of changing legal interpretation.

THE GOLDBLATT CASE

Max Goldblatt, in 1967, filed the first case challenging the Dallas at-large election system. His political activism in Dallas began by his writing letters to the editors of the daily newspapers in the city and articles for newspapers in small surrounding communities. In succession, beginning in 1967, he ran for the Dallas City Council and lost; filed a lawsuit against the city, challenging at-large elections, and lost the lawsuit; ran for the council two more times, and lost both; ran again in 1980, and served three terms; and then lost the mayoral race in 1985.

The 1967 Dallas City Council election was the last held under a 6-3 plan—six candidates running in a district of their residence, and all nine voted on at large.[4] In the April 4, 1967, council election, Goldblatt, owner of a hardware store, challenged, for Place 3, the candidate, Jesse Price, who was backed by the Citizens Charter Association. Price, president of Southwest Consulting and Development Corporation, was active in local Democratic politics. Neither he nor Goldblatt had run for a council seat previously.

Goldblatt carried his residence district by a vote of 2,192 to 1,287, or 63 percent of the vote. Price outpolled him in the remaining five districts, and he lost the election with 38 percent of the vote. In 1969 Goldblatt again challenged Price for the Pleasant Grove seat. Under the new 8-3 plan, this seat became Place 7. The Citizens Charter Association dropped Price in 1969 and did not back a candidate in the hotly contested three-way race between Goldblatt, Price, and Jack C. Adkins, a twenty-one-year-old advertising employee. Goldblatt again lost to Price.

Goldblatt chose not to run in 1971 or 1973. In 1975 he did run, with the

---

4. By referendum in 1968, unrelated to the case filed, the council was enlarged to include eight residence districts and three districts with no residence requirements, with all eleven elected citywide.

backing of the Citizens for Representative Government and the Dallas Progressive Voters League. He lost to L. A. Murr, the incumbent supported by the CCA.

Over a ten-year period, then, Goldblatt ran three times and was defeated each time. Only in the 1975 campaign did he have the support of a slating/endorsement group. After his defeat in 1967 Goldblatt filed the first suit in Dallas against the at-large system for electing city council members.[5] In the original complaint, he alleged that the at-large system was unconstitutional and denied the plaintiff, and all citizens in his district, equal protection of the law, in violation of the Fourteenth Amendment to the U.S. Constitution. The court pointed out that the plaintiff would not be entitled to relief under Supreme Court rulings, since, in 1967, the six districts were substantially equal in population, ranging from 135,184 to 140,221.[6]

Goldblatt amended his complaint, adding the allegation that the at-large plan for electing council members resulted in "a scheme to perpetuate and preserve control of the City Council . . . by a group known as the Citizens Charter Association." Thus, he argued, "the Dallas election law does not pass constitutional muster because the people are effectively denied representation by an invidious discrimination against their choices."[7]

To meet the constitutional test of "invidious discrimination,"[8] the following proof was offered: in all but two of the nineteen Dallas administrations since 1931, the controlling majorities were nominated and elected by the CCA; since 1939, in fifteen elections, 135 CCA candidates had run against 210 independents, and the CCA candidates had consistently won control of the council; and, in that time, only 4 of the 210 independents had been successful.[9]

The court's decision to uphold the at-large election system was based on the following principles:

1. One-person-one-vote was the constitutional test under the Equal Protection Clause and the "democratic ideals of equality and majority rule."[10]
2. A residence requirement in a multi-member district [used here as analogous to election in an at-large city] was constitutional and councilmen represented the city and not the district of residence, since "districts are used merely as the basis of residence for candidates, not for voting or representation."[11]

5. *Goldblatt* v. *City of Dallas,* 279 F.Supp. 106 (1968).
6. Id., at 107 (citations omitted).
7. Ibid.
8. *Reynolds* v. *Sims,* 377 U.S. 533 (1964).
9. *Goldblatt* v. *City of Dallas,* 279 F.Supp. 106, 108 (1968).
10. Id., citing *Reynolds* v. *Sims* at 562, 566.
11. Id., citing *Fortson* v. *Dorsey,* 379 U.S. 433, 438 (1965); and *Dusch* v. *Davis,* 387 U.S. 112, 115–117 (1967).

3. The "one man–one vote" rule was followed automatically, "when Representatives are chosen as a group on a statewide basis, as was a widespread practice in the first 50 years of our Nation's history."[12]
4. The Equal Protection Clause demanded that "the plan must be such as not to permit the systematic frustration of the will of a majority of the electorate of the State."[13]
5. "There is no right per se to select representatives from any given size district or unit."[14]
6. The decision on the basis for selection [that is, at-large or district] "is a matter, in the beginning, of political or governmental policy and judgment. . . . The selection of a system, so long as it is not proscribed by the federal Constitution, is, of course, not the business of the court."[15] This later point was emphasized by citing *Baker* v. *Carr:* "The federal courts are, of course, not forums for political debate, nor should they resolve themselves into state constitutional conventions or legislative assemblies."[16]

On these bases District Judge Joe Ewing Estes held, on January 26, 1968, that the 6-3 at-large election plan for the Dallas City Council "made no distinction on the basis of race, creed, or economic status or location" and did not constitute "invidious discrimination" in violation of the equal protection clause.[17] The Dallas 6-3 plan therefore met all constitutional tests.

After some procedural sparring, Goldblatt appealed to the U.S. Court of Appeals, Fifth Circuit.[18] He based his appeal on his "essential theory" that the CCA, as "powerful millionaires," used the at-large system to perpetuate and to preserve control of the city council through use of "their power, influence, position, and money to back their own hand-picked candidates."[19] This system, Goldblatt asserted, denied equal protection to voters, because it permitted the influence of the CCA to be applied citywide, so as to defeat the will of the voters of a particular district, as well as to defeat independent candidates who could not financially compete with the wealth of the CCA.[20]

Goldblatt used data from 1931, the year that the 6-3 plan was initiated, to 1967, which showed that only fifteen non-CCA candidates were elected in seventeen elections. The effect, he concluded, was "to stagnate public interest and allow the dictates of a few to control the will of the majority."[21]

12. Id., citing *Wesberry* v. *Sanders,* 376 U.S. 1, 7–8 (1964).
13. Id., citing *Burns* v. *Richardson,* 384 U.S. 73, 99 (1966).
14. Id., citing *Reed* v. *Mann,* 237 F.Supp. 22, 24–25 (1964).
15. Ibid.
16. *Baker* v. *Carr,* 369 U.S. 186, 259–260 (1962).
17. *Goldblatt* v. *City of Dallas,* 279 F.Supp. 106 (1968); citing *Dusch* v. *Davis,* at 116.
18. *Goldblatt* v. *City of Dallas,* 414 F.2d 774 (5th Cir. 1969).
19. Ibid., 775.
20. Ibid.
21. *Goldblatt* v. *City of Dallas,* 4141 F.2d 774, 775 (5th Cir. 1969).

The court of appeals ruled that "taking the facts alleged as true, no denial of equal protection or invidious discrimination had been demonstrated."[22] The court held that the elected officials represented the entire city and not merely a particular district, and therefore the at-large system did not constitute a denial of equal protection, either per se or in application, "since the 'one man–one vote' principle is automatically complied with because all votes are equal in a city-wide election."[23] In upholding the district court, the court of appeals concluded: "Stripped of legalese, the appellant is complaining because the citizens of Dallas either from apathy or by design have not exercised the power of the ballot to rid themselves of what the appellant regards as an evil political machine. Whether this view is right or not, need not concern us. The wrong of public apathy cannot be righted by judicial compulsion."[24]

THE LIPSCOMB CASES

The case of *Goldblatt* v. *City of Dallas* is important because of its juxtaposition with the second voting rights case, filed in 1971, with Al Lipscomb as lead plaintiff. In the former case, the plaintiff represented an ideological minority that was fenced out of politics; in the latter case, the plaintiffs represented racial minorities who were also a numerical minority at that time. Dallas Legal Services filed the class action suit on behalf of minority residents on March 10, 1971, seeking to enjoin the city from holding elections on April 6, 1971, under an allegedly unconstitutional at-large election plan. The district court denied the request and summarily dismissed the case. The Fifth Circuit considered the case in 1972 in *Lipscomb* v. *Jonsson* and remanded it for trial.[25]

According to Pancho Medrano, the patriarch of the political Old Guard of Mexican descent, several people, including himself, were considered to be named as lead plaintiff, representative of the group. But Medrano was not comfortable filling out the lengthy questionnaire, which contained "all kinds of personal questions, and some were very embarrassing."[26]

After some discussion, according to Medrano, Albert Lipscomb agreed to fill out the questionnaire, and thus he became the lead litigant.[27] History might

---

22. Ibid.
23. Id., at 776.
24. Ibid. Note that *Reese* v. *Dallas County, Alabama,* 505 F.2d 879 (5th Cir. 1974) involved districting that was not racial but political (that is, plaintiffs were not a racial minority as a group; rather, they were residents of what they felt was an underrepresented election district).
25. *Lipscomb* v. *Jonsson,* 459 F.2d 335 (5th Cir. 1972).
26. Quoted in Roy H. Williams and Kevin J. Shay, *Time Change: An Alternative View of the History of Dallas* (Dallas: To Be Publishing, 1991), 103.
27. Ibid.

well have been different had a Hispanic rather than a black been the lead plaintiff, both in the evolution of the case as well as in subsequent racial politics in Dallas. The case made Lipscomb a hero to his community, cemented a power base, and was a key move for his political career.

As with Max Goldblatt, who ran unsuccessfully several times before he was eventually elected to the city council, Lipscomb ran unsuccessfully four times over thirteen years, before he was elected to the council in 1984. He also tried, and lost, for Dallas school board, for Dallas county commissioner, and for the state Senate. In 1971 he was the first black contender for Dallas mayor, placing third in a field of seven candidates.

By his own account, after years of running for public office, Lipscomb thought he had his best chance to win in 1984 in a special election to fill an unexpired term. This time his district had no incumbent, and no candidate could equal his name identification.[28] He won, and went on to win four more terms, serving the maximum of nine years allowed by the city charter. He dropped out for a term, then was reelected in 1995, and served until he resigned in 2000, following his federal bribery conviction.

Some people remember Al Lipscomb as the disarming, physically imposing waiter in the city's executive clubs and hotels, where he became acquainted with Dallas's power elite. Other people identify Lipscomb with his hell-raising years, when he harangued elected officials about social injustices at meetings of the city council, commissioner's court, and school board, and when, occasionally, he was evicted for his outbursts. Some appreciate his commitment to the issues of the minority community and the years he invested in Dallas on the city council. Yet others see him as a person who easily can be used, and so they financially subsidized him, either for his vote or to keep him quiet on a particular issue or to keep him and his constituency as an ally for political purposes.[29]

Before turning to the actions of the courts in the Lipscomb cases, the efforts at political resolution should be considered. Leadership might have averted litigation. In 1971, after black plaintiffs had filed their suit in federal district court, supporters of single-member city council districts appeared to have enough council support to include the proposal on a city charter revisions ballot, for an election originally planned for December 1972. At first, the issue of charter revision gained little public attention. The public hearing in the council chambers on October 4, 1972, drew three speakers, and was over after only twenty minutes.[30] Interest did not grow until former mayor Erik Jonsson

28. Terry Maxson, *Dallas Morning News,* April 23, 1984.
29. In spite of several direct requests over three years by this author, as well as interventions on this author's behalf by other public officials, Al Lipscomb became the only public official who refused an interview.
30. Henry Tatum, *Dallas Morning News,* October 5, 1972.

appeared at a public hearing, at which he said he was opposed to putting the issue on the charter referendum, "unless they [the people] could be properly informed."[31] This statement caused unwanted publicity and aroused the old suspicions of oligarchic direction. Discontent was also fueled when, after prodding from reporters, the Booz-Allen & Hamilton consultants, hired to conduct a study of needed changes in city government, admitted that the city council specifically had instructed them to avoid the issue of single-member districts in their report to the council in November 1972.[32]

The city council decided on January 4, 1973, not to put the question on the charter ballot. Then, on January 15, after several council members and leaders of the CCA had met secretly, the council reversed itself. According to *Dallas Morning News* sources, the city council was concerned about public reaction if the election system were to be excluded from the charter revisions ballot.[33] By this time, however, debates had stalled the process for long enough that a charter election could not be held before the next council election.

The city council was dealing with this charter proposal issue, even as the Lipscomb case was being considered in the courts. The district court had summarily dismissed the case, and the Fifth Circuit had remanded it to the district court for trial. The trial date, set by U.S. District Judge Eldon Mahon for February 19, 1973, had to be delayed until 1974, owing in part to the decision to put an 8-4-1 (eight single-member districts and five at-large districts, including mayor) on the ballot in the city charter revisions election on June 12, 1973. Both the opponents and supporters of single-member districts overwhelmingly rejected the plan.

As the subsequent trial date, set for December 9, 1974, approached for U.S. District Judge Eldon Mahon to hear the suit, sentiment mounted among city council members to instruct City Attorney Alex Bickley to settle the pending single-member district suit. But proponents who favored Bickley seeking a compromise plan, in which all but three of the city council seats would be elected from single-member districts, were unable to muster a majority. The failure to reach a political compromise forced the matter to legal resolution.

Court of Appeals

The district court dismissed the first Lipscomb suit, filed in 1971, and the plaintiffs appealed to the U.S. Court of Appeals, Fifth Circuit.[34] The plaintiffs in *Lipscomb* v. *Jonsson* shifted the argument from "invidious discrimination" against "residence districts," used in *Goldblatt,* to discrimination against a

31. Quoted by Henry Tatum, *Dallas Morning News,* December 24, 1972.
32. Ibid.
33. Henry Tatum, *Dallas Morning News,* January 18, 1973.
34. *Lipscomb* v. *Jonsson,* 459 F.2d 335 (5th Cir. 1972).

"Ghetto Area" in violation of the Fourteenth and Fifteenth Amendments. The plaintiffs alleged that the at-large plan had the "invidious effect of diluting the vote of the Ghetto residents," as voters in that area "have virtually no political force or control over Members of the city Council, because the effect of their vote is canceled out by other well-established and hostile interest groups in other areas of the city of Dallas."[35]

The Fifth Circuit held that the complaint was not subject to summary dismissal by the district judge, as the plaintiffs might succeed in proving that the election plan *was* a purposeful attempt by the white majority to fence ghetto area residents out of the city council. Circuit Judge Wisdom remanded the case to the District Court because, in the interim, the Supreme Court had handed down its decision in *Whitcomb* v. *Chavis* (1971).[36] This ruling opened the possibility that the plaintiffs could succeed in proving that the Dallas City Council election plan was "a purposeful attempt by the white majority or the Dallas city fathers to fence ghetto area residents out of the City Council."[37] The Court of Appeals also left open another avenue raised by the Supreme Court in *Whitcomb*, that is, "whether 'Ghetto Area' residents have been effectively excluded from participation in the process of selecting city council members."[38]

Citing the recent district court decision in the *Texas Legislative Apportionment Cases*,[39] the Court of Appeals noted that the "ghetto residents were frequently ignored in the selection of Democratic Party candidates for the state legislature."[40] Judge John Minor Wisdom continued: "It may be—we cannot say—that election to the Dallas City Council is only nominally non-partisan; that the major parties or *similar political groups* [emphasis added] endorse candidates for election; that there is high correlation between endorsement and victory in the election; and that the interests of the ghetto area are substantially ignored in determining a slate of endorsees."[41] Also relying on the *Texas Reapportionment Cases,* Judge Wisdom noted "that ghetto candidates, and thus the ghetto itself, [might be] . . . effectively fenced out of the City Council election process by the high cost of city-wide campaigning."[42]

The failure by courts to distinguish between municipal election systems and state legislative election systems is clear regarding "slating" in Dallas.

35. Id., at 336–337.

36. *Whitcomb* v. *Chavis,* 403 U.S. 124 (1971).

37. *Lipscomb* v. *Jonsson,* 459 F.2d 335, 338 (5th Cir. 1972). "Dallas city fathers" and "ghetto area" are two value-laden concepts picked up by the court from the plaintiffs' language.

38. Id., at 339. "Access to the political process" standard was first enunciated in *Whitcomb* v. *Chavis.*

39. *Graves* v. *Barnes* and consolidated cases, 343 F.Supp. 704 (1972).

40. *Lipscomb* v. *Jonsson,* 459 F.2d 335, 339 (5th Cir. 1972).

41. Ibid.

42. Ibid.

The party primaries in Texas are closely regulated by state law.[43] Therefore the "nominating" process for a political party in the state is fundamentally different from the "nomination and endorsement" process in Dallas municipal elections. Local groups that form to support one candidate or a "slate" of candidates have no official recognition by the City of Dallas. Furthermore, a candidate need not be "nominated" to have a place on the ballot. Any citizen can self-nominate. The court did acknowledge that there are no primary elections for city office and that every citizen who fulfills the appropriate residence requirement by paying a fee of fifty dollars and producing a petition containing three hundred signatures is entitled to a place on the ballot.[44] But these points were not pursued.

The arguments advanced in the *Goldblatt* and *Lipscomb* cases included economic discrimination because of the high cost of campaigning citywide; the electoral success of a slating group that did not reflect their interests; and the denial of equal protection to a group, in one case a socioeconomic group in a geographical area and, in the other, a racial group in an area defined as "ghetto." A major difference was whether it could be demonstrated that the at-large election system was a purposeful device to further racial discrimination. The Fifth Circuit had ruled in *Goldblatt* that the at-large system did not discriminate on the basis of creed, economic status, location, or race. But race had not been at issue there, as Goldblatt was a disappointed Anglo office seeker, whereas Lipscomb was a disappointed office seeker of African descent. In *Goldblatt* v. *Dallas,* the Fifth Circuit had dismissed the allegation of participation in the slating process as being sour grapes or apathy. In *Lipscomb* it became evidence of less "access."

This shift shows the diversion from the original path of the one-person, one-vote equal protection argument, to the second path, the dilution concept. The latter concept involves election schemes conceived or operated as devices to further racial discrimination and to diminish the opportunity to participate in the political process. This second, and later, path of argument can be followed through its application to cases filed in Dallas.

Lipscomb on Remand

After the Fifth Circuit's decision to remand *Lipscomb,* both the U.S. Supreme Court and the Fifth Circuit Court of Appeals handed down important decisions

43. A unique aspect in Texas is that the state pays for the primaries of the two major political parties. Democratic and Republican county chairmen conducting primaries file expense reports with the Secretary of State for reimbursement (statement by Douglas Caddy, former director, Elections Division, Office of Texas Secretary of State, in U.S. Congress, House, Committee on the Judiciary, Subcommittee on Civil and Constitutional Rights, *Hearings on Extension of the Voting Rights Act,* 97th Cong., 1st sess., May–July 1981, part 2, 1206).

44. *Lipscomb* v. *Jonsson,* 459 F.2d 335, 336 (5th Cir. 1972). At the time, more signatures were required than is the case today.

that established standards of proof.[45] On January 15, 1975, after an evidentiary hearing, U.S. District Judge Eldon B. Mahon made a preliminary oral finding of dilution, which rendered the exclusively at-large system of voting unconstitutional.[46] On January 17, after certifying a plaintiff class consisting of all black citizens of the City of Dallas, the district court orally declared that the system of at-large elections to the Dallas City Council unconstitutionally diluted the voting strength of black citizens.[47] Dallas was afforded an opportunity to present an apportionment plan that would meet constitutional standards. Testimony was heard on the merits of the city's proposal the week of February 4, 1975.[48]

In the meantime, on January 20, the city council passed a resolution, which stated that the council intended to enact an ordinance to provide for eight council members to be elected from single-member districts, and for the three remaining members, including the mayor, to be elected at large. The plan was submitted to district court on January 24, 1975. It had the advantage of retaining the traditional eight residence districts, changing only the voting rules to election by the district rather than by citywide voting.

On February 8, after conducting an extensive remedy hearing, the court announced in an oral opinion that the city's plan met constitutional guidelines, and thus was acceptable, and that a written opinion would be issued in the near future. The city council formally enacted the promised ordinance on February 10, 1975. The court issued a memorandum opinion containing its findings of fact and conclusions of law on March 25, and again sustained the city plan as a valid legislative act.[49] The city council election on April 1, 1975, was held under the 8-3 mixed plan. The electorate subsequently approved this plan in a referendum conducted in April 1976, thus incorporating it into the city charter. Although the change was a choice forced by court decision, at least it was a plan that had been adopted by the council and approved by the voters.

Al Lipscomb's district under the 8-3 plan was District 6. In the first election under the new mixed plan, with six council members elected from districts, Lipscomb ran in a three-way race. George Allen, the black CCA-backed incumbent, carried the single-member district without a run-off.[50] After

45. *White* v. *Regester,* 412 U.S. 755 (1973); *Zimmer* v. *McKeithen,* 485 F.2d 1297 (5th Cir. 1973). The Fifth Circuit applied these standards in one subsequent case, *Turner* v. *McKeithen,* 490 F.2d 191 (5th Cir. 1973).

46. *Lipscomb* v. *Wise,* 399 F.Supp. 782, 784 (1975).

47. Petitioners did not appeal this ruling and did not question it at the Supreme Court.

48. Several plaintiffs, including all plaintiffs of Mexican descent, were dismissed from the case for failure to respond to interrogatories. Subsequently two citizens of Mexican descent attempted to intervene. The district court denied their application but, later, did permit several citizens of Mexican descent to participate in the remedy hearing, held after the at-large election system was declared unconstitutional.

49. *Lipscomb* v. *Wise,* 399 F.Supp. 782 (1975).

50. The third candidate was Clifton Todd.

George Allen resigned in September 1975, the council on three straight ballots failed to produce a vote sufficient to appoint a replacement. The mayor declared the slot open. In a special election on December 9, 1975, seven candidates ran for the open seat. Of the top three black vote getters, Al Lipscomb came in third, with 822 out of 3,785 votes.[51] Twice more Lipscomb failed to gain elective office and evidently was not "the representative of their choice," even though the election was now by single-member districts rather than at large.

This case is significant; it caused a kaleidoscopic change in Dallas politics. In applying the developing case law on dilution, Judge Mahon determined that the Dallas at-large election system indeed involved unconstitutional dilution of the black vote. His bases were the existence of past discrimination in general, which precluded effective participation of minorities in the electoral system; the customary lesser degree of access to the process of slating candidates than was enjoyed by the white community; bloc voting, with blacks bloc voting in their own areas yet losing citywide; and a high correlation between CCA endorsement and victory citywide.[52]

Judge Mahon did find, however, that "at-large voting, especially on the municipal level, has been an integral part of Texas local governments and that at-large voting schemes have their genesis in reasons other than those racially motivated."[53] He noted that a plan, which provided for three council members to be elected at large, was not constitutionally defective, considering the favorable impact that at-large representation would have on the vote of Hispanics, and considering the legitimate governmental interest to be served by having a citywide viewpoint present on the council. This governmental interest, he observed "is the need for a city-wide view on those matters which concern the city as a whole, e.g., zoning, budgets, and city planning," as well as "downtown revitalization projects, convention business and airport services."[54]

Since a factor in the developing case law was the unresponsiveness of legislators to particular minority concerns, which could contribute to the demonstration of dilution,[55] Judge Mahon spent time on this issue. The judge concluded that "if present responsiveness of the city to the particular interests of the black community (or for that matter the brown or white communities) were the sole issue which determined dilution, then I have little doubt that there would be no finding of invidious discrimination."[56] He continued:

> There has been ample demonstration of the fact that Dallas is acting for the needs of all its citizens—parks, street services, police and fire protec-

51. Juanita Craft won the District 6 seat in a runoff over Joe Kirven.
52. *Lipscomb v. Wise,* 399 F.Supp. 782, 790 (1975).
53. Id., at 797.
54. Id., at 794, 795 n. 15.
55. *Zimmer v. McKeithen,* 485 F.2d 1297, 1305 (5th Cir. 1973).
56. *Lipscomb v. Wise,* 399 F.Supp. 782, 791 (1975).

tion, transportation, equal employment opportunity, fair housing and community relations. In these areas and more I find the city to be acting . . . in a responsive manner. . . . This present responsiveness, however, is not enough to justify the present exclusive at-large voting plan when weighted against the other factors which I have found.[57]

Here the result of the developing law forced a choice between different concepts of representation, accepting *descriptive* over *substantive* representation. Similarly the Court rejected out of hand other suggestions, such as "some form of cumulative voting," as "completely void of merit and [that] would do nothing constructive for either the political interest of minorities or the constitutional interests of all citizens of Dallas."[58] Acceptable pathways in the development of case law had already been walled in linearly. Options such as cumulative voting, which were later to be advanced as potentially better remedies than single-member districts for ensuring minority representation, were excluded from any consideration.

Because of the population dispersion of those of Mexican descent and the fact that at the time only four census tracts in Dallas had a population with a Mexican-descent majority, Judge Mahon observed that they must form voting coalitions with either black or white voters. In the case of voters of African descent, a premium seemed to be placed on continued residential segregation. This situation did not escape the judge's notice, and he observed: "It would be indeed ironic if a remedy for dilution of voting strength resulted in a major impediment to minority citizens enjoying their constitutional rights."[59]

The court accepted the argument that at least twenty districts would be required for a district plan to have citizens of Mexican descent constituting a majority in a single-member district. The judge found that this factor favored having some at-large districts rather than an enlarged council.[60] Another

57. Ibid.
58. *Lipscomb* v. *Wise,* 399 F.Supp. 782, 792 n.10 (1975). The most widespread recent use of cumulative voting has been in Texas, where a state law, enacted in 1995, permitted school districts to adopt cumulative voting for the election of members of local school boards. About fifty did so in the 1990s, including Amarillo. See Kathleen L. Barber, *A Right to Representation: Proportional Election Systems for the Twenty-first Century* (Columbus: Ohio State University Press, 2000), esp. 150–153, for details on recent practice. See also Shaun Bowler, David Brockington, and Todd Donovan, "Election Systems and Voter Turnout: Experiments in the United States," *Journal of Politics* (August 2001), 63:902–915, for an analysis of the effect of cumulative voting on turnout in local elections in Texas and Alabama.
59. Ibid., 793 n. 12.
60. The issue of using an increased size as a remedy was subsequently dealt with in *Holder* v. *Hall,* 114 S. Ct. 2581 (1994), in which the Supreme Court held that the size of a government body cannot be attacked under Section 2 of the Voting Rights Act because it is not a "standard, practice, or procedure." At some threshold point any minority group could have a safe district by increasing the size of the legislative body.

advantage to having some at-large districts was pointed out by council member George Allen in a later case. He testified that blacks and Hispanics who lived in small pockets in Far North Dallas, in East Dallas, in the Love Field area, and scattered throughout the city, rather than in the "ghetto area" in which safe districts could be carved, might stand a chance to win in an at-large district.[61]

Altogether three plans were presented to the court in *Lipscomb* v. *Wise.* The city plan, the one accepted by the court, was the 8-3 plan. The plaintiffs presented two plans. The 10-1 called for ten single-member districts and a mayor elected at large; the alternative plan, an 11-0, provided for eleven council members elected from districts, with the mayor selected by the council members from among their number. The blacks favored an all single-member district plan, with the possible exception of the mayoral position. They continued to hold this position until a 14-1 plan, described below, was achieved.

Unlike an at-large system, single-member districts raise the issue of drawing the district lines. In the original suit filed in 1971, the plaintiffs stated two objections to the city council election procedure. In addition to the dilution issue, they argued that the city had failed to redraw the residence districts for election, which violated a provision of the charter requiring the districts to be redrawn every two years. Further, it was argued that the unadjusted districts resulted in "substantial disparity of population among the various districts." After the city council redrew district lines in 1972, the plaintiffs abandoned this contention.

Judge Mahon noted that there was some "initial concern by the Court by the relatively high concentration of black voters in District 6 (73.60 percent) and District 8 (87.30 percent)," as to whether this concentration presented cluster dilution. He determined that "racial gerrymandering was not the purpose or intent of the district lines," and also noted that testimony in this case led him to comprehend that "there is no agreement on whether the political interest of a minority group are best maximized by an overwhelming majority in a single district, bare majorities in more than one district or a substantial proportion in a number of districts."[62]

Return to the Court of Appeals

Following the district court ruling, the city sank further into a representation quagmire through a series of complications, which arose from interpretations of case law and from coincidental timing. The plaintiffs appealed, joined by Adelfa B. Callejo, as intervenor for Mexican-descent voters.

The case was heard before Fifth Circuit Judges Tuttle, Goldberg, and Clark, with Judge Tuttle writing the opinion.[63] The Fifth Circuit held that since

61. *Wise* v. *Lipscomb*, 437 U.S. 535, Appendix, 30–31 (1978).
62. Citing *Turner* v. *McKeithen*, 490 F.2d 191, 197 n. 24 (5th Cir. 1973).
63. *Lipscomb* v. *Wise*, 551 F. 2d 1043 (5th Cir. 1977).

Dallas did not challenge the district court's ruling that the all at-large system unconstitutionally diminished the voting strength of Dallas's black citizens, the problem lay merely in selecting an appropriate remedy, as a federal common law of voting rights remedies had developed.

Because the courts have yet to rule on the application of the multi-member state legislative district analogy to city government, had the city preserved this issue, the question might have been settled in this case. By this time, however, the city's decision to abandon the fight for a determination of the constitutionality of the at-large system had become a political decision rather than a legal one.[64] Other avenues for more appropriate remedies had been closed.

The black plaintiff-appellants contended that the district court's decision should be reversed because it employed three at-large seats and because the district lines concentrated black voters in an impermissible small number of districts, resulting in "cluster dilution." Representatives of the Hispanic community asked that the court remand for findings on alleged unconstitutional dilution of the voting strength of Dallas's Hispanic citizens, and for development of an election plan to remedy that alleged violation. The intervenors offered no specific plans, but presented the results of the April 1, 1975, election, and other evidence of dilution, to show that they could not benefit from at-large voting.

The appellate court did reverse, holding that the district court had erred by evaluating Dallas's actions only under constitutional standards, rather than by applying the teaching of *East Carroll Parish School Board* v. *Marshall* (1976). This case had established that, absent exceptional circumstances, judicially imposed reapportionment plans should employ only single-member districts.[65] With regard to the Hispanic dilution issue, the circuit court held that because the Hispanic plaintiffs had been dismissed from the lawsuit for failure to comply with discovery orders, a determination had not yet been made that their access had been unconstitutionally impaired. Thus the situation of the Hispanic voters did not constitute a "special circumstance."

The case was remanded with instructions that the district court require the city to be reapportioned into an appropriate number of single-member districts. The court stated that the city might provide for the election of the mayor by citywide election, if desired.[66] In the course of its opinion, the court of appeals adhered to the prevailing standard for determining "effective access to the political process," namely, representation "by the minority-preferred candidate," interpreted to be a person of one's own race. This meant that the principle that seats are to be proportionate to the population was to be enforced, and that single-member districts in court-ordered plans were to be preferred.

64. The assistant city attorney at the time, Joseph G. Werner Jr., affirmed this situation in a telephone interview with the author on June 27, 1997.

65. *East Carroll Parish School Board* v. *Marshall,* 424 U.S. 636 (1976).

66. *Lipscomb* v. *Wise,* 551 F. 2d 1043, 1049 (5th Cir. 1977).

U.S. Supreme Court

On July 20, 1977, the Dallas City Council voted 6-5 to appeal the Fifth Circuit's order. On August 30, 1977, Supreme Court Justice Powell stayed the Court of Appeals' judgment, pending the disposition of the city's petition for certiorari and resolution by the Supreme Court.[67] Subsequently the Court did grant certiorari, with oral arguments scheduled before the Court on April 26, 1978.[68] On April 10 the Justice Department filed a brief that the district court "departed from remedial principle established by this court and thus deprived respondents of the relief to which they were entitled," and that "the charter amendment is not effective as law because it has not been submitted for pre-clearance" by the Justice Department under the Voting Rights Act Amendments of 1975. The brief said that "until such preclearance is obtained, the 1976 charter amendment [8-3 plan] has no force or effect."[69] Presumably, then, eleven members of the city council were serving illegally, which meant that their actions as city officials had no force or effect.

The distinction between a legislatively enacted and a judicially imposed reapportionment or redistricting plan is significant here. Plans imposed by court order are not subject to the requirements of VRA Section 5 preclearance, but the case law does require that federal courts, absent special circumstances, employ single-member districts when they impose remedial plans. But legislatively enacted plans in covered jurisdictions *are* subject to Section 5 preclearance by either a declaratory judgment from the U.S. District Court for the District of Columbia or by submitting the change to the Attorney General, in which case, the established preference, again, is for single-member districts. The likely overall outcome is that any option other than single-member districts will be ruled invalid, though no court had at the time—nor has since—declared at-large elections, per se, unconstitutional.

The Supreme Court noted that "while this Court has found that the use of multi-member districts in a state legislative apportionment plan may be invalid if 'used invidiously to cancel out or minimize the voting strength of racial groups,' . . . we have never had occasion to consider whether an analog of this highly amorphous theory may be applied to municipal governments. Since petitioners did not preserve this issue on appeal, we need not today consider whether relevant constitutional distinctions may be drawn in this area between a state legislature and a municipal government."[70]

The Court did uphold the city's 8-3 plan, ruling that the ordinance was properly considered to be a legislative plan, rather than a court-ordered plan, contrary to the ruling by the court of appeals. The Court also held that the

67. *Wise* v. *Lipscomb*, 434 U.S. 1329 (1977).
68. *Wise* v. *Lipscomb*, 434 U.S. 1008 (1978).
69. *Dallas Morning News*, April 11, 1978.
70. *Wise* v. *Lipscomb*, 437 U.S. 535, 550 (1978).

impact of the VRA on the city ordinance, and on the charter amendment approved by referendum, would be open on remand to the circuit court. Section 5 of the VRA, which had become applicable to Texas while this case was pending on appeal, barred implementing the challenged ordinance absent preclearance. Since the Fifth Circuit Court of Appeals had not dealt with that issue, it needed to be considered by that court on remand.

There was no majority rationale in this important Supreme Court case. Justice White announced the judgment of the Court and delivered an opinion, in which Justice Stewart joined. Justice Powell filed an opinion, in which Justices Burger, Blackmun, and Rehnquist joined, concurring in part with the reasoning and concurring with the judgment. Justice Rehnquist filed a separate opinion in which Justices Burger, Stewart, and Powell joined. Justice Marshall filed a dissenting opinion, in which Justices Brennan and Stevens joined. The confusion generated by plurality opinions, when the Court does not give a "comprehensible message," takes on a new dimension when it affects the political careers of individuals and the public policy of a major city. Just where these ambiguous matters stood was a cause of uncertainty in the city and frustration for the voters.

Justice Marshall, with whom Brennan and Stevens joined, dissented on the basis "that the plan ordered by the District Court here must be evaluated in accordance with the federal common law of remedies applicable to judicially devised reapportionment plans."[71] They argued that, as the council did not challenge the finding that the at-large election of all its members was unconstitutional, a plan that replicated the offending feature for three council members was as unconstitutional as the original plan. The dissenters believed that the court of appeals correctly held that at-large voting in the City of Dallas should not have been approved as part of the remedy by the district court.

After the Supreme Court remanded the case, the city filed suit in the U.S. District Court for the District of Columbia, requesting a declaratory judgment that the 8-3 plan did comply with the Voting Rights Act. The court of appeals, on remand, held that the issue of preclearance was not rendered moot by the city seeking a declaratory judgment, and remanded the case to the district court for any further relief necessary.

Election Stay

Meanwhile, Elsie Faye Heggins filed suit to enjoin the city from conducting its scheduled April 7, 1979, city election, until the council redistricting suit was settled in the D.C. court, and until the U.S. Justice Department was satisfied.[72]

71. Ibid.
72. *Heggins* v. *City of Dallas,* 469 F.Supp. 739 (1979). Heggins had lost the election for a council seat in 1977, but later, in 1980, she won in a special election.

The three-judge court issued an injunction, holding that the city could not conduct elections until the city's election plan had received preclearance, as
required by the Voting Rights Act.[73] The city conceded that it could not conduct elections for the eight single-member districts until precleared but insisted
that no preclearance was necessary for the three at-large places, which showed
no change from what was in effect in 1972. The court did not accept this argument, and concluded that "although the constituencies for the at-large places
remained constant, the influence on an election of the votes cast by each Dallas
voter has been altered drastically."[74] This ruling appropriately acknowledged
the interrelatedness of all elements in an electoral system.

The court also acknowledged that "there is confusion in the case law
about the precise remedy to be accorded to plaintiffs in a case of this nature."
In some instances an injunction had been deemed proper, and in others the
courts have "refused to enjoin elections despite a finding of coverage under
the Act."[75]

In examining "this apparent division of authority," the court concluded
that "the courts which have chosen not to enjoin elections have grounded their
decision in equitable considerations having to do primarily with the timing of
the plaintiff's claim."[76] In the Dallas case, the plaintiffs had filed their action
nearly four weeks before the deadline for candidates to file their nominating
petitions. So, in the court's view, the candidates had not yet expended time
and money in their campaigns.

The court ordered the city to submit details concerning the three at-large
places to the Attorney General or to the District Court for the District of
Columbia for preclearance, and to postpone the scheduled election pending
further order of the court. Current members of the city council were to continue in office until the lawful election of successors, and the court retained
jurisdiction for rescheduling the elections after the city obtained preclearance
of an election plan.[77]

District Judge Robert M. Hill, dissenting in part, laid out the dilemmas
that the tension between the judicial system and the VRA often produce. He
succinctly summarized what had transpired to that date:

> The city's current election plan was adjudged constitutional. . . . The Fifth
> Circuit upheld the constitutionality of the plan, but reversed on the ground
> that the plan did not comply with strict standards required of a judicial
> plan. The Supreme Court reversed, holding that the plan was "legislative"

73. The Voting Rights Act of 1965 authorizes the use of three-judge district courts and
direct appeal to the Supreme Court.
74. *Heggins* v. *City of Dallas,* 469 F.Supp. 739, 741 (1979).
75. Id., at 742.
76. Ibid.
77. Id., at 743.

rather than "judicial," but did not disturb the holding that the plan was constitutional. The city held an election under the plan in April of 1975, after the federal district court had declared it to be constitutional. Thereafter, on September 23, 1975, Section 5 of the Voting Rights Act became applicable to the State of Texas. In April of 1977, the current members of the city council were elected under the plan, which had not been precleared.

In sum, he argued, "the city has a constitutional election plan under which council members were lawfully elected in 1975. In 1977 council members were elected under the plan in violation of Section 5 of the Act, and in 1979 the city seeks again to hold an election under the plan, which could be presumed to be constitutional." "Meanwhile," he said, "the voters of the city are disenfranchised and city government operates under a cloud, if it operates at all. I do not believe Congress intended this to be the normal result." Further, he suggested that "a reading of the cases reveals that enjoining an election for an indefinite time until preclearance is obtained is the exceptional remedy rather than the normal one."[78]

Judge Hill pointed to a pragmatic complication: "In sum, the city's charter provides for a special election if more than four council members resign at any one time. Under the court's order, vacancies are to be filled in the manner prescribed by law. Of course, any election under the current plan is prohibited. Thus if the city council resigns, en masse, the city would have no government until the court could devise a plan for the holding of special elections. Since the court has retained jurisdiction only for the purpose of rescheduling elections when the city obtains preclearance of its election plan, it may not even have power to devise an interim plan."[79]

These dilemmas were avoided, however, as the U.S. Attorney General granted "preclearance" to the "new" 8-3 plan on November 19, 1979, and city council elections were scheduled for January 19, 1980, a delay of almost ten months, because of the stay entered by the three-judge court in Dallas.[80] The DOJ's Civil Rights Division investigation did not support the conclusion that the 8-3 plan had been adopted to discriminate against minority groups because of their racial or language minority status. In the view of the DOJ, the position of minorities had been enhanced over what it had been under the previously existing at-large system. The results of recent elections suggested that minority voters might reasonably expect to influence the election of persons to the at-large seats.[81] Following preclearance, the city moved to dismiss the declaratory

78. Id., at 744–746.
79. Id., at 747.
80. Letter, Drew S. Days III, Assistant Attorney General, Civil Rights Division, to Lee E. Holt, Dallas City Attorney, November 19, 1979, published as Appendix to *City of Dallas* v. *United States,* 482 F.Supp. 183, 186–187 (1979).
81. Id., at 187.

judgment suit in the U.S. District Court, District of Columbia, as moot. It seemed that the city was finally able to resume elections according to a voter-approved election plan.

Redistricting under the 8-3 Plan

As soon as the 8-3 plan had been precleared, and elections finally held in January 1980, the city had to turn to the controversial issue of drawing new district lines based on the 1980 census. The city received the census tapes in April 1981. According to the data, 29.4 percent of the city's 904,078 residents were black, and 12.3 percent were Hispanic. City Council member Elsie Faye Heggins served notice that the city must create a third black council district, or face a new federal lawsuit to strike down the current election system.

Heggins and officials of the Frederick Douglass Voting Council, a black activist group, said that they were prepared to go back to court to seek additional minority representation. Heggins also said that she would again fight for a plan in which voters within specific districts elected at least ten of the eleven city council members.

City staff developed several redistricting alternatives for consideration by the city council. According to City Secretary Robert Sloan, the staff found it impossible to devise a districting plan that would guarantee three black seats and a Hispanic seat on the council. Shifts in population since 1970 contributed to the problem.

According to a report by the city's Office of Management Services, released May 11, 1981, Heggins's district had lost 22 percent of its population during the previous ten years. Census figures indicated that minority population shifts from the inner city to previously all-white neighborhoods did not lend themselves to creation of a fourth minority district. With citywide integration, blacks faced the same problems that Hispanics had faced for many years: dwindling racial concentrations that make it difficult to draw safe districts.[82]

With these shifts in minority population, Don Hicks (Anglo), Max Goldblatt (Anglo), and Ricardo Medrano (Hispanic), whose districts surrounded those of the two black council members, Fred Blair and Elsie Faye Heggins, said that they did not intend to have a third black district carved from their districts. The demographics also drove a wedge between the blacks and Medrano. Medrano opposed creation of the safe black district proposed by Heggins's coalition of black leaders, because it would become close to impossible for a Hispanic to be elected. Other council members spoke of "communities of interest," meaning they opposed creating a third black district, if it meant dividing recognized areas such as Pleasant Grove, Oak Cliff, Oak Lawn, or old East Dallas. The first city council workshop to discuss drawing new dis-

82. *Dallas Morning News,* May 12, 1981.

trict boundaries deteriorated into a tense stalemate between the council's two black members and the rest of the council. Mayor Jack Evans abruptly stopped the workshop an hour ahead of schedule.

To avoid political uproar over the creation of a third black council district under 8-3, other suggestions surfaced. One was an 8-2-1 plan suggested in different variations by Mayor Evans, Don Hicks, and Wes Wise, by which voters from four northern districts would elect one at-large council member, and voters in the four districts in southern Dallas would elect the other; the mayor would be elected citywide. An 8-4-1 plan would have four area council members from the southwest, southeast, northwest, and northeast quadrants of the city. The 10-1 plan also was proposed. But a plan that changed the 8-3 system could not be voted in until the charter election in April 1983, when the next council election was scheduled.

The offices of the city secretary, the city attorney, and management services prepared a lengthy report, which contained eleven reapportionment plans. This document was submitted to the city council on October 9, 1981. The report was designed to demonstrate the effects of the 1980 census, and to serve as a starting point for the city council to develop and to select a final districting plan.

On March 24, 1982, the city council passed an ordinance to reapportion the eight single-member districts. Three days later, on March 27, this new 8-3 plan was submitted to the DOJ for preclearance under Section 5 of the VRA. In spite of complaints from minorities that the new boundaries would not permit a third black council member to be elected, preclearance was granted three months later, on June 25, 1982.[83] The approved redistricting plan included two "safe" black districts with at least 84 percent minority population and one district with a combined minority vote of 64.9 percent, with Hispanics making up 33.2 percent of the district.

The following year, the three minority members on the city council (Blair, Heggins, and Medrano) said that fighting to get a change in the 8-3 plan in the council was a losing cause. They indicated that they would be forced either to take their fight beyond council chambers to a referendum petition or back to federal courts.

Efforts by minorities to gain more representation continued. In August 1986 a group of Hispanics began meeting with members of the Mexican American Legal Defense Fund to examine the possibility of boosting Hispanic voting strength by increasing the council's eight single-member districts to ten. According to René Martinez, who chaired most group meetings, a position paper was prepared to submit to Mayor Starke Taylor. It included two plans, a 10-1 and a 10-3, in which a district with 50 percent Hispanics was possible.[84]

83. Chronology from *Williams* v. *City of Dallas,* 734 F.Supp. 1317, 1354, 1359 (1990).
84. *Dallas Morning News,* August 17, 1986.

The Dallas Homeowners League backed the 10-1 proposal in September. By October 1 the Dallas City Council had unanimously agreed to study the redrawing of the eight district boundaries, with the clear majority favoring a look at ten districts.[85]

Later in October a city council committee recommended that Dallas hold an election in May to consider revisions to the city charter, including the number of single-member districts. By January the list of alternative plans had grown to twenty-five; the council's municipal affairs committee rescinded its recommendation to hold an election in May 1988, because most of the issues to be decided had not been narrowed for an election.[86]

THE WILLIAMS CASE

On May 18 Roy Williams and Marvin Crenshaw filed a lawsuit against the city in U.S. District Court, contending that the three at-large council districts and eight single-member districts weakened black voting strength "for the purpose of discriminating against African American voters."[87]

Meanwhile, the Supreme Court held, in *Mobile* v. *Bolden,* that the "intent" standard, rather than the "effects" standard, governed voting rights dilution cases.[88] On June 29, 1982, three days after Dallas received preclearance of its 8-3 plan based on the 1980 census, the 1982 VRA Amendments, which in effect overruled *Bolden,* became effective. Under its new Section 2 standard, proof of "discriminatory effects alone" of the 8-3 system, without regard to whether it was "intentionally adopted or maintained for a discriminatory purpose," could establish that the 8-3 system violated Section 2 of the Voting Rights Act.

Political Efforts at Resolution

Before turning to the *Williams* lawsuit, the simultaneous political efforts to settle the districting issue should be noted. In March 1988 Mayor Annette Strauss appointed a seventy-six-member commission, known as Dallas Together, and charged it with "bringing Dallas together by identifying the root causes of the racial tensions being experienced in our city."[89] The commission formed five study panels, including one on "Political Participation," chaired by Ray Hutchison, a lawyer, former State Republican Chairman, and former state legislator.

85. *Dallas Times Herald,* October 2, 1986.
86. *Dallas Morning News,* February 5, 1988.
87. *Williams* v. *City of Dallas,* 734 F.Supp. 1317 (1990).
88. *City of Mobile* v. *Bolden,* 446 U.S. 55 (1980).
89. "Final Report of Dallas Together," January 1989, 2.

The commission members spent many hours in meetings, including forty-seven meetings from March 1988 through January 1989, plus many meetings of study panels. The final report of the Hutchison study panel recommended that the Dallas City Council appoint a charter advisory committee to study the composition of the council, additional powers for the mayor, and higher pay for council members.

Following recommendation, the city council appointed a fourteen-member committee, which included two Hispanic and five black members. Two black members, council members Al Lipscomb and Diane Ragsdale, appointed themselves.[90] The mayor appointed Hutchison to chair the advisory committee, and requested its recommendations by June 1, for an August referendum. This committee first met on March 15, 1989, and immediately disagreed over procedures, which signaled the acrimony that was to plague every discussion, until the final committee vote two months later.[91]

Meanwhile, in May, a new council was elected that included only three members who favored eliminating all at-large seats with the exception of the mayor's. They were Lori Palmer and two blacks, Diane Ragsdale and Al Lipscomb. The other eight favored retaining at-large posts in some form. As council members discussed districting issues, charter advisory committee members were engaged in heated debates and negotiations. While all this occurred, the *Williams* lawsuit was proceeding through its discovery phase. The city council realized it would likely be considering recommendations from the charter advisory committee at the time the federal court was scheduled to hear the *Williams* lawsuit in September.

The charter committee finally adopted a recommendation for a 10-4-1 election system for the city, ten members to be elected from single-member districts, four from overlay districts, which would cover quadrants of the city, and the mayor elected at large. In the final committee vote, four blacks voted against the mixed 10-4-1 plan; one black, two Hispanics, one Vietnamese, and six Anglos voted for the plan. When council member Al Lipscomb's heavy lobbying for a united front among minorities failed, he attacked Phap Dam, the only committee member of Asian descent, saying, "A sellout is a sellout is a sellout." Lipscomb added: "You can't stick me in my back with a knife one day and then on August 13 pull it out and say, 'Let's start over again.'" Dam responded: "I'm not a racist. I'm not a sellout. I'm not an Uncle Tom. I'm just Phap Dam. I voted with the whites because I thought this was best for minorities."[92]

90. Anglo council member Jerry Rucker also appointed himself. Many viewed self-appointment by council members as a conflict of interest.

91. For more detail on the Charter Advisory Committee by a participant-observer, see Royce Hanson, *Civic Culture and Urban Change: Governing Dallas* (Detroit: Wayne State University Press, 2003), chap. 11.

92. Quoted by James Ragland, *Dallas Morning News,* August 8, 1989.

The city council received the recommendation and called a charter election for August 12, 1989, on the 10-4-1 system, as well as on a provision to delay the next city council election from May to November 1991, so as to be able to use the 1990 census for drawing the new districts. The 10-4-1 system was approved by the voters by a two-to-one margin. The heaviest vote against it was in minority precincts, but the turnout of minority voters was less than 9 percent. Citywide turnout was about 14 percent. Although no minority elected officials backed the 10-4-1 plan, the Hispanic and the Asian chambers of commerce, the Hispanic Women's Network of Texas, and the Asian American Voters Coalition did support the plan. Most of the Hispanic organizations and all of the city's black organizations backed a single-member district system.[93]

The strategy of the organizers of the "Vote No" to the 10-4-1 campaign was to focus local and national attention on racial friction in the city and to try to get voters angry enough to go to the polls. "Are they outraged enough to go to the polls and vote? That's the question," said Peter Johnson, executive director of the local Southern Christian Leadership Conference. Similarly the strategy of another opposition group, Citizens for Democracy, was to use slogans, songs, and symbols reminiscent of the 1960s civil rights era. Although these strategies did not get minorities to the polls, they did gain national coverage, including stories in *Time* magazine, *The Washington Post,* and *USA Today,* as well as television exposure.[94]

The city submitted the voter-approved 10-4-1 plan to the DOJ and asked for approval in concept until the 1990 census results became available. The city requested that the May 1991 election be delayed until November to ensure that the 1990 census data would be available in time to draw the district lines to submit for DOJ preclearance.

With the definitive citizen vote favoring 10-4-1, the city filed a motion with the court in the *Williams* case, arguing that the question concerning the 8-3 system was moot, now that the city had abandoned it. The district court, nevertheless, proceeded with the trial to determine whether the 8-3 system violated Section 2 of the VRA.

The city did not hear from the DOJ until October 1989, when the Attorney General refused to approve the mixed plan, because no lines had been drawn for the ten local districts or for the four quadrants. Nor was the issue of a delayed election date resolved.

Williams v. City of Dallas

On May 18, 1988, two months after Mayor Strauss had appointed the Dallas Together Commission, Roy Williams and Marvin Crenshaw filed their suit.

93. James Ragland, *Dallas Morning News,* August 13, 1989.
94. James Ragland and Catalina Camia, *Dallas Morning News,* August 11, 1989.

They were seeking an 11-0 plan, charging that the city's 8-3 mixed system for electing council members was unconstitutional, and in violation of the new Section 2 of the VRA.[95] The Ledbetter Neighborhood Association, claiming that the 8-3 plan also discriminated against Hispanics, intervened on August 25, 1988.[96] A motion followed on February 2, 1989, for preliminary injunction to stay the city council elections scheduled for May 6, 1989.

Like Al Lipscomb, Marvin Crenshaw and Roy Williams first came to public attention as self-described gadflies at the podium of city council meetings. Similarly their initial efforts to win council seats met with defeats prior to their filing suit. Unlike Lipscomb, however, neither has subsequently won elective office.[97]

Crenshaw and Williams saw their suit take them from "well-known gadflies" to "heroes" after the 14-1 victory in court.[98] In a lengthy article in the *Dallas Morning News* in 1989, staff writer Ed Housewright quoted Williams as saying: "This is a pinnacle in my life. . . . My life will never be the same. This will be a landmark decision."[99] Al Lipscomb, at the time serving as a member of the city council, was quoted by Housewright as having said that the "lawsuit will authenticate their legitimacy. . . . They will have to be respected and accepted."[100] But at a later time in a talk show broadcast, Crenshaw charged that Lipscomb had offered him $9,000 or $10,000 in 1988 not to file the lawsuit. Williams backed up the allegation, also on the talk show.[101]

On April 6, 1989, Judge Buchmeyer denied the motion to stay the election scheduled for May 6, 1989.[102] He relied on a Fifth Circuit case, which stressed

95. *Williams* v. *City of Dallas,* 734 F.Supp. 1317 (1990). At the time of the suit, both plaintiffs had lived in Dallas for about twenty years, with Williams, ironically, living in north Dallas. Neither had full time jobs. Williams said he worked as a "spiritual counselor"; Crenshaw said his occupation was "lobbyist for justice."

96. The Ledbetter Neighborhood Association comprised mainly Hispanic residents of West Dallas.

97. Crenshaw ran unsuccessfully for city council Place 9 in 1983, Place 8 in 1984, Place 11 (mayor) in 1987 and 1989, Place 4 in 1991, in a special election to fill the remainder of a term in Place 7 in 1992, and for Place 7 in 1993. Williams ran unsuccessfully for at-large Place 9 in 1987 and 1989, for a single-member district in 1991, and for mayor in 1995.

98. Williams and Shay, *Time Change,* 160.

99. Ed Housewright, *Dallas Morning News,* September 4, 1989.

100. Ibid.

101. James Ragland, *Dallas Morning News,* October 17, 1990.

102. U.S. District Judge Jerry Buchmeyer presided over several controversial civil rights cases in Dallas, including a desegregation suit filed by low-income residents against the Dallas Housing Authority and the U.S. Department of Housing and Urban Development. He was named to the federal bench by President Jimmy Carter in 1979, and then succeeded U.S. District Judge Barefoot Sanders in 1995, as chief judge of the Northern District of Texas. Judge Sanders presided over the district court supervision of school desegregation.

Reportedly Dallas Housing Executive Director Alphonso Jackson asked the Superinten-

that district courts should not enjoin state or municipal elections if "other corrective relief will be available at a later date, in the ordinary course of litigation."[103] In the argument, Judge Buchmeyer assumed that the plaintiffs could establish that the 8-3 system was in violation of the VRA by "packing" in Districts 6 and 8 and "cracking" in Districts 1 and 2.

The trial, held in September 1989, lasted two weeks. Six months later, after the voter referendum on 10-4-1 had passed, Judge Buchmeyer ruled that the 8-3 plan did violate Section 2 of the VRA, and that the city was required to hold a special election for city council as soon as possible.[104] The findings of fact in the lengthy opinion are laborious, but the two main reasons for holding the 8-3 system invalid were, first, that blacks and Hispanics were "denied access to the three at-large seats because they cannot raise—*from their own communities*—the amount of money (at least $150–200,000) that is required for an effective at-large, city-wide campaign in Dallas"; and, second, that "blacks have been unfairly prohibited from electing more than two single-district council members by 'packing' them into two districts with 75–87 percent concentration and 85–91 percent total minority population (Districts 6 and 8)—and by splitting the remaining black population in Dallas between Districts 1 and 7 to prevent the creation of a third black district."[105] Judge Buchmeyer concluded that these discriminatory effects blatantly violated Section 2 of the VRA and "must be remedied by a special City Council election to be held *as soon as possible.*"[106] The standards the judge applied were that districts should be designed for racial minority candidates to be able to raise sufficient money from their racial minority communities to win, and that seats proportionate to population should be maximized.

The judge ordered the city to submit within thirty days a legislative plan for holding a special interim election. He set guidelines that required a single tier of single-member districts, which precluded the 10-4-1 plan. According to the city attorney at that time, the staff worked in around-the-clock sessions to meet the order. With the tight schedule, there was little time for public participation. Only one public hearing was held, and it was on the day the proposed 12-1 plan was selected, April 23, 1990.[107]

---

dent of the Dallas Independent School District, Marvin Edwards, what he thought of Judge Barefoot Sanders. Edwards replied that he had never met the man. Jackson responded, "What do you mean you never met him? I have lunch with my judge (Judge Jerry Buchmeyer) once a week!" Reported by Ruth Miller Fitzgibbons, "On the Edge," *D* magazine (September 1991), 18:68.

103. *Chisom* v. *Roemer,* 853 F.2d 1186 (5th Cir. 1988).

104. *Williams* v. *City of Dallas,* 734 F.Supp. 1317, 1318 (1990).

105. Id., at 1318.

106. Ibid.

107. Analeslie Muncy, "Redistricting from Hell: The Dallas Experience," paper presented at the National Institute of Municipal Law Officers Annual Conference, San Diego, California, October 29, 1991.

The staff generated 10-1, 12-1, and 14-1 plans, based on 1980 census data. From these plans, the council finally selected a 12-1 plan to provide five districts with black populations ranging from 61 percent to 63 percent, and one predominantly Hispanic district with a Hispanic population of 50 percent.[108] This 12-1 plan was submitted to the court in May 1990 as the city's interim plan, and to the DOJ for preclearance. Two plans, then, had been submitted to the Department of Justice and both were pending—the voter-approved 10-4-1 plan and this court-required, single-tiered, single-member district plan, the 12-1 plan. The only approved plan was the 8-3 plan, precleared by the DOJ in 1982, and held in violation of the Voting Rights Act in March 1990, but replaced by a charter election on the 10-4-1 plan in the 1989 charter election.

The Justice Department sent a letter in June 1990, requesting that voluminous additional information on the 12-1 plan be provided within sixty days. Again, city staff was forced into around-the-clock sessions. Sentiment on the city council shifted toward trying to settle the lawsuit. After intense negotiations, the city and the plaintiffs agreed on a 14-1 plan, which would be based on 1990 census data, when it became available, with a city charter election on the plan to be held on December 8.[109] This deal almost fell through, when the plaintiffs insisted on appointing four of the fifteen members of the panel, which would draw the new council district boundaries. Mayor Strauss broke the impasse by consenting to appoint one redistricting commission member "agreeable" to the plaintiffs, and a second one agreeable to the Hispanic intervenors.[110]

The voters negated the agreement by defeating the 14-1 plan by a narrow margin in the December charter election. In a sworn statement, Mayor Annette Strauss said that Judge Buchmeyer had told her that if the voters rejected the 14-1 proposal, he would order a May election under a 14-1 or 15-0 redistricting plan.[111] Given the judge's disposition, and since the voter's choice for the mixed constituency 10-4-1 plan was clear, the city withdrew its 12-1 submission to the Justice Department in January 1991. The city asked that the DOJ reconsider the earlier request to change the city council election from May to November 1991, so as to allow time to prepare a plan, using 1990 census data, for DOJ preclearance. At the same time, the city council appointed a new

108. The acrimony at meetings of the charter advisory committee also characterized the arguments during the accelerated schedule of council meetings. Inflammatory personal attacks made national, as well as local, news.

109. See the chart in Muncy's "Redistricting from Hell," developed to explain the complex settlement agreement necessitated by the possibilities resulting from contingencies concerning availability of 1990 census data.

110. David Jackson, *Dallas Morning News,* August 12, 1990.

111. A federal appeals judge, to whom the Strauss affidavit was submitted, ruled that Judge Buchmeyer's discussion with the mayor did not influence his decision to order a 14-1 city council election plan but that the conversation was "ill advised" (*Dallas Morning News,* April 3, 1991).

redistricting commission to draw district lines, upon release of the 1990 census data.

Because of the failure of the settlement agreement, however, the court held a remedy hearing in January 1991. Judge Buchmeyer commandeered the city's redistricting commission, and ordered an interim election under a 14-1 plan, based on 1990 census data. In a summary of the opinion, announced in open court on conclusion of the remedy hearing, February 1, 1991, he explained his reasoning:

> Under both state law and city charter, the City of Dallas is required to hold its next City Council election on May 4, 1991. . . . Yet, the City Council does not have any legal plan for use in a May 4, 1991 election. . . . There was no appeal of the *Williams* decision [that the 8-3 system violated Section 2 of the Voting Rights Act] . . . [and] there is serious doubt that the City Council would be able to obtain Justice Department approval of anything in time to hold an election in November 1991 [which was the delay requested by the city].[112]

The council had not appealed the *Williams* decision in favor of working out a political solution, and had submitted the 10-4-1 plan to the DOJ after the referendum vote. However, in October 1989, the Attorney General had refused to approve it, because no lines had been drawn for the ten local districts or the four quadrants. Judge Buchmeyer observed that the city should have drawn lines based on the 1980 census as "illustrative" so that the Department of Justice could approve the concept of the 10-4-1 plan and an election delay, with final lines to be drawn after receipt of the 1990 census data. This provided the city with hindsight only, as there was no assurance that the Justice Department would have approved "illustrative" lines.[113]

During the remedy hearings, the attorneys for the city had requested that the voter-approved 10-4-1 plan be used for the May 1991 election, which would have given the plan a test for fairness. However, shortly after he had issued his opinion, Judge Buchmeyer met with the attorneys of all parties to make sure they understood that unless the city council obtained DOJ approval for a plan and a November election, the district court would have no alternative under the law but to order an interim election for May 4, 1991, under a 14-1 or 15-0 plan. Buchmeyer noted his doubt that the DOJ would approve the 10-4-1 plan, primarily because it was not fair to Hispanics.[114]

In 1979 a three-judge court had delayed city council elections for ten months, until the city's plan had received preclearance required by the VRA.

112. *Williams* v. *City of Dallas*, 1991 U.S. Dist. LEXIS 1669 [unpublished opinion].
113. *Williams* v. *City of Dallas*, 734 F.Supp. 1317, 1378; 1991 U.S. Dist. LEXIS 1669 [unpublished opinion].
114. *Williams* v. *City of Dallas*, 1991 U.S. Dist. LEXIS 1669 [unpublished opinion}.

This time the city had requested, and was denied, a six-month delay to obtain preclearance. Judge Buchmeyer also thwarted the efforts of the city to have its recently appointed redistricting commission draw the lines for a May election. In his view, the commission's participation might make the 14-1 plan a "legislative" plan, which would need DOJ approval before it could be used. This might delay the election. Since a court-ordered interim plan need not be submitted for DOJ approval, the judge had commandeered the redistricting commission as a court-appointed committee.[115]

Resulting public reaction in Dallas was sufficiently heated that Judge Buchmeyer acknowledged that "some of those who voted in favor of the 10-4-1 plan in August 1989 and against the 14-1 plan in December 1990 are, quite understandably, upset and frustrated and bewildered about how their democratic 'right to vote' could be taken away. The plain answer is this: the city did not obtain the required approval."[116] He held that the city would violate the VRA if it did not hold an election on May 4, 1991, and, as it had no legal plan, he was ordering an interim election under a 14-1 plan, based on 1990 census data.

Judge Buchmeyer exacerbated the discontent in the community by his style. The *Williams* opinion provides several examples of judicial use of scorn and impugnation.[117] Judge Buchmeyer's language and sarcasm appear to be unnecessarily pejorative. Repeatedly he referred to minority candidates, who had served with CCA-backing, as having been "permitted" to serve. This connotation could have been offensive to minority candidates elected from single-member districts who had previously been endorsed by the CCA, such as George Allen. Other than city council members and the chairman of the charter advisory committee, the only ones Judge Buchmeyer specifically named as "credible" witnesses were racial minorities. Specifically, he named the plaintiffs' and the intervenor's expert witnesses as credible, but he discounted the testimony of the city's expert witness.[118]

Judge Buchmeyer also impugned the prior decision of a district judge, even to the point of inaccuracy: "Judge Mahon issued an oral opinion. In it, he found that the city-wide, at-large system of electing members to the Dallas City Council—which had continued, in different forms, for almost 70 years

115. Ibid.
116. Ibid.
117. For a study of judicial rhetoric, see Richard Delgado and Jean Stefancic, *Failed Revolutions: Social Reform and the Limits of Legal Imagination* (Boulder, Colo.: Westview, 1994), chap. 9. An alternative, more favorable, interpretation might be that Judge Buchmeyer was attempting humor, or was following his advice to young lawyers to "be yourself." Jenny Martinez, who wrote a biographical profile of Judge Buchmeyer for the Dallas Bar Association's website, said of him: "Lawyers who have practiced in his court know that he is a kind and patient man who provides a fair forum" (Jenny Martinez, "Judicial Profiles," Dallas Bar Association, April 2002).
118. *Williams* v. *City of Dallas*, 734 F.Supp. 1317, 1330 (1990).

(from 1907 to 1975)—was unconstitutional *because this system was intentionally adopted and maintained to dilute the voting strength of African-Americans"* [emphasis added].[119] Judge Mahon did not state in his opinion, at the page cited or at any other page, that the at-large system was unconstitutional for the reason Judge Buchmeyer declared.

Further, Judge Buchmeyer's opinion is riddled with untested assumptions:

1. In response to the argument that at-large seats can provide a citywide view: "[it is] a City Manager who has the responsibility to provide a 'city-wide' view on policy issues being determined by the Council."[120]
2. In response to the argument that voters have more than one person to contact if there is a mixed plan of single-member and at-large districts: *"This is not an argument to be tossed aside lightly; it should be thrown away with great force."*[121]
3. He identified Marvin Robinson, who "was selected as the 'test case' for the black community as an *excellent choice."* He emphasized, with underlining and italics, that since the race by Marvin Robinson in 1983, *"no serious* black candidate has ever run for an at-large seat."[122] Verna Thomas, who was in a runoff for a seat in 1984, might take exception.
4. With regard to the election of a Hispanic to an at-large seat under the 8-3 system, Judge Buchmeyer countered that this outcome "was due to very atypical circumstances which will not reoccur."[123] He stated that witnesses for the plaintiffs and the intervenor testified that it was not possible for a black or Hispanic candidate to win one of the three at-large seats: *"This testimony is credited because it is true and it is supported by other credible evidence"* [emphasis added].[124]

Yet, four years later, a black candidate won the at-large election as mayor of Dallas.

Meanwhile, the commandeered redistricting commission approved a fourteen-district city council map on February 22, 1991, to submit to Judge Buchmeyer. The districts included five majority black districts and two majority Hispanic districts. To achieve this, several of the districts were bizarrely shaped, barely contiguous in places, and computers were used to split voting precincts to achieve the desired minority percentages. Bob Sloan, the city secretary and elections administrator, expressed concern over voter confusion, with the thirty to forty voting precincts, which had been split, some falling into

119. Id., at 1340, citing *Lipscomb* v. *Wise,* 399 F.Supp. 782, 784 (1975).
120. *Williams* v. *City of Dallas,* 1328.
121. Ibid.
122. Ibid., 1324, 1362.
123. Ibid., 1381.
124. Ibid.

as many as three new council districts.[125] Voting districts, which are split between council districts, can make it difficult for a precinct judge to determine which ballot should be given to a voter.

On February 25 the city council agreed to forward two versions of plans, one with ten single-member districts and one with four single-member quadrant districts, to the DOJ to keep the voter-approved redistricting alternative alive. Slight variations in boundaries distinguished the two versions from each other, but the racial percentages were the same. Of the four quadrant districts, whites had majorities in two, blacks in one, and Hispanics in the other. In the ten single-member districts, whites had majorities in five, blacks in three, and Hispanics in two.

On February 27 Judge Buchmeyer approved the redistricting commission's 14-1 plan, but he refused to grant a stay and ordered a May 4 election using the 14-1 plan. The city council, on a 7-4 vote, appealed the judge's order. On March 15, 1991, a three-judge panel of the Fifth Circuit Court of Appeals overturned Judge Buchmeyer's order and granted the city's request to stay the May 4 council elections. This delay would allow the U.S. Justice Department to act on the city's request for preclearance of a 10-4-1 plan, which was submitted March 6, 1991. Judge Buchmeyer insisted that, even if the DOJ, or a declaratory judgment from a three-judge panel in Washington, D.C., did approve a 10-4-1 plan, he would have to hold a trial on the merits of the 10-4-1 plan. The whole process "could take years," he said.[126]

On May 6, 1991, the DOJ rejected the council's 10-4-1 election plan. Mike McKool Jr., a private attorney hired by the city to help with the case, said that a Justice Department attorney had told him that the DOJ did not object to the 10-4-1 concept per se; rather, it objected because the specific proposals submitted by the city did not provide sufficient minority representation.[127]

Some council members wanted to send a revised map to meet the DOJ concern, but supporters of 10-4-1 were unable to gain a council majority on one to submit. At the May 20 council meeting, supporters of 14-1 believed they could settle the three-year-old lawsuit with a plan that included five predominantly black districts, two Hispanic districts, a mostly white district in Oak Cliff, and six other predominantly white districts. Some council members objected to having to split traditional neighborhoods in Oak Cliff and Pleasant Grove to achieve this.

On a 6-5 vote, the council restored these split neighborhoods by reducing black districts from five to four. This set off vicious personal attacks by council members. If the public session was shocking, the closed council session that followed was said by its participants to have been even rougher.[128] This 6-5

125. James Ragland, *Dallas Morning News,* March 11, 1991.
126. Quoted by James Ragland, *Dallas Morning News,* February 28, 1991.
127. David Jackson, *Dallas Morning News,* May 7, 1991.
128. Ibid., May 25, 1991.

council vote stopped negotiations toward a settlement. The council planned to seek DOJ approval for its 14-1 plan with four black districts, and plaintiffs planned to seek judicial imposition of a 14-1 plan containing five black districts.

By mid-June attorneys warned that the Department of Justice probably would reject the 14-1 plan that the city had submitted, because it included only four predominantly black districts. Most council members did not want Judge Buchmeyer to impose some other 14-1 plan; they said that they would vote for a 14-1 if agreement could be reached on a specific 14-1 plan that the majority could support.[129]

According to the 1990 census, blacks comprised 29 percent of the Dallas population. Five single-member seats on the council would mean 33.3 percent representation, and four seats would mean 26.7 percent. On June 16, 1991, the city council adopted a redistricting plan designed to elect five blacks and two Hispanics. It passed, despite the objections of Pleasant Grove residents, whose area was split among four predominantly black districts.

On August 2, 1991, the U.S. Department of Justice approved Dallas's 14-1 redistricting plan, a four-year mayor's term, and the city's request for a November 5 election. But the saga had not yet ended. Because the election in November 1991 under 14-1 was an interim election, the city either had to ratify 14-1 in a charter election on May 1, 1993, a year and a half after the first elections were held under the plan, or hold yet another election under court order. The voters ratified 14-1.

CONCLUSIONS

The court-mandated election in *Williams* v. *City of Dallas* (1990) closed a major chapter in Dallas voting rights litigation. Litigation may reoccur, but it would be over redistricting or enlarging the size of the city council. Not one of these core Dallas cases centered on impediments that prevented minorities from registering and voting. Rather, the focus was on underrepresentation of minorities in elected office, attributed to the at-large election system.

The major change in the election system in Dallas did not result from a court-determined failure in substantive representation (the "responsiveness" standard) nor did it result from failing the "intent" standard. Only when the "results" standard took precedence, and the city was caught between court and DOJ timing, did the city lose the remainder of its at-large districts, with the exception of mayor.

This experience of the City of Dallas provides perspective on the conflicts created between the body of law under the Fourteenth and Fifteenth Amend-

129. *Dallas Morning News,* June 20, 1991.

ments and that under the Voting Rights Act of 1965, with its successive amendments. The city was placed in an untenably defensive position, trying to comply with two continually moving targets simultaneously. Interpretations of both bodies of law were evolving; the standards and rules under neither were clear.

The significance of timing is a factor to be considered in resolving complex social issues under the constraints imposed by law. Had the city been permitted to delay the 1991 election until the interested groups in the city could negotiate the drawing of boundaries using 1990 census data, and had the Department of Justice then been able to provide timely review of the 10-4-1 plan, this tortuous path, and the outcomes, might have been different.

The Dallas litigation experience emphasizes the delicate balance that prevails between the principle of majoritarianism and the principle of protecting the rights of minorities. A majority of voters in Dallas repeatedly voted for a compromise system—that is, a mixed plan, whether 8-3 or 10-4-1. For years the minorities were frustrated by dominance of a conservative majority. When the situation changed, majorities were frustrated when their votes did not count in city charter referenda elections. Neither group, when in a better position of power than the other, sought a fair compromise.

Other important factors in the politics of a community are the characteristics of its candidates, other key figures, and leadership values. Elected minority officials first achieved power through civil rights organizations, the church, and grass-roots political organizations, which submerged the voices of the middle-class minority professionals. The particular qualities of the candidates must also be considered. How much should a candidate's loss in an at-large election be attributed to race, if the candidate also loses, subsequently, in a racially "safe" single-member district? Leadership styles and personalities may be the most important factors in determining the way in which competing interests of multiple groups in a city are resolved. Yet the law cannot accommodate personality theory. This should prompt judicial restraint before a new gate into the "political thicket" is entered.

Three other points in the case law should be noted. By embedding a theory of descriptive representation into the common law of remedies, the federal courts may have foreclosed opportunities to pursue fundamental remedies for ensuring fair representation for all citizens, and for improving race relations. Second, the litigants raised unequal financial resources as an issue. To date, the federal courts still have not established a test of this concept under the Fourteenth Amendment's equal protection of the laws clause. The district court, however, did use unequal financial resources for campaigning as part of its rationale for single-member districts.

A third matter concerns the politics of coalition. The district court acknowledged that, owing to population dispersal, "Chicano politics in Dallas must be the politics of coalition." This observation would apply, presumably, to other emerging minority groups as well. Ironically Texas came under the Voting Rights Act in 1975 as a result of the Spanish-language minority in Texas, yet the remedy in the litigation was designed for blacks, and perhaps it even disadvantaged Hispanics. Whether the court-imposed remedy in Dallas indeed put Hispanics, or other racial and ethnic minorities besides blacks, at a disadvantage is examined in the next chapter.

PART III
The Legacy of Legislation and Litigation

6
Electoral Effects of the VRA in Dallas

Given the opportunity, we will speak for ourselves.
—Frederick Douglass

I could not have been elected from a single-member district.
—Dallas Mayor Ron Kirk

Electoral consequences in Dallas of the Voting Rights Act reveal shortcomings in some assumptions in voting rights cases on which the remedy of single-member districts is based. Congress and the federal courts have shifted emphasis from protecting individual voting rights to ensuring representation for groups, but no methodology exists to infer how individual members of groups vote in particular elections.

Some data based on race, such as voting-age population, can be disaggregated to the voting district (precinct) level from the census data. But data on actual votes cast by individuals of different races are unavailable at any level because of the secret ballot. This renders suspect inferences on racial bloc voting and voter turnout by race, used as bases for findings of vote dilution.

Gary King has designed an ecological inference technique in an attempt to solve the ecological fallacy problem. King notes that because of the inadequacy of methods that had previously been used for inferring individual behavior from aggregate data, "in some situations the wrong policies are being implemented: the wrong districts are being redrawn, and the wrong electoral laws are being changed."[1]

Yet, this is what resulted from VRA enforcement by the federal courts and the U.S. Department of Justice, especially after the 1982 VRA Amendments. The three main arguments, discussed earlier, which thread through the voting

1. Gary King, *A Solution to the Ecological Inference Problem: Reconstructing Individual Behavior from Aggregate Data* (Princeton, N.J.: Princeton University Press, 1997), 9. While new and different methods for estimating patterns of racial bloc voting and voter turnout by race may be more reliable, no statistical methodology can verifiably solve the problem of unavailable data.

rights cases in Dallas are a general history of discrimination; restricted access to the process of slating candidates by the Citizens Charter Association, given its record of electoral success; and the high cost of citywide campaigning. Based on their findings, the courts determined that the at-large election system in Dallas unconstitutionally diluted the voting strength of minorities. Major concerns for the DOJ and the courts were to maximize the number of minority districts and to determine the appropriate percentage of minority population to be included in each district in order to devise "safe" districts for electing minorities and yet avoid either "packing" or "cracking."

Given my argument that the federal courts blundered in prescribing a generic remedy for underrepresentation of minority groups, the consequences in Dallas of that mistake are considered in this chapter. Since the system-wide outcomes from a change in only one part of an election system cannot be measured by current social science methods, a qualitative and logical approach is used.

First, the positions of the federal government regarding the main themes in the court litigation are evaluated. The city's history of discrimination, as shown in chapter 3, was more complicated than courts were able to consider. This chapter examines the concerns of the courts over access to slating by the Citizens Charter Association and access to campaign contributions. Redistricting is also covered, as both the courts and the DOJ grappled with the complicated task of devising minority-dominant districts in Dallas.

The sixteen elections in Dallas from 1967 to 1997 are the subject of the second part of the chapter. Were there differences between results in the four at-large elections (1967–1973), the eight mixed-system elections (1975–1989), and the four single-member district elections (1991–1997)? What were the intended and unintended consequences of changes in election systems? In order to make these assessments, the chapter analyzes the number of minorities elected under the three election systems. A further question is explored: Did a change in election districts bring changes to other parts of the political system, specifically regarding the types of candidates and electoral competitiveness?

BALLOT ACCESS

A "test of proof" to determine discriminatory treatment in voting rights cases is ballot access. In *Smith* v. *Allwright* (1944) the Supreme Court ruled against the white primary in Texas, because nomination by the Democratic Party was tantamount to election. The courts in the Dallas voting rights cases were concerned as to whether racial and ethnic minorities had access to nomination by the CCA, which was effectively tantamount to election from 1931 to 1975.

The Texas white primary in partisan elections differed from City of Dallas nonpartisan elections. Texas law governing ballot access in state elections serves, in general, as a barrier to independent candidacies and third parties. In Dallas, ballot access is easy under city regulations. No candidate appears under a party or slating group label on the ballot; only the candidate's name is listed. Anyone who meets the specified qualifications for candidacy has equal access to a place on the ballot through self-nomination, by filing a petition. The position on the ballot is by lot.[2]

Political parties have no basis in the U.S. Constitution; they developed extra-constitutionally. Similarly slating groups have no basis in the Dallas City Charter; they developed extra-legally.[3] Rules and regulations regarding political parties were gradually incorporated into state law in Texas; but no city rules and regulations govern nominations by slating groups, and the city's charter specifically prohibits partisan elections.

While CCA support may have been important for a successful candidacy under the at-large election system, nomination for the city council has been by petition under all three election systems—at-large, mixed, and single-member district. Anyone who wishes to become a candidate files an application for a place on the ballot, which is accompanied by a petition signed by a modest number of qualified voters who reside in the candidate's district.[4] The required number of signatures changed in 1983, but the basic procedure for the three election systems has largely remained the same.

Dominance of the Citizens Charter Association

Slating by the CCA concerned the courts, because the CCA dominated elections for more than four decades. During the CCA era, from 1931 to 1977, political contests were generally between the "ins," who were conservative Democrats and powerful business leaders allied with the CCA, and the "outs," who were the minorities, liberals, Republicans, and assorted dissidents.

2. A candidate for Dallas City Council must:

Be a United States citizen;

Be 18 years of age or older on the first day that the new council member is sworn in;

Not be in arrears in the payment of taxes or other liabilities due the City of Dallas;

Have not been determined mentally incompetent by a final judgment of a court;

Have not been finally convicted of a felony from which the person has not been pardoned, or otherwise released from the resulting disabilities;

Have resided continuously in Texas for twelve months prior to the filing deadline;

Have resided continuously in the City Council district to be represented for six months prior to the election. ("City of Dallas Candidates Guide," January 8, 2002)

3. Political parties and slating groups are neither unconstitutional nor illegal. Both developed as political overlays to legal provisions.

4. From 1930 until 1983 the City of Dallas required candidates to submit signatures of 300 persons qualified to vote in their race. The city council in 1983 brought the city into compliance with state law, which required 25 signatures. Apparently previous city attorneys believed that the state law applied only to partisan elections, not to Dallas nonpartisan elections.

In two-party systems, few independents or third-party candidates win in national or state partisan elections. Similarly few independents would be expected to win in nonpartisan elections with strong slating groups. This was the case during the at-large period, when slating groups were active in Dallas.

From 1935 to 1975 the candidates slated by the CCA controlled the Dallas City Council. In 1971, however, after Erik Jonsson stepped down as mayor, populist Wes Wise defeated CCA candidate Avery Mays, and was reelected in 1973 and 1975. In 1975 independents picked up five of the eleven seats. And then the CCA lost control of the council in 1976, when Robert Folsom asked the group not to support him in the special election for mayor, which he won. In the next election, in April 1977, the CCA, for the first time since 1931, ran no slate in a regular city election.

If there is a candidate slating process, despite whether members of the minority group have been denied access to that process, it may be relevant to a Section 2 VRA claim. The courts, in finding the at-large system in Dallas to be discriminatory, relied heavily on the testimony that black candidates needed the support of the dominant CCA to win.

Differentiation needs to be made between "denied access" to the ballot or to the slating process and "denied slating" by a winning slating group. Did blacks and Hispanics in Dallas have equal access to a place on the ballot, with or without being named to a slate? Since there was a slating process, were they "denied access" to slating by the dominant group? If not, did the plaintiffs have valid objections to the minority candidates slated by the CCA?

Losing elections per se is not a basis for court challenge. Continuous success by a dominant political party—such as the Democratic Party in the South from the end of Reconstruction to the 1980s—has not been challenged. The successful record of the CCA slating group in the City of Dallas is analogous to one-party dominance in state and national elections.

Exclusion from CCA support solely on the basis of race is required for a claim under the Fifteenth Amendment and Section 2 of the VRA—not on the basis of partisan or ideological leanings or socioeconomic factors. Because the plaintiffs frame the questions, and blacks and Hispanics are protected groups under the VRA, they blamed the loss of elections in the era of CCA dominance and at-large elections on a claim of racial discrimination. But did racial minorities lose elections because of their race or for other reasons, such as ideological leanings?

From 1964 on, Texas blacks have consistently given the Democratic national ticket more than 90 percent of their vote.[5] The more conservative party, the Republican Party, carried Dallas County in all presidential elections from 1968 through 2000. Voting data for the 1972 presidential election and the

5. Chandler Davidson, *Race and Class in Texas Politics* (Princeton, N.J.: Princeton University Press, 1990), 44.

1971 city council election illustrate the ideological divide in voting in Dallas. In voting precincts that were more than 50 percent black, the Democratic presidential candidate (George McGovern) won, 70 percent to 29 percent, over the Republican candidate (Richard Nixon) in 1972. In twenty-two of the forty-six majority black precincts, McGovern carried the precinct by more than 90 percent of the vote.[6] (See Figure 6.1.)

In the 1971 council election those same majority-black precincts voted 30 percent for the populist, Wes Wise, 30 percent for the black, Al Lipscomb, and 27 percent for the conservative CCA candidate, Avery Mays. The combined vote of the populist candidate and the black candidate of 61 percent, and the 27 percent vote for the conservative CCA candidate,[7] roughly corresponds with the presidential vote for McGovern (70 percent) and for Nixon (29 percent) in the majority-black precincts.

Moreover, endorsement by a city's sole or dominant newspaper has not been a basis for a claim under the Fifteenth Amendment or the Voting Rights Act. The *Dallas Morning News* supported the CCA slates in the years prior to the demise of the CCA in 1977, and it has generally supported the more conservative candidates since then. *News* endorsement has correlated as effectively with victory in city council elections as did slating by the CCA. In the elections from 1977 to 1997, of the 104 contested races, the "success rate" of *News*-endorsed candidates was 80 percent. This compares to the figure used in testimony in *Lipscomb* v. *Wise* (1975) of an 85-percent success rate for CCA-endorsed candidates after 1959.

Several races, however, warrant further attention. The pattern of *News* support for candidates in the majority-black districts after the demise of the CCA shows that the business community (as represented by the CCA and the *News*) supported more conservative candidates than did the voters in those districts. Of the twenty-one races in which the *News*-endorsed candidates lost, fourteen were in minority-dominant districts. (See Table 6.1.)

In one instance (District 4 in 1991), the *News* endorsed a conservative black candidate, Lonnie Murphy, over the liberal white candidate, Larry Duncan, who won the district, and subsequently was reelected unopposed three more times.

6. The available racial classification data are based on census tracts, but to analyze voting data one must use voting units. Given the ecological fallacy, majority-black precincts provide the best data proximate to individual voting patterns. Karen F. Lentz correlated census data with precincts to identify the majority-black precincts.

7. The other 12 percent was divided among four minor candidates. The 1971 council election year and the 1972 presidential election were selected for three reasons: their proximity to an official census, the fact that they preceded the litigation, and because the CCA was still an active slating group. In addition to the usual white conservative, a "liberal" white and a black entered the 1971 race. Hence blacks in Dallas did vote for a liberal white.

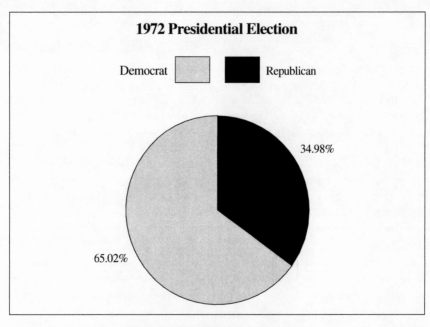

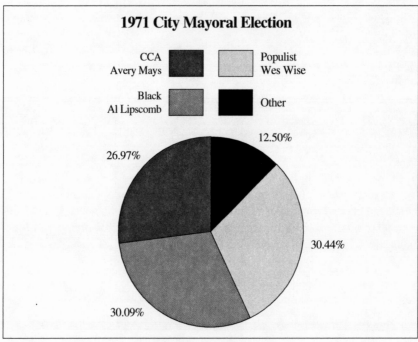

Figure 6.1. Vote in Majority Black Precincts Compared: 1971 City Council Election and 1972 U.S. Presidential Election

Table 6.1. Post-CCA *Dallas Morning News* Endorsements, by District

	1	2	3	4	5	6	7	8	9	10	11	12	13	14	15
1977	w	w	u		w	L	w	w	w	u	w				
1980		u	u	w	w	L	L	u	w	u	w				
1981	u	L	u	w	w	L	w	w	w	w	w				
1983	w	w	w	w	u	w	w	w	w	w	w				
1985	w	u	w	w	L	u	w	w	w	w	w				
1987	w	L	w	u	w	w	u	L	w	w	w				
1989	L	L	w	u	L	u	w	u	w	w	L				
1991	L	w	w	L	w	L	w	L	w	u	w	w	w	w	w
1993	u	w	w	w	w	L	w	w	w	u	w	w	L	w	
1995	w	u	u	u	L	w	w	w	w	u	u	u	u	w	w
1997	w	u	w	u	w	w	L	u	u	u	w	w	u	u	

Key: w—DMN endorsement wins; u—unopposed; L—DMN losses.

Most *News* "losses" were in District 6, which was 59 percent black in 1977. In that year, the *News* endorsed Osborn Caldwell over the black community worker, Juanita Craft, who won. In both 1980 and 1981 the *News* supported Mabel White over the winning Elsie Faye Heggins, but then endorsed Heggins in 1983. In 1991 the *News* endorsed Barbara Mallory, but Mattie Nash won; then, in 1993, it endorsed Nash, and Mallory won.

In District 8 the *News* endorsed Lipscomb in 1985 and 1995 but endorsed the more temperate candidates, Lonnie Murphy and Glenn Mills Jr., in 1987 and 1991. Lipscomb was unopposed in 1989 and 1997.[8]

These examples support the argument made by plaintiffs that, at least in certain areas of Dallas, minorities were unable to elect "candidates of their choice" during the era of at-large elections and CCA dominance. Had these candidates who were not endorsed by the CCA or by the *News* been running at large, they would likely have carried their districts, only to lose citywide. Thus single-member districts have enabled some candidates, who would have been the "outs" in CCA versus anti-CCA races, to be elected.

A plausible argument can be made that the real divide in Dallas is along political and socioeconomic, rather than racial, lines. After the implementation of single-member districts, few politicians emerged who could appeal to both middle-class blacks, and to blacks at the lower end of the economic scale, those who were attracted to the politics of confrontation.[9] This does not mean that race no longer matters.

The electoral success of the CCA and its bias toward candidates with conservative views should not have been a basis for the courts to determine at-large districts to be racially discriminatory.[10] The CCA represented the majority view in Dallas, as did the Democratic Party in Texas during the same period. Whether members of minority groups were *excluded* by the CCA from consideration as slated candidates is a separate matter, to be considered next.

Minority Access to Slating

A judicial standard for determining "effective access to the political process" is representation "by the minority-preferred candidate." Although the term

8. Lipscomb could not run in 1993 because of term limits.

9. Black officials, the former city manager John Ware and the former mayor Ron Kirk, each pointed out that class, not race, is the political divide in Dallas (interviews by the author with John Ware, December 16, 1997, and Ron Kirk, October 23, 1997).

10. In *Thornburg* v. *Gingles*, 478 U.S. 30 (1986), Justices White and O'Connor wrote concurring opinions in which they observed that when differing political or socioeconomic characteristics of whites and minorities explain racially polarized voting, Section 2 does not protect that cause of minority voter electoral failure. See Scott Yut, "Using Candidate Race to Define Minority-Preferred Candidates under Section 2 of the Voting Rights Act," *The University of Chicago Legal Forum,* (1995) 1995:579–580.

minority-preferred candidate has been defined differently in various court cases, it has generally been interpreted to mean a person of one's own race. But since the plaintiffs successfully argued that blacks who were elected under the at-large system—blacks elected with the support of the CCA—were not candidates "of their own choice," the role of blacks in the CCA needs to be examined.

In the 1960s changes in Dallas politics had begun to occur, even before Dallas Legal Services filed the Lipscomb suit that initiated the inexorable route to single-member districts. The business leadership tried for several years to incorporate minorities into the nomination process, perhaps because of pressure or the realistic response of Dallas's business establishment to changing times.

Prospective black candidates found themselves between Scylla and Charybdis. Blacks constituted a minority of the voters in the city, so they needed the support of the CCA to be successful. Blacks did not want to be identified with the CCA, however, as their larger agenda for gaining power was based on an insurgent strategy of attacking the CCA. But minorities could not agree on candidates, either to gain CCA endorsement or to field as consensus independents. This internal conflict in itself should have dispelled any premise of monolithicity, which sustained testimony on bloc voting data. The plaintiffs' position assumed that a black "minority-preferred" candidate, one not selected by the CCA for its slate, should be the one to represent a monolithic black interest.

In 1974 Tom Unis, who had served on the city council from 1957 to 1959, testified that when he had been president of the CCA (from 1965 to 1969), he had tried to encourage well-known blacks, including Pettis Norman, Bobby Hayes, and Frank Clarke, to run on the CCA slate. His organization, Unis said, was unsuccessful, because "there was a reluctance on the part of the black leadership to be identified with the CCA." Unis could recall a black on the CCA executive committee at least as early as 1969, and could not recall an instance in which the CCA had turned down a black who actively sought CCA endorsement. If the black community had agreed on a candidate while he had been president, Unis said, the CCA would have endorsed that individual.[11] The inability to agree on a candidate may have been a factor that caused blacks, in minority-dominant districts, to lose elections in those districts to whites.[12]

11. Quoted in the *Dallas Morning News,* December 16, 1974. However, no black was elected to membership in the Dallas Citizens Council until 1981, when Comer Cottrell was elected. Cottrell, president of Pro-Line Corporation, a cosmetics firm, had relocated to Oak Cliff from Los Angeles in 1980. He was a conservative businessman and a Republican.

12. In 1991 a white won in District 4, competing against eight blacks. In 2001 a white won in District 6 against five blacks. However, the "divided black vote" theory does not hold in 1991, because there was a runoff in which the white candidate won. In 2001 there was no runoff.

Similarly Hispanics did not unite behind candidates, although they did offer names to the CCA. For example, in 1973 the Dallas Coalition of Mexican-American Organizations suggested five names, including two former council candidates, Frank Hernandez and Manuel Almaguer. The CCA selected none of the Coalition's suggestions. For Place 9, the CCA ran Pedro Aguirre, who won. Manuel Almaguer, whom the Coalition had suggested to the CCA, ran as an Independent, but lost to CCA candidate Charles Terrell for Place 10.

In the 1977 special election to fill Place 10, some Hispanic leaders and members of the white business political power structure met in an effort to find a suitable consensus candidate. The hoped-for show of unanimity by Hispanics was broken when Ricardo Medrano declared his candidacy. In a split vote, a group of Hispanics decided to put attorney Joe Montemayor forward as its minority-coalition candidate.[13] Then, a third candidate, Rita Solon, entered the race. The Reverend S. M. Wright of the Interdenominational Minister's Alliance, a black who had pledged black support for a Hispanic candidate, was faced with a quandary. He could not determine which candidate was "minority-preferred."

Court testimony focused on the discriminatory effect of blacks and Hispanics needing CCA endorsement to win. Not to be overlooked is the record which shows that the same applied to whites. White council hopefuls were disappointed when they did not gain CCA backing, because the CCA chose to back black candidates. Forrest Smith, a tax attorney for Mobil, led the campaign for the Dallas bond program, a civic endeavor that historically had been a punched ticket for council candidacy. He had also worked within the ranks of the conservative Democrats and the CCA, and indicated his availability. Although high on the CCA's list of potential candidates in 1973, he failed to gain a spot on the ticket after a black, Joe Kirven, signaled his willingness to run.[14]

Similarly twenty years later, in 1995, and under a different election system, 14-1, Darrell Jordan also might have felt abandoned by the Dallas business leaders. He had invested heavily in civic endeavors and fit the CCA mold. But the key business leaders in the inner circle of the Dallas Citizens Council decided to support a black candidate, Ron Kirk, for mayor.

Race-Based Candidate Strategies

A number of candidate strategies were directly influenced by likely court action. White candidate Max Goldblatt, Hispanic candidate Frank P. Hernandez, and black candidates Al Lipscomb, Marvin Crenshaw, and Roy Williams

13. Ron Calhoun, *Dallas Times Herald,* September 8, 1977.
14. *Dallas Morning News,* December 22, 1975.

all pursued litigation to secure their political fortunes. They believed that they could win in single-member districts, when they did not win in at-large districts under a slating system.

The Hispanic and black plaintiffs, however, were not the "candidates of choice" in their own minority communities, nor was the white candidate the choice in his district.[15] Having failed in the political process, they each sought political power through the courts. Hernandez, an attorney who filed the court case on behalf of the Hispanic intervenors, ran three times and lost; black litigants Marvin Crenshaw and Roy Williams ran several times without winning—even in single-member districts. Al Lipscomb, another litigant, ran five times for the city council and lost, including in a single-member majority-black district, before he finally won a special election in 1984, on his sixth try.

These examples suggest that single-member districts did not answer the plaintiffs' complaints; only one plaintiff—Al Lipscomb—eventually was elected. When a reporter asked litigant Roy Williams if the 14-1 plan worked, Williams responded: "It was disappointing when neither of us were not [sic] elected to the City Council. The City of Dallas would be a different place had the two of us been elected."[16] The other party he referred to was Marvin Crenshaw.[17] More recently Crenshaw has said that the city council is not representative of the people "as long as those of us who were plaintiffs in the lawsuit . . . aren't able to be elected to the seats we created."[18] Since blacks defeated both Williams and Crenshaw in single-member districts, neither of them can argue that they were the "minority-preferred candidates."

Hispanics also pursued a strategy of playing to the courts to attain their goals of a larger council and single-member districts. According to a *News* political reporter, some Hispanics opposed putting forward a strong candidate in the special election for at-large Place 10 in 1977. Their reasoning was linked to the ongoing single-member redistricting suit, in which Hispanics contended that the 8-3 plan denied them representation. The *News* reporter's source noted that if a black-white-brown coalition succeeded in electing a Hispanic candidate, that victory would uphold U.S. District Judge Eldon Mahon's opinion that Hispanics could gain representation in city government through coalition politics.[19]

Candidates who were not litigants also entered council races, especially at-large races, to "prove" to the courts that a black could not win in an at-large

15. Anglo Max Goldblatt claimed that, with single-member districts, he would win District 7. When single-member districts were instituted in 1975, however, L. A. Murr, the CCA-backed candidate, defeated him.

16. Raymond Nowicki, *Black Economic Times,* August 16–22, 2001.

17. Crenshaw ran unsuccessfully for the city council seven times, including in the 2001 election.

18. Nora Lopez and Michael Saul, *Dallas Morning News,* June 7, 1999.

19. *Dallas Morning News,* September 7, 1977.

district. As noted earlier, Judge Buchmeyer opined in *Williams* v. *Dallas* (1990) that Marvin Robinson, who "was selected as the 'test case' for the black community," was "an *excellent choice.*" Robinson was a lawyer, a former school administrator, and a Xerox corporation executive, who had moved to Dallas in 1970. He entered the 1983 Place 9 at-large race as a first-time candidate with five other candidates. He had neither name recognition nor unified support in the black community. During the campaign Robinson indicated that his defeat could serve as grounds for a lawsuit to challenge the city's three at-large council seats. Robinson lost in the runoff to the plurality winner, Jerry Rucker. Jesse Jones, president of the Progressive Voters League, commented on Robinson's failure to incite enthusiasm among grass-roots minorities: "His lifestyle was the posture of a North Dallas type and that was kind of misunderstood in the black community."[20]

Rucker, a lawyer and president of Rucker Construction Company, was a conservative north Dallas Republican. His campaigning skills and his three terms on the city council were sufficient to attract groups wanting him to run for Congress, attorney general, and mayor, all of which he declined.[21] Robinson, a relative newcomer to Dallas, could hardly compete with Rucker's name identification, his incumbency, and his base of support.

In summary, the shortcomings of assumptions in voting rights cases of a monolithic black vote and of exclusion from the political process are evident. The CCA did not refuse to slate blacks based on race; rather, the CCA chose to slate only those blacks who adhered to its philosophy or were willing to work within the group to achieve CCA goals. The self-proclaimed leaders in the minority communities were unable to build coalitions to elect consensus candidates of "their choice."

CAMPAIGN FINANCE

Economic discrimination because of the high cost of campaigning citywide was another pillar used to support the allegation of discriminatory impact of at-large districts in the Dallas voting rights cases. The courts have not established that a candidate has a right to equal financial resources, even under the Fourteenth Amendment's "equal protection of the laws" clause. In *Williams* v. *Dallas* (1990), however, U.S. District Court Judge Buchmeyer held the 8-3 system invalid, in part, because "it is simply not possible for black or Hispanic candidates to raise—*from their communities*—the large amounts of money needed for an at-large City Council race." Judge Buchmeyer continued: "Therefore, the only way that a minority candidate could win an at-large race

20. *Dallas Times Herald,* April 17, 1983.
21. Skip Hollandsworth, "King Ruck," *D* magazine (July 1986), 13:52, 54.

in Dallas under the 8-3 system was to obtain substantial support from the white community." In the Judge's view, dependence on white donor support meant that minorities would not be able to choose their own candidates.[22]

The theory that racial minority candidates would raise their campaign funds from their own communities under a single-member-district system proved to be invalid in practice. Minority candidates continued to be financed by white donors who lived outside the candidates' districts. Names of prominent white members of the Dallas community listed in campaign finance reports of minority candidates often are the same names that appear as contributors to other endeavors in Dallas, such as the Dallas Symphony or the medical centers. According to a political consultant, "their political contributions are perceived as an extension of philanthropy."[23]

In 2001 a *News* analysis identified contributions to Dallas City Council candidates of $1,000, the maximum allowed by ordinance, by donors who lived outside the candidates' districts. A majority of contributions reported were to candidates in southern Dallas from donors in northern Dallas. The *News* found no southern donors who contributed to northern candidates.[24] Kathy Nealy, a black political consultant to the former mayor Kirk and to southern sector candidates, observed that, as campaigning has become more expensive, southern residents have come to accept the necessity for candidates to raise money "all over town."[25] Thus what was a key issue for the courts in determining at-large districts in Dallas to be discriminatory became a nonissue in practice, after the court-ordered institution of single-member districts.

The flow of funds from white donors not only to minority candidates but also to minority council members has a continuous history in Dallas politics, both before and after single-member districts. Council member Al Lipscomb reported that, after he won a seat in 1984 on his sixth try, money started to come in from developers and other business interests. Similarly, in the 1990s, business money was a means to help Mayor Ron Kirk maintain a business-minority-coalition hegemony during his administration.

A major difference in the support for black mayor Tom Bradley of Los Angeles and Dallas's Ron Kirk lay in the sources of financing. Funds for the Bradley campaigns in Los Angeles came "from Black professionals, West Side liberals, and associated politicians."[26] A black professional/liberal support

22. *Williams* v. *Dallas,* 734 F.Supp. 1317, 1327, 1382–1383 (N.D.Tex., March 28, 1990).

23. Carol Reed, *Dallas Times Herald,* February 20, 1983.

24. For example, in the 2001 contest between Elba Garcia and Steve Salazar, Salazar received about 29 percent of his money from ZIP codes that were wholly or partly within his district; Elba Garcia received about 18 percent from within her district (*Dallas Morning News,* April 17, 2001).

25. *Dallas Morning News,* April 24, 2001.

26. Raphael J. Sonenshein, *Politics in Black and White: Race and Power in Los Angeles* (Princeton, N.J.: Princeton University Press, 1993), 121.

base is largely absent in Dallas politics. Minorities in southern Dallas, and affluent white and minority business leaders, have developed a seemingly unlikely alliance—one based on voting as a business transaction. One group has the votes, needed by the business leadership, especially for big public-works referenda; the other has money, attractive to the vote brokers.[27]

The cost of campaigning has not been an issue solely for minorities. Until 1979, when a new city ordinance, passed in 1977, became effective, there had been no limits on campaign contributions. Wes Wise, who proposed limits on campaign contributions in 1974, acknowledged that his proposal was intended to cut the strength of the well-financed campaigns run by the CCA, in order to narrow the advantage they held over independent candidates. Of the eleven-member city council at the time, only Wise and Gary Weber had been elected without CCA backing.

This first campaign finance ordinance limited campaign contributions from an individual or a political committee to $500 and required financial disclosure of sources of contributions that exceeded $1,000. These limits were increased in 1984 to an individual contribution of $1,000 to a single-member district candidate, and $5,000 for the mayoral at-large position. A political action committee (PAC) may contribute up to $2,500 to a single-member district candidate and up to $10,000 to a candidate for mayor.

Successful black and Hispanic candidates, then, whether under at-large or under single-member districts, have received white business support. The demise of the CCA did not mean the end of major business support for candidates in Dallas City Council elections. The same individuals who supported CCA candidates continued to support candidates for the council. The major difference is that, when candidates were slated by the CCA, the voter knew which candidates the business leadership was backing. With single-member districts and the demise of slating groups, the interested voter would have to know which names to look for in the campaign finance reports filed by each candidate in the Office of the City Secretary. Thus information as to the support base of particular candidates is less transparent to voters than it was when candidates were slated.

REDISTRICTING

Drawing district lines, a nonissue in at-large elections, is crucially important with single-member districts. Not only must the people involved in the redistricting process attempt to balance competing political interests, but they also

27. Reporter Jim Schutze documents how the process works in "Absentee Minded," *Dallas Observer*, August 30, 2001. He points out that "for less than $12,000 paid to the right people, you can buy . . . just enough votes . . . to win you a $125 million taxpayer subsidy for your new sports arena or a $246 million city bond issue for your next big public-works construction job."

must respond to shifting legal requirements of the federal courts and the Department of Justice.

Population numbers, reported by the U.S. Census Bureau, controls redistricting nationwide. In recent years political stakes in the numbers have become so high that accuracy of the decennial census has itself become a political issue.[28]

Experiences in Dallas illustrate the dilemmas government bodies face because of changes in the law and the politics of redistricting. In Dallas, in 1975, Judge Eldon Mahon ordered that a combination of eight single-member and three at-large districts be used in the April 1, 1975, election. The district lines that had served only as residence districts, and were based on the 1970 census, were changed to election districts. Judge Mahon found that "the eight districts of the city's plan follow natural and rational boundaries and that no gerrymandering is present."[29] Equally important, Mahon found that the 8-3 plan maintained common community interests and kept the south Dallas area intact. This new 8-3 election system was used in the 1975 and 1977 regular city elections and in two special elections (Figure 6.2).

In August 1979 the Justice Department agreed to accept the Dallas City Council's proposed election plan, which had been drawn under court order, provided lines were redrawn to ensure black or Hispanic majorities of at least 79 percent in three districts. This requirement initiated the pattern of race-conscious districting that continues to the present day.

Juanita Craft, a black leader who had labored for decades in the NAACP civil rights movement, served on the city council from 1975 to 1979. She said it was wrong for the City of Dallas to lump a majority of the city's blacks and Hispanics into three districts. "We have all worked for years to make Dallas a place of community neighborhoods without regard to race," she said. "But now we are going in and cutting up those neighborhoods with redistricting plans that are trying to separate the races again."[30]

Redistricting after the 1980, 1990, and 2000 censuses continued the practice of drawing district lines that crossed natural boundaries and neighborhood boundaries in search of minority population to increase the safety margins for minority candidates and, especially, for minority incumbents[31] (see Figures

28. In 2001 Republicans generally urged that the initial raw count, or "headcount," be used for redistricting. Most Democrats and civil rights groups urged that the raw count be statistically adjusted to account for the estimated 3.4 million people who were missed, primarily minorities, the poor, and children. The Secretary of Commerce made the final call that the Census Bureau's unadjusted data would be used as the official redistricting data.

29. *Lipscomb* v. *Wise*, 399 F.Supp 782, 796 (1975).

30. *Dallas Morning News,* September 7, 1979.

31. The Dallas City Charter mandates that the council appoint a redistricting commission to recommend a districting plan to the council. The council has forty-five days to approve, or modify and approve, the plan. If the council does not act in forty-five days, the submitted plan becomes final.

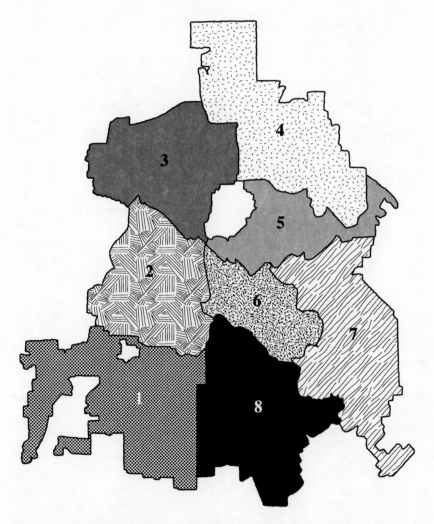

Figure 6.2. 1971 Dallas City Council Districts

6.3–6.5). The dilemmas the city council faced in each exercise in redistricting has been different because of conflicting and changing legal standards.

The city council elected in 1980 was faced with the inherently political task of producing the first districting plan not drawn under a court order. Dallas's population of 904,078, according to the 1980 census, meant that the ideal size for each of the eight districts was 113,010 persons. If seats were to be allocated according to population, blacks would have three, representing 29.4 percent of the city's residents; Hispanics would have one, representing the 9.2

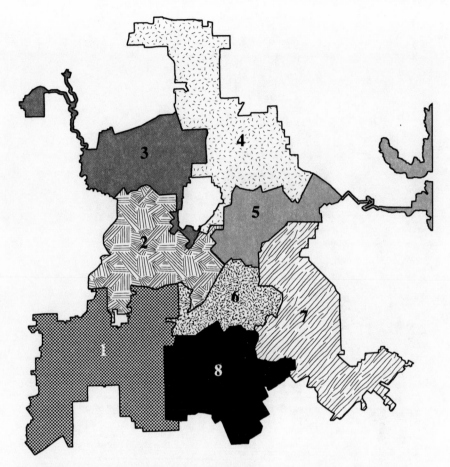

Figure 6.3. 1981 Dallas City Council Districts

percent Hispanic population. City Secretary Robert Sloan said that the staff
was unable to devise a fair districting plan that could guarantee three black
seats and a Hispanic seat on the council because of minority population residence patterns.

The problem was exacerbated by incumbent Elsie Faye Heggins's District
6, which could not exist as it was in 1970, because it had lost black population
to three neighboring districts. A second majority-black district, based on the
1970 census, was incumbent Fred Blair's District 8.

The three council members whose districts surrounded Districts 6 and 8
had experienced increases in black population. Nevertheless, they would not
allow a third black district to be carved from their districts, which now had a

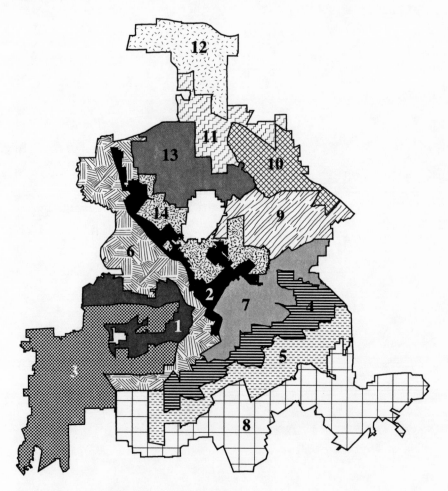

Figure 6.4. 1991 Dallas City Council Districts

combined total of 76,000 blacks—more than 25 percent of the city's blacks.[32] Other council members did not want to create the third black district from their districts, if it meant dividing their neighborhoods.

The demographics drove a wedge between minorities. Council member Ricardo Medrano opposed creation of the safe black district in the Heggins-Blair proposed plan, because it would make it "extremely difficult" for a Hispanic to be elected.[33] When the council turned down all plans for a third black

32. *Williams* v. *Dallas* at 1323. The three council members in the surrounding districts were Don Hicks (District 1), Max Goldblatt (District 7), and Ricardo Medrano (District 2).

33. Bill Turque, *Dallas Times Herald,* June 26, 1982.

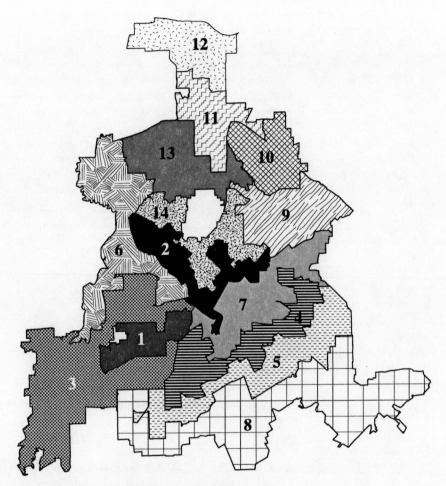

Figure 6.5. 2001 Dallas City Council Districts

seat, council members Heggins and Blair warned that Dallas would face a new federal lawsuit to strike down the current election system.[34] But the DOJ did approve the council's redistricting plan, despite complaints from minorities that the new boundaries would not permit a third black council member to be elected. No further lawsuits were filed until 1988.

By the late 1980s the Justice Department had adopted an aggressive role, and often would reject redistricting plans that did not maximize the number of minority districts. This caused government bodies to adopt districting plans

34. Henry Tatum, *Dallas Morning News,* June 26, 1982.

made up of irregularly shaped districts that snaked across terrain, so as to capture racial and language minority voters—sometimes block by block.

Voters had approved a 10-4-1 plan and had defeated a proposed 14-1 system, when the district court held a remedy hearing in the lawsuit that was filed in 1988, which challenged the 8-3 system. The judge commandeered the city's redistricting commission to draw a 14-1 plan for the court. Believing that the will of the voters should be given deference, the city council submitted two 10-4-1 plans to the court, along with the mandated 14-1 plan. The 10-4-1 plans each produced four predominantly black districts and three predominantly Hispanic districts. The 14-1 plan had five predominantly black districts and two predominantly Hispanic districts. The court rejected both 10-4-1 plans and ordered an election under the court's 14-1 plan.[35]

The city immediately submitted its two 10-4-1 plans to the DOJ for preclearance and appealed to the Fifth Circuit Court of Appeals, which stayed the district court's order to allow the city time to pursue preclearance of its legislative plan. When the DOJ rejected the 10-4-1 versions, the city prepared and submitted a 14-1 plan with four predominantly black districts and two predominantly Hispanic districts. The DOJ indicated that the 14-1 plan would probably need five black districts to obtain preclearance.

The city complied and carved out five majority-black districts. This necessitated, according to the city attorney, an "extreme level of gerrymandering." The amended plan was achieved by using computer-generated maps, color coded to show, block by block, the percentage of minority population. The result "was intricately carved districts in the most peculiar shapes."[36] Four of these racially gerrymandered districts are shown in Figure 6.6.[37] Districts 6 and 8 were majority black; District 2, Hispanic; and District 14, white. Preclearance was granted, and Dallas held its first election under the 14-1 plan on November 5, 1991.

In 1993 the legal environment changed dramatically. The Supreme Court recognized a racial gerrymander claim in *Shaw* v. *Reno* as a violation of the Fourteenth Amendment's "equal protection of the laws" clause. In a series of rulings that challenged redistricting maps after the *Shaw* decision, the Supreme Court restricted the DOJ's interpretation of its Section 5 power.[38] These cases established two broad principles for avoiding a charge of "racial gerrymander-

35. Analeslie Muncy, "Redistricting from Hell: The Dallas Experience," paper presented at the annual conference of the National Institute of Municipal Law Officers, San Diego, California, October 19, 1991.

36. Ibid.

37. The five districts drawn as black districts were Districts 4, 5, 6, 7, and 8.

38. *Shaw* v. *Reno*, 509 U.S. 630 (1993) and its progeny: *Miller* v. *Johnson,* 515 U.S. 900 (1995); *United States* v. *Hays,* 515 U.S. 737(1995); *Bush* v. *Vera,* 517 U.S. 952 (1996); *Shaw* v. *Hunt,* 517 U.S. 899 (1996) ("Shaw II"); and *Abrams* v. *Johnson,* 521 U.S. 74 (1997).

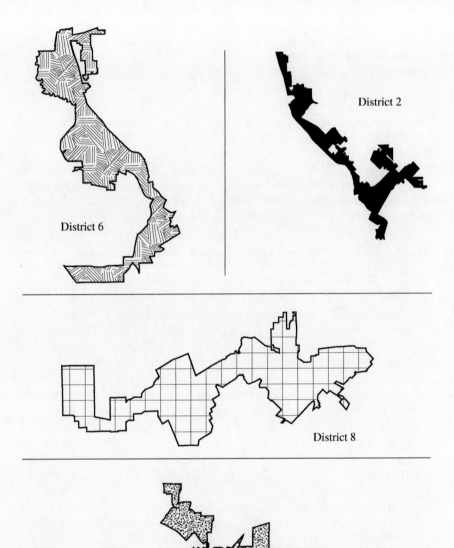

District 6

District 2

District 8

District 14

Figure 6.6. Four 1991 Gerrymandered Dallas City Council Districts

ing." Race cannot be the *predominant* consideration in drawing districts, unless a compelling reason can be shown. Second, if race is only one of many factors considered in drawing a district, then the legislative body need not meet the same constitutional standard under the Fourteenth Amendment's guarantee of equal protection that it would need to meet were race the predominant factor.

Following the 1990 census the Dallas redistricting commission had drawn bizarrely shaped minority districts to obtain preclearance; this plan created a dilemma for the 2001 redistricting commission. After *Shaw* v. *Reno* and its progeny had been decided by the Supreme Court in the mid-1990s, the city's 2001 redistricting commission had to find a balance between tilting toward the VRA's race-based protections in Section 2 (non-dilution) and Section 5 (non-retrogression) to obtain DOJ preclearance, on the one hand, and, on the other, tilting toward race neutrality to avoid potential lawsuits under the Fourteenth Amendment (prohibition of racial gerrymandering after *Shaw*).[39]

The Section 5 requirement that *changes* in voting rights had to be pre-cleared before they could become effective created a practical problem. It became necessary to measure the 2001 redistricting plan against the existing 1991 plan to determine whether the new plan would cause a retrogression in the political power of racial and language minorities. Yet the 1991 plan in itself was constitutionally suspect under the mid-1990s series of Supreme Court decisions that disallowed the use of race as the "predominant" factor in districting.

Districts drawn to maximize safe minority districts could not be changed if the change would cause "retrogression," and yet they had to be drawn so as to avoid a challenge that race was used as a predominant factor. A comparison of the geography of District 2 in the 1991 plan and the 2001 plan shows that the redistricting commission "smoothed" boundary lines to create a visual impression that minority voters were not captured block by block, as they had been in the two previous plans[40] (see Figure 6.7). In so doing, the commission hoped to avoid a charge of using race as the predominant factor.

The findings in Dallas presented in this chapter show the shortcomings in some of the assumptions in voting rights cases on which the remedy of single-member districts was based. These assumptions included, first, that minority candidates failed to win in citywide elections because of the lack of access by minority "candidates of choice" to CCA slating; and, second, with single-

---

39. *Shaw* v. *Reno*, 509 U.S. 630 (1993). The term *retrogression* refers to a reduction in the voting strength of a racial or ethnic group resulting from a redistricting plan or other change in election procedures, and is the primary test for evaluating a change under Section 5 of the Voting Rights Act.

40. These are the author's observations at public meetings of the Redistricting Commission. The U.S. Department of Justice subsequently precleared the redistricting plan of 2001.

1991   2001

Figure 6.7. Comparison of Dallas City Council District 2 in 1991 and 2001

member districts, racial minority candidates would be able to raise sufficient campaign funds from their own communities so as not to be obligated to white donors. After court-ordered single-member districts were instituted, the legal mandates requiring that district lines be drawn after each decennial census to comply with case law and with Justice Department requirements for preclearance became moving targets. In general, these legal mandates required that districts be drawn to provide "safe" council districts for minorities, and to protect incumbents, at the sacrifice of neighborhoods and communities of interest.

Considered next is the impact on election outcomes. To what extent did single-member districts increase the representation of minorities? Was there a change in the qualifications of candidates? Did elections become more or less competitive?

FACES AND PLACES

The only "circumstance" that Congress specifically identified in the Voting Rights Act to consider for a finding of minority vote dilution was the extent to which members of a protected class have been elected to office. This factor closely approaches contradiction of the VRA proviso that Section 2 does not establish "a right to have members of a protected class elected in numbers equal to their proportion in the population."

The 1982 amendments radically changed the VRA by moving the "effects" standard to the fore, replacing the "intent to discriminate" criterion. The phrase "an opportunity to elect candidates of their choice" also emerged from the 1982 Amendments to the VRA (Section 2b), and later from the 1986 Supreme Court decision in *Thornburg* v. *Gingles*.[41]

Parties opposing a results test argued that it would inevitably lead to a requirement for proportional representation of minority groups on elected bodies. This reasoning was valid, as "underrepresentation" has to be related to some standard that defines "representation." As a practical matter, and for lack of another standard, both the courts and the DOJ have used seats-in-proportion-to-population as the standard for evaluating redistricting plans.

Opponents of using the results test as the standard of measurement for fair representation also argued that devising seats in the same proportion as minorities in a population would be divisive in local communities, by emphasizing the role of race in politics. Political scientist Rory A. Austin found that "the use of district elections to ensure minority representation carries the undesirable effect of increased polarization." In contrast, factors other than race, such as partisanship, unite black and white voters in at-large elections.[42]

In the 1970s, in Dallas, a flurry of race cards was played in council elections. However, busing, particularly in 1977, became the only major citywide campaign issue. More frequently the complaints were of "racist" campaign literature. For example, during the intense mayoral race between Gary Weber and Robert Folsom in a special election in 1976, a Folsom flyer urged "all white voters" to go to the polls because "your vote for Bob Folsom is vitally important to override the huge black bloc vote expected this Saturday."[43]

In the 1990s the existence of single-member districts spawned numerous claims that the districts drawn as minority districts should be reserved for minority candidates. This view did not diminish in the new decade. In the May 2001 election, race surfaced in the ad campaigns in two predominantly minority districts in which white candidates were running.

In the contest for the District 4 seat against white candidate Larry Duncan, a supporter of black council member Maxine Thornton-Reese told listeners to a radio ad: "Remember to vote for the person who looks like you." William Blair Jr., the radio ad spokesman and publisher of the *Elite News,* said that the ad had an obvious message: "Blacks should vote for a black person." Ed Oakley, a white running for the mostly black West Dallas District 6, had four opponents, all of whom were black; he faced similar campaign radio ads. Roy Williams, a black candidate, called Oakley's candidacy "nothing but a ploy by the white business community and this city's establishment to take power from African-Americans and Hispanics."[44]

41. *Thornburg* v. *Gingles*, 478 U.S. 30 (1986).
42. Rory A. Austin, "Measuring the Effects of Local Electoral Structures," paper presented at the annual meeting of the American Political Science Association, Boston, 1998.
43. Ron Calhoun, *Dallas Times Herald,* June 2, 1976.
44. Dave Michaels and Gromer Jeffers Jr., *Dallas Morning News,* May 4, 2001.

In assuming a monolithic black interest that could only be represented by black elected officials, and in requiring single-member districts to ensure the election of a proportionate number of minorities, the courts and the DOJ reinforced a racially divisive view of representation and fostered the notion of a "right" to be elected based on race.

Changes from one census to the next in proportionate racial shares of total city population also have intensified racial divisiveness over redistricting. In 1991 increases in minority population pressured the redistricting commission to create more "safe districts" for minority candidates. In 2001 the decline in the black share and the increase in the Hispanic share of the city's total population drove the redistricting effort. A struggle for power ensued as blacks tried to save their former number of safe seats, and Hispanics tried to increase their number of safe Hispanic seats.[45] However, the Hispanic population was not concentrated sufficiently to enable the redistricting commission to draw compact districts for Hispanics in proportion to their share of the city's total population.

The City Project Director advised the commission that staff was "not able to meet the objective of five African American districts and three Hispanic districts with the requested [population] percentages."[46] Similarly a coalition that proposed a map on behalf of a majority of the black commission members was unable to "save" five districts. The final recommendation of the redistricting commission, adopted by the Dallas City Council and later approved by the DOJ, consisted of four districts that were 53 to 59 percent black and three districts that were 71 to 80 percent Hispanic.[47]

Minority Election Successes

The court-preferred remedy of single-member districts as a replacement for at-large districts was intended to lead to the election of more blacks to public office and, after the 1982 VRA Amendments, to more Hispanics being elected. The predominant view, based on data gathered in the 1970s and early 1980s, attributed the dramatic increase in the number of blacks elected to office nationwide to changes to single-member districts.

More recent research, using varied methodologies and later data, suggests that at-large elections no longer have the effect of underrepresenting minorities. Using 1988 data, Susan Welch found that at-large elections represent blacks much better than a decade ago, although there is still a small gap

45. This author served as a member of the 2001 Dallas Redistricting Commission.

46. Approved Minutes of the Called Meeting, City of Dallas Redistricting Commission, May 22, 2001.

47. The population percentage used for Hispanics took into account citizen-eligible voting-age population figures.

between representation afforded by at-large and by district systems, while the impact of local election structures on Hispanic representation is less clear-cut and seems to vary from region to region.[48] A study four years later confirmed Welch's finding that the differences between district and at-large election systems are not as well defined as earlier studies suggest. The form of electoral system was found to be "an interactive variable, serving to enhance or depress minority representation given the presence of such other variables as residential segregation, percentage of minority population, and income ratios."[49]

An increase in the number of blacks elected to office in Dallas followed a change from at-large to single-member districts.

Table 6.2 shows the numbers of minorities elected under the at-large, mixed, and single-member district systems. Blacks held 11 percent of the seats under the at-large system, 18 percent under the mixed 8-3 system, and 30 percent of the seats under the 14-1 system. If single-member seats and at-large seats are considered separately under the 8-3 and 14-1 systems, the figures for minorities are 25 percent and 29 percent, respectively, of the single-member district seats. The percentage seat gain for minorities with the change from eight to fourteen single-member seats was not as great as blacks had argued and as the courts had assumed would occur, especially if one considers that the single-member election districts were racially gerrymandered to create "safe" seats.

In comparing minority seats under the three different electoral systems in Dallas, Table 6.2 shows that as early as 1969 minorities were not excluded from at-large councils, and certain residence districts were considered to be "minority seats." In the last three elections under the at-large system (1969, 1971, and 1973), and with CCA slating, Place 8 was a black seat and Place 9 was a Hispanic seat on the council, a combined minority representation of 14 percent of the seats on each of those three councils.

In the eight elections under the 8-3 system from 1975 to 1989, blacks consistently won two single-member district seats, Districts 6 and 8, or 25 percent of the single-member council seats. Hispanics won only two single-member seats and one at-large seat, or 3 percent of the total of eighty-eight seats during that period. Under 14-1, Hispanics consistently have won two seats (Districts 1 and 2), or 14 percent of the seats; and blacks have consistently won four seats (Districts 5, 6, 7, and 8), or 29 percent of the seats. If one considers the single

48. Susan Welch, "The Impact of At-Large Elections on the Representation of Blacks and Hispanics," *Journal of Politics* (November 1990), 52:1050–1076. Further, her findings indicate that Hispanics appear to do better in mixed systems than in either single-member districts or at-large systems, while mixed systems have not improved black representation to the same degree as at-large systems.

49. J. L. Polinard, Robert D. Wrinkle, Tomas Longoria, and Norman E. Binder, *Electoral Structure and Urban Policy: The Impact on Mexican American Communities* (Armonk, N.Y.: M. E. Sharpe, 1994), 60.

Table 6.2. Council Seats Held by Race

Districts	1	2	3	4	5	6	7	8	9	10	11	12	13	14	15
At Large															
1967	W	W	W	W	W	W	W	W	W	W[b]	B[b]				
1969	W	W	W	W	W	W	W	B	H	W	W				
1971	W	W	W	W	W	W	W	B	H	W	W				
1973	W	W	W	W	W	B	W	B	H	W	W				
Mixed 8-3															
1975	W	W	W	W	W	B	W	B	W[c]	W[c]	W[c]				
1977	W	H	W	W	W	B	W	B	W[c]	W[c]	W[c]				
1980[a]	W	H	W	W	W	B	W	B	W[c]	W[c]	W[c]				
1981	W	W	W	W	W	B	W	B	W[c]	W[c]	W[c]				
1983	W	W	W	W	W	B	W	B	W[c]	W[c]	W[c]				
1985	W	W	W	W	W	B	W	B	W[c]	W[c]	W[c]				
1987	W	W	W	W	W	B	W	B	W[c]	H[c]	W[c]				
1989	W	W	W	W	W	B	W	B	W[c]	W[c]	W[c]				
Single Member 14-1															
1991	H	H	W	W	B	B	B	B	W	W	W	W	W	W	W[c]
1993	H	H	W	W	B	B	B	B	W	W	W	W	W	W	W[c]
1995	H	H	W	W	B	B	B	B	W	W	W	W	W	W	B[c]
1997	H	H	W	W	B	B	B	B	W	W	W	W	W	W	B[c]

Key: W—white; B—black; H—Hispanic.
[a] The 1979 election was postponed due to litigation.
[b] Appointed under new charter adopted in 1968.
[c] At large seats.
Source: Official Election Returns, City of Dallas

at-large seat under the 14-1 system (that of mayor), whites won 50 percent of the seats and blacks won 50 percent. However, the mayoral position has been a four-year term since 1991, so only two mayors were elected during the period.

The consistent wins in racially gerrymandered single-member districts confirm that the strategy pursued by the federal courts and the DOJ did increase the number of blacks and Hispanics elected to the Dallas City Council. The two at-large wins by minorities, and the two minority wins in a single-member district not drawn as a safe minority district, indicate that racial attitudes in Dallas have not precluded crossover voting and coalition building as successful strategies.

Simple numerical comparisons of minority seats under the different election systems do not take into account either demographic or attitudinal changes in Dallas over the thirty-year period. Table 6.3 shows, by race, the decennial census figures, which are the bases for redistricting, and the number of seats each racial or ethnic group would have had if seats had been allocated proportionately to each group's share of the total population. Table 6.3 also shows the actual seats held by racial groups, before and after the institution of single-member election districts in 1975.

Even though census figures for Hispanics are either unavailable or not comparable for all the census years, one can plausibly conclude that the population under "other" would be large enough that any seats unassigned after proportionate allocation to whites and blacks could be claimed as Hispanic.[50]

Under slating and at-large elections, blacks were "underrepresented," by one seat, from their proportionate share of seats; they were also short by one seat after 1975, the first election to use the former residence districts as election districts, and prior to attempts to draw safe minority districts. In 1983 and 1993, the first elections after the use of decennial census data for redistricting to correct minority underrepresentation, blacks were also "underrepresented" by one seat until 1991, when they held seats at least in proportion to or in excess of their population share.

The Supreme Court's "one person, one vote" legal standard is based on using total population figures in crafting districts that are equal in population. Interpretative law, however, is mixed as to whether total population or voting-age population or citizen voting-age population should be used to determine the population size needed in a district as a practical matter for a protected minority group to be able to elect a candidate of its choice.

50. The census data are suspect for Hispanics, as the Spanish origin column in the 1970 census and the 1980 census is not part of the racial groups. In the 1990 census most Spanish/Hispanic origin groups are reported under "Other." In the 2000 census, for the first time, persons who identified themselves as Hispanic also answered the race question, as Hispanic or Latino were not considered a race category. Also, for the first time in the 2000 census, a multiracial category was added, which concerned protected racial groups, depending on the size of the group, in bringing a claim under the Voting Rights Act. Consequently data in different censuses are not comparable.

Table 6.3. Comparison of Number of Council Seats Proportionate to Population with Actual Seats Held by Race/Ethnicity (by percentage)

1960

	Census Population	%	Seats/Pop.	1967	1969	1971
White	548,473	80.70%	9	10 (90.91%)	9 (81.82%)	9 (81.82%)
Black	129,249	19.02	2	1 (9.09)	1 (9.09)	1 (9.09)
Other	1,962	0.29	0	0 (0.00)	1 (9.09)	1 (9.09)
Total	679,684		11	11	11	11

1970

	Census Population	%	Seats/Pop.	1973	1975	1977	1980	1981
White	626,247	74.16%	8	8 (72.73%)	9 (81.82%)	8 (72.73%)	8 (72.73%)	9 (81.82%)
Black	210,238	24.90	3	2 (18.18)	2 (18.18)	2 (18.18)	2 (18.18)	2 (18.18)
Other	7,916	0.94	0	1 (9.09)	0 (0.00)	1 (9.09)	1 (9.09)	0 (0.00)
Total	844,401		11	11	11	11	11	11

1980

	Census Population	%	Seats/Pop.	1983	1985	1987	1980	1991
White	555,270	61.42%	7	9 (81.82%)	9 (81.82%)	8 (72.73%)	9 (81.82%)	9 (60.00%)
Black	265,594	29.38	3	2 (18.18)	2 (18.18)	2 (18.18)	2 (18.18)	4 (26.67)
Other	83,214	9.20	1	0 (0.00)	0 (0.00)	1 (9.09)	0 (0.00)	2 (13.33)
Total	904,078		11	11	11	11	11	15

1990

	Census Population	%	Seats/Pop.	1993	1995	1997
White	479,980	47.65%	7	9 (60.00%)	8 (53.33%)	8 (53.33%)
Black	290,882	28.88	4	4 (26.67)	5 (33.33)	5 (33.33)
Hispanic	210,240	20.87	3	2 (13.33)	2 (13.33)	2 (13.33)
Other	25,775	2.56	0			
Total	1,007,338		14	15	15	15

Note: All seats listed in "Other" were held by Hispanics.

Proportionate-to-population seat conclusions would change, if based on "voting-age population" or "citizen voting-age population," rather than on total population. Dallas Hispanics have a higher proportion of noncitizens and a lower proportion of age-eligible citizens than do blacks and whites. Using 1990 census figures and the 1993 number of council seats, blacks were 30 percent of the Dallas population, 20 percent of the voting-age population, and held 29 percent of the council single-member seats. Hispanics constituted 21 percent of the Dallas population, 13 percent of the voting age population, and held 14 percent of the council seats.

The 1960 census data, on which the 1967 at-large election (the first election covered in this study) was based, show that had the seats been proportionate to total population in Dallas, blacks should have held two seats, rather than one, and whites nine seats, rather than ten.

The 1990 census data, on which the 14-1 single-member districts are based, show that had the seats been proportionate to total population, blacks should have held four seats, Hispanics three, and whites seven. In all four elections from 1991 to 1997 blacks held four seats, Hispanics two, and whites eight. Five districts were drawn as majority-black districts, two as majority-Hispanic, and six as majority-white. One district did not have a majority of a racial or ethnic group. The redistricting commission in 1990 was unable to draw the third majority-Hispanic district because of the dispersed residence patterns of the Hispanic population.

Contrary to the courts' assumptions that blacks vote as a bloc and whites vote as a bloc, and that a minority candidate always loses in citywide races, a black was elected mayor to two four-year terms in 1995 and 1999. Nor was the monolithic black vote theory confirmed in District 4, drawn as a majority-black district. A white was elected to the District 4 seat for the maximum four two-year terms, beginning in 1991.

Increases in elected minorities that might have occurred because of changing demographics, changing attitudes, and emphasis on coalition building, had the city's political system not been disrupted by court-ordered single-member districting, cannot reasonably be tested. Clearly, however, neighborhood-based, rather than race-based, districting has been a top priority for many citizens, including minorities, despite that crucial decision by the courts.

During the public hearings held by the 2001 Dallas Redistricting Commission, citizens of all races testified that they did not care about the color of the skin but, rather, wanted someone who would represent their neighborhoods and their issues. The commission was repeatedly urged not to split neighborhoods so as to draw minority districts, and to make whole again neighborhoods divided in the 1991 redistricting.

Nevertheless, because of case law and DOJ preclearance requirements, the 2001 Redistricting Commission focused most of its attention on drawing "safe" minority districts and avoiding "retrogression," while at the same time taking care not to use race as the "predominant" factor.[51] A major dilemma was to craft safe Hispanic districts, containing a minority population of about 80 percent, in order to compensate for low voting-age population and yet avoid rejection of a plan because of "packing."

Candidate Characteristics

Other issues related to representation are more subtle than counting the number of individuals of a particular race elected to a city council before and after a change in districting. Did court-forced changes in districting result in different types of candidates elected to office—candidates with different motivations, backgrounds, and credentials?

Max Weber distinguished between persons involved in politics on a marginal basis, as an avocation, and persons who either "live for" or "live off" politics and for whom politics is a vocation or a "calling."[52] Most candidates sponsored by the CCA seemed, in Weberian terms, to have been involved in politics as an avocation. They were civic leaders, whose civic and business interests were mutually reinforcing. Their civic contributions were premised on building Dallas, which redounded to benefit their private businesses. The characteristics of CCA candidates, in fact, were such that some candidates continued to be referred to as "in the CCA mold" after the CCA's demise. Typical of the "CCA mold" was Robert Folsom, a developer who lived in north Dallas and was drafted to serve. He told an Oak Cliff Republican Club that he had "absolutely no political ambitions." Having had a successful career, he continued: "Dallas has been good to me. I simply want to put back in some things I took out."[53]

Motivations of "nonpolitical" candidates, who seek office as a civic obligation, differ from the motivations of those who seek to establish careers in politics or those who run for reasons of self-aggrandizement, such as public recognition or political and perhaps derivative economic power in the community.

An evident change in Dallas politics, with the demise of slating groups for recruiting and supporting candidates, has been the election of "politicians," rather than "citizen-legislators." Candidates who self-select and develop their own candidate-oriented campaign organizations are often ones who "live for" and "live off" politics. Persons enamored with being players in the game of politics consider their job to be full-time and spend more time in the arena than those who view their office as an avocation and a community service.

51. Protecting incumbents did not receive much attention during commission deliberations, because it was adopted as a criterion at the outset.

52. "Politics as a Vocation," *Max Weber: Essays in Sociology,* trans. and ed. H. H. Gerth and C. Wright Mills (New York: Oxford University Press, 1958), 77–128.

53. *Dallas Morning News,* March 5, 1976.

A few candidates in Dallas have run to register a personal opinion or to seek attention. From 1967 to 1997 twenty candidates ran three or more times without being elected. Five of these "perennials" were white, seven were black, and eight were Hispanic. Another motivation, evident during the voting rights litigation in Dallas, was to run, expecting to lose, as a strategy to influence courts.

With one exception, all the members of the Dallas City Council who have resigned from the council to run for another political office, or who have run for another office after their tenure on the council, have done so in recent years, after single-member districts.

Three mayors resigned their positions to run for Congress: Earle Cabell in 1964, Wes Wise in 1976, and Ron Kirk in 2001. Cabell won and served one term before being ousted by Alan Steelman; Wise lost in the Democratic primary; and Kirk lost his bid in 2002 for election to the U.S. Senate. Council members who ran for Congress after serving on the council included Glenn Box, who lost in the Republican primary in 1995; Lucy Patterson, who lost in the Republican primary in 1982; and Donna Halstead, who lost her race for the U.S. Senate in 1996.

Except for Steve Bartlett, who had served as U.S. Congressman, no elected council members held prior elective office. Only Ron Kirk, who was appointed as Secretary of State of Texas by Governor Ann Richards, had prior experience in statewide office.

Another meaningful change under single-member districts has been in the employment backgrounds of individuals elected to the city council (Table 6.4). Under at-large councils from 1967 to 1973, more than half the council members were engaged in business, many with executive experience. Businessmen continued to dominate councils under the mixed system from 1975 to 1989.

Under the 14-1 single-member district system, the change in backgrounds has been striking. Since 1991 about half the council members have either been attorneys or in a group comprised of homemakers, civic volunteers, or unem-

Table 6.4. Council Member Occupations by Election System (by percentage)

	At-Large	Mixed	14-1
Business experience			
(large & small business, real estate, investments)	60	56	15
Legal experience			
(attorneys)	14	13	23
Other employment experience	14	18	43
(public relations, government, education)			
Other experience	12	14	20
(homemaker, volunteer, unemployed)			

ployed members. Another 43 percent bring a variety of other employment experiences to the council, such as communications/public relations, education, medicine, and government service. The number of members in business dropped to 15 percent.

In contrast, in the 105th Congress (1997), the number of businesspeople outnumbered lawyers in the House for the first time since the *Congressional Quarterly* began to keep records in 1953 of members' occupations.[54] In state legislatures nationwide in 1993, more than a third of the legislators were lawyers or other professionals and nearly a third were in business occupations.[55]

The low percentage of lawyers during Dallas's at-large system and CCA slating could be the result of law and accounting firms not being invited into the Dallas Citizens Council until the 1980s.[56] In the CCA years the individuals who served on the city council had the means to do so. Prior civic service and success in one's business or profession were the sine qua non for selection. Financial independence and the confidence bred by success made council members more naturally secure than those who have sought the financial benefits of power in recent years.

The path to elected office also changed. Most CCA candidates were citizens who had served as board chairs of community organizations, such as the United Way and the Chamber of Commerce. After 14-1, service on the city's boards and commissions has been the dominant "career route" for election to the city council.

Before 14-1, with few exceptions, mayors had been self-employed or independently wealthy, which helped in a job that paid $50 per meeting until January 2002.[57] One exception was Wes Wise, mayor from 1971 to 1976. Developer Trammell Crow provided him with a job at the World Trade Center as vice president of international relations at $22,000 a year.[58] The first two mayors elected under the 14-1 system, Steve Bartlett and Ron Kirk, were politicians; both received financial support through business or professional opportunities. Ron Kirk stepped down as Texas Secretary of State to run for mayor. In January 1995 he joined the law firm of Gardere, Wynne, and Sewell, one of the city's large law firms, as a partner at a salary of $227,000.[59]

54. Allan Freedman, "Lawyers Take a Back Seat in the 105th Congress," *Congressional Quarterly* (January 4, 1997), 27.
55. Virginia Gray and Herbert Jacob, *Politics in the American States: A Comparative Analysis,* 6th ed. (Washington, D.C.: CQ Press, 1996), 174.
56. When Mike Boone, a co-founder and partner at Dallas's second-largest law firm, assumed office in January 2001, he was the first attorney to serve as president of the Dallas Citizens Council.
57. By referendum in May 2001, council pay was increased to $37,500 (mayor, $60,000), effective January 2002.
58. *Dallas Morning News,* March 30, 1975.
59. Patricia Kilday Hart, "Mr. Happy Man Goes to Washington," *Texas Monthly* (August 2002), 30:100.

By the 1980s, with single-member districts, many of those living in Dallas had become dismayed by the quality of candidates for Dallas City Council. The lists included perennial candidates, unemployed activists, and parochial interest advocates. Rarely did professionals or leaders experienced in large organizations enter the fray in single-member districts. In 1987 political analyst Carolyn Barta suggested a reason: broad-based potential candidates with management backgrounds do not wish to spend the time, suffer the hassle, or endure the poor image of the city council.[60] Moreover, broad-based candidates have difficulty winning in single-member districts dominated by parochial interests.

In the black communities, black candidates successful in single-member districts have had, for the most part, different styles from those who ran at large. Former at-large, CCA-supported council member George Allen stressed the importance of having someone on the council who could carry influence with the city's business leadership. Tony Davis, president of the Pylon Salesmanship Club, a group of black businessmen, concurred: "I didn't see Lipscomb on the horizon. We prefer someone who will work with the council to get things done . . . it doesn't make you a leader to stand up and talk about what is wrong."[61]

The accommodationist approach of George Allen and Juanita Craft during their service on the council in the 1970s contrasted markedly with the race-conscious styles of Elsie Faye Heggins, Al Lipscomb, and Dianne Ragsdale in the 1980s. This change was partly a reflection of altered circumstances. At the national level the new members of Congress, such as William Clay, Shirley Chisholm, and Louis Stokes, who formed the Congressional Black Caucus in 1971, "incorporated the assertive, race-conscious style of the civil rights activist into their congressional behavior," and encountered senior colleagues "whose political circumstances strongly discouraged race-conscious stridency."[62]

Candidates of both the race-conscious style and the deracialized style have run in minority districts in Dallas in the past decade. These divergent perspectives characterized the 1993 race between Charlotte Mayes, who ran as a conciliation candidate, and Diane Ragsdale, who claimed to be the "minority-preferred" candidate.[63]

60. *Dallas Morning News,* February 23, 1987.

61. *Dallas Times Herald,* August 13, 1976.

62. Robert Singh, *The Congressional Black Caucus: Racial Politics in the U.S. Congress* (Thousand Oaks, Calif.: Sage, 1998), 54–55.

63. Mayes won a regular election and a runoff in 1991 against Ragsdale and then survived a Ragsdale-instigated recall election in 1992, a first for the city. Mayes, a customer service representative for American Telephone & Telegraph Company, campaigned as a candidate of conciliation. Ragsdale claimed to be the "minority-preferred" candidate and alleged that Mayes was a token black candidate fielded by the white establishment.

In fact, in 1991 there were four runoffs in predominantly minority districts; in one, a white was one of the candidates. Political consultant Lorlee Bartos observed that in the other three races the contest was between a black urban professional and an old-time black ward politician.[64] This division within Dallas's black community is, in part, between newcomers who have come to Dallas with companies relocating to the area and blacks who grew up in Dallas's segregated neighborhoods. The plaintiffs in districting litigation usually represented the latter group.

In sum, the change from an at-large election system to single-member districts in Dallas resulted in candidates with far different motivations, backgrounds, credentials, and, in some instances, style than was the case formerly.

Electoral Competitiveness

In the United States a presumption exists that healthy democratic political systems have competitive elections. Among the indicators of competitiveness are the pool of candidates, the percentage of seats contested, the margin of victory, and the voter turnout.

In Dallas the number of candidates running for a seat on the city council has not changed significantly. Under each of the three election systems, the number of candidates per seat has averaged three. With the demise of the slating group that dominated electoral success for so long, a proliferation of candidates expecting to win in single-member districts could be anticipated. However, there were fewer candidates (fifty-eight) in the two elections following the introduction of single-member districting (1975 and 1977) than candidates (seventy-one) in the two elections preceding single-member districts (1971 and 1973). The size of the council remained constant at eleven seats.

Minorities cannot be expected to hold seats proportionate to their population if they do not run for office. The size of the candidate pool is therefore a factor in analyses of election trends. The success rates, or "wins" in proportion to the number of candidacies, were virtually identical under all three districting election systems: 35 percent, 34 percent, and 36 percent, respectively, under at-large, mixed (8-3), and single-member (14-1) district systems (Table 6.5). When the success rates are disaggregated by race, whites have a higher percentage of wins relative to candidacies than do either blacks or Hispanics. The success rate of black women has been approximately equal to that of white men since 1975. The comparatively low success rate of black men is because of a greater than average number of black male candidates who have run for seats that blacks are most likely to win, and not because they have lost to white candidates.

Competitiveness can also be viewed as the percentage of districts with

64. *Dallas Morning News,* November 12, 1991.

Table 6.5. Election Success Rate of Candidacies by Race

	White	Black	Hispanic	n/a	Total
1967–1973					
Candidates	79	22	8	10	119
Elected	35	4	3		42
Success	44.30%	18.18%	37.50%		35.29%
1975–1989					
Candidates	178	66	11	3	258
Elected	69	16	3		88
Success	38.76%	24.24%	27.27%		34.11%
1991–1997					
Candidates	76	65	21		162
Elected	33	17	8		58
Success	43.42%	26.15%	38.10%		35.80%

contested races. During the era of CCA dominance under the at-large system, more seats were contested and fewer candidates polled less than 15 percent of the vote than under either the 8-3 or 14-1 district systems. This may be explained by the fact that the CCA candidates were actively challenged in that system by other organized candidate groups and by independents (Table 6.6).

Of the 188 seats in sixteen elections from 1967 through 1997, 39, or 21 percent, were uncontested. Under the at-large, the mixed, and the single-member district systems, the percentages were, respectively, 17 percent, 20 percent, and 24 percent. Fewer minority seats, however, have been uncontested under single-member districting (10 percent in 8-3 and 8 percent in 14-1) than white seats (21 percent in 8-3 and 31 percent in 14-1).

With single-member districts, the number of candidates who polled less than 15 percent of the vote, referred to as "non-serious" candidates, has increased: 26 percent under at-large, 40 percent under 8-3, and 35 percent under 14-1. This finding is counterintuitive, since fewer seats have been contested and because single-member districts were intended to provide low-budget, parochial-interest candidates opportunities to win. The ease of ballot access does give individuals opportunities to run for a variety of personal reasons. Many of the "non-serious" candidates raised no money and expended no funds on campaigning.

Incumbency is another factor that reduces electoral competitiveness. From studies of the U.S. Congress and of state legislatures, incumbent members of legislative bodies have a high probability of reelection if they choose to run. Similarly, in Dallas, in 117 races from 1967 to 1997 incumbents lost only 8—an incumbent success rate of 93 percent. No incumbents lost under the at-large election system. Six incumbents lost under the mixed 8-3 system for a

Table 6.6. Noncompetitive Election Comparisons

	Seats	Candidates	Nonserious[a]	Run-offs	Incumbents	Unopposed Incumbent	Reelected Incumbent	Nonincumbent	Unopposed Nonincumbent
At Large									
1967	9	20	1	0	5	4	5	4	0
1969	11	28	1	1	5	1	5	6	0
1971	11	27	6	1	7	2	7	4	0
1973	11	44	23	2	5	0	5	6	0
Total	42	119	31	4	22	7	22	20	0
Percent			26	10	52	32	100	48	0
Mixed 8-3									
1975	11	28	8	1	8	1	6	3	1
1977	11	30	11	2	10	2	9	1	0
1980	11	29	10	2	3	0	3	8	3
1981	11	28	19	0	9	2	9	2	0
1983	11	50	30	4	4	0	3	6	0
1985	11	32	11	3	10	1	8	1	1
1987	11	34	16	1	7	3	7	4	0
1989	11	26	6	2	8	3	8	3	1
Total	88	258	102	15	59	12	53	28	6
Percent			40	17	67	20	90	32	21
Single-Member 14-1									
1991	15	57	27	4	6	0	6	9	0
1993	14	43	15	4	9	2	8	5	0
1995	15	35	11	0	12	6	11	3	0
1997	14	27	4	0	9	4	9	5	2
Total	58	162	57	8	36	12	34	22	2
Percent			35	14	62	33	94	38	9

[a] Nonserious candidates received less than 15 percent of the vote.
Note: In the 1967 election the Council was comprised of 9 seats; thereafter, 11.

success rate of 90 percent. Two incumbents were defeated under 14-1 for an incumbent reelection rate of 94 percent. No incumbent mayor has been defeated.

Competitive elections have a high percentage of close races, evidenced in elections that are won by vote margins of 10 percent or less. Since Dallas has a majority vote requirement in nonpartisan local elections, the percentage of runoff elections is a good indicator of closely contested races.[65] Under the at-large system, 10 percent of the races resulted in a runoff, 17 percent under the mixed system (8 percent of at-large seats and 20 percent of single-member district seats), and 14 percent under 14-1. Under 14-1 there have been no mayoral runoffs and no runoffs in the 1995 or 1997 elections. Under the at-large system when a dominant slating group was the main player, fewer sufficiently contested elections and therefore fewer runoff elections might be expected, as was the case. Conversely, under the 14-1 system, more close contests than under either at-large or mixed-system elections might be expected, but that result is not supported by the findings.

Some of the most heated contests have been in the minority districts, where electoral fraud has escalated. To attribute election fraud to single-member districts would be erroneous, although stakes have become higher in those districts. The battle for political control of black inner-city precincts in District 6 goes back at least to the late 1960s. Feuds involving charges of vote fraud have led to lawsuits, fights over precinct chairmanships in Democratic primaries, and disputes over control of the Martin Luther King Community Center.[66] In 1980 State Representative Clay Smothers asked state election officials to conduct a full-scale investigation into irregularities, claiming to want an end to two decades of outright cheating at the polls in thirty black precincts in Dallas County.[67]

The controversy over a large number of absentee ballots cast by senior citizens in the District 6 city council race in 1984 was a prelude to an escalation of allegations of absentee ballot fraud, particularly after eligibility requirements were dramatically loosened in 1985 to allow the disabled to vote absentee without having a doctor's certification.

Attention to absentee ballot fraud peaked in 2001, when a judge threw out

65. The majority requirement was one of the "proofs" used in court that an electoral system was discriminatory to minorities. The argument that minorities could prevail in the first election but were defeated in a runoff election is not substantiated in Dallas elections. In nineteen cases, or 70 percent of the time, the plurality winner in the election also won the runoff. In none of the eight cases in which the plurality winner lost the runoff was a minority candidate contesting a white candidate. This was true under at-large and single-member district systems. For an analysis of three legal challenges to runoff elections pursued under the Voting Rights Act, see Charles S. Bullock III and Loch K. Johnson, *Runoff Elections in the United States* (Chapel Hill: University of North Carolina Press, 1992).

66. *Dallas Times Herald,* January 30, 1979.

67. *Dallas Morning News,* February 12, 1980.

thirty-two ballots, voiding the election of a black incumbent in District 4.[68] The judge had determined the ballots to be illegal in that race, in which a white candidate, former four-term member of the city council Larry Duncan, was defeated by sixteen votes. The incumbent, Maxine Thornton-Reese appealed, but the state appeals court upheld Duncan's challenge to the election, and a new election was scheduled for July 27, 2002, which Thornton-Reese won.

In 2001 in District 6, after a prior pattern of "winking" at the abuse of absentee ballots in minority districts, election officials threw out between 150 and 200 absentee ballots, delivered to the county elections department by Dwaine Caraway's campaign. Caraway was running for the District 6 seat in 2001 vacated by his wife, Barbara Mallory Caraway, because of term limits. A white candidate, Ed Oakley, won the seat.

Another indicator of competitiveness is turnout, with the closest races typically having the highest average turnout.[69] Democratic theory places a great deal of emphasis on voter turnout. Analysis of voter turnouts, as a percentage of registered voters under the three election systems, shows that at-large, 8-3, and 14-1 have respective average turnouts of 16.2 percent, 19.32 percent, and 21.7 percent. The turnouts from 1967 to 1997 were erratic, ranging from 10.56 percent to 24.83 percent under at-large; from 13.19 percent to 24.32 percent under 8-3; and from 7.10 percent to 36.2 percent under 14-1.[70] (See Figure 6.8.)

However, the voter turnout trend, as a percentage of registered voters, was generally upward until it peaked in 1991. After 1991 the trend has been dramatically downward under 14-1.[71]

In contrast, a generally downward trend can be detected in turnouts, as a percentage of voting-age population, in national elections. In presidential elec-

68. State District Judge Richard Mays decided incumbent council member Maxine Thornton-Reese's slim sixteen-vote victory over former District 4 council member Larry Duncan was obtained through fraudulent means and ordered a new election.

69. See the summary chart of victory margin compared to turnout in U.S. House races in 2000, in "Dubious Democracy 2001: Overview" (Takoma Park, Md.: Center for Voting and Democracy, 1999).

70. These figures represent the percentage turnout of registered voters. Figures for 1967 and 1969 are unavailable. Voting turnout in national elections are generally reported in the popular press as a percentage of the voting-age population. Caution must be used when dealing with this population because the Bureau of Census uses three separate sets of figures to determine the voting-age population, based on different bases for estimations. Moreover, voting-age population refers to the total number of persons in the United States who are eighteen years of age or older, regardless of citizenship, military status, or felony conviction.

71. A study of 118 cities determined that at-large elections prove more competitive than district elections (Norman R. Luttbeg, "The Origins of Competition in Municipal Elections: A Study of 118 Randomly Chosen Cities with Populations of at Least 25,000," paper prepared for the annual meeting of the American Political Science Association, San Francisco, 1996).

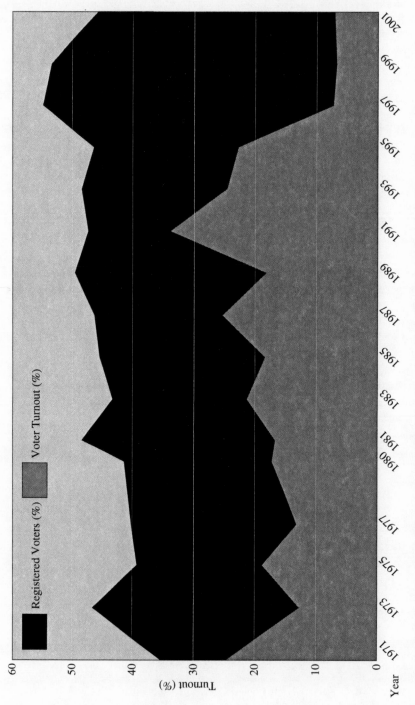

Figure 6.8. Voter Turnout as Percentage of Registered Voters and Registered Voters as Percentage of Population, 1971–2001. *Note:* The courts enjoined the city from holding the 1979 election pending settlement of a redistricting suit and DOJ preclearance of an election plan.

tions from 1968 to 1996, turnouts ranged from 60.9 percent in 1968 to 49.0 percent in 1996 but remained between 50 percent and 55 percent in the other six elections. Similarly turnouts in congressional elections ranged between 44.9 percent and 55.1 percent in presidential election years, and between 33.1 percent and 45.4 percent in off-year congressional elections.

In Dallas the extreme variations of voter turnout are likely candidate- and issue-dependent, rather than having a correlation with the different election systems. The very low 7.10 percent turnout in 1997 was no doubt partly owing to the lack of a mayoral campaign, and the fact that six candidates (43 percent) were unopposed. Two newcomers, even, were elected without opposition, in addition to four incumbents. In 1999, a year with a low turnout of 6.7 percent, the incumbent mayor did not have major opponents and five of the fourteen council races had unopposed incumbents.

The highest turnout between 1967 and 1997, in 1991, can be attributed to the first election under 14-1, with all the seats contested. According to election officials, the statewide constitutional amendment to create a lottery also led to the record turnout.[72]

CONCLUSIONS

A greater number of minorities have been elected to office in the United States and in Dallas since the VRA was passed. Consistent wins in racially gerrymandered single-member districts affirm that the remedies imposed by the federal courts and the U.S. Department of Justice indeed achieved the intended result of increasing the number of blacks and Hispanics elected to the Dallas City Council. Occasional at-large wins by minorities, and Anglo wins in minority districts, however, suggest that election politics in Dallas has not precluded successful coalition building and crossover voting.

The evidence presented is anecdotal and idiosyncratic. Although the data may tend to support persuasive arguments, whether identical results might have been achieved without requiring the city to abandon all, or even some, of its at-large districts cannot be empirically validated. Any projection of what "might have been" the result under a different election system is subject to what can be called a "mirage fallacy," because each election result is due to specific circumstances at a particular time.

The findings in Dallas reveal that a change to single-member districts did attain descriptive representation, but it does not seem to have stimulated greater electoral competitiveness, an increase in voter turnout, or a general perception of improvement in the quality of city governance. Furthermore, the findings reveal shortcomings in some assumptions in voting rights cases on

72. *Dallas Morning News,* November 6, 1991.

which the remedy of single-member districts was based. Reliance by plaintiffs, courts, and the DOJ on aggregate data, used to convert population figures by race to votes, and then to seats, rested on an assumption of a black interest being monolithic and needing to be represented by black elected officials. But neither the data nor the outcomes support these assumptions.

In assuming a monolithic black interest, and by requiring minority single-member districts to ensure the election of minorities proportionate to their share in the total population, the courts and the DOJ reinforced a racially divisive view of representation. Federal requirements incubated the expectation among black and Hispanic citizens that representation from districts drawn as minority districts was "guaranteed" to minority candidates. Racist campaigns against white candidates in minority districts resulted.

The theory that racial minority candidates could raise sufficient campaign funds from their own communities and not be obligated to white donors proved to be invalid. Minority candidates have continued to receive financial support from white donors who live outside the candidates' districts. Campaign funds continue to flow from northern to southern Dallas despite the end of at-large elections and despite the demise of the CCA.

Nor does the evidence support the assumption that the failure of the CCA to slate candidates, whom the plaintiffs and their witnesses viewed as minority "candidates of choice," was racially discriminatory. The CCA bias was toward minority candidates with conservative views. Supreme Court justices have observed that when differing political and socioeconomic characteristics of whites and minorities explain racially polarized voting, Section 2 of the Voting Rights Act does not protect that cause of minority electoral failure. This issue was not addressed in the litigation involving Dallas elections.

Creating race-based districts also subordinated the practical need for candidates to build a broad base for electoral success. Forcing Dallas to abandon all at-large districts, except for the mayoral election, deprived the council of voices of every race with a broad constituency base. The pendulum was forced from one extreme to its opposite in order to constitute councils comprised of members who speak for special constituencies. A mixed system has the potential to balance the voices of the majority, with opportunities for the voices of minorities to be heard.[73] A system in which both perspectives can be heard is preferable to a system that excludes one in favor of the other. The Supreme Court in *Williams* v. *City of Dallas* checkmated that option for Dallas.[74]

73. Morris L. Ernst has written a thought-provoking letter, "The Right To Be Heard vs. the Right to Vote," *American Bar Association Journal* (1965), 51:508.
74. *Williams* v. *City of Dallas*, 499 U.S. 945 (1991).

7
Governance Consequences

The more things change, the more they stay the same.
—Alphonse Karr

Court-mandated single-member districts accomplished the intended result in Dallas of increasing the number of minority members elected to the Dallas City Council. This change in the election system also had an impact on governing institutions and processes in the city, including consequences not anticipated and some, no doubt, unintended. The fundamental question in this chapter is whether a court-forced change in one part of a city's governmental system had a detrimental effect on the whole of a city's governance. In particular, did the change jeopardize the council-manager form of government? Did it affect relations between officials (mayor, council members, and administrators)? And did the move to a single-member district election system change the relationship between official and unofficial policy makers?

COUNCIL-MANAGER FORM OF GOVERNMENT: MODIFIED

The Progressive reform movement was a reaction against the cronyism and corruption of ward politics. The proponents of reform intended that the recommended institutional changes make the operation of government more economical and efficient, as well as oriented more toward promoting the good of the community as a whole rather than toward neighborhood special interests.[1] Clean government was another anticipated consequence of the recommended reforms.

In proposing a "Model City Charter," the National Municipal League recommended that the model council-manager form of government be adopted as a package and that cities not selectively choose from among its elements. The elements of the package included at-large elections, nonpartisan elections, selection of the mayor by the council, a merit system in personnel, and city

1. Adoption by Dallas of the reform institutions is described in chapter 2.

planning. The courts, by ending at-large elections in Dallas, one element in the package, may also have undermined the council-manager form of government itself.

As a replication of a corporate model of organization, the council-manager form of government comfortably fit a city with the business-oriented traditions of Dallas. Except for a voter-approved change in 1949 to direct election of the mayor by voters, rather than by the council, this governing model went unchallenged in Dallas for more than half a century, after its adoption in 1931.[2]

However, after court intervention, few of the other recommended reform elements in the National Municipal League's "Model City Charter" remained in their intended form in Dallas. Nonpartisan elections remain, but some district elections are de facto partisan. District-elected council members, who interfere with personnel matters, compromise both the merit system in personnel and the responsibility of the city manager to make appointments. City planning takes a back seat to any issues of the moment, and city planning that does occur is often spearheaded by the private sector, rather than by the council and city staff.

Single-member districts are not inherently incompatible with the council-manager form of government. Experiences of other cities suggest that single-member districts need not signal the death of council-manager government. Ten cities in the top thirty-five in population in the 1990 census operated under the council-manager plan.[3] All ten cities are generally considered to be better managed and to be better places to live than cities with a "strong mayor" form of government—such as Detroit and New Orleans. In a detailed analysis of the practice of urban public management in thirty-five of America's largest cities, the two cities ranked highest by *Governing* magazine were council-manager cities, Austin and Phoenix.[4] In Austin the seven-member city council is elected at large; all serve staggered three-year terms, with a two-term limit. In Phoenix

2. The change to direct election of mayor resulted from a power move spearheaded by mayoral aspirant J. B. Adoue Jr. to strengthen the mayoral position vis-à-vis the city manager. Adoue became the first directly elected mayor. He flexed this new political muscle and violated the spirit of the council-manager charter by infringing on the city manager's turf. Adoue made it known that he wanted to replace the city's police chief with his own; ultimately he drove the city manager, Charles B. Ford, to resign.

3. Two of these have at-large (Austin) or mixed (Kansas City, Missouri) systems. The others have single-member districts. The ten cities include San Diego, Dallas, Phoenix, San Antonio, San Jose, Austin, Fort Worth, Oklahoma City, Kansas City, and Charlotte, North Carolina.

4. The Government Performance Project, conducted by researchers at *Governing* magazine and academics at the Maxwell School of Citizenship and Public Affairs, Syracuse University, graded thirty-five cities. To each city the researchers assigned an average grade, as well as grades for financial management, human resources, information technology, capital management, and managing for results. Dallas received a C+ average grade. Its highest grade was B+ on financial management and its lowest grade was D+ on information technology (*Governing* [February 2000]).

the mayor is elected at large; the eight council members, from districts, serve staggered four-year terms, with a two-term limit.

If single-member districts did not cause other changes to be made to the city charter, in what ways has the operation of council-manager government in Dallas been modified by the institution of single-member districts?

Changed Expectations

The courts' means to ensure greater proportionate representation of minorities changed the composition of the city council, which, in turn, altered the way the council functions as a representative institution. This altered mode occurred primarily because of a shift in the way the role of the representative is viewed. One general view holds that the appropriate role for a representative is that of agent—to act to carry out the will of the representative's constituents. Another view regards the appropriate role to be that of trustee—to act on the representative's own judgment of what may be in the general public's interest.[5]

Most council members elected at large view a representative as a trustee of the interests of the city as a whole. Public interest is believed to be greater than the sum of individual interests, so the representative should strive to reflect that common interest on behalf of all citizens. Most council members elected from single-member districts fight for special interests specific to their districts, and are expected to do so by their constituents. Here representatives, viewed as agents of their constituents, presumably mirror the constituency.

In accepting a theory of representation closer to the "mirror-of-the-constituency" view, the courts have been employed to enhance correlations in legislative bodies between blacks and, to a lesser extent, Hispanics, and their proportionate numbers in the populations. The same consideration has not been introduced for Americans of Asian descent or for other racial or ethnic minorities. Similarly the lack of representation in terms of gender and socio-economic status has not been addressed through litigation or legislation. Nor do legislative bodies mirror their constituencies in terms of backgrounds—doctors, teachers, clergymen, plumbers, and so on.

A manifestation of the changed view of the role of the representative in Dallas has been a shift in focus by councils from large-policy issues to an emphasis on constituency service. The former role is usually less time-consuming and hence more conducive to a part-time, civic-duty concept of representation. The division of responsibilities between council and city staff, between policy making and administration, characteristic of the council-manager form of government, was more clearly understood by council members under the at-large district system.

5. See Hanna Fenichel Pitkin, *The Concept of Representation* (Berkeley: University of California Press, 1967), for a classic study of various meanings of representation and aspects of the role of the representative.

The divisiveness created by Dallas single-member district representatives, competing for the interests of their geographical areas, emerged in the first council elected under the 8-3 single-member district plan in 1971. Mayor Wes Wise, the first mayor elected under the 8-3 plan, was a proponent of single-member districts. He had second thoughts, however, after his experiences with the new system. He complained that indigenous interests of a council member's constituency "seem to pervade everything" and created a serious problem with the city council's inability "to come together on some important issues of our day."[6]

The change from a long-term to a short-term perspective by council members immediately became apparent to the city manager, George Schrader. After the election district change, he observed that the council "less and less is giving its attention to policy issues and long-term concerns, and more to specific operational considerations—patching the streets, traffic signals and stop signs, picking up the garbage." With the council becoming increasingly concerned with day-to-day operations, Schrader said that he frequently had to tell the staff to "make sure we are prepared for the future."[7] This observation continues to hold true; it was exacerbated by the shift from 8-3 to 14-1.

Most notable among other sources of divisiveness on single-member district councils was the new socioeconomic diversity among the council members. Political columnist Carolyn Barta observed that the vocal and confrontational "Diane Ragsdales and Al Lipscombs are not personality blips on this city's radar screen." Rather, she asserted, "they represent a constituency—the underclass—that will continue to be represented on the council."[8] Barta noted that middle-class minorities, who would be elected under a different council configuration, are unelectable in the underclass districts. Mayor Ron Kirk endorsed this premise, when he said he could not have been elected from a single-member district.

Even so, minority council members representing less affluent districts, but with different political styles, have not regularly voted as a bloc. For example, the council that took office on February 6, 1980, was often described as Elsie Faye Heggins and her ten opponents, though it included two other minority members, Fred Blair and Ricardo Medrano. Heggins even had difficulty getting a second for her motions, let alone mustering serious support from the rest of the council. Both the *News* and the *Herald* carried accounts throughout her term of the conflicts between her and Mayor Folsom. Folsom was reported to have said that some day Heggins would learn that she had to work with the other ten council members to accomplish anything of significance for her predominantly black constituency.[9] Fred Blair (1980–1983), on the other hand,

6. Dotty Griffith, *Dallas Morning News,* November 6, 1975.
7. Terry Mason, *Dallas Times Herald,* May 31, 1981.
8. Carolyn Barta, "Dallas Needs a Change," *Dallas Morning News,* January 30, 1989.
9. *Dallas Times Herald,* April 10, 1980.

like George Allen (1969–1975), was adept at working with "the Establishment" to get things done.

Single-member districts were successful in bringing both the haves and have-nots to the same council table, so that both voices could be heard. The income of a district has been called the key variable in constituency orientation.[10] In a study of eleven cities, Heilig and Mundt found that, regardless of city or race, council members from the city's low-income districts viewed taking care of the personal problems of their constituents, and looking out for their area's share of city benefits, as vital aspects of their job. Upper-income representatives were found to focus more on policy questions.[11]

Max Wells, the council member from the affluent north Dallas District 4 from 1989 to 1997, said that he probably received less mail and phone calls than other council members, because the district he represented was more homogeneous than most, and it was the highest educated and in the newest part of the city. He added that he had to hold fewer Town Hall meetings than most council members, because he received less demand for them.[12]

Additional change was noticed with the transition from the 8-3 combined district/at-large council to the 14-1 councils. Glenn Box, who served under both 8-3 and 14-1, said that people did not expect as much detailed work from their elected officials under the former. "Knowing about a pothole in Lakewood—you didn't have to worry about that," said Box, but "you can't do that under this system." City Manager Hart agreed: "I think the expectations of constituents with respect to the Council members are higher, and we need to adjust to those expectations."[13]

Cronyism and Corruption

For many citizens of Dallas, a disturbing consequence of court modification of the council-manager form of government with single-member districts was the resurfacing of cronyism and corruption, which had characterized Dallas under the ward form of government prior to 1931. Progressive movement reformers had hoped that institutional changes would eliminate the corrupting influence of money and privileged access to governmental outcomes. Candidates slated by the Citizens Charter Association were required to pledge "to protect the council-manager form of government and to fight any trace of scandal, personal selfishness and political bias." To a large extent, the reforms did elimi-

10. Peggy Heilig and Robert J. Mundt, *Your Voice at City Hall: The Politics, Procedures, and Policies of District Representation* (Albany: State University of New York Press, 1984), 85–91.

11. Ibid.

12. Max Wells, author interview, March 5, 1996.

13. Lori Stahl, *Dallas Morning News,* June 27, 1993.

nate illegal graft. Clean government became a source of pride in Dallas for elected officials, business leaders, and citizens alike.

"I seen my opportunities and I took 'em," was defined by George Washington Plunkitt of Tammany Hall as "honest graft." Such opportunities might include being "wired in" to receive the contracts for public work projects, or to buy land where a public park or a highway was to be developed. Plunkitt observed, correctly, that big fortunes in politics had come from honest graft, rather than through illegal activities.[14]

Dallas city leaders viewed "honest graft" as fueling progress while enhancing their profits, rather than as a corrupting influence. Business leaders saw and made opportunities. Through council-adopted policies, these businessmen benefited from public works contracts, tax policy, and zoning flips. As Mayor Kirk said with regard to allegations of "sweetheart deals" during his tenure as mayor, "If something is good for the city, why should we get so concerned that someone makes money?"[15]

An effect of the change to single-member districts was that ethical expectations changed. Some members of the new groups represented at the council table expected their share of "spoils." These parties were not sufficiently affluent to take advantage of "honest graft" opportunities on a large scale, so petty cronyism and "dishonest graft" began to permeate politics. Some district representatives used their positions for private gain and dispensed patronage, especially jobs and contracts, with missionary zeal. These were also the opponents of a strengthened ethics code.

Commonplace in commentary on official corruption in the United States is that instances of bribery, office buying, and other gross forms of malfeasance have over time given way to a variety of more subtle forms of quid pro quo and conflict of interest. The reverse seems to have been true in Dallas.[16] On rare occasions during the years of at-large elections and CCA dominance was there a hint of scandal, either in the bureaucracy or among elected officials. So infrequently, in fact, that as late as 1985, when architects Jerry Stewart and W. Bryan Thruston accused Robert Gahl, chief of the city's building inspection division, of soliciting a bribe from them, City Manager Charles Anderson "was absolutely horrified."[17] Anderson's assistants gathered facts, and within days Gahl was arrested.[18]

14. William L. Riordin, *Plunkitt of Tammany Hall* (New York: E. P. Dutton, 1963), 3–6.

15. Ron Kirk, author interview, October 23, 1997.

16. Andrew Stark, "Beyond Quid Pro Quo: What's Wrong with Private Gain from Public Office?" *American Political Science Review* (March 1997), 91:108–120.

17. Craig Holcomb, former city council member, in Robert Tomsho, "High Profile: Charles Anderson," *Dallas Morning News,* August 12, 1984.

18. Gahl was sentenced to four years in prison for soliciting and accepting a bribe of about $16,000.

A great deal changed in the ensuing decade. Charles Anderson, who later served as executive director of the Dallas Area Rapid Transit (DART) from 1986 to 1991, resigned that post because he would not deliver special favors requested by some city council members. He said that council members had asked him to direct DART contracts to a company where a council member worked, to hire a council member's friend for a DART job, to build an unjustified rail line through a council member's district, and to construct a bus ride lot, also not warranted, in a particular council district. "I knew special interest politics was the name of the game in Dallas, Texas, and DART was the victim," he said.[19]

Even so, change in the degree or kind of corruption under different circumstances cannot be proved. Walter Lippman was correct to observe that one can only record the exposure of corruption, as it would be impossible to write a history of political corruption.[20] The vehicles for exposing scandal and corruption in municipalities are the efforts of a vigilant press, government investigations, and aggressive prosecutors. In Dallas the U.S. Attorney for the Northern District of Texas, Paul Coggins, promised that local officials would face prison terms if they exploited their office for personal gain. "Public corruption . . . will spread if you allow it to spread," he said. "It has spread in some areas in Dallas because we addressed it later than some other cities have."[21]

The *Dallas Morning News* had not played the role of government watchdog for years. It was the investigative reporting of Laura Miller, who broke the story on the patterns of payments to Lipscomb in the weekly *Dallas Observer*, that sparked the federal probe,[22] and an aggressive U.S. Attorney who did not let it die. The *Observer* and *D* magazine, with fewer resources, both out-report the *News* on fundamental governance issues in Dallas.[23]

FBI investigations that resulted in the conviction of two council members in the 1990s shocked the city out of its complacency. In 1997, for the first time in Dallas history, a city council member, Paul Fielding, was forced to leave

19. *Dallas Morning News,* April 5, 1992.
20. Walter Lippmann, "A Theory about Corruption," *Vanity Fair* (November 1930), 35:61.
21. Lori Stahl, *Dallas Morning News,* March 2, 1998.
22. Laura Miller, "Clueless," *Dallas Observer,* May 30, 1996.
23. Wick Allison, editor of *D* magazine, in expressing frustration over the failure of the *News* to report the truth on a racially volatile school board meeting: "Are they so stuck in the 'he said/she said' mode that they cannot recognize, much less report, the truth? Don't diving ratings and sinking circulation offer up a clue that pablum isn't what the city wants? Doesn't conscience tell them it isn't what the city needs?" (Wick Allison, *D* magazine [March 1997], 24:6). *Observer* reporter Schutze believes the reporting failures are because the *News* worries "that analysis—any reporting on the local scene at a fundamental level—runs the risk of rubbing their own interests wrong or the interests of their peers" (Jim Schutze, *Dallas Observer,* February 3, 2000).

office. Two years later council member Al Lipscomb also was forced to leave office. Fielding was white; Lipscomb was black. The two were political and business allies.[24]

The Paul Fielding trial in April 1997, according to prosecutors, produced "a shocking pattern of strong-arm tactics against clients and friends, bald-faced influence peddling and outright extortion of business contacts."[25] Testimony showed that Fielding had used his council position to get work for his clients. Specifically, federal authorities said that he had extorted a $1 million cleaning contract from EDS (Electronic Data Systems), in return for a favorable vote in a zoning case.

Prosecutors had secretly recorded tapes of Fielding and Lipscomb discussing forming a "minority front" sanitary supply company to gain public contracts, and of Fielding discussing making threats of racial strife, so as to force Dallas-area companies into business deals. Faced with mounting evidence against him, Fielding opted to resign from the council, and pleaded guilty to single counts of mail fraud and conspiracy to commit extortion. He was sentenced to forty-one months in federal prison.

In 1999 a federal grand jury indicted Al Lipscomb on charges of selling influence at City Hall, accusing him of bribery and conspiracy. Less than two months after the sixty-five count indictment, Lipscomb won reelection to the council with 79 percent of the vote; and Mayor Kirk reappointed him as chairman of the council's committee that oversees the city's municipal courts.

In January 2000 the Lipscomb trial, transferred to Amarillo by U.S. District Judge Joe Kendall, focused on the accusation that Lipscomb accepted $1,000 monthly cash payments from Yellow Cab Company owner Floyd Richards in exchange for voting on issues to benefit Yellow Cab. Lipscomb had not reported financial ties to Richards in annual disclosure forms submitted to the city prior to the indictment, nor had he recused himself from votes on taxicab issues. Lipscomb pleaded not guilty, and Richards, who was indicted on the same charges, initially pleaded not guilty but later agreed to a plea bargain and testified against Lipscomb.

Evidence prepared by the prosecution, not used during trial and later released by the judge, included allegations that Lipscomb had accepted four payments in 1992 from the owner of a topless club, Caligula XXI.[26] This revelation, long rumored but hitherto unconfirmed, reverberated through the city, because for years homeowners and businesses along Northwest Highway had fought to have the topless bars, such as the Caligula, closed. Tim Dickey, a leader in the Bachman/Northwest Highway Community Association, wrote to

24. Lipscomb (joined by County Commissioner John Wiley Price) exhorted the black community to support incumbent Fielding's election to the council in 1985.
25. Editorial, *Dallas Business Journal,* April 18, 1997.
26. Jim Schutze, *Dallas Observer,* March 2, 2000.

council member John Loza that he had heard "people in the Northwest High-way community talk for several years about the fact that certain council members have protected sexually oriented businesses and other clubs." Dickey wrote, "I had a police officer from the Northwest division tell me he could do nothing about violations among sexually oriented businesses and other clubs because of orders from downtown."[27] Frequently, at the open microphone at city council meetings, the same complaint had been made.

What Dallas citizens would not have known, without having read investigative reporter Jim Schutze's account in the *Dallas Observer*, is that exhibits the U.S. Attorney had prepared for Lipscomb's trial included evidence that several Caligula employees had been arrested in late 1991 and 1992 for selling cocaine. These arrest records had been presented to a city board when Caligula's license had been suspended for fifteen days in May 1992.[28] Terrell Bolton, later to be named Dallas Police Chief, was also implicated in the Lipscomb-Caligula connection. Cindy Schoelen, former secretary to Dallas Police Chief Terrell Bolton, and Dallas Police Lieutenant John Sullivan told an *Observer* reporter that they "testified to a grand jury that Bolton ordered Sullivan to a meeting in 1993 with Lipscomb and Nick Rizos, owner of the Caligula XXI topless club . . . to discuss what Rizos considered 'police harassment' of the club."[29] In a March 3, 2000, deposition, Sullivan testified under oath that Bolton ordered him to have patrol officers "back off enforcement" at Caligula.[30]

Lipscomb was found guilty on all sixty-five counts of conspiracy and bribery on January 25, 2000. In letters to the editor, as well as in response to the informal poll on the *News* web page, asking how citizens graded the city council, people expressed outrage that only two council members, Donna Blumer and Laura Miller, had called for Lipscomb's resignation, after he had been convicted. Lipscomb indicated that he might try to remain on the council until his sentencing. He resigned on February 3, 2000, and was sentenced on April 27, 2000, to forty-one months. Then, unexpectedly, Judge Kendall said that, because Lipscomb was "elderly and infirm," he would be confined to his home and not sent to prison.[31]

The compassionate sentencing punctured the politically and racially charged atmosphere in the city. U.S. Attorney Paul Coggins said that his office had faced "tremendous pressure" from Lipscomb's supporters, some of them high-ranking officials, to be lenient with Lipscomb. "He had a lot of supporters in high places," Coggins said. "Many of them weighed in at various stages of the process . . . but the evidence was such that we would have indicted any-

27. Henry Tatum, *Dallas Morning News*, February 23, 2000.
28. Jim Schutze, *Dallas Observer*, March 2, 2000.
29. Thomas Korosec, *Dallas Observer*, August 1, 2002.
30. Jim Schutze, *Dallas Observer*, March 22, 2001.
31. Mark Wrolstad, *Dallas Morning News*, April 30, 2000.

one else who had this much evidence against them. We couldn't ignore it."[32] When, on the last day of the Clinton presidency, an attempt by friends and supporters to obtain a presidential grant of clemency failed, Coggins said that he would have strongly opposed a clemency recommendation had the pardon attorney's office asked, because "public corruption is a serious matter, and these were serious crimes that should carry serious consequences."[33]

During the trial, many citizens were disturbed by the parade of city leaders who testified that they had routinely provided money to Lipscomb but did not seem at all chagrined by their admission. A prosecutor said he had been shocked to see Dallas city leaders say on the stand that they handed out cash to public officials regularly. *D* magazine reported that Mayor Ron Kirk had been moved to tears when he had testified as a character witness on Lipscomb's behalf.[34]

The editorial page editor noted that "for years, it has been acknowledged with a wink that business and civic leaders routinely funneled cash to some minority council members."[35] The irony was missed that the city's newspaper was culpable. It had exposed the wink-wink system only after the public revelation by city officials and other civic leaders, who acknowledged, in testimony for the defense during the trial of council member Lipscomb, that giving cash to minority council members was customary. The newspaper not only failed to report corruption in city politics but implicitly condoned influence peddling by endorsing candidates known to be on the take.[36]

Two black leaders in Dallas, County Commissioner John Wiley Price and the Reverend Zan Holmes, testified in Lipscomb's defense that taking secret cash payments from white benefactors was a time-honored tradition among civil-rights activists. Secret cash payments may have been "a time-honored tradition" in Dallas, but that was not the case nationwide. David Garrow, author of a Pulitzer Prize–winning biography of Martin Luther King Jr., and a law professor at Emory University, told a *News* reporter that he had pored over thousands of documents and had conducted hundreds of interviews in researching the life of Dr. King. Garrow said he had "never found an example of a civil-rights leader who accepted confidential cash payments for his or her own benefit."[37] But, according to Royce Hanson, former dean of social sciences at the University of Texas at Dallas, "You have to look at the motives on both sides" in the underground history of Dallas whites paying off Dallas minorities. "You have to think of this not simply as a matter of extortion but as a question of social control."[38]

32. Michael Saul, *Dallas Morning News,* January 30, 2000.
33. Todd Bensman, *Dallas Morning News,* January 20, 2001.
34. *D* magazine (March 2000), 20.
35. Rena Pederson, *Dallas Morning News,* January 30, 2000.
36. The *News* repeatedly endorsed Lipscomb in his races for a seat on the city council.
37. Craig Flournoy, *Dallas Morning News,* January 28, 2000.
38. Ibid.

While the city council, even after the Lipscomb trial and conviction, continued to condone a system of nepotism, to excuse city staff who subverted bidding processes, and to resist the adoption of a strong code of ethics, some citizens did express disappointment and outrage. For example, Anthony Bond, founder of the Irving branch of the NAACP, said he was shocked and saddened that more people were not demanding that Lipscomb step down.[39] "I have always known Al was guilty and that he should resign and save the taxpayers money on a useless trial. I love Al as a human being and for the good that he has done, but bought-off black politicians are hurting African-American communities."[40]

Ethics Codes

Changes in the political climate in Dallas and the ensuing scandals focused attention on the need to strengthen the city's code of ethics. During the 1970s, efforts to adopt a conflict of interest ordinance for both elected and appointed city officials failed. In 1975 council member Lucy Patterson created a controversy, because she received a salary for teaching in the Department of Sociology at North Texas State University at the same time that she was paid $50 a week for her council service. She gave up the council pay. Greater controversy in the 1975 campaign followed, when mayoral candidate Bob Folsom refused to reveal his real estate interests. In 1976 the council adopted an ordinance requiring council members to make a limited disclosure on personal finances in a "financial involvement statement," to be submitted to the City Secretary's office.

Former City Attorney Analeslie Muncy recalls that she drafted strengthened provisions for the city's code of ethics at least twice during her 1982 to 1991 tenure, in response to questionable incidents involving former employees.[41] In 1996 council member Larry Duncan was asked about the extent of corruption in city departments. He cited cases he considered to be conflicts of interest by a department head, but then he observed that "by and large, though, overall it's surprising how little of that I actually bump into."[42]

In recent years citizen concern has escalated over conflicts of interest and other improprieties by elected and other high-ranking officials. Councilman Al Lipscomb, who could not seek reelection in 1993 because of term limits, drew complaints from his former colleagues for soliciting a chlorine supply contract from them, shortly after he stepped down from the council.[43] When city attor-

39. Tim Wyatt and Michael Saul, *Dallas Morning News,* January 29, 2000.
40. Michael Saul, *Dallas Morning News,* December 24, 1999.
41. Analeslie Muncy, author query (telephone), January 2, 2001.
42. Larry Duncan, author interview, April 22, 1996.
43. The term limit provision in the Dallas City Charter applies to consecutive terms. Lipscomb sat out one term and then ran again in 1995.

neys determined that he had not violated the ethics code, the council revised the law, so as to restrict former officials from doing business with City Hall for one year after leaving office.

The appearance of impropriety by high-ranking city officials in sweetheart deals with the private sector called the city's ethics code into question again in 1998 and triggered a two-year debate on City Hall ethics standards. After City Manager John Ware announced, on June 5, 1998, that he was leaving City Hall in sixty days to head a newly created investment company financed by Tom Hicks, council member Laura Miller initiated the move to strengthen the ethics code.[44]

On June 6, 1998, a few days after the Ware-Hicks liaison became public, the *Dallas Morning News* broke the story that three years earlier (August 1995), Tom Hicks had invited the mayor's wife, Matrice Ellis-Kirk, to join the board of the Hicks-owned Chancellor Broadcasting Company, only two months after Kirk had taken office as mayor.[45] The mayor's wife accepted the seat on the board. Mayor Kirk subsequently chaired the heavily financed pro-arena campaign—"Yes! For Dallas"—which won a slim victory in January 1998. Matrice Ellis-Kirk is an accomplished professional in her own right, but the timing of the board appointment added fuel to the public's skepticism over the cozy relations between mayor, manager, and team owners.

For Dallas's Stanley Marcus, the front-page story on Matrice Ellis-Kirk was "a clarion-like challenge to the voter of Dallas about the existing council-approved ethics code for officials."[46] As Marcus observed, "A part of the great immigration that Dallas has enjoyed in the past has been due to the reputation this city has earned—'No corruption, no payoffs, no governmental financial scandal.'"[47] He expressed concern that after the *News* broke the story on June 6, no stories or editorial columns appeared in the paper in the following days.

Responding to a query from a *News* reporter, the executive director of Common Cause of Texas, Suzie Woodford, concurred with Marcus's view. "This kind of cozy, cozy arrangement between the major players should raise questions and concerns," she said. "It may not be against the law and it may not be against the code of ethics. But it certainly is a huge appearance of impropriety. . . . It certainly does not pass the smell test."[48]

44. Hicks, CEO of Hicks, Muse, Tate & Furst, owns the National Hockey League's Dallas Stars, the Chancellor Broadcasting Company, and other enterprises. The announced departure came within two months after Ware, together with Mayor Kirk, negotiated, behind closed doors, the city's $230-million arena deal with Hicks and Dallas Mavericks owner Ross Perot Jr. The deal included raising a highly controversial $125 million from taxpayers.

45. Todd J. Gillman, *Dallas Morning News,* June 6, 1998. In addition to the $12,000/year seat on the board, she bought securities in the company at a preferred price reserved for corporate officials, from which she was reported to have profited more than $500,000.

46. Stanley Marcus, "Viewpoints" column, *Dallas Morning News,* June 17, 1998.

47. Ibid.

48. Todd J. Gillman, *Dallas Morning News,* June 6, 1998.

Questions were also raised by Mayor Kirk's acceptance of a $36,000-a-year board appointment at Brinker International—the Dallas-based parent of Chili's and other restaurant chains. John M. Nash, president of the National Association of Corporate Directors, a nonprofit group that advises directors of their duties, agreed with council member Donna Blumer that the Brinker post could create "a perception problem" for Mayor Kirk. "It's not unknown but not very common" for incumbents to join corporate boards, Nash said. "Generally speaking, they tend to be ex-office-holders."[49] Kirk's immediate predecessors, Annette Strauss and Steve Bartlett, both of whom also had ties to the Dallas business community, did not accept new board appointments while on the city council.

When she was a reporter for the *Dallas Observer,* council member Laura Miller was the first to expose Al Lipscomb's transgressions in print.[50] Following the Ware-Hicks announcement, she proposed a tough ethics code to the council. As on previous occasions, she was not in step with Mayor Kirk and a majority of the council, who felt that her proposed changes were too stringent. Al Lipscomb even suggested that her changes were racially motivated: "When someone black or Chicano gets a chance for a better job opportunity, all of a sudden something went wrong."[51]

The council responded to public discontent and the Miller proposal by appointing a fifteen-member task force to review the city's ethics rules. Three minority council members (Don Hicks, Barbara Mallory Caraway, and John Loza) appointed individuals to the task force who had faced questions about their own ethical records (Chris Luna, Dwaine Caraway, and Judge Dan L. Wyde). The task force grappled with the issues for more than eight months, before making its recommendation to the city council in August 1999.

Three white council members indicated that they supported the task force recommendation, as submitted; they were Laura Miller, Donna Blumer, and Sandy Greyson. The five black council members indicated that they did not think the existing code needed changing. Subsequently some of them took actions that would have been prohibited had the recommended revisions been adopted. Contrary to the proposed nepotism rule, for example, Barbara Mallory Caraway re-nominated her husband, Dwaine Caraway, to the Park and Recreation Board in September 1999; then Maxine Thornton-Reese nominated her daughter to the South Dallas/Fair Park Trust Fund Board; two months later Don Hill nominated his wife to the Municipal Library Board.[52] The latter told a *News* reporter, "We really feel that it's an attack on how we are trying to

49. Ibid. Already questions had been raised over a downtown law firm subsidizing Mayor Kirk's full-time service on the city council with an annual salary in six figures.

50. Laura Miller, *Dallas Observer,* May 30, 1996.

51. Nora López, *Dallas Morning News,* October 8, 1998.

52. Council members usually defer to a colleague's nomination for appointments to a board or commission.

develop our minority political community."[53] Contrary to the position taken by the black council members, a *News*-commissioned poll in March 2000 revealed that residents of *all* races overwhelmingly supported the three major strong provisions of the proposed ethics code—an ethics review board, a ban on family appointments, and the detailed financial disclosure required of state legislators.[54]

Nevertheless, during this time, the leading candidates campaigning to fill Lipscomb's District 8 seat on the council in the May 6, 2000, special election, spoke out against a strengthened ethics code. In an interview with an *Observer* reporter, Sandra Crenshaw, who had served one term on the council when term limits had forced Lipscomb to sit out, conceded that she accepted use of a truck, received free car repairs, and often stopped at the Yellow Cab office for a drink before and after council meetings—all while sitting on the council and championing the cab company's position in votes and interviews. She apparently agreed to a limited immunity deal and testified for the state before the grand jury that indicted Lipscomb.[55]

James Fantroy, who later won Lipscomb's seat, told voters at a campaign debate, "I don't need an ethics code to keep me honest. Now that we're getting to be the majority, all of a sudden we have to have ethics down there."[56] In September 1989, according to Ken Nichols, the commission's interim director, the Texas Commission on Private Security ordered Fantroy to pay a $3,000 fine for cheating on the state licensing exam, operating a security and investigation company without a license, and illegally carrying a weapon.[57]

The two-year ethics debate ended on June 28, 2000. After weakening the major provisions, the council passed the new code. Single-member district representatives, who sought to build personal political and economic power bases, viewed a strong ethics code as an attempt by representatives of affluent districts to keep them submerged.

Single-member districts did not cause corruption. The political climate that condoned corruption was created in part by the cumulative expectations in a city with a history of "buying off" dissent in the minority communities. L. A. Bedford, attorney, civil rights activist, and former judge in Dallas, explained: "I'll give Dallas credit for being slick. Dallas knew how much to give—just enough. What do you want? O.K., we'll give you a bone. Then you'd go along for a period of time. It was disheartening for those who believed in the law."[58]

53. Nora López, *Dallas Morning News,* December 16, 1999.
54. Michael Saul, *Dallas Morning News,* June 29, 2000.
55. Peter Calvin, *Dallas Observer,* April 27, 2000.
56. Ibid.
57. Ibid.
58. L. A. Bedford, remarks at a public forum, "Civil Rights in Dallas: A Reappraisal," J. Erik Jonsson Central Library, February 11, 1997.

A consequence of single-member, gerrymandered districts in the cultural context of Dallas was the election of some representatives, who held the view that opportunities for graft came with political power, and that acceptance by them of dishonest—even illegal—graft would be condoned. Behaviors based on these expectations, cultivated by the underground history of whites paying off minorities in Dallas, surfaced into the spotlight when those holding elected office accepted payoffs. The promise of council-manager government, to end the cronyism and corruption of the former ward system of government, was undermined by single-member districts, from which parochial-interest candidates could be elected.

Relations Between Officials

A body of literature on the operation of council-manager governments centers on the manner in which power is shared between mayor and council and manager, and on the structural features that affect distribution of power. Although the interplay of power often depends more on those who exercise it than on structure, dissatisfaction with the operation of Dallas city government under a single-member district system has expressed itself frequently in calls to change the structure.

The power of the mayor, the relations between the mayor and the council, between the mayor and the city manager, between the council and the city manager, and between members of the council all were affected in one degree or another by the change to single-member districts.

Mayor-Council Relations in Dallas

One structural feature that often causes contention is the manner of electing the mayor. It can be argued, plausibly, that the power of a mayor may be enhanced more by direct election citywide than election by a council. Nevertheless, the political skills of a mayor are likely to be more important than this structural feature. Former Dallas City Manager John Ware does not consider the manner of election of the mayor to matter at all. He served in four council-manager cities; in three the mayor was elected at large, and in the fourth by the city council. Ware found no difference but rather that a particular individual's acumen mattered most.[59]

Some minorities pressed for the Dallas mayor to be elected by the council under the 15-0 plan, which had been proposed at the time 14-1 was adopted in 1991. In the time-honored American practice of tinkering with the political system when different outcomes are desired, this plan had not been proposed

59. John Ware, author interview, December 16, 1997.

to reduce the power of the mayor. Rather, the minorities anticipated a better opportunity for electing a black mayor from among the council members who had been elected from single-member districts than from the at-large system in a white-majority city. Ironically had minorities won the 15-0 plan, it seems unlikely that Dallas would have had a black as mayor before the turn of the century.

The change to single-member districts did have an impact on attitudes toward mayoral power. The first councils elected from all single-member districts were so contentious that little was accomplished; the mayor had difficulty even maintaining decorum. Steve Bartlett was the first mayor to confront a council that viewed the role of representatives differently from how it was perceived previously. Bartlett's style exacerbated the discord. Not only was there conflict between Bartlett and the city manager, but Bartlett's difficulty in building coalitions often also put him at variance with members of the diverse new council. On occasion Bartlett announced city programs before consulting the city manager or council, which intensified dissatisfaction.

In reaction to chaos at City Hall, a movement developed to enhance the Dallas mayor's power. Henry Tatum, the associate editor of the *Dallas Morning News* editorial page, frequently penned support for a strong mayor for Dallas. Tatum wrote:

> The hard truth is that Dallas mayors no longer can push through projects with little more than bluff and bluster. There was a time when the person in the city's top elected spot had the clout and financial backing of the business community behind his every effort. But those days are gone. . . . [T]he mayor needs more power—pure and simple.

He proposed that the mayor be given veto authority and expanded appointment powers, so that the mayor could do more than just "bargain with them to get his programs approved."[60]

Tatum represented the views of business leaders, who publicly expressed their frustrations that, under the new single-member district councils, Dallas could not "close a deal." With only two years experience under a single-member district council, the Dallas Citizens Council was so concerned that it commissioned a study of the governance structure. That report, presented to the Citizens Council Board in March 1994, concluded that, under the manager/council form of government in Dallas, the City Council "is hindered by the lack of a mechanism by which it can exercise real power."[61]

The minorities on the council viewed the mayoral power issue differently.

60. Henry Tatum, *Dallas Morning News,* November 27, 1996.
61. Donald C. McCleary, "Dallas' Form of Government," a report prepared for the Dallas Citizens Council, March 1994, 16. McCleary was Managing Partner at Gardere & Wynne.

Members considered an increase in the power of the mayor as an attempt to diminish their own power, turning the clock back on the gains of 14-1. Council member Barbara Mallory Caraway viewed a call for additional power for the mayor as "a selfish approach to silence individuals and become a dictatorship."[62]

Business leaders were unwilling to wait on a possible change in the rules; they took steps to change the players. Members of the Citizens Council, who had supported bringing U.S. Congressman Bartlett back to Dallas to run as mayor, had hoped that he could tame the council. Frustrated by inaction and unpredictability and embarrassed by the behavior in council meetings during his first term, the Citizens Council abandoned him for a second term.

The inner circle of top Dallas businessmen decided to back Ron Kirk, a Democrat, who, as secretary of state, was the first black to hold statewide office. When word of the backing of Kirk began to make the breakfast/luncheon circuit rounds of the "fantastic four hundred," a member of the Citizens Council executive committee expressed surprise, saying: "I didn't know [Kirk had been anointed], and I'm a member of the Executive Committee!"[63]

Kirk won easily, without a runoff, and was able to create a black/conservative white biracial coalition for several reasons. The white business leadership saw the potential for winning votes and support of blacks to achieve economic policy goals; a moderate black mayor could calm the racial turmoil detrimentally affecting business in the city; and blacks would see an opportunity for economic gain and would take pride in supporting a black for mayor.[64]

Mayor Ron Kirk quickly fulfilled his supporters' expectations of strong leadership, and early in his tenure he established dominance of the council. Being the first black mayor worked with advantage among both blacks and whites. Kirk also had the advantage of a strong economy and increasing tax base, as well as an engaging personality and adroit political skills.

When council members objected to some of his tactics, Kirk responded: "The train is moving, and the easiest way to not get run over is to get onboard." Most council members did get onboard. Exceptions were Paul Fielding, Larry Duncan, and Donna Blumer during Kirk's first term, and Donna Blumer and Laura Miller during his second term.

62. Remarks by Barbara Mallory Caraway to the Greater Dallas Planning Council, January 23, 1997.

63. This was an off-the-record comment to the author. *Fantastic four hundred* is a term that former city manager John Ware used in my interview with him, December 16, 1997, to describe "the same people we meet everywhere we go," while the rest of the citizens in the city are "getting on with their lives."

64. In Los Angeles, similarly, Tom Bradley was a moderate black mayor who appealed both to racial minorities, who saw continued growth as the foundation of new jobs, and to the conservative white leadership, who hoped for racial harmony while not jeopardizing business interests. For a detailed account, see Raphael J. Sonenshein, *Politics in Black and White: Race and Power in Los Angeles* (Princeton, N.J.: Princeton University Press, 1993).

Being a black politician created constituency problems for Kirk, as it had for the two professionally trained black city managers. Richard Knight, city manager from 1986 to 1990, observed in 1979:

> Black people have traditionally viewed city halls as large imposing structures that represent the "system." A black manager should therefore try to include those who have felt left out. But he must also have the courage to say "no" to some of the demands or requests from individuals or interest groups who expect special treatment because the manager belongs to their racial group.

Shortly after his appointment as city manager, he was more adamant: "I think we can ill afford to make decisions based on something being a black issue, a brown issue or a white issue. As a city administration, we will deal with those issues because they are human issues. Period."[65]

Three years later, when the second black city manager, John Ware, assumed office, vocal black leaders in the community tested him. His reaction was similar to that of Knight. John Wiley Price called Ware to tell him he was bringing fifty people to City Hall. Ware responded that his office was not large enough to accommodate them, but that Price could bring five, and if Price were to make an appointment, Ware would try to fit it in. Price then threatened a sit-in at City Hall; so Ware told him to go ahead, but that it would not affect him, although it might disrupt traffic. For several Sundays thereafter, Price wore a placard to church: "He's a Brother, but He's the Other."[66] But there were no demonstrations at City Hall or at Ware's home.

The 97 percent black vote for Mayor Kirk in 1995, and the subsequent honeymoon period, kept discontent among the Old Guard black leadership private for the first two years of Kirk's administration. This quiet finally broke down in 1997, when County Commissioner John Wiley Price and NAACP president Lee Alcorn led protests on Saturdays in March and April outside the mayor's home. Mayor Kirk fumed over the protests that invaded his private life at his home rather than at City Hall.[67] The major complaint expressed was that the mayor was not addressing the interests of blacks and was a pawn of white business interests. The catalyst was Mayor Kirk's public statement that disruptive protesters at school board meetings should be arrested.[68]

This public rift reflected the division in the black community between the

65. Chris Kelley, "High Profile," *Dallas Morning News,* May 3, 1987.

66. John Ware, author interview, December 16, 1997. Also see Anne Belli Gesalman, "High Profile," *Dallas Morning News,* May 1, 1994.

67. Henry Tatum, *Dallas Morning News,* March 12, 1997.

68. Public education in Dallas is governed by an independently elected school board, which has been embroiled in conflict for decades. See Glenn M. Linden, *Desegregating Schools in Dallas: Four Decades in the Federal Courts* (Dallas: Three Forks, 1995). Recent conflicts have been racial power plays to name the superintendent.

natives "who have been in Dallas and are professional victims of racism, and the newcomers, who are entrepreneurial."[69] The two groups have different styles for bringing about the changes desired: marches and protests versus working through the system.

Mayor Ron Kirk favored increasing the mayoral powers. He proposed that the mayor, with the council's consent, rather than the city council itself, hire the city manager, city attorney, and city secretary, with the mayor alone being given the authority to fire these officers. A two-thirds majority of the council could overturn these mayoral decisions.

Mary Poss, mayoral aspirant and loyal Kirk supporter, proposed a mayoral veto of council decisions on policy matters, with a two-thirds veto override provision. Since at least 1982 the issue of giving the mayor veto power with a two-thirds override by the council had been discussed. Faced with opposition on the council from minorities, Kirk, like Bartlett before him, backed away from proposals to strengthen the mayor through charter changes, as did the Citizens Council and the *News*. Councilman Al Lipscomb observed: "It'll pull power away from the neighborhoods and give it right back to the master. We'll be right back to square one: powerless."[70]

When Kirk and Poss did not get their proposals on the ballot to strengthen the power of the mayor, Kirk wanted to halt a pending charter election in favor of a charter review commission. The *Dallas Morning News* weighed in with an editorial in support of Kirk's position.[71] The council voted to proceed with the May charter election but did approve by an 8-6 vote a Kirk-authored resolution, which urged the successor council, taking office in June 1997, to name a thirty-member City Charter Review Commission to study changes. Such a panel was not created, although Kirk was reelected to a second term as mayor.

Although Mayor Kirk did not get the formal increase in authority he had sought, the mayor in Dallas is not just "first among equals." The mayor has the right to name the members and chairs of the city council standing committees, control the agenda that goes before the full council, and appoint more members of boards and commissions than other council members. Since 1991 the mayor has had a four-year rather than a two-year term but with a two-term limit, while council members each have a two-year term, with a limit of four successive terms.

Although Ron Kirk did not gain *formal* veto authority, his use of *informal* veto authority illustrates the opportunities available to leaders with the clout and political skills to exercise expansive powers. And in Dallas, when the mayor and the city manager do work in tandem, and have the support of the leadership of the Citizens Council, the Greater Dallas Chamber of Commerce,

---

69. Interview by author of a black leader, who asked to remain anonymous.
70. Christopher Lee, *Dallas Morning News,* January 1, 1997.
71. Editorial, *Dallas Morning News,* February 28, 1997.

and the *Dallas Morning News,* they can plow a path to their goals, regardless of the government structure.

An example is what happened to a council member's "share" of bond election money. Council member Larry Duncan had spent two years asking his constituents what they wanted to spend their next bond-election budget allocation on; he drew up their list. Besides phasing in the spending on land for a new branch library in their district, flood-control projects and an ambulance bridge at a rail crossing were on the list. City Manager Ware, however, took all the district's share of the bond allocation for the library. In a council briefing, Kirk explained to Duncan that a wealthy patron such as Margaret McDermott might stop donating so generously to the city's library system if the city did not make tough choices, and show participation with some of its own money.[72] The "tough choice" was to take the district's bond money share and allocate it to a citywide library project.[73]

Single-member districts did not materially affect the position of mayor in the council-manager form of government. However, the greater diversity of interests represented on a council elected from single-member districts increases the challenges to mayoral leadership.

Mayor-Manager Relations

Since the first mayor was elected citywide in 1951, sufficient mayors and city managers have served to discern whether single-member district elections per se have affected relations between the city manager and the mayor. Of the nine city managers and twelve mayors since 1951,[74] some mayors have been the acknowledged leaders; a few even have driven city managers from office.[75] Some city managers also have taken a dominant lead.[76] These "dominations" pertained under both at-large elections and single-member district elections.

The change to single-member districts in Dallas does not seem, materially, to have affected the institutional balance of power between the mayor and city

72. Margaret McDermott, one of Dallas's generous and gracious philanthropists, would not, in all likelihood, have approved of such a ploy.

73. Jim Schutz, *Dallas Observer,* March 12, 1998.

74. City Managers Ford, Crull, McDonald, Schrader, Anderson, Knight, Hart, Ware, Benavides; and Mayors Adoue, Thornton, Cabell, Jonsson, Wise, Harrison, Folsom, Evans, Taylor, Bartlett, Strauss, and Kirk.

75. The mayors who drove out city managers were J. B. Adoue (1951–1953), Eric Jonsson (1964–1971), and Steve Bartlett (1991–1995). Jonsson wanted a city manager more willing to fulfill grand plans than Elgin Crull; Bartlett not only had trouble working with a woman but was faced with Jan Hart, a strong professional willing to resist a mayor's invasions of a city manager's turf.

76. These include city managers George Schrader (1972–1981), who served with Mayors Wes Wise, Adlene Harrison, and Robert Folsom; and John Ware (1993–1998), who served with Steve Bartlett and cooperatively with Ron Kirk.

manager. Thus the relative power of these two city official positions can be attributed to strength of personality and political skills rather than to the structure of government. The strong exercise of power has been seen in a white mayor (Jonsson) and a black mayor (Kirk), as well as in a white city manager (Schrader) and a black city manager (Ware). In each case, these leaders also had the critically important support of Dallas business leaders.

Council-Manager Relations

The council-manager form of government establishes a division between the policy-making responsibility of the council and the administrative role of the manager and city staff. While this separation of powers is seldom clear-cut, the principles on which the division of responsibility is based are understood and respected by at-large councils. Council members view their service as part-time, and details of administration remain, for the most part, within the province of city officials and staff.

With the introduction of three single-member districts in Dallas in 1975, City Manager George Schrader, who served under both at-large councils and the first council elected under 8-3, observed that almost immediately the dividing line between his administrative duties and the duty of the council to set overall guidelines no longer existed. "Single-member districts have tended to make the council much more aware of the daily problems in their districts," he said. At the same time, according to Schrader, the city council's increased involvement with constituents' demands made the council less attentive to policy areas.[77]

Council members who served at the time made similar observations. One said, "[The city manager] can do more policy initiating with single-member districts than before. The council sometimes doesn't even realize what he is doing." Another member observed that the lack of unification on the city council made it easier for Schrader to manipulate them: "He has gained too much power in policy decisions because we really don't always know what we are deciding."[78] The city manager did not appear to usurp the council's responsibility for establishing general policy guidelines; rather, the council members abrogated that role.

The contrast was accentuated with the change from 8-3 to 14-1. Jan Hart, city manager from 1990 to 1993, spanning the transition to 14-1, had trouble with an inexperienced council, and with Mayor Bartlett, over the policy/administration distinction in the council-manager form of government. Few of the council members elected from single-member districts had served on cor-

77. Lyke Thomson and Henry Tatum, "Who has the power?" *Dallas Morning News,* January 30, 1977.

78. Ibid.

porate or nonprofit boards, where they could have gained an understanding of their policy role. They faced changed expectations of their constituents, who wanted a more hands-on, responsive representation. Many members elected to the council—unlike the at-large representatives—were unemployed or minimally self-employed, and thus had more time to devote to city business.

As council members responded to the political pressures, they chose to approach department heads directly to express concerns. City Manager Jan Hart responded by establishing strict rules, not allowing staff members, except for the city manager or one of four assistant city managers, to talk to council members. After Hart resigned, council members extracted from her successor, John Ware, an agreement to allow council members to talk to staff directly but for informational purposes only.[79] The separation of information seeking and pressure application was not, and cannot be, easily enforced.

After they had gained a seat at the council table, minorities wanted more power and chafed under the constraints of council-manager government, especially the restriction on dealing directly with department heads. Council member Don Hicks, a black lawyer who represented parts of southern Dallas, was vocal in expressing dissatisfaction with the council-manager system. He believed it to be unresponsive to his district's needs, and wanted council members to have more control over solving problems and spending money in their own districts.

Again, changing the system of government became a hot topic. By the time of the city council retreat in 1993, Mayor Bartlett reversed his position, which favored discussing a change. "There is no groundswell of support for changing the council-manager system," he said. "It's been a hot topic in the press and among analysts, but I think the public is generally satisfied with the council-manager system."[80] The appointment of the new city manager, John Ware, was partially responsible for the change in Bartlett's and others' attitude. "We're working with our first 14-1 city manager and things are changing, so there's kind of feeling to wait about a year and see how things are going," said council member Larry Duncan.[81]

Three years later Don Hicks was still complaining that the council-manager system had not adequately addressed problems in his district, such as poverty, housing, and code enforcement. "I believe if I had a ward system and my district got its share of taxes for five years, I could make more impact on the district than what I have right now," he said. "I want a radical change."[82] His position failed to garner support, and was not picked up or supported by members who served on later councils.

79. Laura Miller, *Dallas Observer,* October 7, 1993.
80. Sylvia Martinez, *Dallas Morning News,* November 21, 1993.
81. Ibid.
82. Todd J. Gillman, *Dallas Morning News,* November 24, 1996.

Several factors contributed to a significantly increased workload for council members: their greater involvement in operational details; the city manager's increased participation in the setting of policy; more constituent contact, with greater demands for highly detailed information from staff; and the enlarged size of the council. Members often complained that they put in a forty- to sixty-hour week, which qualified their work as a full-time job, warranting full-time pay. A salary for a full-time job finally did receive voter approval in May 2001.[83] This completed the transition from the concept of council service as a part-time civic duty to a full-time political job, a significant modification of the council-manager form of government from its original intent.

The principles on which the division in council-manager government is based, between the policy-making responsibility of the council and the administrative role of the city manager and city staff, have either not been understood and respected or have been ignored by council members elected from single-member districts. This, too, had the effect of eroding the "wall of separation" between the responsibilities of the council and those of the city manager and city staff.

Intra-Council Relations

Single-member districts have had significant effect on council organization. Little attention had been focused on the largely ceremonial officer positions, until Mayor Pro Tem Adlene Harrison became mayor, when Wes Wise resigned to run for Congress in 1976. Seeing the possibility for succeeding to the office, council members jockeyed for leadership positions. With single-member districts, race-consciousness moved to the forefront in the selection of officers.

After the 1991 adoption of 14-1, the fifteen-member council had an unwritten rule that each of the three major ethnic groups would be represented in the three leadership positions on the council. Under Mayor Bartlett, black Al Lipscomb was mayor pro tem and Hispanic Chris Luna was deputy mayor pro tem; during the next two years, Hispanic Domingo Garcia was mayor pro tem, and black Charlotte Mayes served as deputy mayor pro tem. It was a long-standing tradition that the public vote should be unanimous, even though the competition engaged in private might be nasty, which it was in 1993. In that year Luna and Garcia competed for mayor pro tem; finally, Luna declined the nomination so as not to split the council.

83. The mayor's salary was raised to $60,000 per year and a council member's salary to $37,500. The campaign literature, which supported a salary increase, indicated endorsement by all the area's chambers of commerce, plus the Stemmons Business Corridor, the Dallas Citizens Council, the African American Pastors Coalition, and the *Dallas Morning News*.

In 1995 the race-based positioning breached tradition. It became public, in an embarrassing first-day defeat for the new mayor. The election of Kirk demonstrated, in the minds of some, the folly of race-based traditions. The election of a black as mayor placed the council in an awkward situation, with regard to the tradition of a white and a Hispanic filling the other two slots. After the swearing-in, and following form, council member Max Wells was chosen mayor pro tem by acclamation, after Donna Halstead had backed out of the race to keep from splitting the council over the white officer slot.

But the debate over whether Charlotte Mayes (black) should remain as deputy mayor pro tem for a second term caused Ron Kirk, as his first official action as mayor, to call the group into a closed, executive session. There the fifteen-member council argued over who would get the slot. Certainly they had wrestled over such matters before, but they had never dragged the division into public view. Backers of Charlotte Mayes wanted her to keep the deputy mayor pro tem title. They claimed that, with a black mayor, the city should stop striving for constant tri-ethnic parity in leadership posts.[84]

Other colleagues argued that Dallas should move beyond symbolic inclusiveness, choosing its leaders regardless of race or ethnicity. Barbara Mallory Caraway, a black council member, said that she had struggled before deciding to back Hispanic Chris Luna over her friend Mayes. But, she said, "race *does* matter. And those of us that say that race doesn't matter are fooling ourselves." In the end, Mayes lost to Luna, who became deputy mayor pro tem on a 10 to 5 vote.[85]

The tri-ethnic pattern of leadership also became the accepted practice on council-appointed boards and commissions. In fact, if there were insufficient positions to accommodate all three ethnic groups on a particular board, a new leadership position was to be created.[86]

The committee structure of the council is important in Dallas. Scant research exists on current roles taken by committees of city councils. Political scientists John P. Pelissero and Timothy B. Krebs found, in their 1997 study of city councils in large American cities, that legislative committees have little impact on policy.[87] In Dallas, however, council committees not only play a

84. Lori Stahl, *Dallas Morning News,* June 10, 1995.

85. Todd J. Gillman and Sylvia Martinez, *Dallas Morning News,* June 6, 1995. Mayes won the backing of Fielding, Lipscomb, Larry Duncan, and Donna Blumer.

86. For example, in 1993, the mayor appointed Lois Finkelman (white) as president of the Park and Recreation Board. When René Martinez (Hispanic) challenged Evelyne Long (black) for the number 2 slot in October 1993, however, shouting and accusations of racism erupted at the board meeting. Later, when the officers were elected, the board reelected Long as vice president and created a second vice president's post to which Martinez was elected.

87. John P. Pelissero and Timothy B. Krebs, "City Council Legislative Committees and Policy-making in Large United States Cities," *American Journal of Political Science* (April 1997), 41:499–518.

significant role in shaping city policy and laws, but they also serve as gate-keepers in the policy process. If an item does not win approval from a committee, it is unlikely to be heard by the full city council. And if it should win committee approval, the council normally defers to the committee because of the sheer volume of items on the council's bi-weekly voting agenda.[88] Further, it is often at committee meetings, which are open to the press and to the public, where council initiatives are brought to public attention prior to a council decision.

Thus council members covet the chairmanships of these committees, and the structure of the committees strengthens the mayor's role in policy making. The mayor has sole authority to form council committees, assign members, and name chairmen and vice chairmen. The authority to form council committees also can be used to abolish committees. When Mayor Kirk assumed office in 1995, the entire committee system was in jeopardy. According to council member Donna Blumer, Mayor Kirk suggested to her and other council members that he believed committees should be abolished altogether. Blumer responded by writing a column for the *News;* she argued that, "while the rule changes may appear slight to the casual observer, they could be an early indication of how our new mayor intends to establish 'predictability'—by gaining virtual control of the agenda for himself and his inner circle, limiting debate and public exposure on controversial issues, and working toward a rubber-stamp vote by an inadequately informed council."[89]

Kirk abandoned the idea, but he avoided having policy conflicts aired at council meetings by assigning chairmanships only to his supporters. In 1995 he said that he tried to assign a council member to at least one of the committees she or he had set as a priority. Blumer responded that the mayor had denied her request to sit as a voting member on the three committees she had listed as her priorities.[90]

Kirk also stripped Donna Blumer, Larry Duncan, Charlotte Mayes, and Paul Fielding, all having voted against his choice for mayor pro tem, of their chairmanships and vice chairmanships. Only Al Lipscomb, who had supported Mayes over Luna, escaped punishment. For months, Blumer and Fielding complained that Kirk was hurting their north Dallas constituents by denying them key committee assignments, especially since no north Dallas council member was represented on the Transportation Committee, which was wrestling with proposals to expand the LBJ Freeway in north Dallas. Mayor Kirk said that the moves were part of a larger effort to reduce City Hall's public quarrels, which sully Dallas's image in business circles.[91]

88. A typical agenda has approximately one hundred items that require a vote.
89. Donna Blumer, Op-Ed, *Dallas Morning News,* June 14, 1995.
90. Miriam Rozen, *Dallas Observer,* November 22, 1995.
91. Todd J. Gillman, *Dallas Morning News,* March 6, 1996.

In 1997 the mayor again promoted allies, including the council's four newcomers, to become chairs or vice chairs of a committee. He left out the two detractors, council veterans and four-termers Larry Duncan and Donna Blumer. "I wasn't surprised by this," Blumer said. "We all know around City Hall that we dissent at our peril, and I have dissented on several occasions and I've done it publicly."[92]

In the 1999 appointments, Donna Blumer, with Laura Miller, one of the mayor's most vocal critics, were the only returning council members who did not receive a chairmanship. This time, however, four-termer Donna Blumer was appointed vice chair of the Health, Youth, and Human Services Committee. Subsequently, though, Blumer resigned her vice chairmanship, to show her opposition to the mayor's decision to exclude council colleague Laura Miller from a leadership position. "I feel the mayor has written off District 3," Blumer said. "If it were any other council member, I would take the same position." Blumer explained that she believed it was time for council members to take a stand against the mayor's practice of appointing only his supporters to leadership posts. "The mayor doesn't pick his team," she said. "The voters pick his team."[93]

Other mayors may or may not pursue Mayor Kirk's use of committees, but the use Kirk made of them illustrates the flexibility available to the mayor under the city charter. Kirk's approach was to use the committee structure as a way to gain control of 14-1 councils with diverse and conflicting interests.

The council officers and the council committees may not have captured the attention of many citizens, but behavior in council meetings did. From the public's perspective, a major, visible change in Dallas's city politics with 14-1 was that conflict moved from behind closed doors. During council meetings, the media could focus their cameras and stories on confrontations, grandstanding, outrageous racial epithets, and even physical attacks. In a city accustomed to decorum, disgust with the council grew. According to one *News* editorial, council meetings looked more like "wrestling events at the Big D Sportatorium than orderly functions for municipal business."[94]

The chaos in meetings caused the disaffected, including strong potential candidates, who did not want to be part of this new scene, to withdraw from city politics. The new public behavior could not be attributed to any change in law; Texas has had an Open Meetings Act, which covers municipal governing bodies, since 1967.[95] Rather, the single-member district council members, schooled in the confrontational political style, benefited from public controversy and the accompanying media attention.

92. Todd J. Gillman, *Dallas Morning News,* March 19, 1997.
93. Michael Saul, *Dallas Morning News,* July 31, 1999.
94. Editorial, *Dallas Morning News,* February 14, 1997.
95. The Texas Open Meetings Act has been amended several times since 1967; in 1993 it was codified as chapter 551 of the state's Government Code.

The absence of a circus-like atmosphere in the years before single-member districts cannot be attributed to agreement within the at-large councils. Elizabeth Blessing, an Independent on the council from 1961 to 1965, said that members often fought vigorously behind closed doors, but they then united so that the public would see efficient and effective council behavior. George Allen, the four-term CCA candidate, provided confirmation. He said that Mayor Erik Jonsson controlled, using the respect that the council had for him: "Erik was just straight. Straight in his life, straight in his business dealings, straight in his thinking. Nobody including a Heggins or a Lip [Al Lipscomb] would have talked to Erik Jonsson in a public meeting like she [Elsie Faye Heggins] talked to [Mayor Robert] Folsom."[96] Allen continued, describing how Jonsson did not like public controversy:

> He could sit quiet longer than anybody I've ever seen to be a public official. He wouldn't say a word. He'd let us go at it. Finally when it seemed like we've gotten it out of our system, maybe still pouting a little bit or moaning about it, you know, he'd say, "All right. Are we through with it now?" And if one would say, "Well, no, . . ." He'd say, "Now don't tell me you don't know. Let's get through with it in here because I don't want to hear that out there. When we go out there, we're going to be together . . . don't you go out there acting like a circus or something because a lot of people sitting out there came to see just such conduct."[97]

During the years of the 8-3 councils, 1976 to 1990, but especially after 1991 with the 14-1 councils, meetings sometimes dragged on for fifteen hours, votes were tabled and delayed for months, while efforts were made to achieve consensus. As political columnist Carolyn Barta observed: "Individual agendas have become the stuff of which council meetings are made, with members constantly testing the bounds of the council-manager system. Some members consistently offend, others retreat for fear of offending."[98]

Bartlett, the first mayor elected under the 14-1 plan, campaigned on a promise to restore decorum at City Hall, but he was unable to maintain control over council meetings. Sometimes it became quite ugly. In 1993, after Jan Hart had selected Ben Click as chief of police, an infuriated Don Hicks called the city manager a "queen," part of an elitist conspiracy "like the one in Nazi Germany." For Hicks, who was black, the appointment of a white chief was tantamount to racism. "The process is flawed as far as African Americans are concerned," Hicks said. "This is a cram down, and I'm not going to take it quietly." He said Hart's pick of a white outsider to head the Dallas Police

96. Oral history interview with George Allen by Gerald Saxon (1981), "Dallas Mayors Oral History Records Project," J. Erik Jonsson Branch, Dallas Public Library.
97. Ibid.
98. Carolyn Barta, "Dallas needs a change," *Dallas Morning News,* January 30, 1989.

Department was part of a deliberate effort to exclude input from black elected officials.[99] That Hart was following the Dallas City Charter in a matter as important as the selection of a police chief was disregarded. Almost equally egregious was that Mayor Bartlett did not use the tools of the chair to put a stop to the outrageous public attack.

The continued fractiousness of councils was a reason for a desire by some for a black to be elected mayor. Ron Kirk, given his political skills, monetary motivations, sense of humor, and pragmatism, seemed a sound choice to be the first black mayor of Dallas. He was appropriate for bridging the black community and the white business establishment at that time. Although Kirk had a bumpy start in parts of the black community, they soon quieted when they found that he could not be intimidated by his own race.

Kirk's election was seen as a mandate for reining in the council. With the support of the business community and with minorities not wanting to embarrass the first black mayor, Kirk was able quickly to consolidate control over council meetings by changing some of the city council rules of procedure. Five resolutions to do so were passed in 1995. The first was a proposal to control the agenda. Until Steve Bartlett's term, council members had approached the city manager directly to place items on the agenda. Mayor Bartlett had caused a stir when he had sought to have final say over everything that was to be entered onto the agenda. Opposition to this move had prompted the council to adopt a three-member rule for items to be added to the agenda.

Mayor Kirk caused a similar stir by changing to a five-member rule. Kirk's supporters noted that to require five signatures on an agenda item is not unreasonable, given that eight votes were required to adopt legislation. "It is not in their [citizens] best interest for us to be here—12 to 15 hours at a council meeting—debating issues that do not have the support of a significant number of the council," Donna Halstead argued.[100]

Deputy Mayor Pro Tem Chris Luna agreed: "History has shown that the issues we spend an inordinate amount of time on were driven by three council members and only get support of three council members." Luna pointed to a push by Donna Blumer, and colleagues Paul Fielding and Domingo Garcia, to put a nonbinding referendum on a new sports arena on the ballot. After much debate, the measure had been defeated by a vote of 12 to 3. This conflict also illustrates the alternative view, as expressed by Donna Blumer, however. The five-member rule "is a clear attempt to stifle those with minority views who might force council members into a debate or vote they would like to avoid," she said.[101]

In 1998 the mayor lost on an issue regarding control of the agenda for

99. Lori Stahl and Sylvia Martinez, *Dallas Morning News,* June 17, 1993.
100. Sylvia Martinez, *Dallas Morning News,* June 13, 1995.
101. Ibid.

briefing meetings, which occur on the Wednesdays alternate to the voting meetings.[102] When council member Laura Miller wanted the council to be briefed on proposed revisions to the city's code of ethics, Mayor Ron Kirk thwarted her effort to get the issue onto the agenda. Miller succeeded in passing a new policy, one the mayor had opposed. The council voted 9 to 6 to require the mayor to put an item requested by five council members on the briefing agenda. Prior to this resolution, the mayor and the city manager controlled that agenda. Kirk responded that he did not believe the resolution would weaken the office of the mayor. "As long as I stay my sweet, persuasive self, if I can find eight votes, I will be OK," he said.[103]

While considered heavy-handed by some, Mayor Kirk, by force of personality, assisted by the changes in the rules of procedure that he initiated, did rein in the council.

RELATIONS BETWEEN OFFICIALS AND SELF-APPOINTED POLICY MAKERS

Beyond the governance structure, the extra-legal decision making in the city should be considered with regard to assessing whether single-member districting has affected the regime. Recall from chapter 4 that regime theorists define an urban regime as "the informal arrangements by which public and private interests function together in order to be able to make and carry out governing decisions."[104] In Dallas, the strongest "informal arrangements" have been between city government and business. Indeed, the city mantra has been, and is, "The business of Dallas is business."

When the president of General Motors said, "What is good for General Motors is good for the country," a national outcry ensued. In contrast, when Dallas leaders justify policies based on the assertion that what is good for business is good for the city, as they often do, citizens with differing voices are silenced as being naive or are discounted as troublemakers. Some abandon their causes and climb aboard for economic gain. Cynicism is a by-product when citizens discover that business leaders and public officials have disguised their ambition as "public interest."

With society being market-driven, the systemic bias is toward capital; hence much of the literature on cities focuses on the business-government nexus. Economic prosperity does substantially assist in the solving of pressing problems confronting a community. Mayors and city managers would prefer

102. At briefing meetings, the council receives reports but does not formally take votes.
103. Michael Saul, *Dallas Morning News,* October 22, 1998.
104. Clarence N. Stone, *Regime Politics: Governing Atlanta 1946–1988* (Lawrence: University Press of Kansas, 1989), 6.

functioning in cities with expanding tax bases rather than those facing nose-diving economies. The interests of political leaders and business leaders, therefore, coincide in tending toward economic development. City officials depend on capital investment for city priorities, and elected officials depend on financial support from the business community. In turn, business depends on the government for policies that favor the economic interests of business.

But when a price mechanism breaks down, the capitalist economic system breaks down. How can public goods such as safe streets, unpolluted air, and social services to the needy be priced? Citizens have a common interest in an economically prosperous city with a free market economy; they have a common stake in a socially just society. Can these dual priorities compete realistically? With a balance of influence, perhaps they can. With sufficient support to back noneconomic public policy initiatives strongly, public officials can sometimes say no to business and yes to other constituents.

That balance of influence has been absent in Dallas. Bringing the representatives of the disadvantaged and of neighborhoods to the council table through single-member districts did not redress the inequality of interests. The economic weight of the Dallas Citizens Council and the Chamber of Commerce, when they mobilize on an issue, together with the support they have from the city's dominant communications engine, the Belo Corporation, totally overwhelms public good priorities.[105] Bond issues and trophy projects, which fuel businesses that depend on real estate, development, and construction projects, receive primary attention. Affordable housing, human services, youth programs, and pollution abatement languish for lack of funding and attention.

Frustrated citizens tend to demonize the wealthy major business leaders, who play a leading role in setting the agenda in Dallas. Partnering requires two sides. Blame falls equally on city staff and city council members, who arrange and execute unsound ventures on behalf of business leaders, at the expense of taxpayers. On the other hand, much collaboration and partnering between the private, the public, and the nonprofit sectors that has widespread beneficial impact does occur in Dallas. Many remarkable and constructive examples, from community policing and neighborhood block watches to business-school partnerships and mentoring programs, can be cited.

Some collaboration is stimulated by grants from foundations and some by businesses and individuals through direct financial support and in pro bono services. But Dallas associations and groups of like-minded individuals have not been sufficiently sizable, nor have they had the resources or the staying

---

105. Dallas-based Belo owns the *Dallas Morning News,* WFAA-TV (Channel 8) and Texas Cable News (Channel 38), and media properties nationwide, as well as having influence over many radio stations, TV channels, and newspapers outside Belo ownership, nationwide.

power to generate large and ongoing support for unprofitable, social public policy initiatives.

In the final analysis, the dominant role in Dallas played by the major business leaders with vested interest in city programs and policies has not fundamentally changed with single-member districts. Although they themselves may not serve on the city council any longer nor recruit candidates for election slates, they still determine who is to be mayor and who is to receive funding or other perks. With the demise of the Citizens Charter Association, and its public backing of a slate of candidates, voters now do not know who receives the support of the Citizens Council members and of their political offshoot, the Breakfast Group. During its time, the Citizens Charter Association at least provided a cue to voters and stimulated the organization of opposing slates.

In the early days of single-member districts, after the demise of the Citizens Charter Association, traditional business leadership stumbled as it searched for new ways to control unwieldy councils and public images embarrassing to the city. Part of the disarray can be attributed to the economic free-fall in the mid-1970s, which complicated the local and national political scene. By the early 1980s business had regrouped; City Manager Charles Anderson could claim that there seemed little Dallas could not do: "In a matter of a few phone calls, I could put together a team of business and civic leaders to do just about anything." Under Anderson's watch, the city approved its largest bond issue in history, reached an agreement with the state to widen a city artery, North Central Expressway, and landed the 1984 Republican National Convention.[106] By the 1990s a team of business and civic leaders—largely behind closed doors—gained approval for a new sports arena, the long-argued Trinity River development project, and a bid for the 2012 Olympics.

A city council member summed up the situation for his constituents in this way:

> If one does not think the business community can still get things done, just take a look at *financial* interest issues. When dollar and cents business issues are important to a particular large business, they bring down the sky in influence and pressure on the political system. On the other hand, if it is recruiting a candidate, taking the time to know an issue and its impact on the tax base or infrastructure system, business leaders shrug and say "it's single member districts—we can't do anything about it." If, however, those issues line the pocketbook or infringe on the market advantage of a particular company, the Council will come under very great organized across-the-board pressures such that even the most staunch and aggressive

106. *Dallas Morning News,* April 5, 1992.

civil rights advocate will say "I can't take *this* pressure" and give their vote to the particular corporate interest.[107]

CONCLUSIONS

The change to a single-member district election system required few adjustments in the City Charter, but the change modified the functioning of Dallas's council-manager form of government. Generally members elected from single-member districts became more involved with day-to-day government operations and less attentive to policy direction. Through ignorance, or by intent, many council members ignored the division of responsibility between council and city manager, inherent in the council-manager form of government. Constituency service, and responsiveness to special interests, assumed priority; a level of cronyism and corruption, not characteristic in Dallas for half a century, developed.

Representatives from single-member districts altered the dynamics of the struggles for power and turf between the mayor and the council and the city manager. Public views of the council changed, as conflicts moved from behind closed doors to the council table.

On the other hand, the informal relationships between public and private interests, as well as the public policy initiatives taken by key business leaders, were not altered in any fundamental way by single-member districts. The dominant role played by major business leaders in the city has not fundamentally changed. The bedrock of government and politics in Dallas is still the city's cultural context and the long-standing business-government partnership. The more things change, the more they stay the same.

107. Jerry Bartos, "Newsletter to Constituents and Friends," May 26, 1993.

8
Policy Results

You won't find the fingerprints.
—Dallas City Manager John Ware

Culture might be defined as what matters to a society. And certainly a good
measure of what matters is how we spend our money.
—David McCullough

When citizens press for change in their election system, they hope to achieve
policy outcomes different from those produced by the status quo. Chapter 6
explained the changes in election results in Dallas that can be attributed to the
court-ordered single-member district system. The "mirror-the-constituency"
view of representation accepted by the courts, discussed in chapter 7, presumes
that policies adopted by a council, which includes members of minority
groups, will be responsive to the interests of those minorities. The fundamental
question in this chapter is whether the election outcome ("who is elected")
makes a difference in policy making. If the answer is yes, then the courts' pre-
scription for Dallas's election system had the unintended consequence of alter-
ing yet another element in the whole of the city's politics, its policy agenda.

Over the last three decades, scholars have generated a body of literature
on connections between government structures and public policies. Those who
have studied the impact of minority representatives on policy outcomes have
reached conflicting conclusions on the effect, if any, made by who is elected.[1]
The finding, often attributed to an increase in the number of minority representatives, is an increase in minority employment in government.[2] Even in this
case, some scholars have found that when they control for the minority per-

1. For a path-breaking study, see Robert Lineberry and Edmund Fowler, "Reformism
and Public Policy in American Cities," *American Political Science Review* (September
1967), 61:701–716.
2. See, for example, James W. Button, *Blacks and Social Change: Impact of the Civil
Rights Movement in Southern Communities* (Princeton, N.J.: Princeton University Press,
1989), 128–135, 162–164.

centage of the population, the results do not have statistical significance.[3] Without establishing linkages between who gets elected and policy outcomes, the difference that electoral structure makes cannot be determined.

Meanwhile, in the absence of proven linkages, researchers can identify factors in various circumstances that *seem* to be related to policy outcomes. Anecdotes are the bearers of narratives that explain, represent, and illustrate wider realities. From this perspective, what changes in Dallas's policy agenda might be attributed to a change in electoral structure? In particular, did council policies become any more responsive to the expressed interests of minorities with an increase in minority representation on the legislative body?

Top-down agenda setting by the economic elite, as well as bottom-up issues introduced by minority representatives, are considered. To assess changes in the elite's agenda that might have resulted from single-member districts, Dallas's responses to planning and zoning, and to budget and bond issues, are examined. Regarding the agendas of minorities, the areas investigated include symbolic issues, city employment, equity in the allocation of goods and services, and affirmative action in city contracts.

Political scientist John Kingdon defines *agenda* as "the list of subjects or problems to which governmental officials, and people outside of government closely associated with those officials, are paying some serious attention to at any given time."[4] Roger Cobb and Charles Elder define *systemic agenda* as "all issues that are commonly perceived by members of the political community as meriting public attention."[5]

Thus it is appropriate to determine if new voices at Dallas's council table have changed the agenda "meriting public attention" in Dallas, and whether such changes have been given sufficiently serious attention that policy changes have ensued.

SETTING THE AGENDA: TOP DOWN

An emphasis on economic development and growth in the tax base, which undergirds other policy proposals in Dallas, has changed little with time. Unlike other cities that have had to face problems created by urban sprawl, Dallas is almost totally surrounded by incorporated municipalities. Conse-

3. See, for example, J. L. Polinard et al., *Electoral Structure and Urban Policy: The Impact on Mexican American Communities* (Armonk, N.Y.: M.E. Sharpe, 1994).

4. John Kingdon, *Agenda, Alternatives, and Public Policies* (Boston: Little, Brown, 1984), 3.

5. Roger W. Cobb and Charles D. Elder, *Participation in American Politics: The Dynamics of Agenda-Building,* 2nd ed. (Baltimore, Md.: The Johns Hopkins University Press, 1983), 85; quoted in Sarah A. Binder, "The Dynamics of Legislative Gridlock, 1947–96," *American Political Science Review* (September 1999), 93:523.

quently development of Dallas must occur mainly within its present city limits. Another option for increasing Dallas's tax base is for the city to find ways to share in revenues generated in the region.

Urban sprawl in the neighboring region profoundly affects Dallas. Because the area's population is growing substantially, Dallas's proportion of the region's population will continue in its decline, even if the population within the city limits should increase. Furthermore, the growth in the region has been to the north and west, which has adversely affected the efforts to develop southern Dallas.

Two fundamental, interrelated areas in which to assess changes in the city's traditional issues surrounding economic development are, first, planning and zoning, and, second, bond referenda and annual budgets.

Planning and Zoning

On-again, off-again planning efforts in Dallas illustrate the complexity of the interplay between business interests, mayors, city managers, key city staff professionals, council members, and particular interest groups. This interplay appears to be unrelated in any significant way to whether council members are elected at large or by single-member districts.

Indisputably a common thread throughout the history of Dallas has been the primacy given to unbridled speculative real estate development over quality-of-life considerations, such as green space, human services, and environmental protection. After the state passed enabling legislation in 1927 with respect to zoning, Dallas responded two years later with a zoning ordinance. According to city planner Harland Bartholomew, even this first zoning ordinance reserved a disproportionate amount of land for commercial use.[6] Cultural context, then, as well as historical timing, and special circumstances, all contributed to Dallas being different from cities that had already implemented far-sighted master plans by the 1920s.

Planning in Dallas has flourished and ebbed in response to crises, and to the priority given it by business and civic leaders. This has pertained from the city's first planning effort in 1910 to its most recent in 1994. Planning initiatives have often been in reaction to problems created by lack of planning. Several points are illustrated by this story of planning and zoning efforts in Dallas: the difficult position of city staff planners who have found their professional judgments in conflict with the interests of powerful business leaders; the importance of leadership by the mayor, the city manager, and the newspapers; and, as a consequence, the marginal impact, in general, of a change in election districts on planning and zoning.

6. Harland Bartholomew & Associates, "A Master Plan for Dallas" (St. Louis: H. Bartholomew & Associates, 1943–1945).

In Dallas numerous plans have been commissioned both by the city itself and by private groups. Some have been implemented, but many have gathered dust on library and office shelves. Over decades a few plan proposals have appeared and then reappeared in varied forms.[7]

In 1910 the first major planning effort in Dallas was inspired by George B. Dealey, who used the *News* to push for comprehensive city planning. George E. Kessler, a noted Kansas City landscape architect, was hired to consult with the Dallas Park Board. A planner in the "City Beautiful" tradition, he proposed grand plazas, boulevards, parks, and a civic center, all linked to nearby city neighborhoods.[8] Some of Kessler's recommendations were never implemented; others were completed years later.[9]

After World War II, because of Mayor Woodall Rodgers's determination to make planning a priority for the city, Harland Bartholomew of St. Louis was hired to develop a plan. The Bartholomew Plan of 1946 reiterated many of Kessler's recommendations, and chastised the city for not having implemented them sooner. Like Kessler before him, and like virtually every planner after him, Bartholomew stated that a key reason for traffic congestion, for civic ugliness, and for blight was the city's abdication of its role to "unbridled land speculators" who did not have the greater good of the city at heart. In his report on zoning, Bartholomew stressed the importance of strong neighborhood associations to secure residential areas from commercial encroachments.[10] It was to be forty years before strong neighborhood associations did develop in Dallas to rein in unbridled commercial development. While not caused by the institution of single-member districts, the stronger political voice exercised by neighborhoods and election district change were mutually reinforcing.

A planning crisis, owing to explosive growth of the city after World War II, prompted the appointment of Dallas's first full-time director of planning in 1950. Marvin Springer, who came to Dallas from St. Louis, served until 1959. Twin legacies of the Springer Plan were the 1957 Thoroughfare Plan and an increase in city size, from 117.3 square miles in 1950, to 277.1 square miles in 1960, an increase of 136 percent in one decade.[11] Annexation in the decade of the 1950s was a sensitive political issue, mainly because the Citizens Char-

---

7. Development of the Trinity River is one example.

8. George E. Kessler, "A City Plan for Dallas: Report of Park Board," May 1911.

9. Darwin Payne, *Big D: Triumphs and Troubles of an American Supercity in the 20th Century* (Dallas: Three Forks, 1994), 111–112, 155. Some of the Kessler Plan proposals that were eventually completed include the levee system along the Trinity River, White Rock Lake Park, Central Expressway, Turtle Creek Boulevard, and a Convention Center.

10. Bartholomew, "A Master Plan"; David Firestone, *Dallas Times Herald,* July 25, 1983; and Payne, *Big D,* 210–215.

11. The city later added another 100 square miles, with the annexations of Renner, Kleberg, and Lake Ray Hubbard.

ter Association opposed it.[12] The problems Dallas would be experiencing today, especially in its tax base, had this expansion not occurred, can only be imagined.

Not only were annexation opportunities lost because of CCA opposition, but "deals" also were forfeited in the 1950s and 1960s. In recent years critics have perpetuated a myth that Dallas "can't close a deal" *because* of single-member districts and because of diminished control by the business elite. But "deals" were lost before single-member districting, such as the renowned Las Colinas development and the Dallas Cowboys stadium, both gained by the city of Irving in the 1960s.[13]

Dallas's first citywide planning effort is a legacy of the Erik Jonsson administration. In 1965 Jonsson founded Goals for Dallas, which involved grass-roots participation in establishing goals for the city and became a model for similar planning efforts in other cities. As with many planning efforts, less than two years after Jonsson left office, in 1971, Goals for Dallas was seldom mentioned in city council chambers.[14]

During the 1970s and early 1980s two professional city planners, James Schroeder (1969–1977) and Jack Schoop (1979–1982) tried to direct the explosive growth in Dallas. Both lost their positions in their attempts to stop the onslaught of the developers. Since Schoop left in 1982, Dallas has not had a strong planning voice; professional planners have come and gone.[15]

In the absence of citywide planning, attention turned to specific plans for particular areas, such as Oak Lawn and Deep Ellum. Planning for orderly development for Far North Dallas was not forthcoming, nor was a plan developed for south Dallas areas.

Through the years a problem for the southern sector has been lack of

12. David Dillon, *Dallas Morning News,* July 25, 1983.

13. When developed, Las Colinas, which included corporate headquarters, residences, hotels, restaurants, trademark canals, and a popular mustang sculpture, garnered national prominence.

When Clint Murchison Jr. proposed a downtown stadium, he had difficulty gaining an audience with the Dallas signal callers to review his detailed plans. When he did finally meet with Mayor Jonsson and Robert Cullum, he found them to be committed to preserving the Cotton Bowl and beautifying Fair Park (Blackie Sherrod, *Dallas Morning News,* July 7, 1994).

14. The first Goals program identified 114 goals, with plans for achieving them. Later, twelve committees investigated and evaluated progress in achieving the goals, and issued a report in 1972. The second cycle, begun in 1976 and completed in 1982, identified 205 new goals in seventeen subject areas. In this cycle, goals were set separately in minority communities and were found to be similar to goals set by the community as a whole. This comparison was published in 1978 as "Goals for Dallas Compared for Black Dallas and Mexican American Objectives." In 1983 a 150-member Planning Committee developed the third cycle of setting goals for the community.

15. David Dillon, "Why Can't Dallas Keep a City Planner?" *Dallas Life,* September 19, 1982, 10–20.

development. In 1997 several sponsoring organizations commissioned McKinsey & Company to develop a fact-based view of opportunities for private companies to invest and operate in the southern sector. McKinsey found that the southern sector accounted for 41 percent of Dallas's population and 47 percent of its land area but contributed only 16 percent of the city's tax base. Faced with the reality that no large parcels of land are still available for development in the northern sector, an increase in Dallas's tax base is largely dependent on southern-sector development.[16]

The problem for the far northern section of the city was excessive, unplanned commercial development. Far North Dallas, an area north of the LBJ Freeway (the second loop outside downtown), had been intended for low-density, single-family use. When speculators started to make money by rezoning the land from residential to high-density commercial, insufficient numbers of homeowners lived in the area to resist the changes.[17] Lured by an expanding tax base, impressed by the attractive elaborate drawings of developers, and ignoring how the infrastructure, especially drainage, utilities, and traffic, would be affected by every zoning change, the city council repeatedly acceded to the developers' requests.

By the time Charles Anderson became city manager in 1981, Dallas was changing. Dallas had had single-member district elections to an 8-3 council for six years. The city had had an influx of newcomers, and neighborhood groups had grown stronger. For years, land speculators had profited from land flips under Dallas's policy of cumulative zoning. Under that policy, a zoning district, such as retail, could contain several uses. Zoning categories were so broad that, for example, in Far North Dallas, the Galleria complex, which contained shops, hotels, and offices, was built on land zoned for warehouse and industrial uses.

Anderson attempted to curtail cumulative zoning with a new set of planning policies, adopted by the council in 1984, that called for sweeping changes in zoning and development rules. After two more years of intense negotiations among business leaders, neighborhood groups, and city staff, a proposed zoning ordinance was forwarded by the Plan Commission in 1986 to the city council, which passed it in 1987.[18]

City councils elected from single-member districts were more neighborhood-oriented than previous councils, but the changed approach to zoning involved more than a modified election structure. Attitudes in Dallas were changing. Conservative Republicans in north Dallas had become disenchanted

16. "Report of the Southern Sector Initiative: Dallas Working Together."

17. Mary Candace Evans, "The Route to the Present," *Parkway* (January 1983), 37–38.

18. The 1987 zoning ordinance was only the second revision since the city adopted a zoning ordinance for the first time in 1929. The first revision was in 1965, before single-member districting.

with the problems created by poorly controlled development, especially traffic congestion. The building boom in the early 1980s produced new projects and introduced new players who did not play by the old "gentlemen's agreement" rules. According to Cay Kolb, a leader in the neighborhood movement, personal agreements were enough with the old-time builders in Dallas. "I might disagree with Trammell Crow, . . . but once we reached an agreement I felt sure he would honor it."[19] By the mid-1980s city planners were finding a disturbing number of cases in which builders did not keep promises made when zoning was granted.

After council members learned that nearly half a billion dollars would be needed for new roads for all the development they had approved north of the LBJ Freeway, they realized that voters would be seeing north Dallas bond issues on their ballots for decades. Not only was the north Dallas debacle a failure by Dallas leadership to act on behalf of the city as a whole, it also justified the claims made for years by south Dallas residents that south Dallas was ignored in favor of north Dallas expenditures, a form of silent subsidy of private interests. Anger over traffic, building heights, and neighborhood protection helped the zoning reform movement win the new ordinance.

A series of high-profile zoning controversies in the 1980s tested the new policies and temperament in Dallas, with mixed results. Even as the council passed the new set of overall planning policies in 1984, calling for sweeping changes in zoning, the council diluted the power of those policies. It approved the Cityplace project, two forty-two story towers in a twenty-story zone in Oak Lawn, an area north of downtown.

Oak Lawn may have lost on Cityplace, but the following year the City Plan Commission killed a $1 billion development proposed for Oak Lawn, which called for a 35 percent increase in density over the existing zoning. For the first time in Dallas's history, the council rejected a developer's large-scale gamble to upzone.

This instance was the forerunner of several others, in which elaborate presentations by sophisticated coalitions of neighborhoods offset the elaborate presentations of developers. A coalition of Oak Lawn neighborhoods spent $35,000 to hire a lawyer, traffic planner, and engineer to prepare its case opposing the upzone proposal.[20] In 1986 the Glen Lakes Homeowners Association thwarted three big zoning requests by mega-developers—the Bass family of Fort Worth, and the Perot family and Raymond Nasher of Dallas.[21] The total

19. *Dallas Morning News,* April 6, 1986.
20. David Firestone, *Dallas Times Herald,* August 10, 1985.
21. The Homeowners Association included real estate lawyers, CEOs, and the developer of Glen Lakes, Vernon Smith. Smith stood behind the Homeowners Association, ignoring the code in Dallas that a developer does not counter another developer (Syd Reagan, telephone interview by author, September 4, 1995).

square footage of the proposed developments on Central Expressway was more than everything else that had been built in Dallas in 1984.

By the mid-1980s neighborhood groups had come of age, and the approval process had changed to one of negotiation between developer, public, and city staff. No longer were big projects approved by the city manager and planning staff, and then sped with green lights through the Plan Commission and the city council. According to Larry Duncan, longtime leader of the Dallas Homeowners League, just five years earlier the approval procedure had been called "urban guerrilla." "Since you couldn't win, you raised hell as loudly as possible to try to attract the media to educate the public." The difference, he said, is that now when a developer comes before the city planning commission, often the first thing they ask him is, "Have you talked this over with the neighborhood?"[22]

But neighborhoods did not, necessarily, have smooth sailing. In 1988, just before the crucial referendum on mass transit, Oak Lawn neighborhood activists caught wind of a scheme by Southland Corporation, a Dallas institution and parent of 7-11 Stores, to escape some financial trouble. In return for Southland's financing of an expensive DART subway station, to be located where Southland wanted it to be, the city was to grant Southland valuable re-zoning for its Cityplace property. Southland would pay the city $24 million for road and utility improvements. When the deal became public, it sounded like "contract zoning"—a swap of money for building rights—which state law prohibits. It was well known, according to a *Herald* editorial, that Southland intended to sell much of its property. In that case, the paper queried, who would make good on the $24 million?[23] Southland filed for Chapter 11 bankruptcy two years later.

Cay Kolb, an Oak Lawn neighborhood activist and former member of the City Plan Commission, called the secret negotiations "the most massive violation of the public trust ever witnessed."[24] Hugh G. Robinson, president of Cityplace Development, a Southland Corporation subsidiary, made the familiar developer argument that all sides stood to gain.[25] But from the neighborhood's perspective, they stood to gain only traffic congestion and high-rise office towers, and stood to lose the neighborhood preservation zoning that had been hammered out in 1983. For the taxpayers, this was yet another instance of clandestine dealings, which could be traced back to secret negotiations between George Schrader and Ray Hunt for the development of the Reunion complex in

22. Jim Schutze, *Dallas Times Herald,* July 1, 1987. Duncan served as a member of the Dallas City Council from 1991 to 1999.
23. Editorial, *Dallas Times Herald,* March 5, 1988.
24. Chris Kelley, *Dallas Morning News,* February 29, 1988.
25. Ibid.

Dallas's first public-private partnership.[26] Single-member districting had little effect on this style of decision making by "shadow government."

With the nosedive in real estate in the mid-1980s, Dallas slid into a period of decline. Then, in the 1990s, some business leaders decided to resume their traditional aggressive role behind the scenes to reenergize the city. Anticipating divisiveness on the first 14-1 council, elected in 1991, the inner circle in the Citizens Council encouraged Steve Bartlett to leave his seat in Congress to run for mayor and to initiate a new planning process. In August 1992 the Dallas City Council unanimously passed a resolution that authorized the creation of the Dallas Plan, as a public-private partnership.

This time the planning initiative formalized the business-government interlocking interests: the nonprofit planning organization was funded by private contributions, yet held official status as a quasi-city agency, housed in the municipal building. In December 1994 the council adopted the Dallas Plan, a thirty-year blueprint for the city, with its preliminary price tag of $6.6 billion. Within its long-range plan framework, the city council was to determine projects annually to be targeted for short-term action and completion.

The rounds of public meetings on the Dallas Plan before it was adopted, and subsequent meetings of the city council regarding annual priorities, generated little citizen interest. Reasons for public apathy varied. Citizens had observed, time and again, their priorities trumped by unofficial private deal making. Cynicism had been fostered by the many occasions Dallas citizens had seen attention given in planning documents to human needs and quality-of-life considerations, only to have the mayor, city manager, and city council focus on big projects geared to economic development. Improvements in the infrastructure, libraries, parks and recreation, and social services always seemed to be postponed. An example of a still awaited project contained in the 1994 Dallas Plan is a unified network of parks, boulevards, and natural reserves, not unlike the Kessler Plan's proposal in 1910.

Further, the Dallas Plan itself, the first plan in Dallas's history to be officially adopted by the city council, is ignored and circumvented. In 1994 the Central Dallas Association, a downtown business coalition, released its study, which proposed renovating Reunion Arena or building a new sports arena downtown. Such a strategy contradicted a Dallas Plan suggestion to build a new arena on the western outskirts of town, in Pinnacle Park. These and other

26. For details, see William E. Claggett, "Dallas: The Dynamics of Public-Private Cooperation," in *Public-Private Partnership in American Cities: Seven Case Studies,* ed. R. Scott Fosler and Renee A. Berger (Lexington, Mass.: Lexington Books, 1982). The Reunion Project, begun in 1973, was a fifty-acre downtown Dallas development that includes a Hyatt Regency Hotel, fifty-story tower, municipal sports arena, and restored Union Terminal Building. Subsequent phases were planned but were not carried out.

recommendations were bulldozed by the decision to build an arena with public subsidy on polluted land purchased by Ross Perot Jr.

Dennis Martinez, Dallas's Economic Development Director, had said in 1990 that "Dallas made the decision very early on that we would look at [sports facilities] more conservatively" than many other cities: "We are not going to give away the store."[27] Assistant City Manager Cliff Keheley had concurred, stating that some cities spend unjustified amounts of municipal money on stadiums, money that should go for fixing streets and building libraries. Even in 1993 Mayor Steve Bartlett had said: "We're not going to subsidize sports facilities, but we don't have to. We have the market."[28]

Yet, by February 1994, the prevailing attitude among those who seem to matter had changed. A group of downtown businessmen with economic interest in building a new sports arena for the Dallas Stars (hockey) and the Dallas Mavericks (basketball) franchises had volunteered to put their expertise in real estate and financing to studying the issue. The leader of the group was John Crawford, a realtor and former chairman of the Greater Dallas Chamber of Commerce. He explained that the strategy was to make the city manager, John Ware, part of the team, so that he would embrace the idea, and devote attention and staff time to it. The council was briefed on the conclusions of the $500,000 study in executive session in October 1994. The study found justification for demolishing Reunion Arena and building a $170 million, 20,000-seat arena on land that belonged to Ray Hunt and was adjacent to Hunt's Hyatt Regency hotel.[29]

Another "behind-closed-doors" maneuver resulted in a city staff study costing $50,000. It focused on an area near the Dallas Convention Center, southeast of Reunion Arena. When the council learned of the study, conducted without its knowledge or authorization, no one claimed ownership; eventually long-time staffer Cliff Keheley lost his job over the matter. A council member privately complained to an *Observer* reporter: "There's no way anybody can fight this. No way. We don't have the information. We're being buffaloed. And we're allowing it to happen because the staff has convinced us that if we don't do a new arena *right now* we'll lose the Mavericks and the Stars." Another council member added, "I'm not convinced we need it, but we're *going* to get an arena."[30]

27. Gayle Reaves, "Sleeping Giant," *Dallas Life Magazine,* February 7, 1993, 19–20.
28. David Jackson and David Hanners, *Dallas Morning News,* December 12, 1993.
29. Laura Miller, *Dallas Observer,* November 3, 1994.
30. Ibid. Nothing had changed since Reunion Arena was built, and the city council was informed that it was legally obligated to pay $1.4 million for work that was never authorized by the council or admitted to by anyone else. Apparently council member Sid Stahl tried in vain to penetrate the decision-making process of the city: "Somebody made the decision to tell the contractor to proceed. I think we are entitled to know who that person is." But the city manager only would say that it was a "team effort" (Jim Henderson, *Dallas Times Herald,* April 12, 1981).

The arena matter became a top priority of the Kirk-Ware tenure at City Hall and commanded most of the city's attention during Kirk's first four-year term. On June 17, 1994, City Manager John Ware authorized the public-works department to issue a formal request for proposals from consultants to conduct the feasibility study for the new Dallas sports arena. (The city council did not approve the study by consultants until five days later.) Two consultants were to be selected—an architectural firm and a construction firm. The council did not know when it approved the study that city officials had already hired Austin Commercial Inc. (ACI), a division of Dallas-based Austin Industries, to partici-pate in the unauthorized arena study. In early August city staff proposed hiring ACI as part of the authorized feasibility-study team. Council member Chris Luna raised a critical question: ACI would surely seek the lucrative arena con-tract, so how could it, objectively, assess whether the city could afford a new arena?[31] To the surprise of few Dallas observers, ACI did win the contract. It was teamed with black-owned H. J. Russell & Co. of Atlanta.[32]

Dallas business leaders and city officials, according to a *News* reporter, claimed that much was at stake—the city's reputation for closing a deal, the opportunity to lure developer Ross Perot Jr. back to his hometown, a potential boon for DART's rail system, the fate of downtown, and Mayor Ron Kirk's national image. "This is one we can't let get away," said political consultant Rob Allyn. "This is a city where growth is cherished. You're talking about something that sort of cuts to the heart of what Dallas is about. Rightly or wrongly, we measure the accomplishments of our leaders in physical terms."[33]

Charles C. Euchner noted that cities today face a host of intractable prob-lems, all of which a mayor cannot expect to confront in a term. A city stadium, Euchner suggested, provides a high-visibility issue that shows the mayor or manager taking charge, and it "provides booty to distribute to development interests, construction unions, bankers, and lawyers."[34] As U.S. Senator Byron L. Dorgan observed: "The only remaining healthy public housing is in sports stadiums for wealthy team owners."[35]

The arena opponents labeled the arena project "corporate welfare," a label that might have struck a chord in lower-income neighborhoods on the south side. For these neighborhoods, tax-subsidized projects always seemed to be

31. Laura Miller, "The Arena Papers," *Dallas Observer,* January 5, 1995.

32. H. J. Russell, Atlanta multimillionaire, founded the construction firm, which is America's fourth-largest minority-owned company. The company continues to qualify for, and benefit from, affirmative action.

33. Lori Stahl, *Dallas Morning News,* May 29, 1996.

34. Charles C. Euchner, *Playing the Field: Why Sports Teams Move and Cities Fight to Keep Them* (Baltimore, Md.: The Johns Hopkins University Press, 1993), which he summarized in *Dallas Morning News,* July 23, 1995.

35. Leslie Wayne, *New York Times,* July 27, 1996. See Neal R. Peirce, *National Jour-nal,* July 20, 1996, 1592.

built in other parts of Dallas, not in theirs. The voters in five predominantly black council districts, however, mobilized by their black leaders, supported the arena by more than 64 percent. According to a south Dallas resident, Mattie David, "So many of us who voted this time had never voted before."[36]

The two Hispanic districts voted against the arena, as did virtually all the precincts in Far North Dallas, which had carried most issues in the past. Mayor Kirk had promised that the arena would bring jobs and economic development, from which minorities would benefit. Perot Jr.'s Hillwood development company had won over the endorsement of several minority leaders, by promising to try in good faith to hire certain percentages of Dallas-based minority firms.

If city decision makers finessed the arena project, which did not benefit southern Dallas, then perhaps long-awaited economic development in southern Dallas might provide an example of a change in policy attributable to minority council members elected from single-member districts. Various attempts to stimulate economic development in southern Dallas had not lacked for support of city officials after the early 1980s.

Mayor Starke Taylor appointed a task force in 1983 to explore housing and economic development in southern Dallas. The resulting report pointed out the need for a nonprofit economic development corporation. The Housing and Economic Development Corporation was officially established on January 1, 1985, to stimulate residential and commercial projects in the southern sector. But the Dallas business community did not come through with key financial support for the agency. This disappointed Mayor Taylor and puzzled Richard Knight, who noted that the business community nearly always found the money for projects it really believed in.[37] The corporation was disbanded in 1987 for lack of funding.[38]

Mayor Taylor's successor, Steve Bartlett, saw an opportunity to generate $100 million in the first year, with 800 permanent jobs, if one of the state's new maximum security prisons were to be built in southern Dallas, near the city's landfill. But Bartlett, supported by south Dallas council member Don Hicks, ran into strong opposition when they met with residents within southern Dallas. The residents were concerned that a prison would reinforce the already negative image of the area.[39] In the face of this opposition, Bartlett and Hicks abandoned the idea.

John Ware, named city manager in 1993, frequently focused public attention on the need for economic development in southern Dallas. Ware's often-repeated refrain in a round of talks to community groups: "The only place Dal-

36. Christopher Lee, *Dallas Morning News,* January 25, 1998.

37. Bert Holmes, *Dallas Times Herald,* January 16, 1987. For example, $3.5 million in private contributions were raised for the 1984 Republican National Convention in Dallas, and private contributions funded the bid for the 2012 Olympics.

38. *Dallas Times Herald,* November 15, 1988.

39. Jim Reid, "A Destiny beyond Myths," *Dallas Morning News,* April 12, 1992.

las can grow is south. I'm not talking race and ethnicity. I'm talking Economics 101."

Major agenda-setting economic development projects in Dallas have not been driven by council members elected from single-member districts. After single-member districts were instituted, planning continued to follow an economics-driven historical pattern, in which the city council, limited by a lack of information, played a marginal role. The economic development that is occurring in south Dallas is largely based on private economic self-interest and competitive advantage.

Zoning has been a somewhat different matter. The major cross-district decisions, such as the zoning reform in the 1980s, resulted from a combination of factors: changing attitudes; bad experiences, such as the obvious excesses in the development of Far North Dallas that overloaded infrastructure; emerging neighborhood associations, which were finding their political voices; and a city manager able to capitalize on this confluence of opportunities to get new policies adopted. As a result, Dallas engaged in what was then considered to be the largest re-zoning of a major American city, with the possible exception of Los Angeles. Because strong neighborhood associations and single-member districts are mutually reinforcing, the role played by neighborhoods on supra-district zoning issues can be attributed tangentially, at least, to the change to single-member district elections.

On the other hand, single-member districts have had a direct effect in changing the way that intra-district zoning cases are handled. Council deference to the district representative in a zoning matter became an immediate practice after single-member election districts were instituted. This practice of "district deference," along with the major re-zoning in the 1980s, dramatically reduced the amount of time consumed in council meetings on zoning matters and attention paid to the Dallas Plan Commission.

While the cause cannot be attributed to single-member districts, the first council members to be accused of seeking financial benefit for their votes in zoning cases were elected from single-member districts. Council member Paul Fielding was indicted on eight felony counts of conspiracy, mail fraud, perjury, and extortion. On one of the extortion counts, the grand jury charged that Fielding pressured Electronic Data Systems (EDS) into signing a $1 million deal with Handy Andy, a minority-owned janitorial service, in exchange for Fielding's vote on re-zoning an EDS property.

Individuals who follow the political scene in Dallas had speculated for years that council member Al Lipscomb's sources of income had to be other than what he could make from selling produce at Dallas Farmers Market, plus the $50 he earned for each council meeting. Former and sitting council members have acknowledged that Lipscomb was "allowed" to posture on issues without direct economic consequences, as long as he "voted right" on business interests, such as zoning. When a "right vote" and the vote expected by his constituency were in conflict, he would leave the council meeting for the vote.[40] Despite Lipscomb's indictment for alleged kickbacks on taxi contracts, the Real Estate Council endorsed Lipscomb for an eighth term. George Shafer, chairman of the endorsement committee, explained: "We really just looked at the service that he's given to the city."[41]

Budgets and Bond Issues

Traditionally, Dallas has followed the pay-as-you-go method to finance capital improvements through bond issues. Dallas has prided itself in maintaining a AAA bond rating, and in exercising fiscal restraint in budgeting. The city has been successful in passing almost all bond proposals by following a consistent pattern of funding the campaigns with private contributions and appointing campaign committees, chaired by a member of the Citizens Council. A funding proposal that is opposed by the Citizens Council will not make it to the city council, much less through it.

The development of proposals for big-ticket projects to be included in bond issues changed little with single-member districts; they are planned behind the scenes and fronted by city staff to the council. What did change were distributive economic benefits. Beginning with the 8-3 council in 1975, and accelerating under the 14-1 council after 1991, council members insisted that one or more of the projects in each proposed bond package must be for their districts. For example, council member Bob Stimson worked behind the scenes for weeks to create a $5 million package of amendments to the 1995 bond issue. Pet projects were spread across council districts. He said that "there are some things in here that I wouldn't vote for individually and other council members wouldn't. But by packaging everything together, everyone on the council was happy."[42]

The 1998 General Bond Capital Improvement Program illustrates the way big-ticket citywide projects are handled. This bond program included eleven propositions, totaling $543.5 million, designed to ratify a three-year cycle of investment based on the Dallas Plan. The package was split into a ten-year Trinity River plan, and a three-year "nuts-and-bolts" program for streets, parks, and other facilities. While some of the funding was spread throughout the city, by far the largest proportion of the program was the $246 million general obligation Trinity River Corridor Project. The Trinity Project included floodways, levees, waterways, open space, recreational facilities, the Trinity Parkway, and related street improvements. This project was the only one to encounter organized opposition.

---

40. Author interviews with two public officials who asked to remain anonymous.
41. Todd J. Gillman, *Dallas Morning News,* April 3, 1999.
42. Todd J. Gillman, *Dallas Morning News,* September 12, 1995.

Few bond issues have failed at the polls, except those related to the Trinity. In 1973 voters rejected a long-standing plan for a 362-mile Trinity River barge canal to the Gulf Coast, a plan that environmentalists denounced as a $1.3 billion boondoggle. In 1978 voters rejected a proposal for an extension to the downtown levee system (minus the barge canal) that would reclaim thousands of acres for industrial development. It, too, was defeated by a coalition of environmentalists and tax reformers. This history caused concern for the Trinity development proposal included in the 1998 bond issue, which influential business leaders were again trying to sell.

The Trinity River Project campaign, labeled "We Love Dallas" by its advocates, raised $347,046. Opponents of the river plan raised $12,050 for their "Save the Trinity" campaign. Much of the "We Love Dallas" money went to Allyn & Co., a public relations firm, and to Kathy Nealy & Associates, a political consulting firm.[43] Nealy is an expert on black voter turnout.

Trinity proposition opponents called the river plan "a poorly developed plan that will consume tax dollars needed for other city priorities." Mayor Kirk branded dissenters as "chronic naysayers" and "rag-tag environmentalists."[44] The mayor called opposition to the Trinity plan by the Dallas League of Women Voters "abominable."[45]

Dallas Morning News executives weighed in on the nonpartisan League of Women Voters' opposition to the Trinity River projects by threatening to halt publication of the group's election *Voter's Guide*.[46] The *News* publisher also intervened in a news story to order that criticism by former Mayor Adlene Harrison be relegated to the bottom of the story on a continuation page and that only endorsement by the Dallas Plan be on the front page. This breach of the line between editorial opinion and news reporting apparently caused the reporter to demand that his by-line be removed unless the story was evenly balanced when published.[47]

Most minority council members elected since 1991 to 14-1 councils have aligned with influential business leaders rather than with middle-class neighborhood groups. The 1998 bond program represents one of the results, a change in voting patterns on big citywide projects in Dallas. Both the sports arena and the Trinity River measures in 1998 won approval without the support of north Dallas. For the better part of the twentieth century, north Dallas taxpayers had provided the leadership and votes to keep things moving at City Hall. For years it was these north Dallas voters who carried most bond issues.

43. Robert Ingrassia, *Dallas Morning News,* April 25, 1998.
44. Christopher Lee, *Dallas Morning News,* May 4, 1998.
45. Robert Ingrassia, *Dallas Morning News,* April 14, 1998.
46. Jim Schutze, *Dallas Observer,* August 27, 1998.
47. *Dallas Observer,* May 14, 1998. The Dallas Plan is a private city-planning group that maintains offices in City Hall. The former mayor, Adlene Harrison, also served as Regional Administrator of the U.S. Environmental Protection Agency from 1977 to 1981.

By 1998 north Dallas voters had become less engaged in municipal issues and more cynical over city government's use of their tax dollars and over city staff fronting for the economic elite. A finding in a 1999 survey of citizens' attitudes was that a higher percentage of whites than either blacks or Hispanics believed that they had no influence on elected officials. Further, almost 80 percent of newcomers to Dallas (defined as less than six years in residence) live north of I-30.[48] The recent election patterns reflect not so much a higher turnout among minorities as a lower turnout in north Dallas.

The Trinity proposal passed by 2,357 votes, with 51.6 percent of the 73,675 voters who cast ballots on the measure supporting it. It was the black precincts in southern Dallas that carried the proposal. Adlene Harrison, former director of the regional Environmental Protection Agency (EPA) and former Dallas mayor, who worked to defeat the river plan, said that she thought city leaders had created the impression that the Trinity project would be a boon to southern Dallas. "I agree that it's healthy to get people involved," she said. "But I do think it's bad if you take advantage of them just to get their vote."[49]

While many black business and civic groups and ministers backed the arena and the Trinity projects, both to support the city's first black mayor and in expectation of the promised jobs and contracts for minorities, some expressed opposition. During the campaign, Dallas NAACP president Lee Alcorn accused Kirk of pursuing the river plan at the expense of more pressing minority needs, such as housing and neighborhood redevelopment. "We really were up against a wall trying to fight this establishment," Alcorn said. "It's a tough battle because we're fighting people who are after billions of dollars." The NAACP, however, dropped its opposition after owners of the Dallas Mavericks and Dallas Stars agreed to set satisfactory minority contracting goals.[50]

Annual budgeting remains staff-driven, although, under single-member districting, more voices at the table try to stake claims to resources for their districts. Most of the budget is fixed, constrained by ongoing commitments. For the major function areas of city government, little maneuver room exists for council decisions, except at the margins. Perhaps 5 percent of the total budget affords council members options among political preferences. When the tax base is expanding, council members dream up a wish list on behalf of their constituents. When it is contracting, they negotiate where they either have to make cuts or increase taxes or both.

As with zoning, council members defer to colleagues on pet projects to be funded in their districts. Some minority council members find this practice insufficient. They have pressed to administer their "share" of the money. Don

48. Audience Research & Development, Dallas, "A Study of Dallas Citizen Attitudes: Management Summary" (August 1999).
49. Robert Ingrassia, *Dallas Morning News,* May 4, 1998.
50. Ibid.

Hicks, who wanted to control and distribute his district's proportionate share of the city budget, complained that council members had little latitude to spend money in their districts and had to bow to the priorities of City Manager John Ware. "We ought to fairly well have an opportunity to make a mark or do a special project, as long as it's a legitimate project," Hicks claimed.[51]

The budget process apparently went smoothly during Mayor Ron Kirk's two terms, largely because the city had money to allocate rather than having to make cuts. In the 1996–97 budget, there was a 3.8 percent increase in the city's tax base, along with increased sales tax and franchise tax revenues. Because of a growing tax base, the city manager was able to include a cut in the tax rate by 2.8 percent in the 1997–98 budget, while increasing spending by more than $59 million. But in these years, as in other years, city staff manipulated the technical tax rate versus the property values to obfuscate real tax increases. Further, after a new city manager was appointed to succeed John Ware, it became clear that Ware had used one-time funds for ongoing expenses and the budget was not as flush as it had seemed. Ron Kirk cavalierly dismissed this practice: "We all like to spend money and didn't question where it came from."[52]

Usually the city budget changes very little after council members agree on amendments proposed by city staff. In recent years one or two council members have packaged a consolidated plan of budget amendments, developed through a series of memos and negotiations. This effort, and questioning of staff recommendations, depends on whether one or two members of the council have the interest and the expertise. While this allocative decision making, according to the "rule of 14," is essentially a norm of inclusiveness, the practice does not necessarily go smoothly. In 1997 the "consolidated" plan that council members developed during a series of memos upset council member Don Hicks. He complained at the exclusion of his $1.3 million request for recreation center repair in his southeastern Dallas district: "This is why I wish I had my own damn money for my own damn district," he said, accusing his colleagues of forming "cliques" to get what they wanted.[53]

A trend in budgets, first emerging in the mid-1980s, has been an increasing commitment to social services for low-income residents, such as housing, day care, and special programs for the young and elderly. Still, city spending for human services was 0.5 percent of the total budget in 1989, and 1.9 percent in 1998. Even these funds intended for low-income residents do not necessarily reach them. A "wired-in" network that focuses on political control, patronage, and jobs has developed in minority communities. An example is the South Dallas/Fair Park Trust Fund, created by the Dallas City Council in 1989. The

51. Christopher Lee, *Dallas Morning News,* September 23, 1997.
52. Ron Kirk, remarks to the Dallas Summit, September 21, 1999.
53. Robert Ingrassia and Christopher Lee, *Dallas Morning News,* September 16, 1997.

fund was to provide loans and grants for economic development, community improvements, emergency home repairs, and job-related community services for the thirteen census tracks that compose the South Dallas/Fair Park area. The support of city staff was provided to the board of the trust, whose members are appointed by the city council.

Once again, Dallas's inability to develop effective grant-assisted programs for low-income residents in impoverished neighborhoods was demonstrated.[54] After three years $700,000 remained idle in the fund; less than $70,000 in grants had been provided to eligible recipients. The representative of District 7 had much to say about how the money from the Trust Fund was to be spent—a feature of single-member districts. So, because they were not sure who would control the purse strings at City Hall after the 1993 election, residents who applied for grants said that they were skittish about taking sides in the District 7 race.[55]

Shortly after Charlotte Mayes won the District 7 seat, the South Dallas/Fair Park Advisory Board, the city board that oversees the program, recommended that forty-one individuals and businesses be awarded grants. No information was given beyond the name of each recipient and the dollar amount of each grant. As Chris Luna observed, "there is no city employee who can confirm that these businesses even exist."[56]

These applicants were recommended, even though city staff indicated that none met all the guidelines and some owed taxes. A review by the *News* showed that for every recommended grant, one or more application requirements or documents were missing, and that the board had recommended at least ten grants without staff review. A council member said it was "damn close to political handout money," because Dwaine Caraway, chairman of the city advisory board, had helped run District 7 Charlotte Mayes's city council reelection campaign.

Single-member districting, then, has had little effect on the big-ticket items in bond issues or in the ordering of major priorities in annual budgets. One consequence of single-member districting for budgets and bond issues has been to provide each district representative with some funds for pet projects in his or her district. In addition, some council members, especially those representing minority districts, have pursued opportunities to establish a direct network for personally seeing to the distribution of city funds. A second important consequence has been the development with single-member districts of a pattern of co-dependency between the economic elite (and their city staff surro-

54. In the late 1980s Dallas was forced to return a portion of its federal affordable housing funds, because the money went unspent for too long. Then, in the 1990s, the city staff let tens of millions of dollars approved under the Community Development Block Grant and Neighborhood Renaissance programs go unspent.

55. *Dallas Morning News,* July 26, 1992.

56. *Dallas Morning News,* August 13, 1992.

gates) and minority council members in an exchange system of promised benefits for votes on big-ticket projects and tax abatements.

SETTING THE AGENDA: BOTTOM UP

While blacks, Hispanics, and other minorities, as groups, may not be monolithic, there are commonalties in the respective views of these groups. In the present context, minority members on a city council do bring issues to the agenda that are high priority for them but may not be similarly viewed by whites as a group. In her award-winning book on black representation in Congress, Carol M. Swain states that "broad patterns of objective circumstances and subjective orientations characterize American blacks, and striking differences continue to exist between black and white Americans well over a century after abolition and a quarter of a century after the enactment of civil rights legislation."[57]

Swain distinguishes between objective and subjective interests of blacks. The former are interests attributed (sometimes incorrectly) to an individual or group, such as employment status. The latter are closely connected with the feelings, emotions, and temperaments of the people involved. "The perception of subjective interests may be influenced by cultural and psychological needs that lie outside the range of normal political activity—for example, the need of African Americans to feel that their contributions as a group are valued by society at large."[58] This need for appreciation and recognition surfaced frequently in heated public policy controversies in Dallas.

Symbolic Issues and Long-Standing Grievances

Identity politics dominated the discussion of many issues that reached the city council table in the 1980s and 1990s. Not only did the presence of minority council members after single-member districting add new items to the agenda, they often used race-based demands as a political foil to projects important to the white business community. This situation occurred with Dallas Area Rapid Transit, with the Trinity Corridor Development Plan, with the new sports arena, and even with the Dallas bid for the Olympics in 2012.

The first black representatives to be elected to the city council in Dallas, George Allen and Juanita Craft, both of whom served on at-large councils, addressed racial issues but in a low-key way. Allen successfully secured a civil rights city ordinance and an open housing ordinance. These ordinances went

57. Carol M. Swain, *Black Faces, Black Interests: The Representation of African Americans in Congress* (Cambridge, Mass.: Harvard University Press, 1995), 7.
58. Ibid., 6.

beyond federal civil rights acts in eliminating the exceptions in the federal legislation. Allen and Craft were moderates, who worked quietly and effectively
to secure white support for their goals.

In contrast, minority representatives elected from single-member districts
have tended to be more responsive to the subjective interests of their constituents. Virtually every issue coming before the council has been given a racial
litmus test by some of the minority representatives.[59]

Black council members, more so than Hispanic members, have sought
credibility by concentrating on eliminating long-standing race-based issues
and grievances. The early council meetings with single-member districts were
long and contentious. Some white council members failed to appreciate that
whatever constituents self-define as their interests or concerns are valid issues
and should be taken seriously.

Perhaps even more troublesome to some white council members, and to
their white constituents, was the confrontational style of black council members from single-member districts. This attitude had not been characteristic of
representatives, including blacks, elected to at-large councils.

For a group beginning to feel empowered, a council seat provided an ideal,
press-attentive, bully pulpit. Black council members found that by posturing
for the press, they could get a sound bite on the evening news. By this means,
they enhanced their status, sending a message to their districts that they were
standing up for their race. Council meetings became dominated by long
debates on symbolic issues and the airing of long-standing grievances. The
council spent hours arguing over issues, such as renaming streets for black
leaders or withdrawing city pension funds from companies doing business with
South Africa.

The decorum of previous years in council chambers disappeared, and rules
were flouted.[60] Verbal abuse became standard fare in council arguments, and,
at times, the arguments became physical.[61]

Such symbolic issues did not abate by the 1990s under the 14-1 council
structure, adopted in 1991. In 1994 perennial mayoral candidate Marvin Crenshaw collected two misdemeanor assault charges. The first was for scuffling
with a security guard at a planning meeting. The second was for attempting to
strike council member Bob Stimson, who opposed renaming a ten-mile stretch
of an avenue after slain Black Muslim leader Malcolm X.

59. Elsie Faye Heggins, Al Lipscomb, Diane Ragsdale, Don Hicks, Barbara Mallory-
Caraway, and Domingo Garcia, particularly, have been known for it.

60. In a meeting in 1997 Al Lipscomb persistently brought up the police department's
handling of a matter, a subject that was not on the agenda, a potential violation of state
open meetings law (Christopher Lee, *Dallas Morning News,* February 4, 1997).

61. Diane Ragsdale's shouting match with a white woman in a debate over the police
review board almost ended in fisticuffs (Payne, *Big D,* 378). Housing Director Alphonso
Jackson's disagreement with council member Paul Fielding did end in an actual fistfight.

Two stories illustrate the complexity of developing policies on issues that are of subjective interest to blacks: the Craft home location and environmental pollution.

Craft Home Location

A three-year controversy over the location and preservation of long-time civil rights activist and former council member Juanita Craft's home illustrates how a decision can become entangled in interests that are totally unrelated to the substantive issue.

Highly respected Juanita Craft spent a lifetime fighting for civil rights. Chandler Vaughan, who formed the Juanita Craft Foundation, observed that Craft had an uncanny ability to work with white leadership to achieve her goals; when she called, she received responses.[62] After her death in 1985, white and black council members agreed to honor her. A heated controversy arose concerning the "appropriate" site.

In the three years between 1985 and 1988, the City Park Board studied alternative sites for the Juanita Craft home, which she had willed to the city. Her stated desire, "but not a condition of this gift," was that the house be moved to Old City Park. Although Old City Park was operated by the Dallas County Heritage Society, the City of Dallas contributed some of its funds. The Old City Park officials rejected the home, because it had been built in 1922. They said that it would not fit in with the restored historical buildings of the pioneer and Victorian days (1840 to 1910) that had been moved to the Park. The house was also turned down by the Fair Park Museum, because of "architectural conflicts and spacing requirements." An alternative was to leave the house in its original location, which was viewed as costly from the standpoint of security. Almost by default, in April 1987, the Park Board endorsed a plan to relocate the home to a lot next to the South Dallas Cultural Center, near Fair Park.[63]

This recommendation created severe reaction, because the Cultural Center is located just outside the gates of Fair Park. The location symbolized for some in the minority community the historical exclusion of blacks from Fair Park on all days except for Negro Day, as well as the failure to respect Craft's wishes. For the black member of the Park Board, Vivian Johnson, it was a test of how the white community perceived the credibility of Dallas's black leadership "to determine what goes on within its borders."[64] For some in the white community, it exemplified that "whenever a council member doesn't get his or her

62. Ruth Miller Fitzgibbons, "The Craft House: Legacy of Love, Symbol of Mistrust," *D* magazine (April 1988), 15:35.
63. James Ragland, *Dallas Morning News,* February 5, 1988.
64. Judy Howard, *Dallas Morning News,* March 7, 1988.

way, allegations of racism are used to bludgeon the rest of the council."[65] The issue was resolved by a 6-1 vote on the Park Board. The Craft home would be left at its original site, and converted into a learning center and a community meeting place. This decision angered some community leaders, including Vivian Johnson, who wanted the city council and the Park Board to force Old City Park officials to accept the house.

Environmental Pollution

A long-standing grievance of minorities in Dallas was environmental pollution in West Dallas, which they viewed as environmental racism. The entangled issue involved a business investment made prior to the location of a public housing unit there; a low-income public housing unit, created to solve a housing shortage for blacks and to clear out a slum area; the U.S. Environmental Protection Agency; city agencies that had not aggressively pursued their available options; and residents, whose health interests were sacrificed to the political self-interests of some of their leaders.

Nationwide, minorities have alleged "environmental racism," charging that their neighborhoods are deliberate targets of pollution and toxic waste dumping. Low-income populations certainly have suffered environmental problems disproportionately, but whether it has been driven by racism or by economics is arguable. In West Dallas heavy polluters and low-income housing ended up where land and resources were cheap. City officials responded more favorably to the business interests of the polluters than to the health interests of the low-income residents. Race came into play indirectly, because of the segregated housing that existed.

When Dallas was founded a wedge-shaped site, between Walton Walker Boulevard on the west, the Trinity River on the north, and I-30 on the south, became known as West Dallas. The area was considered to be a prime location by the French and Belgian immigrants who situated their "La Reunion" commune on the site. This utopian enterprise failed in 1858. The land was available after the Civil War for black freemen, small ranchers, and cowboys, who surged into the area and into neighboring Oak Cliff. Their attempts to make a success in West Dallas also failed.

Then, when the railroad came, city leaders wanted to move the stench and inconvenience of unloading cattle from the downtown railhead, so they built a rail spur three miles into West Dallas in 1870. Thus began a pattern of using West Dallas as a dumping site—first for cattle and then as a trash dump. By the end of the nineteenth century, the area had turned into an industrial site, known as "Cement City." Thousands of poor workers came for jobs in the cement plants, lead smelters, brick factories, rock quarries, and gravel pits.

65. Philip Seib, Viewpoints, *Dallas Morning News,* March 9, 1988.

Many, including Mexicans who had come north to work on the railroads, settled in the area.[66]

In 1929 D. H. Murph and his two partners found West Dallas to be a suitable spot for their lead smelter. It became one of the largest units in the United States, eventually occupying sixty-three acres. The cheap land in this area, which was outside the city limits, also attracted absentee landlords. They capitalized on the severe housing shortage, created by the substantial migration of black workers from East Texas farms in the 1940s. The landowners built and rented thousands of shacks and "shotgun houses," with no running water or indoor plumbing. The area's population more than quadrupled, from 6,000 to 24,000. City leaders had little interest in assuming the burden of annexing the area, until federal funds were promised for public housing.

In 1950 eleven homes of blacks who had moved into white areas in Dallas were bombed. Whites demanded action to maintain segregated housing. The Dallas Housing Authority built 3,500 units to replace old slums as a solution to the "Negro housing problem." The policy of federal agencies at the time was to leave the decision on segregation to the local public housing authorities that administer the housing assistance programs. Thus, in effect, units for blacks, for whites, and for Hispanics were segregated.[67]

In 1952 the city annexed West Dallas, including the West Dallas Housing Project, which eventually totaled 460 acres.[68] The 1952 annexation included the smelter. Thus the largest public housing tract in the nation was fifty feet from the property line of one of the nation's largest lead smelters. Further, these two sites lay in the direct line of the prevailing southerly winds, with the housing downwind of the smelter.

This historical evolution is supported by the findings of a study of environmental injustices in South Carolina. The South Carolina study found that inequitable environmental situations are more the result of state and regional migration patterns and market dynamics than racism.[69]

As early as 1968 the City of Dallas enacted one of the nation's first local lead ordinances to limit emissions, to be accompanied by fines for violations. But the city failed to enforce the regulation. The lead smelter issue came to public attention in the early 1980s. Mayor Starke Taylor appointed a task force from the Dallas Alliance, a private, nonprofit business-oriented organization, to recommend solutions. The chair, Jack Miller, and two members of the task force, Adelfa Callejo and Rebecca Olind, all were critical of the city for not doing the job themselves. "It never belonged to the private group," according

66. Jim Reid, "A Destiny Beyond Myths," *Dallas Morning News,* April 12, 1992.

67. Richard West, "The Forgotten City," *D* magazine (July 1984), 11:160.

68. *Dallas Morning News,* August 30, 1992.

69. Jerry T. Mitchell, Deborah S. K. Thomas, and Susan L. Cutter, "Dumping in Dixie Revisited: the Evolution of Environmental Injustices in South Carolina," *Social Science Quarterly* (June 1999), 80:229–243.

to Jack Miller. "The people who are paid to protect the public health and the people who are elected to protect the public health should have done their jobs to begin with."[70] Residents who lived near the smelters had already voiced many of the report's conclusions and recommendations, but the Dallas City Council had failed to act.

The issue became a choice between closing the public housing and relocating the low-income residents or forcing the smelter either to install adequate pollution control equipment or close down. West Dallas residents saw the replication of a familiar pattern—*namely,* solving a problem by forcing low-income residents to move from their homes, without adequate compensation for replacement housing. The residents knew the similarity to the occasions when Baylor Hospital had wanted to expand, when Love Field had expanded, when Fair Park had needed to expand, when Central Expressway had been built, and when the State-Thomas development had needed the land that was formerly a freedman's town. Appointing a task force to come up with recommendations that the city itself should have handled was also a familiar pattern in Dallas. There seems to have been no difference in results, whether council members were elected at large or from single-member districts.

The smelter, which opened in 1936, was closed in 1984. The RSR Corporation shut its doors rather than spend $600,000 for lead emission control equipment.[71] In the half century of the smelter's existence, the city had dragged its feet, federal government and state government officials had passed the buck back and forth, and there had been lawsuits, congressional investigations, highly publicized cleanups, multiple studies, and self-aggrandizement by profiteers and politicians.

These failures to resolve a substantive issue predated the institution of single-member districts and continued afterward. What can be attributed to single-member districting is the political incentive to maintain residential segregation. The council representative of West Dallas wanted the district to retain a black population large enough for blacks to maintain political control of the district. The stance taken by Mattie Nash, a black council member, and the Reverend R. L. Curry, a local black minister, was a betrayal of West Dallas residents. They accomplished this betrayal by capitalizing on the political ambitions of Jack Kemp.[72]

In 1985 seven black women had sued the U.S. Department of Housing and Urban Development (HUD) and its local partner, the Dallas Housing Authority, to break up racially segregated federal housing in Dallas. This class-action

70. *Dallas Times Herald,* July 1, 1983.

71. Richard West, "The Forgotten City," 160.

72. This account of the West Dallas public housing project is based largely on a nine-month investigation by the *Dallas Morning News,* as reported by staff writers Randy Lee Loftis and Craig Flournoy in a two-part series in *Dallas Morning News,* May 9, 1993, and May 10, 1993.

lawsuit provided federal authorities with the opportunity to make rent vouchers available to public housing tenants, to demolish most of the dilapidated housing, and to offer the land for redevelopment. Under a court-approved settlement of the suit in 1987, the Dallas Housing Authority renovated 832 apartments. The rest of the residences were to be demolished, to be replaced by rent certificates. The City of Dallas, which had not been a defendant in the suit, delayed the pending demolition, which landed the city in court. Judge Jerry Buchmeyer ruled, in August 1989, that a handful of city officials had obstructed the settlement. He pointed to Mattie Nash, then a Housing Authority board member and later elected to the council in 1991, as a principal opponent of demolishing and replacing the project.

In March 1990 Nash and other opponents of the demolition saw an opportunity to reverse the 1987 settlement and preserve the West Dallas Project. HUD Secretary Jack Kemp agreed to a private meeting with the group, and was convinced to commit to a $67-million plan to retain and renovate two-thirds of the units.

Just days before the meeting with Kemp, a group of ministers, headed by the Reverend R. L. Curry, had formed a for-profit construction company, expecting to win millions of dollars of West Dallas contracts. For Mattie Nash, the long-range benefit was political, because Hispanics were then a majority in West Dallas. Adding hundreds of black families to the project meant that blacks would remain the community's political leaders. Racial and economic segregation was desirable in this case, said Nash. "We don't have a problem living together, and we want everybody to know that we want to live together. If they want to call it segregation, we want segregation."

Harry Jones, the city's top housing official, said that the project was approved to satisfy politicians, not the community, and was made without any discussion with the city. "I felt quite candidly," he said, "that what Kemp did was try to build his own 'rainbow coalition' for some future run at the presidency." The Reverend R. L. Curry, spokesman for the group that secured Kemp's private commitment, concurred: "It comes down to politics. I don't mind saying that we played a better game." Other facts add credibility to these views. The Kemp plan was opposed by the Southwest regional HUD official, by the top City of Dallas housing official, and by government officials who knew that doubling the number of poor minority families in an impoverished minority neighborhood would intensify racial and economic segregation. Furthermore, the plan violated HUD's own regulations. This was resolved by one of Kemp's top deputies, who granted waivers exempting the project from those regulations.

Mattie Nash also lobbied against designating West Dallas as a Superfund site to receive federal cleanup money. She was worried that the stigma of such a declaration might jeopardize plans to house more people there. Buck Wynne, regional administrator of the EPA, who claimed that Nash frequently lobbied him, also advanced this view. Wynne told her that the EPA had no choice, because West Dallas was still contaminated with lead from the smelter. Other supporters of the housing plan insisted that the problem was minor or nonexistent. A HUD memo of July 1991 shows that the director of the Dallas Housing Authority, Alphonso Jackson, "assured us that there were no problems with lead" in the project. Jackson also told the *News* that the concerns regarding lead were "nonsense."

But the concerns were not "nonsense" to people living in the area. The Reverend R. T. Conley had begun sounding the alarm on possible lead contamination as early as 1968, after his children had developed strange illnesses. His persistence had helped prompt the first cleanup in 1984 and the eventual shutdown of the smelter. He had struggled for years to get medical screening for residents, especially children. Toward that end he had joined Luis Sepulveda in forming the West Dallas Coalition for Environmental Justice. The coalition's work brought about a new cleanup effort early in 1992.

In spite of the public rhetoric about jobs, neighborhood revitalization, and shelter for the homeless, the city council heard in executive session that the reason for saving the project was to get the city out of expensive litigation. This revelation was sobering for the council, for the settlement of the housing lawsuit in 1990 had cost the city $118 million, the largest involving Dallas to that time. Attorneys, rather than housing experts, drew up plans for the Kemp-supported 2,000-unit project. They inserted a provision to shield the city and the federal government from liability for past racial discrimination.

The council voted 12 to 2 for the plan, with Charles Tandy and Jerry Bartos, both white, voting against it. The Hispanic council member, Domingo Garcia, said he voted in favor only because the city attorney had advised the council that it would protect the city from legal liability. The council was not told at the time that 1,200 renovated units would replace 1,200 vouchers.

That the result might have been different had the city not been structured in single-member districts cannot be proven. But, clearly, the residents in the West Dallas Housing Project were not protected by "one of their own," in contradiction of the presumption of courts in mandating single-member districts. A survey by Richard Scotch, a sociology professor at the University of Texas at Dallas, had found that 80 percent of the families on the public housing waiting list did not want to live in the West Dallas project, even if it were renovated.[73]

Fortunately for the health of residents, a new HUD Secretary, Henry Cisneros, rejected his predecessor's scheme. Cisneros outlined a $62-million plan to demolish two-thirds of the 3,500-unit project and rebuild the rest. He promised to replace the units with rent subsidy certificates and hundreds of new public housing apartments in middle-class, predominantly white neighbor-

73. Ibid., May 10, 1993.

hoods. HUD was finally released from the 1985 lawsuit on March 8, 2001, when it reached a settlement to provide 3,205 rent-subsidy vouchers, to be used in predominantly white areas, and $9.6 million to administer the vouchers and to provide assistance.

These stories of subjective interests of blacks, manifested in symbolic issues and long-standing grievances, span the change from at-large to single-member district elections. Single-member districts gave minority council members an opportunity to give official voice to their concerns in the public arena. The expressed policy results being sought, however, cannot be attributed to the district minority representatives in these cases. Further, with regard to West Dallas public housing, the community's expressed interest was thwarted by the district representative's self-interest.

Minority Employment in City Government

A finding often attributed to an increase in the number of minority representatives is an increase in minority employment in government. Except in the cases of the police and fire departments, and contrary to findings in the literature, increasing the number of minorities in city government seldom has been a source of controversy for minority council members in Dallas. Nor did appointments of minorities to key executive and administrative positions at City Hall require pressure from minority council members or from a black city manager or mayor.

In the early litigation in the 1970s on at-large elections, courts made no finding of racial discrimination in city employment in Dallas. A plausible explanation is that the city manager form of government, the professional and progressive attitudes of city managers, and the lack of comparable opportunities for other employment in Dallas, had been contributing factors.

George Schrader was city manager from 1973 to 1981, during the tenure of the first three councils elected under the 8-3 mixed districting plan. He increased the city's percentage of black managers to 6.5 percent. He was followed in office by one of his assistants, Charles Anderson, who served from 1981 to 1986. Anderson raised the city's black managers to 10 percent in six months.[74] Anderson (1981–1986) appointed Dallas's first black assistant city manager, Levi Davis, and the first Hispanic assistant city manager, Samuel A. Moreno.

Diversity among the top leadership positions that began in the early 1980s gave minorities the experience required for consideration for top spots. This aspect is important in Dallas, because all city managers since 1950 have been selected from City Hall ranks. While these appointments cannot be attributed

74. George Rodrigue, "Two City-Management Styles: Schrader and Anderson," *D* magazine (April 1982), 9:150.

to single-member districts, minority council members did compete to see if they could get a member of their own group selected as city manager.

Council members, with limited opportunities for patronage in a council-manager system, have pressed for patronage opportunities wherever a possibility arose. Mayor Evans reported that council members tried to prevail on Manager Anderson regarding personnel matters. "I try to stop that whenever it comes to my attention," Evans said, "because it endangers the city's system of government."[75]

The concern over "representation" in the leadership positions did not abate in the 1990s. When Dallas's second black city manager, John Ware, named Clifford Keheley to the number 2 spot in the city manager's office in 1993, Chris Luna, Domingo Garcia, and other Hispanic leaders expressed their displeasure.[76]

Minorities criticized Ware for re-engineering City Hall, because it eliminated several positions and demoted some city employees, which hurt minorities. By reducing the number of city departments from twenty-six to eighteen, Ware achieved savings that topped $1 million. County Commissioner John Wiley Price complained that there were "more people of color in positions of authority before he got there."[77] Cross-sectional analyses of the number of minorities in city positions do not capture these changes in the status of minorities, which may be influenced as much by professional management practices or economic factors as by political will or having a black in a top position.

The story of minority employment and leadership positions in the police and fire departments in Dallas has been a different matter. Affirmative action policies for the police and fire departments created great attention and controversy for the city council. At the time that the 1988 affirmative action plan in employment was under consideration, the city's first black city manager, Richard Knight, was in office. Knight said that his black experience made him opposed to an affirmative action plan that many minority leaders favored as a way to increase the minority composition of the police department from 18.4 percent to 41 percent—Dallas's minority population according to the 1980 census.[78] The plan that was adopted, renewed in 1993 for five years and in 1998 and 1999 for one year, states that within the pool of new hires, one-third should be black and one-third Hispanic, and that one-third of each new class should be female. The plan establishes promotional targets to be met for minorities and women within each rank.

Until the city council approved the affirmative action plan in 1989, promotions in the police and fire departments had been made based on exam scores.

75. Ibid., 152.
76. Ted Benavides became the city's first Hispanic city manager in 1999.
77. Sylvia Martinez, *Dallas Morning News,* November 7, 1994.
78. Robert V. Camuto, *Dallas Times Herald,* June 22, 1987.

But the affirmative action guidelines of 1993 recommended that 50 percent of the promoted officers be black, Hispanic, or female to meet its promotion goals. Higher-scoring whites would be passed over.

This policy of "skip" promotions spawned bitter reaction among white and minority officers in the police and fire departments, and led to a series of lawsuits, with mixed rulings. By 1998 the percentage of black and Hispanic employees at the officer rank in the police department was virtually proportionate to the city's black and Hispanic populations.[79]

The naming of a chief of police has been another source of contention on the council through the years, though the city manager has sole responsibility for making the appointment. Dallas went outside the department to hire chiefs in 1988 and 1991 largely because community leaders felt that an officer who had been brought up through the Dallas system would be unable to address problems in the department. The two who were hired—Mack Vines and Bill Rathburn—had not previously served in Dallas.

By 1993, with minority candidates on the executive staff inside the department, minorities pressured to promote from within. The appointment in June 1993 of Ben Click, yet another white officer who had not previously served in Dallas, created a furor. Council member Don Hicks, who repeatedly had pressed for the appointment of an insider, threatened to place the city manager's performance review on the council agenda. "I don't guess it's any secret I'm unhappy with her exercising her discretion in the latest decision," he said. When other council members reminded their colleague that the city charter gives the city manager authority to name all department heads, including the police chief, Hicks responded: "We as city officials should have something to say."[80]

Tension decreased during Ben Click's tenure as police chief from 1993 to 1999. Black leaders who had been vocal critics of the police, such as former city council members Diane Ragsdale and Fred Blair, conceded, in retrospect, that hiring chiefs from outside the department had eased racial tensions in the city. Diane Ragsdale acknowledged that "each has come in here and set the tone that police abuse will not be tolerated and that you will be disciplined accordingly if you do it," Ragsdale said. "Ten years later, things are much better, even the relationship with minority communities," she added.[81]

But before Chief Ben Click announced his resignation in 1999, John Wiley Price and other black leaders again exerted pressure for the selection of the department's first black chief. Others favored a nationwide search, and observed that the era of fast promotions had molded an executive staff of less experienced officers, unqualified to assume the top position. A former top Dal-

79. Stephen Power, *Dallas Morning News,* February 7, 1998.
80. Sylvia Martinez, *Dallas Morning News,* June 15, 1993.
81. Robert Ingrassia, *Dallas Morning News,* October 27, 1996.

las police official, who spoke on condition of anonymity, told a *News* reporter that "they were done a great disservice by achieving those promotions without the experience and training and actual doing of the job at the mid-levels that is required of a well-rounded police administrator."[82] All the leading inside candidates represented minorities—two were black, one Hispanic, and one a white female.

Dallas City Manager Ted Benevides went inside the department and, without interviewing him, named Assistant Chief Terrell Bolton the city's first black police chief in 1999.[83] County Commissioner John Wiley Price, who reportedly had lobbied the city manager to appoint Chief Bolton, said that he did not expect to picket the department anymore, with Chief Bolton in charge.[84] He and other black elected leaders rallied around Bolton to shield him from criticism over a continuous series of questionable actions. These included his demotion, without cause or due process, of nine of the seasoned members of the command staff when he took charge in 1999, and a massive fake-drug scandal in late 2001 that resulted in innocent working-class Mexican immigrants wrongfully jailed. Bolton's action in the former instance cost the city taxpayers millions in legal settlements and, in the latter, still under federal investigation, the likelihood of years of legal battles.[85]

While Dallas has had no large-scale riots, two issues in particular, a strong civilian review board to deal with police brutality and shootings, and the affirmative action policy of "skip" promotions for minorities, created volatile situations. Single-member districts resulted in the election of blacks, who could then give official voice to these issues and capture headlines from the podium of their elected posts. In one instance, council member Al Lipscomb helped to attract a hearing of the House Subcommittee on Criminal Justice to Dallas in May 1987. The congressional hearing brought Dallas's problems to national attention;[86] the result was "an intentional quieting down after the hearings because Dallas doesn't like adverse publicity."[87]

Redistribution of Goods and Services

In the 1970s social scientists produced a large body of literature on the subject of local service delivery. Much of it focused on the question of equality in the

82. Dave Michaels, *Dallas Morning News,* July 29, 1999.

83. Bolton was an assistant chief at the time of his appointment to chief, after having been triple-promoted.

84. Frank Trejo, *Dallas Morning News,* August 21, 1999.

85. For an account of Chief Bolton's credibility problems and his protection by a bloc of black politicians and activists (including Mayor Pro Tem Don Hill, John Wiley Price, and Lee Alcorn), see Thomas Korosec, "Dallas' Chief Problem," *Dallas Observer,* January 16, 2003. Also see Jim Schutze, "Who Controls the Cops?" *Dallas Observer,* December 19, 2002.

86. See, for example, Peter Applebome, *New York Times,* February 1, 1988.

87. Emerson Emery, chairman of the Citizens-Police Paramedic Complaint Committee, *Dallas Times Herald,* December 6, 1987.

distribution of those services among racial and income groups. Some authors found significant changes in the provision of public sector services resulting from the political success of racial minorities. Political Scientist James Button analyzed six cities in Florida. He found that the political success of blacks produced significant changes in availabilities of public-sector services, such as police and fire, streets, and parks and recreation. He also discovered that capital-intensive services showed more change than labor-intensive services from the late 1950s to the mid-1980s.[88]

As noted in chapter 5, Judge Mahon devoted much time to the issue of Dallas's responsiveness to particular interests of the black and Hispanic communities. He found the city to be "acting in a responsible—in a responsive manner" regarding parks, street services, police and fire protection, transportation, equal employment opportunity, fair housing, and community relations, as well as other areas.[89]

Even so, the political success of blacks under single-member districting brought heightened attention to the provision of services to minorities in Dallas. The change from the at-large system to election from single-member districts focused council members' attention on obtaining their "fair share" of goods and services.

In 1989 Mayor Pro Tem Diane Ragsdale demanded a study on the delivery of city services to the southern and northern parts of town. In response, city staff presented reports in 1990 and 1991 to the city council on selected service delivery data, and the criteria used in providing these services. The analyses indicated that the format for service delivery was geographically neutral, and that the criteria for service delivery were applied equally in all parts of the city.[90]

Statistical comparisons, again, can prove to be misleading without in-depth analysis. The 1990 study prepared by the Public Works Department had found that 16 percent of the residential streets in Dallas were "non-standard," that is, asphalt or gravel, with no curbs and gutters. The greatest concentration of nonstandard streets was in the less affluent, southern part of town.[91] "This is an example of the gross inequities we have been talking about for years," said council member Al Lipscomb, who represented Southeast Oak Cliff.[92] In many affluent areas, however, residents prefer to keep asphalt streets with no curbs to preserve a rural character.

According to the 1990 study, rather than the concentration of poor streets in poor neighborhoods being from conscious policy or program by design, the

---

88. James W. Button, *Blacks and Social Change: Impact of the Civil Rights Movement in Southern Communities* (Princeton, N.J.: Princeton University Press, 1989).

89. *Lipscomb* v. *Wise,* 399 F.Supp. 782, 791 (1975).

90. Briefing Meeting, Dallas City Council (April 15, 1992), 92-1355; Clifford V. Keheley memorandum to City Council, April 10, 1992.

91. Mike Todd, *Dallas Morning News,* February 7, 1990.

92. *Dallas Morning News,* February 8, 1990.

situation may have resulted from development occurring before annexation. The study noted that as areas north of downtown began to grow in the 1960s, developers were required to meet city street standards. In contrast, residential areas that were developed earlier kept their asphalt or gravel streets.

Rebuilding streets in Dallas has been done traditionally at the request of neighborhoods. Residents petition the city for the construction, and pay part of the cost through assessments. This cost sharing is part of the problem in poor neighborhoods. The city, by law, must assess property owners for a formidable share of the cost of adjacent street and alley repairs. As this assessment could force poorer homeowners from their neighborhoods, they seldom petitioned the work.

A major aim of the federal Community Development Block Grant Program (CDBG) was to provide grants to poor neighborhoods to help them pay off their street-repair assessments. The money, however, often did not go to poor neighborhoods, as intended. In his investigation of the misuse of CDBG funds in Dallas, reporter Jim Schutze found that the $22 million in federal funds that was supposed to go to neighborhood improvements mostly went to pork-barrel projects for well-wired special interests, recommended by council appointees to Dallas's Community Development Commission. Fully one-third of the CDBG money went to a handful of nonprofit agencies, not even into the nonprofits' programs to help people. Rather, the money went toward new buildings to house the nonprofits. Objections were raised at a 1999 council meeting on block grants by white council members Lois Finkelman, Sandy Greyson, Alan Walne, and Laura Miller—not by "black representatives protecting their poor constituents." Council member Finkelman asked, "What if the nonprofits go out of business?"[93]

After the initial study of service delivery by the Public Works Department in 1990, city staff then worked to routinize data collection throughout city departments, and to develop uniform reporting areas for an annual review of service delivery. The council was briefed on the first of these annual City Services Analysis Data Reports on April 15, 1992.[94] The data confirmed some inequities among the city's ten regions but found no concentration in any particular area of the city. In contradiction to the data, a perception of inequity in city services still existed, according to the report. This contention was substantiated in a survey of 1,200 area residents, conducted by the *Dallas Morning News*. In the 1991 *News* survey, 88 percent of blacks, 64 percent of Hispanics, and 49 percent of whites believed that Dallas provided better services to white neighborhoods than to predominantly black or Hispanic neighborhoods.[95] Per-

93. Jim Schutze, *Dallas Observer*, May 13, 1999.
94. *City Services Analysis Program* (File No. 92-1355); City Council Briefing, April 15, 1992.
95. *Dallas Morning News*, October 13, 1991.

ception of inequities in the distribution of services is not unusual; it has been reported in other cities.[96]

Even when city council members agree that they want the city to deliver municipal services fairly, they often disagree about what constitutes fairness. For some, fairness might mean delivery of services in equal proportions across council districts. For others, fairness might mean distribution according to need. Minority representatives claim that minorities have suffered in comparison with north Dallas, and so they should receive more resources. The city staff has tried to build a consensus on the meaning of "equity," particularly with regard to the needs of different neighborhoods.[97]

Another indicator of inequitable distribution of services might be found in the relative size of expenditures in particular function areas that may be more important to minorities than to whites. Local governmental expenditures for nine function areas for the fiscal years from 1978 through 1998 provide data.[98] Shifts in the ratio composition of governmental expenditures by function appear to have been based on factors other than single-member districts or greater representation of minorities on the council.

Rather, increases and decreases in spending by function seem to be explained by circumstances at particular times, such as a downturn in the national and local economies in the mid-1980s or a program of federal grants that had to be matched, such as in the case of low-income housing. In some instances, the city manager may receive a policy directive from the council, such as occurred when Charles Anderson attended to increasing human services.

In the literature on notable racial differences in policy preferences, blacks have been found to favor redistributive programs more than whites. A manifestation of this in Dallas is in the demands minorities make for a "fair share" of city contracts and for an equitable share of budget and bond issue benefits. The institution of single-member districts led to each council member contesting for his or her share of allocations, distributed across eight districts from 1975 to 1990, and then fourteen districts after 1991.

Minority Contracting

According to 1998 revenue data, the largest black-owned businesses in the City of Dallas were Davis Automotive at $80 million, owned entirely by Richard O. Davis, and Pro-Line Corporation, an ethnic hair-care products firm at $55 mil-

---

96. Lyndon B. Johnson School of Public Affairs, *Local Government Election Systems, Policy Research Project Report Number 62* (Austin: University of Texas, 1984), 52.

97. City Services Analysis Program (File No. 92-1355), 1992.

98. Figures provided by the City of Dallas, Controller's Office, Financial Reporting Section.

lion, 64 percent owned by Comer and Isabell Cottrell. The largest Hispanic business was El Fenix Corporation, a restaurant chain at $33 million, owned by the Martinez family. None of these businesses were built on city contracts.

In the private sector a group of area business leaders, under tri-ethnic leadership, organized the Dallas Together Forum in 1993 to increase minority involvement in the business community. The participating companies signed a covenant to set hiring, promotion, and purchasing goals. They pledged to voluntarily disclose progress in reaching those goals. Minority members of the Forum pressed for more advantages. They requested that CEOs in the Forum contract to mentor a minority company, treat it as a subdivision of their company, and bring it to the level of $20 to $30 million. When told that this could not be done because of legal issues, the minorities extracted a commitment from the CEOs to provide contract opportunities to move fifteen black businesses in Dallas into the top 100 minority-owned businesses in the United States by the following year. A similar commitment to "mentor" fifteen Hispanic businesses was made.

The "volunteers" who were to be made into millionaires were minority members of the Forum. A Hispanic leader was reported to have said, "We have enough minority businesses; we need to make the ones we have big." The editor of a black business newsletter said, "I'm certainly ready any minute to be one."[99] After initial press coverage and reports of success, corporate participation in the Dallas Together Forum had declined by 1997. But the effort paid off for a number of black and Hispanic business owners in Dallas.

In the public sector the fair division of lucrative city contracts in major city projects has been perhaps the most volatile and frustrating issue for minority members on the Dallas City Council. Dallas first established voluntary minority contracting goals in 1978, and periodically modified its good-faith-effort plan as new data became available. Under the plan, bidders/proposers for the city's construction, professional services, or procurement contracts are required to meet—or to demonstrate and document their efforts to meet—established goals when competing for City of Dallas contracts.[100] The plan pinpointed administrative accountability and responsibilities within the city, formalized the certification and goal-setting process, and established guidelines to ensure adequate demonstration of good-faith efforts to obtain the participation of the Minority- and Women-owned Business Enterprise.

99. Member of the Dallas Together Forum, who asked not to be named (author interview by telephone, February 23, 1998).
100. Federal law forbids quotas, but the U.S. Supreme Court ruled in 1989 that goals for contracting with minorities and women can be established provided that availability studies show that a group has been discriminated against. The first disparity study prepared by Dallas city staff, released in 1992, set off its own round of controversy about whether it overestimated or underestimated the number of minority-owned firms for setting contracting goals.

Council members are constrained by federal law and state law on minority contracting programs, by conflicts over interpretation of the city's good-faith-effort plan, and by disagreements over the data on which goals are set. Reports by city auditors in Dallas have noted a number of problems in city staff oversight of the minority contracting program. Audits in 1994 and 1995, for example, found that city staff overstated participation toward the city's minority contracting goals by counting work that passed through minority-owned firms to white subcontractors.

The Dallas good-faith-effort plan works similarly to the joint-venture plan in Atlanta. A contractor in Atlanta believes that the extra 15 percent, a common fee to a minority firm for use of its name, plus the extra paperwork, plus the search for a qualified partner, plus a premium for lack of competition causes a building job at $60,000 in "unenlightened Gwinnett county" to cost the city of Atlanta $100,000.[101]

Certification as minority-owned, a requirement for participating in government contracts, has been another source for controversy. The process is time-consuming and requires heavy paperwork. Some minority-owned companies choose not to participate, which leads to undercounting availability, which has a negative impact in setting goals. The certification program was instituted to try to eliminate front companies. In the investigations of Paul Fielding and Al Lipscomb, the first sitting council members to be indicted in the city's history, Lipscomb appeared in tapes made by the FBI. The taped conversation alluded to setting up fake minority-front companies. Lipscomb was heard to say that he was "the 800-pound gorilla" who could serve as the front man for such scams in the future.[102]

In 1991 three minority Dallas City Council members, Don Hicks, Domingo Garcia, and Chris Luna, formed a task force to review the city's record with minority vendors. The task force recommended that the city raise its goal for minority contractor awards from the 17 percent set in the 1988 plan. "That's part of the impact of 14-1," Garcia said. He added that he would like to see the minority contracting target raised to 35 or 40 percent.[103]

In 1993 a goal of 37.3 percent was set for the city's construction money to go to minority-owned firms. But a city-ordered consultant's report found that City Hall overestimated the number of minority-owned firms when it set those goals. Based on the consultants' findings, 16.58 percent of the city's construction money should have been the benchmark for contracts to minority-owned firms. Under both federal and state law, cities cannot set minority contracting goals that are higher than the share of minority-owned firms in the city or they are open to lawsuits. The consultants' report opened a new round of conflicts over goals.

101. *The Economist,* April 15, 1995, 22.
102. Jim Schutze, *Dallas Observer,* April 16, 1998.
103. *Dallas Morning News,* January 23, 1992.

The story of the contract controversies that affected the mass transit project, DART, is representative of the complexities in "fair share" minority contracting. Pursuant to state-enabling legislation, the regional transportation authority was created by fifteen cities (Dallas and its neighbors) in August 1982. A public referendum passed with 58 percent of the vote. The Dallas City Council would have no direct control over many decisions at DART, but it would appoint fourteen of the board's twenty-five members. The suburbs and Dallas County Commissioners would appoint the remaining eleven members.

For some, especially Dallas real estate developers, mass transit was viewed as an economic development tool to steer business and population growth back into the central city. For others, it was a social service agency to further personal agendas of jobs, contracts, and political power. Neither group accorded the transportation needs of the region with priority. Between the 1983 vote creating DART and the 1988 bond issue vote, various interests battled for their own claims.

In January 1992 the city council gave DART permission to break ground on the rail transit system. But some council members warned that they would move quickly to shut down the rail project if DART failed to live up to its promise to increase the number of contracts awarded to minority and female contractors. Attacks on DART started in January, shortly after the first 14-1 council was seated in 1991; frustrated members stunned DART by denying a routine easement. Thereafter, even the smallest council agenda item related to DART opened the door for diatribes on alleged insensitivity to minorities, wasteful spending, and management problems. Previous councils did have disagreements with DART, but the squabbles after the new 14-1 council was seated were far more intense, primarily because of conflicts over the equitable distribution of contracts.

By March 1992 DART came close to splitting because of a rift over an $18.6 million DART rail-bridge contract. The transit agency had awarded the contract to an Austin construction company, whose initial list of subcontractors did not include companies owned by blacks. Shortly after the primary contractor had hired black-owned businesses, Hispanics, led by council members Domingo Garcia and Chris Luna, became incensed. They thought that Hispanic companies were to sacrifice part of their subcontracts to benefit blacks. This was a misunderstanding, as profit margins and work tasks of the Hispanic companies were not affected by the black-owned business participation. The angry Hispanic council members, backed by council colleagues Paul Fielding and Al Lipscomb, proposed a six-month moratorium on DART rail work.

Board members representing the suburbs, which were contributing 40 percent of DART's revenue, said that the moratorium would affect agency revenues by $50,000 for each day that rail work was delayed. Eleven suburbs threatened to pull out of DART if the moratorium passed, saying that they would not be held political hostage to Dallas. Ray Noah, a DART board member from the City of Richardson, said, "We need to ask Dallas if they are willing to hold DART hostage to every private, personal political agenda that is being pushed."[104]

In May 1993 a DART study determined that the agency's minority contracting goals were not achievable. Just ten days earlier, a rancorous debate at City Hall had erupted over a similar conclusion. The study reported that DART's target levels were too high and had discouraged prime contractors from submitting bids or had forced them to inflate their bid prices to accommodate women and minority-owned firms.[105] After decades of feuds and false starts, Dallas opened an 11.2-mile section in June 1996. This portion included the downtown transit mall and two branches into mostly black and Hispanic neighborhoods south of downtown. The transit agency's records showed that the light-rail bill was already "about $200 million higher than it would have been without the bickering that has dogged the project since 1983."[106]

The minority contracting issue has not been limited to the major development projects. Consider the ordeal in 1999 of Robert Troy, an experienced architect and a professor of architecture but a new city employee who did not know he was supposed to avoid paper trails that might limit his bosses' political options to act on instructions from higher-ups.[107] Troy brought charges that the Cultural Affairs Director Margie Reese, who is black, bypassed the selection process to steer a $500,000 consulting contract to Johnson McKibben, a local architectural firm that had served as the minority-owned partner on several major projects, including the new downtown sports arena. Troy's professional ethics were compromised, because he was in charge of a committee that was supposed to choose among fourteen architectural firms invited to bid on the contract. From his experience, he knew the costs in time and money for firms to even bid on a project, assuming it to be a fair process.

The city auditor, Robert Melton, investigated the claims and confirmed that top city officials had rigged the deal. But the city council members, especially Veletta Lill, Barbara Mallory Caraway, and Maxine Thornton-Reese, went after the messengers, Troy and Melton. The council supported Margie Reese, as did the Cultural Affairs Commission, whose members wore large campaign buttons with the slogan "We Love Margie!" at the September 16 meeting, attended by Troy. After the Margie Reese affair, and because of other audit reports that had been unpopular with certain city council members, Melton resigned. He claimed that in Dallas he "criticized operations contrary to the message the City Council wanted to put out. . . . I was under constant pressure from a few of the council members to make unethical moves."[108]

104. Catalina Camia and Nita Thurman, *Dallas Morning News,* March 4, 1992.

105. *Dallas Morning News,* May 29, 1993.

106. Curtis Howell, *Dallas Morning News,* June 8, 1996.

107. This account is based on reports by Jim Schutze, *Dallas Observer,* September 23, 1999; November 4, 1999.

108. Deborah O'Neil, *St. Petersburg Times,* August 3, 2000.

CONCLUSIONS

Experiences in Dallas give credence to the importance of minority voices being present in legislative bodies. Minority council members elected from single-member districts gave voice to long-standing subjective grievances. And because racial minorities, in general, adhere to a view of the elected representative as agent, rather than as trustee, they tend to contact their representative more and believe that they have more influence on their elected officials than do their white counterparts.

The practice of colleague deference, which developed with single-member district representation, has afforded individual council members opportunities to respond to some of the budget priorities of their communities and to control intra-district zoning requests. Bond issues, at the margins at least, now reflect single-member districting by distributing some projects by district.

Unlike many other cities, affirmative action in minority employment in city government has not been a major issue in Dallas, except in the police and fire departments. Minority council members, however, have tried to influence appointments of particular individuals at City Hall and on major boards, such as that of DART. Minority groups have competed aggressively to have representatives of their groups in official leadership roles, especially in the city manager's office and in the police department.

It has been established that minority council members elected from single-member districts, especially under 14-1, have made a difference in securing contract benefits. In unprecedented numbers blacks and Hispanics have been represented in city contracts, and minorities have been appointed to boards and commissions where they could keep a watchful eye on contract and employment opportunities. Larry Duncan, a former council member, believes that "rotating seats on the city council, the airport board, the school board, the DART board and elsewhere" enable a small coterie of players to control the distribution of contracts and other tribute in Dallas.[109] This distribution of economic rewards seems to have gone to the large, established minority companies and to those who are politically "wired-in." The same, of course, was also true of established white companies, such as Austin Commercial, discussed above.

A paradox, really, under 14-1, is that more attention has been devoted to the redistribution of economic resources among districts, and to political leadership, than to ensuring that funds intended for low-income residents reached them in a fair manner. This situation prevailed, because a new network of contacts developed in minority communities to the purse-string holders, who controlled funds and patronage.

The main public policy consequences of election by single-member dis-

109. Jim Schutze, *Dallas Observer,* June 27, 2002.

tricts, then, have been to give voice to subjective issues, to afford minority participation to a greater degree in contracts than formerly, and to enable minority council members to claim economic benefits for their districts, at least at the margins, in budgets and bond issues.

On the other hand, city politics continues to be dominated behind the scenes by the interlocking directorate of an economic elite/government alliance. The presence of minorities on the council has had only minimal effect on substantive issues important to minorities, such as affordable housing, social services, and economic development in southern Dallas.

Conclusions

The best way out of a racial dilemma does not require a fixed course without
regard to wind or wave but a route that allows the political process to sort
alternatives until the country finds policies with which it can live.
—Paul E. Peterson

The Voting Rights Act of 1965 is landmark legislation in the history of civil
rights in the United States. It ended de jure voting discrimination and effectively achieved its initial objective to eliminate barriers to black registration
and voting. Any negative consequences of the Voting Rights Act were caused
primarily because the federal government pushed beyond protecting the right
of blacks to register and to vote, to requiring federal preapproval of prospective
voting changes in selected jurisdictions, to including Hispanics under the
umbrella of remedies designed for blacks, and, finally, to requiring that representation of two minority groups, blacks and Hispanics, be maximized in proportion to their numbers in the population.

How to measure, and to remedy, discrimination once the issues moved
beyond the ballot was not obvious. Congressional attempts to devise standards
for subtle de facto discrimination failed. A review of the transformation of the
original Voting Rights Act of 1965, and its subsequent amendments, illustrates
the shortcomings of developing statutory law additively. New provisions
appear to have been considered independent of their effect on the extant body
of law. The target was not clear, even kept changing, and public support
declined as public officials muddled through complex questions. A national
consensus could not be built on shifting goals.

Paradoxes that emanate from the intertexture of this study include the tensions between the norm of a color-blind society and the practice of classification by race; between individual rights and group rights; and between the
principle of majoritarianism and the tenet of protecting the interests of minorities. Such paradoxes can only be understood and temporized, not definitively
resolved.

The experience of Dallas demonstrates the difficulties created for a city by
the tensions between the original Voting Rights Act (and Fifteenth Amendment

268

right to vote issues) and subsequent VRA Amendments (and Fourteenth Amendment equal protection of the laws issues). Both bodies of law have continuously evolved since 1965; the standards and rules under neither are clear. A city should not be placed, as Dallas was, in the untenable position of trying to comply with two continually moving targets of federal law simultaneously.

The results of voting rights litigation have been equally as mixed as legislative results. As long as the courts treated voting rights as an individual right, they were able to develop manageable standards. Voting rights case law went awry when the courts attempted to prescribe legal solutions for representational inequities of groups and became ensnared in an undefined concept of minority vote dilution. Moreover, no methodology exists to infer how individual members of groups vote in particular elections (the ecological fallacy). This problem renders suspect inferences on racial bloc voting and voter turnout by race, used as bases for findings of vote dilution.

As voting rights litigation evolved, courts became mired in making policy choices among competing theories of representation, conflicting testimony of expert witnesses, and inconclusive debates on empirical and methodological questions. The Supreme Court has yet to develop a coherent theory of representation to guide federal court decisions, or to resolve the quandary of an appropriate balance between group rights and individual rights.

To enforce nondiscrimination, or negative remedies, is clearly within the jurisdiction of the courts. But they do not have expertise or tools to determine affirmative remedies for resolving racial issues. I am not suggesting here either a reduction in concern with minority political participation or the abandonment of a legal strategy; rather, recognition that the judicial process has internal constraints is in order. This recognition frees a society to think outside narrow channels in order to develop holistic strategies for resolving complex, multifaceted racial issues.

Another paradox that can be accommodated in a variety of ways, but never definitively resolved, is how to balance majority and minority interests. Majority rule is often considered to be a defining principle of democratic government on practical grounds. But if the will of the majority, or the greater number, is to prevail, how far may the preferences of those in the minority be ignored? Or be given advantage?

Rather than balancing constitutional-democratic goals, the legal approach tipped the scales to favor race-based remedies, group voting rights, and a districting system that tilts toward parochial interests.

A plausible explanation for dissatisfaction with the results is that case law channels elements of representation narrowly, focusing on those that can be quantified and thus made to *seem* manageable. Courts likely made single-member districts the preferred choice because of the nature of the adversarial process. Plaintiffs attacked at-large districts as discriminatory and posited single-member districts as the panacea. Other options were foreclosed from consideration.

The litigation experience in Dallas reemphasizes that the balance between the principle of majoritarianism and the equally important principle of ensuring that the minority has an opportunity to hold the majority to account is delicate. When forced to do so, a majority of Dallas voters attempted to find a compromise by repeatedly voting in favor of a mixed system of at-large and single-member districts. The courts, however, thwarted the voters' preferences.

Even though the courts lack a standard for balancing majority and minority interests, or a proven method for determining what districting requirements best serve minority interests, a federal judge commandeered the city's redistricting commission and ordered a 14-1 single-member district plan. While it is within the purview of the courts to find city election plans constitutionally defective, federal courts are not forums for political debate and should not resolve themselves into charter commissions.

Given the trajectory of the developing case law and the U.S. Department of Justice guidelines under the Voting Rights Act, the black plaintiffs and their constituents in Dallas had little incentive to work toward a compromise. The judicial bias for single-member districts, therefore, sabotaged the efforts of citizens of all races to find a political accommodation to the new realities of federal law and to rapidly changing demographic patterns. Furthermore, by embedding a theory of descriptive representation into the common law of remedies, the federal courts may well have foreclosed opportunities to pursue more fundamental remedies for ensuring fair representation for all citizens and for improving race relations.

Moreover, the findings in Dallas reveal that a number of the assumptions on which the federal government's preference for single-member districts were based are unsupported by either the data or the outcomes. A federal judge in 1990 voided a compromise mixed system on the assumptions, repudiated shortly thereafter, that a black could not win an at-large seat in Dallas, and that single-member districts would enable minorities to raise campaign funds from their own districts and not be beholden to white donors. Ron Kirk won the citywide contest for mayor in 1995 and was reelected in 1999, and minority candidates continue to be funded by sources outside their districts.

Reliance by plaintiffs, courts, and the DOJ on aggregate data, used to convert population figures by race to votes and then to seats, rested on an assumption that a monolithic black interest needed to be represented by black elected officials. In assuming a monolithic black interest, and by requiring minority single-member districts to ensure the election of minorities proportionate to their share in the total population, the courts and the DOJ reinforced a racially divisive view of representation, and eliminated incentives to form cross-racial coalitions and to engage in collaborative politics. Federal requirements incubated the expectation among black and Hispanic citizens that representation from districts drawn as minority districts was "guaranteed" to minority candidates. Racist campaigns against white candidates running in minority districts resulted.

Evidence does not support the assumption that the failure of the CCA to slate candidates, whom the plaintiffs and their witnesses viewed as minority "candidates of choice," was racially discriminatory. The CCA bias was toward minority candidates with conservative views. Supreme Court justices have observed that when differing political and socioeconomic characteristics of whites and minorities explain racially polarized voting, Section 2 of the Voting Rights Act does not protect that cause of minority electoral failure. This issue was not addressed in the litigation involving Dallas elections. Furthermore, the demise of the slating group did not mean an end to the influence of major business support for candidates in Dallas City Council elections, but did mean that business influences lost their transparency.

Given the flawed assumptions on which the single-member-district remedy was premised, were the intended results from the districting change achieved? Single-member districts as a replacement for at-large districts did have the intended consequence of more blacks and Hispanics elected to public office in Dallas. Because of the fragility of democracy as process, not only is the opportunity for minorities to have their voices heard fundamentally fair, but a participatory voice is also in the self-interest of the majority. Michael Suk-Young Chwe has shown mathematically that Marquis de Condorcet's idea of information aggregation, "much more than merely a justification of majority rule," enables democracy to be seen "not only as the fair resolution of conflicting interests but also as a collective enterprise in which each person's participation benefits everyone else."[1]

The two at-large wins by minorities, and the two minority wins in a single-member district not drawn as a safe minority district, indicate that racial attitudes in Dallas have not precluded crossover voting and coalition building as successful strategies. Increases in elected minorities that might have occurred because of changing demographics, shifting attitudes, and emphasis on coalition building, had the city's political system not been disrupted by court-ordered single-member districting, cannot reasonably be tested. Clearly, however, the crucial decision by the courts to impose a 14-1 system that required "safe" districts for minorities undercut the neighborhood-based districting desired by many citizens, including some minorities.

A number of the other consequences of single-member districts are evident. Council members elected from single-member districts have had different motivations, backgrounds, credentials, and, in some instances, style than members elected at large. Political careerists, some of whom ran for reasons of self-aggrandizement, replaced council members who served as part-time "citizen-

1. Michael Suk-Young Chwe, "Minority Voting Rights Can Maximize Majority Welfare," *American Political Science Review* (March 1999), 93:85–97.

legislators," guided, in general, by noblesse oblige. Councils comprised of members from diverse employment experiences, as well as homemakers, civic volunteers, and the unemployed, replaced councils on which businessmen, many with executive experience, dominated. Council composition is yet another instance in which a system of all single-member districts changed the council from one end of a spectrum to the opposite end rather than achieving some balance in the middle.

Creating race-based districts also subordinated the practical need for candidates to build a broad coalition for electoral success. Forcing Dallas to abandon all at-large districts, except mayor, deprived the council of voices of every race with a broad constituency base. The pendulum was forced from one extreme to its opposite to constitute councils comprised of members who speak for parochial interests.

The path to elected office also changed. Most CCA candidates were citizens who had served as board chairs of community organizations, such as the United Way and the Chamber of Commerce. After 14-1, service as council appointees on the city's boards and commissions has been the dominant career route for election to the city council.

By the 1980s, with single-member districts, many citizens of Dallas had become dismayed by the quality of candidates for Dallas City Council. The lists included perennial candidates, unemployed activists, and parochial-interest advocates. Rarely did professionals or leaders experienced in large organizations enter the fray in single-member districts. Perhaps most discouraging is the finding that single-member districts create an incentive to maintain racial separation, as evidenced when some West Dallas leaders sacrificed the interests of public-housing residents in order to ensure a black-dominant election district.

For many citizens of Dallas, a disturbing consequence of single-member districts is that cronyism and corruption, which had characterized Dallas under the ward form of government prior to 1931, resurfaced. Candidates slated by the Citizens Charter Association were required to pledge "to fight any trace of scandal, personal selfishness, and political bias." Clean government became a source of pride for elected officials, business leaders, and citizens alike.

This changed. While single-member districts did not cause corruption, some council members elected from these districts have held the view that opportunities for graft is one of the rewards of political power. Behaviors based on these expectations, cultivated by the underground history of whites paying off minorities in Dallas, finally came to public attention with the convictions of two elected officials in the 1990s, and with the opposition among some council members to a strengthened city ethics code.

Districts do not seem to have stimulated electoral competitiveness and voter turnout. The number of candidates running for a seat on the city council has not significantly changed under the three election systems in Dallas. More close contests might be expected under the 14-1 system than under either at-large or mixed-system elections, but the findings do not support that result. During the years of CCA dominance under the at-large system, more seats were contested, and fewer candidates polled less than 15 percent of the vote than under either 8-3 or 14-1. This may be explained by the fact that the CCA candidates were actively challenged in that system by other organized groups and by independents.

Voter turnout trend, as a percentage of registered voters, was generally upward until it peaked in 1991. After 1991 the trend has been dramatically downward under 14-1. One might plausibly assume that single-member districts would have created more voter interest and hence a higher turnout. Extreme variations of voter turnout occurred under all three systems. These swings were likely candidate- and issue-dependent, rather than having a correlation with the different election systems.

Another issue of single-member districting, avoided in at-large systems, is the need to design the districts. Conflicts over redistricting are inherently a product of drawing district boundaries for political advantage, for whatever reason. Before 1975, when districts in Dallas served only as candidate residence districts, there had been no incentive to manipulate the boundaries. Consequently, when residence districts were changed to election districts under court order, but without any redrawing, a federal judge approved the plan. He found that the district lines followed "natural and rational boundaries" and that no gerrymandering was present. Equally important, he judged that the 8-3 court-ordered plan maintained common community interests and kept the south Dallas area intact.

Then, in August 1979, the Justice Department agreed to accept the Dallas City Council's proposed election plan, but only if lines were redrawn to ensure black or Hispanic majorities of at least 79 percent in three districts. This requirement initiated the pattern of race-conscious districting that continues to the present day. Redistricting after the 1980, 1990, and 2000 censuses continued the practice of drawing district lines that crossed natural boundaries and neighborhood boundaries in search of minority population in order to increase the safety margins for minority candidates, and especially for minority incumbents.

Nor does change to single-member districts seem to have stimulated a general perception of improvement in the quality of city governance. Single-member districts are not inherently incompatible with the council-manager form of government, yet few of the recommended reform elements in the National Municipal League's "Model City Charter" remain in their intended form in Dallas. Many election contests are de facto partisan. District-elected council members, who interfere with personnel matters, compromise the city manager's responsibility to make appointments. City planning takes a back seat to any issues of the moment; any planning that does occur is spearheaded by the private sector.

Although the interplay of power often depends more on those who exercise it than on structure, dissatisfaction with the operation of Dallas city government in recent years has expressed itself frequently in calls to change the structure. The difference between the policy-making responsibility of the council and the administrative role of the city manager and city staff have either not been understood and respected, or else have been ignored, by council members elected from single-member districts. The power of the mayor, the relations between the mayor and the council, between the mayor and the city manager, between the council and the city manager, and between members of the council all were affected to some degree by the change to single-member districts.

Other results have included greater involvement in operational detail by council members; greater involvement in the setting of policy by the city manager; increased constituent contact, with greater demands for more detailed information from staff; and an enlarged size of the council. These developments all contributed to a significantly increased workload for council members, which fueled demand for a full-time salary, finally approved by voters in May 2001.

Even though the representatives elected from single-member districts altered the dynamics of the struggles for power and turf between the mayor, council, and city manager, the informal relationships between public and private interests were not altered in any fundamental way by single-member districts. The dominant role played by major business leaders in the city has not fundamentally changed. The bedrock of government and politics in Dallas is still the city's cultural context and the long-standing business-government partnership.

Another measure of the consequences of single-member districts is change in public policy. When citizens press for change in their election system, they hope to achieve policy outcomes different from those produced by the status quo. The "mirror-the-constituency" view of representation, accepted by the courts, presumes that policies adopted by a council that includes minorities will be responsive to the interests of those minorities.

The main public policy consequences for minorities of election by single-member districts have been to give voice to subjective issues, to afford minority participation to a greater degree in contracts than formerly, and to enable minority council members to claim economic benefits for their districts.

The practice of district deference, which developed immediately under single-member districts, has afforded individual council members opportunities to respond to some of the budget priorities of their communities and to control intra-district zoning requests. Bond issues, at the margins at least, now reflect single-member districting by distributing some projects by district.

A paradox, really, under 14-1, is that more attention has been devoted to the redistribution of economic resources among districts, and to political leadership, than to ensuring that funds intended for low-income residents reached them in a fair manner. This situation prevails because a new network of contacts developed in minority communities to the purse-string holders, who control funds and patronage.

Planning continues to follow economics-driven historical patterns, in which the city council plays a marginal role, limited by a lack of information. Zoning has been a somewhat different matter. Because strong neighborhood associations and single-member districts are mutually reinforcing, the role played by neighborhoods on supra-district zoning issues can be attributed tangentially, at least, to the change to single-member district elections.

Unlike many other cities, affirmative action in minority employment in city government has not been a major issue in Dallas, except in the police and fire departments. Civil service precludes city employment patronage opportunities. However, minority council members have tried to influence appointments of particular individuals at City Hall and on major boards, such as that of DART. Minority groups have competed aggressively to have representatives of their groups in official leadership roles, especially in the city manager's office and in the police department.

Consideration of these consequences of the Voting Rights Act, and court litigation that prescribed single-member districts as the preferred remedy for underrepresentation of two minority groups, should be a call for the following:

- Congress should reassess the temporal provisions of the Voting Rights Act;
- Federal judges ought to restrain from prescribing remedies that should be debated instead in constitutional conventions or legislative assemblies; and
- Citizens should move beyond litigation to find ways to further the goal of fair representation in American political institutions through healthy, competitive, political processes.

The future of the Voting Rights Act, now in its fourth decade, seems uncertain. A generation after the development of a national consensus, which supported the initial enactment of the VRA, race relations remain troubled, many of the consequences have proved to be unsatisfactory, and theories and assumptions that underlie the legal rights approach to ensuring fairness in electoral politics are being questioned.

At a minimum, Congress should reconcile the internal conflicts in the Voting Rights Act and should modify or allow the preclearance provision to expire. The shortcomings of Section 5, which will expire in 2007 unless renewed by Congress, have been demonstrated. It has no effect on states that are not covered and, consequently, the de facto discriminatory patterns in other parts of the nation were largely ignored. The attempt to design a formula for determining the jurisdictions to be covered has been shown to be a moving target that has not fulfilled original intent. The preclearance requirement only applied to changes per se; therefore, even in states that were covered by special provisions in the VRA, some discriminatory practices continued to prevail until changes were proposed.

Section 5 also raises serious questions concerning federal-state relations in a federal system of government. This section accorded extraordinary power to the federal government over state and local laws by requiring states and localities to *preclear* any change in law, and by shifting the burden of proof to states and localities to prove that their proposed changes were *not* discriminatory.

If Section 5 is retained, it should apply nationwide. Some advantage was realized in applying the VRA special provisions to states in the south, which had a history of de jure discrimination. But that era is now past history. Had the focus in 1965 been on outcomes, as it came to be later, rather than solely on discriminatory voting laws, it would have become evident that black voters were not represented in proportion to the black population in the legislatures and city councils of northern states. There, the black franchise had been unimpeded by law for at least one hundred years.

If the special provisions are allowed to expire, they can be reinstated by court order if there is a renewal of discriminatory practices. Even so, as 2007 approaches, a wave of rumors may be spread to create alarm and sufficient protest to influence Congress to renew the temporal provisions. There was precedent in 2000, when radio talk show hosts perpetrated the rumor, which spread on the Internet, that the entire Voting Rights Act would expire in 2007, and, as a result, blacks were in danger of losing the right to vote.

Second, the courts should restrain from prescribing affirmative remedies on issues of representation. As there is no perfect machinery for the translation of the popular will, and no ultimately "right answer" among various electoral options, such issues, because of their complexity and subtlety, are the ones most dependent on political compromise. Conversely, they are the ones least conducive to the legal model, in which plaintiffs frame the questions and "rules" frame the answers. Yet the extraordinarily complicated issue of fair representation is one of those infrequent instances in which courts moved beyond proscriptive adjudication to develop affirmative remedies, or prescriptive law.

Judicial restraint should be exercised most when courts contemplate moving beyond proscriptive law. The judiciary lacked resources and expertise to make the political choice of single-member districts the preferred remedy for underrepresentation of minorities. One of the striking features of the papers and comments presented at a Texas Law Review symposium on the electoral process is the sense that courts have often served as an obstacle, rather than the solution, to problems of minority political empowerment.[2]

2. Pamela S. Karlan, "The Rights to Vote: Some Pessimism about Formalism," *Texas Law Review* (June 1993), 71:1737.

When the prescribed legal solution to representational inequities failed to fulfill the hopes of even the protected classes of minority voters, scholars, legislators, and even the courts, in a few instances, began to explore alternative remedies. A vast literature exists now on election systems alternative to majority winner-take-all single-member districts. Especially prevalent are recommendations of various forms of proportional representation in multi-member districts as a race-neutral method of remedying the tensions of racial representation.

Arguments that hypothesize as to the likely results attained under alternative voting systems retain a focus on the election of minority candidates to office, an approach that is useful as a matter of legal strategy since courts and plaintiffs can count winners. The greater need is to move beyond strategies intended to fix the results to strategies that aim to improve the politics that gives rise to the results.

At the least, courts will likely continue to litigate voting rights cases under the extant VRA or a revised Voting Rights Act. Some states and localities, and perhaps even Congress, will tinker with election systems and try new strategies that will have their own advantages and disadvantages. None of these developments will prove to be satisfactory, unless ways can be found to revitalize democratic politics. This requires a commitment both to fair process and to the ideals of the nation's founding documents.

The current emphasis on maximizing the number of safe minority seats, protecting incumbents with districts as safe as possible, and drawing competitive districts only if that cannot be avoided dampens citizen interest in voting. Real "democratization" of urban government requires the restoration of healthy political processes with competitive elections and coalitions forged on the basis of values held in common rather than on safe seats gerrymandered by any particular group criterion.

The present climate, in which compromise is denigrated, pejorative labels are assigned to those with whom one disagrees, and every issue is made adversarial, must be changed to avoid causing deadlock in public life and rendering city government incapable of functioning both responsively and efficiently.

To overcome the dysfunctional consequences of the structural and institutional incentives that have encouraged the separate claims of distinct identities, systemic incentives to encourage cooperation and coalition building must be found. In healthy democratic politics, citizens find common ground through a deliberative process in which they exercise the art of negotiation and compromise.

In a revitalized city, citizens learn that it is de Tocqueville's "self-interest properly understood" to engage in give-and-take, to agree to disagree with respect and civility, and to listen and learn from other voices. It is enlightened self-interest to contribute to a more cooperative, deliberative politics.

In an era of citizen impatience and expectation of quick results, deliberative politics may seem inordinately time-consuming. But cooperative, deliberative politics avoids the demoralizing effects of the wearisome, ubiquitous conflict that appeals to selfishness and opportunism rather than to the "better angels of our nature," to use Lincoln's memorable phrase.

The challenge, then, is to find systemic ways to facilitate cooperation and to achieve an acceptable level of public consensus in order to respond wisely to urban challenges. "The essence of political life," according to Hanna Pitkin, "is precisely the problem of continually *creating* unity, a public, in a context of diversity, rival claims, unequal power, and conflicting interests."[3] In the final analysis, creating unity takes extraordinary leadership and people of good will in both the public and private sectors, people who are committed to making the constitutional-democratic system work for all.

3. Hanna Pitkin, *Wittgenstein and Justice;* quoted by Laura Stoker, "Interests and Ethics in Politics," *American Political Science Review* (June 1992), 86:369.

Appendixes

A. Candidates for the Dallas City Council by Race, Date of Candidacy, and Date of Election, 1967–1997

Name	Race	Candidate	Elected
Ackels, Lawrence E.	White	1971	
Adams, Clara R.	White	1985	
Adkins, Jack C.	White	1969	
Aguirre, Pedro	Hispanic	1973, 1975	
Allen, Billy R.	Black	1977	
Allen, George L.	Black		a1968, 1969, 1971, 1973, 1975r
Almaguer, Manuel	Hispanic	1969, 1973	
Alpert, Emily J.	White	1983	
Ambler, Jess	White	1980	
Anderson, James	Black	1977	
Andrews, Michael L.	Black	1991	
Arrendondo, Roberto	Hispanic	1975	
Aubrey, Richard D.	White	1967	
Aymond, Rex	White	1983	
Baccus, Jasper	Black	1973	
Baccus, Mrs. R.L. (Shirley)	White	1969	
Baldwin, Pete	White	1977	
Baillargeon, Margaret	White	1981	
Ball, James M. (Jim), Jr.	White	1967, 1973	
Ball, Jim	White	1989, 1991, 1993	
Ballard, Moses	Black	1983	
Banks, Richard	White	1981	
Baril, Ruth	White	1977	
Barker, Barry	White	1991	
Bartlett, Steve	White	1973	s1977, 1979, 1991–1995
Bartos, Steve	White	1973	1987, 1989, 1991
Bartram, Webster B.	White	1969	

Key: s—special election; r—resigned; a—appointed to vacancy.

Candidates for the Dallas City Council, 1967–1997 (continued)

Name	Race	Candidate	Elected
Bedford, L. A., Jr.	Black	1980	
Bello, Jamie	Unverified	1975	
Bishop, Brad	White	1980	
Bishop, David E.	White	1973	
Bivins, Ron E.	Black	1991	
Blackburn, Bill	White		s1976, 1977
Blair, Fred	Black	1993	1979, 1981, 1983r
Blessing, Elizabeth	White	1981	
Blumer, Donna	White		1993, 1995, 1997
Bock, Joe	White	1971	
Bodzin, Frank	White	1983, 1989, 1993	
Bolden, Le Roy	Black	s1975	
Borden, Jack F.	White	1983, 1993	
Box, Glenn	White		1989, 1991, 1993
Boyd, Sharon	White	1993, 1995	
Bradshaw, James (Jim)	White	1977	
Brady, Leonard G.	White	1980	
Brannon, Taylor	Black	1993, 1995, 1997	
Brin, R. Nathan	White	1991	
Brown, Herschel	White	1980	
Brown, Lamar D.	White	1969	
Buerger, Jim	White	1987	1989
Burkleo, Joe	White	s1976	
Busch, Ed	White	1981, s1996	
Byrd, Don	White	1989	
Cain, Kathryn	White	1991	
Caldwell, Osborn	Black	1977	
Cantrick, Bob	White	1981	
Caraway, Barbara Mallory	Black	1991	1993, 1995, 1997
Carter, W. S. (Bill)	White	1973	
Chaney, Leo, Jr.	White	s1984	
Chase, Scott	White	1989	
Clark, Harold G., Jr.	White	1969	
Cole, Lorenzo D.	Black	1993	
Collins, Jim	White	1987	
Connolly, John	White	1981	
Cothrum, William E.	White		1967, 1969, 1975, 1977
Craft, Juanita	Black	s1975	a1975, 1977
Corcoron, Stan	White	1983	
Crenshaw, Marvin E.	Black	1983, s1984, 1987, 1989, 1991, 1993	
Crenshaw, Sandra	Black	1995	1993

Candidates for the Dallas City Council, 1967–1997 (continued)

Name	Race	Candidate	Elected
Cullum, Charles G.	White		1967
Cunningham, E. Brice	Black	1977	
Dallas, Dewayne	White	1981, 1983	
Baniel, John	White	1985	
Daniels, Shirley	Black	1985	
Davis, Cedric W.	Black	1993	
Davis, H. L.	White	1980	
Davis, Larry K.	White	1980	
Davis, Marvin	Black	1997	
Dear, Bill	White	1967	
Dearman, J. Edward	Black	s1975	
DeBrucque, William R.	White	1973	
DeGaugh, Tom	White	1973	
Devany, Joseph A. (Joe)	White	1967, 1973	
Dickey, Ben	White	1983, s1984, 1985	
Doyle, August	Black	1983, 1984, 1985	
Duncan, Larry	White	1989	1991, 1993, 1995, 1997
Eddy, Dan	White	1983	
Emory, Emerson	Black	1973, 1975, 1977	
Evans, Jack	White		1981
Evans, John	White	1977, 1991	1985, 1987, 1989
Fain, Douglas	White		1969, 1971
Fair, William W. (Bill)	White	1977	
Fantroy, James (J. L.)	Black	1993	
Fender, Marian	White	1983	
Ferguson, Sherry	Black	1980	
Fielding, Paul N.	White	1985, 1997	1983, 1991, 1993, 1995
Finch, Gordon I.	Black	1973	
Finkelman, Lois	White		1997
Finlan, Owen Henry	White	1987	
Finlan, Richard (Rick)	White	1987, 1991	
Fitzwater, Sid	White	1981	
Folsom, Robert (Bob)	White		s1976, 1977, 1979
Forest, Bill	Black	s1984	
Frazier, Willie (Joe)	Black	1991	
Freeman, Brad	White	1973	
Fugitt, Morris H.	White	1975, 1977	
Fuller, George R.	Black	1993	
Gale, Jennifer	White	1991, 1993	
Galindo, Guillermo M.	Hispanic	1991	
Garcia, Domingo A.	Hispanic	1995	1991, 1993

281

Candidates for the Dallas City Council, 1967–1997 (continued)

Name	Race	Candidate	Elected
Garner, Curtis	Black	1987	
Garner, James	White	1983, 1985, 1989	
Gibbons, Tom	White	1980, 1981, 1983	
Gibson, Colleen	Black	1987	
Giddings, Helen	Black	1983, 1989	
Giles, Artie Fay	Black	1993, 1995	
Gill, Marianne	White	1973	
Gilmore, Jerry	White		1971, 1973
Goldblatt, Max B.	White	1967, 1969, 1975, 1985	1979, 1981, 1983r
Goldsmith, Mrs. C. R. (Taffy)	White	1980	
Gonzales, Al	Hispanic		1987
Gray, Ed	White	1981, 1983	
Green, Herbert, Jr.	White	1971, 1973	
Green, Kenneth R.	Black	1995	
Greyson, Sandra (Sandy)	White		1997
Grunsfeld, Norman	White	1975, s1976	
Guinn, Gene	White	1967, 1969, 1971	
Haggar, Joe	White		1979, 1981
Hall, Stan	White	1985	
Hall, Vincent	Black	1995	
Halstead, Donna	White		1991, 1993, 1995r
Hamilton, Mrs. C. F. (Sybil)	White		1967
Hammond, Jay	White	1971	
Harp, Bud	White	1993	
Harris, James (J. Frank)	Black	1977	
Harris, J. (Jim) C.	White	1977	
Harrison, Adlene	White		1973, 1975, 1977r
Hart, Jim	White	1985	1983
Hauntz, Adolph	Black	s1984	
Hawkins, Teddy Delbert	Black	1991	
Heggins, Elsie Faye	Black	1977	1979, 1981, 1983r
Henderson, Michael W.	Black	1977	
Hernandez, Frank P.	Hispanic	1969, 1980, 1991	
Hicks, Don	White		1977, 1979, 1981
Hicks, Donald W., Sr.	Black		1991, 1993, 1995, 1997
Hicks, Les	White	s1976	
Higginbotham, Rufus (JFK)	White	1991, 1997	
Hill, Lloyd J.	White	1993	
Hoke, Frank A.	White		1967
Holcomb, Craig	White		1983, 1985, 1987

Candidates for the Dallas City Council, 1967–1997 (continued)

Name	Race	Candidate	Elected
Holland, Ted	White		1969, 1971
Hollins, Jurline	Black	1995	
Houston, Horace	White	1971	
Howard, B. D.	Black	1980	
Howell, G. L. (Pete)	Black	1973	
Hughes, George A., Jr.	White	1971, 1973	
Hughes, Robert	White	1969	
Huginnie, Clarence	Black	1969, 1971	
Hutchison, Mike	White	1993	
Hytche, Herbert H. Jr.	Black	1991	
Jackson, Dallas	Black	1987, 1991	
Jackson, Joseph F. (Joe)	White	1977	
Johnson, D. Ellen	Black	s1975	
Jonsson, J. Erik	White		1967, 1969
Jordon, Darrell	White	1997	
Kadane, Sheffield	White		1969, 1971
Kallenberg, Roger	White	1993	
Kennedy, Beverly	White	1993	
Kincannon, Charles P.	White	1985	
Kirk, Ron	Black		1995
Kirven, Joe	Black	s1975	
Kolpien, Alton L.	White	1991	
Lake, Jim	White	s1976	
Lantz, Elaine	White	1995	
Larry, Jerald Henry	Black	1971	
Lee, Jimmy J.	Black	1991	
Leedom, John	White		1975, 1977
Lerouge, Roni	White	1987	
Lesser, Peter	White	1989	
Lewis, James M. (Skip)	White	1985	
Lewis, Mary Louise	Black	1980, 1983	
Liberman, David M.	White	1973	
Lill, Veletta	White		1997
Lipscomb, Al	Black	1971, 1973, 1975, s1975, 1983	s1984, 1985, 1987, 1989, 1991, 1995, 1997
Logan, Perry	White	s1976	
Longoria, Rudi	Hispanic	1973	
Lott, Judy	Black	1973	
Loza, John	Hispanic		1997
Ludwig, Billy Jack	White	s1976, 1981, 1987, 1989, 1991, 1997	
Luna, Chris	Hispanic		1991, 1993, 1995

Name	Race	Candidate	Elected
Lyons, Cully	White	1985	
Mallory (see Caraway)	White		
Malouf, Peter G.	White	1983	
Martin, Art	White	s1976	
Martin, Bill	White	1980	
Martin, David	White	1977	
Martin, Ted	White	1987, 1989	
Marinez, Mrs. Alfred (Anita)	Hispanic		1969, 1971
May, Joe	Hispanic	1985	
Mays, Avery	White	1971	
Mayes, Charlotte	Black		1991, 1993, 1995, 1997
McAlpin, Bill	White	1987	
McCollum, Andy	White	1991	
McDaniel, Craig	White		1993, 1995
McGarvey, William R.	White	1969	
McGrew, Elijah, Jr.	Black	1991, 1993	
McIntyre, Robert C.	Black	1975, 1983	
McKillop, J. M.	White	1969	
McKinney, Jack F.	White		1967, 1969
McNamara, Tim	White	1997	
McVay, J. C. (Bud)	White	1991	
Medrano, F. (Pancho), Jr.	Hispanic	1975	
Medrano, Ricardo	Hispanic	1975, s1977, 1983, 1991	1979, 1981
Menefee, Jerry	White	1971	
Merritt, Alan	White	1997	
Meserole, Otis	White	1983, 1987, 1991	
Meyer, Abe	White		1967, 1969
Meyer, Fred	White	1987	
Middlebrooks, Sharon M.	Black	1997	
Miers, Harriet	White		1989
Milkie, Bill	White		1985
Mills, Glenn, Jr.	Black	1991	
Moeller, Dave	White	1971	
Montemayor, Joe	Hispanic	s1977	
Moody, Joe	White	1993	
Morehead, Gardell Anthony	Black	1985, 1987	
Moser, Jack	White		1967
Mount, Ralph	White	1985	
Murphy, Craig	White	1997	

Candidates for the Dallas City Council, 1967–1997 (continued)

Name	Race	Candidate	Elected
Murphy, Eileen	White	1973	
Murphy, Lonnie	Black	1987, 1991	
Murr, L. A.	White		1973, 1975
Nash, Mattie Lee	Black	1993, 1995	1991
Needleman, Michael David	White	1991	
Nelson, Bill	White	1985, 1987	
Nicol, William F. (Bill)	White		1975, 1977
Nixon, Carl	White	1967	
Niebuhr, Mike	White	s1977, 1981	
Oakley, Ed	White	1993	
Oliphant, Roy E., III	White	1977	
Orndoff, George L.	White	s1977	
Owens, Chester Lee	Black	1995, 1997	
Palmer, Lori	White		1985, 1987, 1989, 1991
Parker, James	Black	1983	
Patterson, Lucy	Black		1973, 1975, 1977
Pemberton, Edna B.	Black	1993	
Poss, Mary	White	1989	1995, 1997
Preston, Greg	White	1983	
Price, Jesse	White	s1976	1967, 1969, 1971
Rabon, Olga Mae	Black	1973, s1975	
Radman, Paul	White	1973	
Ragsdale, Diane	Black	1991	s1984, 1985, 1987, 1989
Ramirez, Alberto (AJR)	Hispanic	1991	
Ranger, Marcus	Black	1973	
Reagan, Darren	Black	1993	
Reaves, Patterson S.	White	1980	
Renfroe, Rose	White	1977, 1983	1975
Rettig, Kathy	White	1981	
Reyes, Brenda	Hispanic	1997	
Reynolds, David	White	1973	
Rich, Kenneth J.	White	1983	
Richard, Jim	White		1983, 1985
Rios, Richard G.	Hispanic	s1984	
Rittenberry, Lee R.	White	1983	
Rizo, Frances	Hispanic	1997	
Robinson, Marvin E.	Black	1983	
Rodriguez, Humberto	Hispanic	1973	
Rodriguez, Raphael	Hispanic	1973	
Rucker, Jerry	White		1983, 1985, 1987
Salazar, Steve	Hispanic		1995, 1997

Candidates for the Dallas City Council, 1967–1997 (continued)

Name	Race	Candidate	Elected
Sanders, Barrot Steven	Black	1980	
Schoelkopf, John	White	1975	
Self, Drexel	White	1969	
Sepulveda, Julia E.	Hispanic	1995	
Sepulveda, Luis Daniel	Hispanic	1995, 1997	
Serna, Fernando	Hispanic	1983	
Sias, Paul	Black	1993	
Simon, Willie B.	Black	1971, 1973	
Simpson, Lee	White		1979, 1981
Skinner, Ed	White	1983	
Smith, Forrest	White	1991	
Smith, Richard (Dick)	White		1975, 1977
Smith, Russell B.	White	1975	1971, 1973
Smothers, Clay	Black	1973	
Sneed, T. A.	Black	1991	
Solon, Rita	Hispanic	1977	
Sparks, John R.	White	1975	
Spears, Helen	Black	1973	
Spears, Patricia	Black	1983	
Stahl, Sid	White		1979, 1981
Steakley, Marvin C.	White	1969, 1975, 1987	
Stedman, Joe	White	1983	
Stewart, Daniel G.	White	s1996	
Stimson, Robert (Bob)	White		1993, 1995, 1997
Storey, Charles H.	White	1975	1973
Strauss, Annette	White		1983, 1985, 1987, 1989
Stuart, Henry	White	1969, 1971	a1968
Svoboda, Betty	White	1983	
Sweeney, John D.	White	1973	
Tandy, Charles	White		1987, 1989, 1991
Taylor, A. Starke, Jr.	White		1983, 1985
Terrell, Charles	White		1973
Teschner, Lisa Saemann	White	1995	
Thomas, Dan	Black	1975	
Thomas, Verna	Black	s1984, 1987, 1991	
Thompson, Carolyn Jean	Black	1993	
Tindell, Elbert C.	White	1983	
Tinsley, John	White	1991	
Tobian, Milton	White	1989	
Todd, Clifton S.	White	1975	
Townsend, Ralph	White	1981	
Tuck, M. (SGT)	Black	1991	

Name	Race	Candidate	Elected
Tucker, Rolan	White		1979, 1981
Tyson, Jim	White	1985	
Urquhart, Ivy Marie	White	1987	
Vanderbilt, Dean	White		1983, 1985, 1987r
Voorhees, Jonathan Van	White	1993	
Wade, David	White	1971	
Wallace, Earnest L.	Black	1981	
Walne, Alan	White		s1996, 1997
Walton, John A.	White	1973	1977
Watkins, Richard (Dick)	White	1983	
Watts, Marvin	Black	1981, 1983	
Weber, Gary	White	s1976	1969, 1971, 1973, 1975
Weiner, Penina (Penny)	White	1993	
Wells, Max W.	White		1987, 1989, 1991, 1993, 1995
Wesson, Tom	White	1997	
White, Mabel	Black	1980, 1981	
White, Lunita Johnson	Black	1991	
White, Leroy, Jr.	Black	1991	
Wilkins, Hank	Black	1991	
Wilkinson, Mark	White	1997	
Wilkerson, Floyd F.	Black	s1977	
Williams, Raymond	Black	1969	
Williams, Roy	Black	1987, 1989, 1991, 1995	
Williams, Thomas (Tom)	Black	1985	
Williams, Tom	White	1987	
Willoughby, John A.	White	1973	
Wilson, W. W. (Bill)	White	s1976	
Wise, Wes	White	1983	1969, 1971, 1973, 1975r, 1981
Woertendyke, Clair	White	1980, 1981, 1983, 1985	
Woods, Adam	Black	1985, 1991	
Wooten, Gwain	Black	1983	
Wright, Jane	White	1989	
Young, Irene M.	Black	1987	
Zareie, David	White	1993	
Zeder, Fred	White		1971

B. Dallas City Council Members, 1967–2001

Place	1967	Place	1969	Place	1971	Place	1973
1	Hoke	1	Holland	1	Holland	1	Storey
2	Meyer	2	Meyer	2	Gilmore	2	Gilmore
7	Price	3	Fain	3	Fain	3	Harrison
6	Cothrum	4	Weber	4	Weber	4	Weber
4	Moser	5	Wise	5	R. Smith	5	R. Smith
3	Cullum	6	Kadane	6	Kadane	6	Allen
9	Hamilton	7	Price	7	Price	7	Murr
10	McKinney	8	Allen	8	Allen	8	Patterson
11	Jonsson	9	Martinez	9	Martinez	9	Aguirre
	Stuart	10	McKinney	10	Zeder	10	Terrell
	Allen	11	Jonsson	11	Wise	11	Wise

Place	1975	Place	1977	Place	1979 (1980)	Place	1981
1	Renfroe	1	D. Hicks	1	Hicks	1	Hicks
2	Nicol	2	Nicol	2	Medrano	2	Medrano
3	Leedom	3	Leedom	3	Haggar	3	Haggar
4	R. Smith	4	R. Smith	4	Tucker	4	Tucker
5	Cothrum	5	Cothrum	5	Simpson	5	Simpson
6	Allen/Craft	6	Craft	6	Heggins	6	Heggins
7	Murr	7	Walton	7	Goldblatt	7	Goldblatt
8	Patterson	8	Patterson	8	Blair	8	Blair
9	Weber/ Blackburn	9	Blackburn	9	Stahl	9	Stahl
10	Harrison	10	Harrison	10	Bartlet	10	Wise
11	Wise		Bartlett	11	Folsom	11	Evans
	Harrison	11	Folsom				
	Folsom						

Place	1983	Place	1985	Place	1987	Place	1989
1	Hart	1	Milkie	1	Tandy	1	Tandy
2	Fielding	2	Palmer	2	Palmer	2	Palmer
3	Richards	3	Richards	3	Bartos	3	Bartos
4	Vanderbilt	4	Vanderbilt	4	Vanderbilt	4	Wells
5	Holcomb	5	Holcomb		Wells	5	Box
6	Heggins	6	Ragsdale	5	Holcomb	6	Ragsdale
	Ragsdale	7	Evans	6	Ragsdale	7	Evans
7	Goldblatt	8	Lipscomb	7	Evans	8	Lipscomb
8	Blair	9	Rucker	8	Lipscomb	9	Miers
	Lipscomb	10	Strauss	9	Rucker	10	Buerger
9	Rucker	11	Taylor, Jr.	10	Gonzales	11	Strauss
10	Strauss			11	Strauss		
11	Taylor, Jr.						

Dallas City Council Members, 1967–2001 (continued)

Place	1991	Place	1993	Place	1995	Place	1997
1	Garcia	1	Garcia	1	Salazar	1	Salazar
2	Luna	2	Luna	2	Luna	2	Loza
3	Tandy	3	Stimson	3	Stimson	3	Stimson
4	Duncan	4	Duncan	4	Duncan	4	Duncan
5	Hicks, Sr.	5	Hicks, Sr.	5	Hicks, Sr.	5	Hicks, Sr.
6	Nash	6	Mallory	6	Mallory	6	Mallory-Caraway
7	Mayes	7	Mayes	7	Mayes	7	Mayes
8	Lipscomb	8	S. Crenshaw	8	Lipscomb	8	Lipscomb
9	Box	9	Box	9	Poss	9	Poss
10	Halstead	10	Halstead	10	Halstead	10	Walne
11	Fielding	11	Fielding	11	Fielding	11	Finkelman
12	Wells	12	Wells	12	Wells	12	Greyson
13	Bartos	13	Blumer	13	Blumer	13	Blumer
14	Palmer	14	McDaniel	14	McDaniel	14	Lill
15	Bartlett	15	Bartlett	15	Kirk	15	Kirk

Place	1999	Place	2001
1	Salazar	1	Garcia
2	Loza	2	Loza
3	Miller	3	Miller
4	Thornton-Reese	4	Thornton-Reese
5	Hill	5	Hill
6	Mallory-Caraway	6	Oakley
7	Chaney	7	Chaney
8	Fantroy	8	Fantroy
9	Poss	9	Poss
10	Walne	10	Walne
11	Finkelman	11	Finkelman
12	Greyson	12	Greyson
13	Blumer	13	Rasansky
14	Lill	14	Lill
15	Kirk	15	Kirk

References

PUBLISHED SOURCES

Abraham, Henry J. *Freedom and the Court: Civil Rights and Liberties in the United States.* 2nd ed. New York: Oxford University Press, 1972.

Allison, Wick. "Ron Kirk Toughens Up: The Mayor, the Mouseketeers, and the Media." *D* magazine (March 1997), 14:6.

Alonso, William, and Paul Starr, eds. *The Politics of Numbers.* New York: Russell Sage Foundation, 1987.

Amy, Douglas J. *Real Choices/New Voices: The Case for Proportional Representation Elections in the United States.* New York: Columbia University Press, 1993.

———. *Behind the Ballot Box: A Citizen's Guide to Voting Systems.* New York: Praeger, 2000.

Ang, Ien. *Watching Dallas: Soap Opera and the Melodramatic Imagination.* London: Methuen, 1985.

Arreola, Daniel D. "The Mexican American Cultural Capital." In Kenneth E. Foote, ed., *Re-Reading Cultural Geography,* 34–47. Austin: University of Texas Press, 1994.

Balinski, Michel L., and H. Peyton Young. *Fair Representation: Meeting the Ideal of One Man, One Vote.* New Haven: Yale University Press, 1982.

Ball, Howard, Dale Krane, and Thomas P. Lauth. *Compromised Compliance: Implementation of the 1965 Voting Rights Act.* Westport, Conn.: Greenwood, 1982.

———. "The View from Georgia and Mississippi: Local Attorneys' Appraisal of the 1965 Voting Rights Act." In Chandler Davidson, ed., *Minority Vote Dilution,* 181–202. Washington, D.C.: Howard University Press, 1984.

Barber, James David. *The Presidential Character: Predicting Performance in the White House.* Englewood Cliffs, N.J.: Prentice Hall, 1972.

Barber, Kathleen. *A Right to Representation: Proportional Election Systems for the Twenty-first Century.* Columbus: Ohio State University Press, 2000.

Benhabib, Seyla, ed. *Democracy and Difference: Contesting the Boundaries of the Political.* Princeton, N.J.: Princeton University Press, 1996.

Benoit, Kenneth, and Kenneth A. Shepsle. "Electoral Systems and Minority Representation." In Paul E. Peterson, ed., *Classifying by Race,* 50–84. Princeton, N.J.: Princeton University Press, 1995.

Berman, David R., and Bruce D. Merrill. "Citizen Attitudes toward Municipal Reform Institutions: A Testing of Some Assumptions." *Western Political Quarterly* (June 1976), 29:274–283.

Bernard, Richard M., and Bradley R. Rice, eds. *Sunbelt Cities: Politics and Growth Since World War II.* Austin: University of Texas Press, 1983.

Binder, Sarah A. "The Dynamics of Legislative Gridlock, 1947–96." *American Political Science Review* (September 1999), 93:519–533.

Blodgett, Terrell. *Texas Home Rule Charters.* Austin: Texas Municipal League, 1994.

———. "Home Rule Charters." *The New Handbook of Texas.* 6 vols. (Austin: Texas State Historical Association, 1996), 2:116.

———. *City Government That Works: The History of Council-Manager Government in Texas.* Texas City Management Association, 1998.

Bowler, Shaun, David Brockington, and Todd Donovan. "Election Systems and Voter Turnout: Experiments in the United States." *Journal of Politics* (August 2001), 63:902–915.

Bradley, Robert B. "Goals for Dallas." In Clement Bezold, ed., *Anticipatory Democracy: People in the Politics of the Future,* 58–87. New York: Vintage, 1978.

Branch, Taylor. *Parting the Waters: America in the King Years, 1954–1963.* New York: Simon & Schuster, 1988.

Brenner, Saul, and Harold J. Spaeth. *Stare Decisis: The Alteration of Precedent on the Supreme Court, 1946–1992.* New York: Cambridge University Press, 1995.

Bridges, Amy. "Boss Tweed and V. O. Key in Texas." In Char Miller and Heywood T. Sanders, eds., *Urban Texas: Politics and Development,* 58–71. College Station: Texas A&M University Press, 1990.

———. *Morning Glories: Municipal Reform in the Southwest.* Princeton, N.J.: Princeton University Press, 1997.

Brischetto, Robert, David R. Richards, Chandler Davidson, and Bernard Grofman. "Chapter Eight: Texas." In Chandler Davidson and Bernard Grofman, eds., *Quiet Revolution in the South: the Impact of the Voting Rights Act, 1965–1990,* 233–270. Princeton, N.J.: Princeton University Press, 1994.

Bullock, Charles S., and Loch K. Johnson. *Runoff Elections in the United States.* Chapel Hill: University of North Carolina Press, 1992.

Butler, Katharine I. "Affirmative Racial Gerrymandering: Fair Representation for Minorities or a Dangerous Recognition of Group Rights?" *Rutgers Law Journal* (spring 1996), 26:595–624.

Button, James W. *Blacks and Social Change: Impact of the Civil Rights Movement in Southern Communities.* Princeton, N.J.: Princeton University Press, 1989.

Cain, Bruce. "Excerpts from Declaration of Bruce Cain in Badham v. Eu." *PS: Political Science and Politics* (summer 1985), 18:561–567.

Campbell, Randolph. *An Empire for Slavery: The Peculiar Institution in Texas, 1821–1865.* Baton Rouge: Louisiana State University Press, 1989.

Canon, David T. *Race, Redistricting, and Representation: The Unintended Consequences of Black Majority Districts.* Chicago: University of Chicago Press, 1999.

Carmines, Edward G., and James A. Stimson. *Issue Evolution: Race and the Transformation of American Politics.* Princeton, N.J.: Princeton University Press, 1989.

Carr, Robert K. *Federal Protection of Civil Rights: Quest for a Sword.* Ithaca, N.Y.: Cornell University Press, 1947.

Center for Voting and Democracy. "Dubious Democracy 2001: Overview." Takoma Park, Md.: Center for Voting and Democracy, 1999.

Childs, Richard S. *The First 50 Years of the Council-Manager Plan of Municipal Government.* New York: National Municipal League, 1965.

Claggett, William E. "Dallas: The Dynamic of Public-Private Cooperation." In R. Scott Fosler and Renee A. Berger, eds., *Public-Private Partnership in American Cities: Seven Case Studies,* 243–292. Lexington, Mass.: Lexington Books, 1982.

Claude, Richard. *The Supreme Court and the Electoral Process.* Baltimore, Md.: The Johns Hopkins University Press, 1970.

Cobb, Roger W., and Charles D. Elder. *Participation in American Politics: The Dynamics of Agenda-Building.* 2nd ed. Baltimore, Md.: The Johns Hopkins University Press, 1983.

Cochran, John H. *Dallas County: A Record of Its Pioneers and Progress.* Dallas: Service Publishing, 1928.

Cotrell, Charles L., ed. "Assessing the Effects of the U.S. Voting Rights Act." *Publius: The Journal of Federalism* (fall 1986) (special symposium), vol. 16.

Cotrell, Charles L., and Jerry Polinard. "Effects of the Voting Rights Act in Texas: Perceptions of County Election Administrators." *Publius: The Journal of Federalism* (fall 1986), 16:67–80.

Dahl, Robert A. *Who Governs? Democracy and Power in an American City.* New Haven, Conn.: Yale University Press, 1961.

Davidson, Chandler. *Race and Class in Texas Politics.* Princeton, N.J.: Princeton University Press, 1990.

Davidson, Chandler, ed. *Minority Vote Dilution.* Washington, D.C.: Howard University Press, 1984.

Davidson, Chandler, and Bernard Grofman, eds. *Quiet Revolution in the South: The Impact of the Voting Rights Act, 1965–1990.* Princeton, N.J.: Princeton University Press, 1994.

Davidson, Chandler, and Luis Ricardo Fraga. "Slating Groups as Parties in a 'Nonpartisan' Setting." *Western Political Quarterly* (June 1988), 41:373–390.

Davidson, Chandler, and George Korbel. "At-Large Elections and Minority-Group Representation: A Re-Examination of Historical and Contemporary Evidence." *Journal of Politics* (November 1981), 43:982–1005.

Davis, Abraham L., and Barbara Luck Graham. *The Supreme Court, Race, and Civil Rights.* Thousand Oaks, Calif.: Sage, 1995.

Davis, Olethia. "Tenuous Interpretation: Sections 2 and 5 of the Voting Rights Act." *National Civic Review* (fall–winter 1995), 84:310–322.

Days, Drew S., III, and Lani Guinier. "Enforcement of Section 5 of the Voting Rights Act." In Chandler Davidson, ed., *Minority Vote Dilution,* 167–180. Washington, D.C.: Howard University Press, 1984.

de la Garza, Rodolfo O., and Louis DeSipio. "Save the Baby, Change the Bathwater, and Scrub the Tub: Latino Electoral Participation after Seventeen Years of Voting Rights Act Coverage." *Texas Law Review* (June 1993), 71:1479–1539.

Delgado, Richard, and Jean Stefancic. *Failed Revolutions: Social Reform and the Limits of Legal Imagination.* Boulder, Colo.: Westview, 1994.

Derfner, Armand. "Racial Discrimination and the Right to Vote." *Vanderbilt Law Review* (1973), 26:523–584.

Dillon, David. "Why Can't Dallas Keep a City Planner?" *Dallas Life,* September 19, 1982, 10–20.

Dixon, Robert G., Jr. *Democratic Representation: Reapportionment in Law and Politics.* New York: Oxford University Press, 1968.

Dulaney, W. Marvin. "What Happened to the Civil Rights Movement in Dallas, Texas?" In John Dittmer, George C. Wright, and W. Marvin Dulaney, *Essays on the American Civil Rights Movement.* College Station: Texas A&M Press, 1993.

Eberstadt, Nicholas. *The Tyranny of Numbers: Mismeasurement & Misrule.* Washington, D.C.: AEI Press, 1995.

Edsall, Thomas Byrne, and Mary D. Edsall. *Chain Reaction: The Impact of Race, Rights, and Taxes on American Politics.* New York: Norton, 1991.

Eisinger, Peter K. "Black Employment in Municipal Jobs: The Impact of Black Political Power." *American Political Science Review* (June 1982), 76:380–392.

———. "The Economic Conditions of Black Employment in Municipal Bureaucracies." *American Journal of Political Science* (November 1982), 26:754–771.

Elkin, Stephen L. *City and Regime in the American Republic.* Chicago: University of Chicago Press, 1987.

Elliott, Ward E. Y. *The Rise of Guardian Democracy: The Supreme Court's Role in Voting Rights Disputes, 1845–1969.* Cambridge, Mass.: Harvard University Press, 1974.

Engstom, Richard L. "Shaw, Miller, and the Districting Thicket." *National Civic Review* (fall–winter 1995), 84:323–336.

Engstrom, Richard L., and Michael D. McDonald. "The Election of Blacks to City Councils: Clarifying the Impact of Electoral Arrangements on the Seats/Population Relationship." *American Political Science Review* (June 1981), 75:344–354.

———. "The Effect of At-Large versus District Elections on Racial Representation in U.S. Municipalities." In Bernard Grofman and Arend Lijphart, eds., *Electoral Laws and Their Political Consequence,* 203–225. New York: Agathon, 1986.

Ernst, Morris L. "The Right to Be Heard vs. the Right to Vote." *American Bar Association Journal* (1965), 51:508.

Euchner, Charles C. *Playing the Field: Why Sports Teams Move and Cities Fight to Keep Them.* Baltimore, Md.: The Johns Hopkins University Press, 1993.

Evans, Mary Candace. "The Route to the Present." *Parkway* (January 1983), 37–38.

Fairbanks, Robert B. "The Good Government Machine: The Citizens Charter Association and Dallas Politics, 1936–1960." In Robert B. Fairbanks and Kathleen Underwood, eds., *Essays on Sunbelt Cities and Recent Urban America,* 125–150. College Station: Texas A&M University Press, 1990.

———. *For the City as a Whole: Planning, Politics, and the Public Interest in Dallas, Texas, 1900–1965.* Columbus: Ohio State University Press, 1998.

Fehrenbach, T. R. *Lone Star: A History of Texas and the Texans.* New York: American Legacy, 1983.

Firebaugh, Glenn. "Are Bad Estimates Good Enough for the Courts?" *Social Science Quarterly* (September 1993), 74:488–495.

Fitzgibbons, Ruth Miller. "The Accommodation." *D* magazine (March 1987), 14:91.

———. "The Craft House: Legacy of Love, Symbol of Mistrust." *D* magazine (April 1988), 15:35.

———. "On the Edge." *D* magazine (September 1991), 18:40–45, 66–69.

Foote, Kenneth E., ed. *Re-Reading Cultural Geography.* Austin: University of Texas Press, 1994.

Foster, Lorn S., ed. *The Voting Rights Act: Consequences and Implications.* New York: Praeger, 1985.

Franklin, John Hope, and August Meier, eds., *Black Leaders of the Twentieth Century.* Urbana: University of Illinois Press, 1982.

Freedman, Allan. "Lawyers Take a Back Seat in the 105th Congress." *Congressional Quarterly,* January 4, 1997.

Glendon, Mary Ann. *Rights Talk: The Impoverishment of Political Discourse.* New York: Free Press, 1991.

Goldman, Eric F. *The Tragedy of Lyndon Johnson.* New York: Knopf, 1969.

Goldstein, Joseph. *The Intelligible Constitution: The Supreme Court's Obligation to Maintain the Constitution as Something We the People Can Understand.* New York: Oxford University Press, 1992.

Govenar, Alan B., and Jay F. Brakefield. *Deep Ellum and Central Track: Where the Black and White Worlds of Dallas Converged.* Denton: University of North Texas Press, 1998.

Grant, Joseph M. *The Great Texas Banking Crash: An Insider's Account.* Austin: University of Texas Press, 1996.

Gray, Virginia, and Herbert Jacob. *Politics in the American States: A Comparative Analysis.* 6th ed. Washington, D.C.: CQ Press, 1996.

Greene, A. C. *The Deciding Years: A Historical Portrait.* Austin: Encino, 1973.

———. *Dallas USA.* Austin: Texas Monthly Press, 1984.

Grofman, Bernard, ed. *Race and Redistricting in the 1990s.* New York: Agathon, 1998.

Grofman, Bernard, and Arend Lijphart, eds. *Electoral Laws and Their Political Consequences.* New York: Agathon, 1986.

Grofman, Bernard, and Chandler Davidson, eds. *Controversies in Minority Voting: The Voting Rights Act in Perspective.* Washington, D.C.: The Brookings Institution, 1992.

Grofman, Bernard, Lisa Handley, and Richard Niemi. *Minority Representation and the Quest for Voting Equality.* New York: Cambridge University Press, 1992.

Guinier, Lani. "The Triumph of Tokenism: The Voting Rights Act and the Theory of Black Electoral Success." *Michigan Law Review* (March 1991), 89:1077–1154.

———. "No Two Seats: The Elusive Quest for Political Equality." *Virginia Law Review* (November 1991), 77:1413–1514.

———. *The Tyranny of the Majority: Fundamental Fairness in Representative Democracy.* New York: Free Press, 1994.

———. "More Democracy." *The University of Chicago Legal Forum* (1995), 1995:1–22.

Halpern, Stephen C. *On the Limits of the Law: The Ironic Legacy of Title VI of the 1964 Civil Rights Act.* Baltimore, Md.: The Johns Hopkins University Press, 1995.

Hamilton, Alexander, James Madison, and John Jay. *The Federalist.* Cambridge, Mass.: Harvard University Press, 1961.

Hanson, Royce. *Civic Culture and Urban Change: Governing Dallas.* Detroit: Wayne State University Press, 2003.

Harlan, Louis R. "Booker T. Washington and the Politics of Accommodation." In John Hope Franklin and August Meier, eds., *Black Leaders of the Twentieth Century,* 1–18. Urbana: University of Illinois Press, 1982.

Hart, Patricia Kilday. "Mr. Happy Man Goes to Washington." *Texas Monthly* (August 2002), 30:78–81, 98–101.

Hazel, Michael V. *Dallas: A History of Big "D."* Austin: Texas State Historical Association, 1997.

———, ed. *Dallas Reconsidered: Essays in Local History.* Dallas: Three Forks, 1995.

Heilig, Peggy, and Robert J. Mundt. *Your Voice at City Hall: The Politics, Procedures, and Policies of District Representation.* Albany: State University of New York Press, 1984.

Hill, Patricia Evridge. *Dallas: The Making of a Modern City.* Austin: University of Texas Press, 1996.

Hill, Steven. *Fixing Elections: The Failure of America's Winner Take All Politics.* New York: Routledge, 2002.

Hochschild, Jennifer L. *Facing Up to the American Dream: Race, Class, and the Soul of the Nation.* Princeton, N.J.: Princeton University Press, 1995.

Hollandsworth, Skip. "King Ruck." *D* magazine (July 1986), 13:52–55, 153–156.

Horowitz, Donald L. *The Courts and Social Policy.* Washington, D.C.: The Brookings Institution, 1977.

Hudson, David Michael. *Along Racial Lines: Consequences of the 1965 Voting Rights Act.* New York: Peter Lang, 1998.

Hunter, David H. *Federal Review of Voting Changes: How to Use Section 5 of the Voting Rights Act.* 2nd ed. Washington, D.C.: Joint Center for Political Studies, 1975.

Hunter, Floyd. *Community Power Structure.* Chapel Hill: University of North Carolina Press, 1953.

Issacharoff, Samuel. "Polarized Voting and the Political Process: The Transformation of Voting Rights Jurisprudence." *Michigan Law Review* (June 1992), 90:1833–1891.

———. "Supreme Court Destabilization of Single-Member Districts." *The University of Chicago Legal Forum* (1995), 199:205–239.

Jacobsohn, Gary J. "The 'Pragmatic Dogma' of the Political Thicket: The Jurisprudential Paradox of 'One Man, One Vote.'" *Polity* (spring 1977), 9:297–301.

Jonas, Andrew E. G., and David Wilson, eds. *The Urban Growth Machine: Critical Perspectives Two Decades Later.* Albany: State University of New York Press, 1999.

Judge, David, Gerry Stoker, and Harold Wolman, eds. *Theories of Urban Politics.* Thousand Oaks, Calif.: Sage, 1995.

Karlan, Pamela S. "The Rights to Vote: Some Pessimism about Formalism." *Texas Law Review* (June 1993), 71:1705–1740.

Karnig, Albert K., and Susan Welch. *Black Representation and Urban Policy.* Chicago: University of Chicago Press, 1980.

———. "Electoral Structure and Black Representation on City Councils." *Social Science Quarterly* (March 1982), 63:99–114.

King, Gary. *A Solution to the Ecological Inference Problem: Reconstructing Individual Behavior from Aggregate Data.* Princeton, N.J.: Princeton University Press, 1997.

Kingdon, John. *Agenda, Alternatives, and Public Policies.* Boston: Little, Brown, 1984.

Kousser, J. Morgan. "The Undermining of the First Reconstruction: Lessons for the

Second." In Chandler Davidson, ed., *Minority Vote Dilution,* 27–46. Washington, D.C.: Howard University Press, 1984.

Krane, Dale. "Implementation of the Voting Rights Act: Enforcement by the Department of Justice." In Lorn S. Foster, ed., *The Voting Rights Act: Consequences and Implications,* 123–157. New York: Praeger, 1985.

Kull, Andrew. *The Color-Blind Constitution.* Cambridge, Mass.: Harvard University Press, 1992.

Land, Kenneth C. "Discriminatory Electoral Practices, Contextual Effects, and a New Double Regression Method for the Courts." *Social Science Quarterly* (September 1993), 74:469–470.

Landsberg, Brian K. *Enforcing Civil Rights: Race Discrimination and the Department of Justice.* Lawrence: University Press of Kansas, 1997.

Lasswell, Harold D. *Politics: Who Gets What, When, How.* New York: McGraw-Hill, 1936.

Leslie, Warren. *Dallas Public and Private: Aspects of an American City.* Rev. ed. Dallas: Southern Methodist University Press, 1998.

Lijphart, Arend. "Electoral Systems." In the *Encyclopedia of Democracy.* 5 vols. Washington, D.C.: Congressional Quarterly, 1995.

———. "Proportional Representation." In the *Encyclopedia of Democracy.* 5 vols. Washington, D.C.: Congressional Quarterly, 1995.

Linden, Glenn M. *Desegregating Schools in Dallas: Four Decades in the Federal Courts.* Dallas: Three Forks, 1995.

Lineberry, Robert, and Edmund Fowler. "Reformism and Public Policy in American Cities." *American Political Science Review* (September 1967), 61:701–716.

Lippmann, Walter. "A Theory about Corruption." *Vanity Fair* (November 1930), 35:61, 90.

Lublin, David. *The Paradox of Representation: Racial Gerrymandering and Minority Interests in Congress.* Princeton, N.J.: Princeton University Press, 1997.

Luttbeg, Norman R. *The Grassroots of Democracy: A Comparative Study of Competition and Its Imact in American Cities in the 1990s.* Lanham, Md.: Lexington Books, 1999.

MacManus, Susan A. "City Council Election Procedures and Minority Representation: Are They Related?" *Social Science Quarterly* (June 1978), 59:153–161.

———. "At Large Elections and Minority Representation: An Adversarial Critique." *Social Science Quarterly* (November, 1979), 60:338–340.

———. "The Appropriateness of Biracial Approaches to Measuring Fairness of Representation in a Multicultural World." *PS: Political Science and Politics* (March 1995), 28:2–47.

Maveety, Nancy. *Representation Rights and the Burger Years.* Ann Arbor: University of Michigan Press, 1991.

McDowell, Gary L. *Curbing the Courts: The Constitution and the Limits of Judicial Power.* Baton Rouge: Louisiana State University Press, 1988.

McKay, Robert B. "Political Thickets and Crazy Quilts: Reapportionment and Equal Protection." *Michigan Law Review* (February 1963), 61:645–710.

Melosi, Martin V. "Dallas–Fort Worth: Marketing the Metroplex." In Richard M. Bernard and Bradley R. Rice, eds., *Sunbelt Cities: Politics and Growth since World War II,* 162–195. Austin: University of Texas Press, 1983.

Merrill, Bruce D. "Citizen Attitudes Toward Municipal Reform Institutions: A Testing of Some Assumptions." *Western Political Quarterly* (June 1976), 29:274–283.

Mills, C. Wright. *The Power Elite*. New York: Oxford University Press, 1956.

"Minisymposium, Political Gerrymandering: *Badham* v. *Eu*, Political Science Goes to Court." *PS: Political Science and Politics* (summer 1985), 18:537–581.

Mitchell, Jerry T., and Deborah S. K. Thomas. "Dumping in Dixie Revisited: The Evolution of Environmental Injustices in South Carolina." *Social Science Quarterly* (June 1999), 80:229–243.

Molotch, Harvey. "The City as a Growth Machine: Toward a Political Economy of Place." *American Journal of Sociology* (1976), 82:309–332.

———. "Growth Machine Links: Up, Down, and Across." In Andrew E. G. Jonas and David Wilson, eds., *The Urban Growth Machine: Critical Perspectives Two Decades Later,* 247–265. Albany: State University of New York Press, 1999.

Monkkonen, Eric H. *America Becomes Urban: The Development of U.S. Cities & Towns, 1780–1980*. Berkeley: University of California Press, 1988.

Morgan, Ruth P. *The President and Civil Rights: Policy-Making by Executive Order*. New York: St. Martin's, 1970.

Municipal Year Book. Washington, D.C.: International City/County Management Association [annual].

New Handbook of Texas. 6 vols. Austin: Texas State Historical Association, 1996.

Olien, Roger. *From Token to Triumph: The Texas Republicans since 1920*. Dallas: Southern Methodist University Press, 1982.

O'Rourke, Terry B. *Reapportionment: Law, Politics, Computers*. Washington, D.C.: American Enterprise Institute for Public Policy Research, 1972.

O'Rourke, Timothy G. "The 1992 Amendments and the Voting Rights Paradox." In Bernard Grofman and Chandler Davidson, eds., *Controversies in Minority Voting: The Voting Rights Act in Perspective,* 85–113. Washington D.C.: The Brookings Institution, 1992.

Parker, Frank R. "*Shaw* v. *Reno*: A Constitutional Setback for Minority Representation." *PS: Political Science and Politics* (March 1995), 28:47–50.

Parker, Robert E., and Joe R. Feagin. "Houston: Administration by Economic Elites." In H. V. Savitch and John Clayton Thomas, eds., *Big City Politics in Transition,* 169–188. Newbury Park, Calif.: Sage, 1991.

Payne, Darwin. *Big D: Triumphs and Troubles of an American Supercity in the 20th Century*. Dallas: Three Forks, 1994.

Pelissero, John P., and Timothy B. Krebs. "City Council Legislative Committees and Policy-making in Large United States Cities." *American Journal of Political Science* (April 1997), 41:499–518.

Perry, H. W., Jr. *Deciding to Decide: Agenda Setting in the United States Supreme Court*. Cambridge, Mass.: Harvard University Press, 1991.

Peterson, Paul E., ed. *Classifying by Race*. Princeton, N.J.: Princeton University Press, 1996.

Peterson, William. "Politics and the Measurement of Ethnicity." In William Alonso and Paul Starr, eds., *The Politics of Numbers,* 187–233. New York: Russell Sage Foundation, 1987.

Phillips, Anne. *The Politics of Presence: Democracy and Group Representation*. University Park: Pennsylvania State University Press, 1993.

————. "Dealing with Difference: A Politics of Ideas, or a Politics of Presence?" In Seyla Benhabib, ed., *Democracy and Difference: Contesting the Boundaries of the Political,* 139–152. Princeton, N.J.: Princeton University Press, 1996.

Pildes, Richard H., and Kristen A. Donoghue. "Cumulative Voting in the United States." *The University of Chicago Legal Forum* (1995), 1995:241–302.

Pitkin, Hanna F. *The Concept of Representation.* Berkeley: University of California Press, 1967.

————, ed. *Representation.* New York: Atherton, 1969.

"Plurality Decisions and Judicial Decisionmaking." *Harvard Law Review* (1981), 94:1127–1146.

Pocock, Douglas C. D. "Place and the Novelist." In Kenneth E. Foote, ed., *Re-Reading Cultural Geography,* 363–373. Austin: University of Texas Press, 1994.

Polinard, J. L., Robert D. Wrinkle, Tomas Longoria, and Norman E. Binder. *Electoral Structure and Urban Policy: The Impact on Mexican American Communities.* Armonk, N.Y.: M. E. Sharpe, 1994.

Polsby, Daniel, and Robert D. Popper. "Ugly: An Inquiry into the Problem of Racial Gerrymandering under the Voting Rights Act." *Michigan Law Review* (winter 1993), 92:652–682.

Pool, William C. *A Historical Atlas of Texas.* Austin: Encino, 1975.

Prewitt, Kenneth. "Public Statistics and Democratic Politics." In William Alonso and Paul Starr, eds., *The Politics of Numbers,* 261–274. New York: Russell Sage Foundation, 1987.

Prince, Robert. *A History of Dallas from a Different Perspective.* [Dallas]: Nortex, 1993.

Rae, Douglas. *The Political Consequences of Electoral Law.* New Haven, Conn.: Yale University Press, 1967.

Ragsdale, Kenneth B. *The Year America Discovered Texas: Centennial '36.* College Station: Texas A&M University Press, 1987.

Ray, Karen. "The Untold Story." *Dallas Life Magazine,* June 8, 1990, 10–11.

Reaves, Gayle. "Sleeping Giant." *Dallas Life Magazine,* February 7, 1993, 19–20.

Renner, Tari. "Municipal Election Processes: The Impact on Minority Representation." *Municipal Year Book 1988* (Washington, D.C.: International City Managers Association, 1988), 55:13–21.

Renner, Tari, and Victor S. DeSantis. "Contemporary Patterns and Trends in Municipal Government Structures." *Municipal Year Book 1993* (Washington, D.C.: International City/County Management Association, 1993), 60:57–69.

————. "Municipal Form of Government: Issues and Trends." *Municipal Year Book 1998* (Washington, D.C.: International City/County Management Association, 1998), 65:30–41.

Rice, Bradley Robert. *Progressive Cities: The Commission Government Movement in America, 1901–1920.* Austin: University of Texas Press, 1977.

Rice, Gwendolyn. "Little Mexico and the Barrios of Dallas." In Michael V. Hazel, ed., *Dallas Reconsidered: Essays in Local History,* 158–168. Dallas: Three Forks, 1995.

Riordin, William L. *Plunkitt of Tammany Hall.* New York: Dutton, 1963.

Robinson, Glenn A. "The Electorate in Texas." In Anthony Champagne and Edward J. Harpham, eds., *Texas at the Crossroads: People, Politics, and Policy,* 68–107. College Station: Texas A&M University Press, 1987.

Robinson, Theodore P., and Thomas R. Dye. "Reformism and Black Representation on City Councils." *Social Science Quarterly* (June 1978), 59:133–141.

Rodrigue, George. "Two City-Management Styles: Schrader and Anderson." *D* magazine (April 1982), 9:99, 148–152.

Rosenberg, Gerald N. *The Hollow Hope: Can Courts Bring about Social Change?* Chicago: University of Chicago Press, 1991.

Rudwick, Elliott. "W.E.B. Du Bois: Protagonist of the Afro-American Protest." In John Hope Franklin and August Meier, eds., *Black Leaders of the Twentieth Century,* 63–83. Urbana: University of Illinois Press, 1982.

Rush, Mark E. *Does Redistricting Make a Difference? Partisan Representation and Electoral Behavior.* Baltimore, Md.: The Johns Hopkins University Press, 1993.

———, ed. *Voting Rights and Redistricting in the United States.* Westport, Conn.: Greenwood, 1998.

Ryden, David K. *Representation in Crisis: The Constitution, Interest Groups, and Political Parties.* Albany: State University of New York Press, 1996.

Savitch, H. V., and John Clayton Thomas, eds. *Big City Politics in Transition.* Newbury Park, Calif.: Sage, 1991.

Scheingold, Stuart A. *The Politics of Rights: Lawyers, Public Policy, and Political Change.* New Haven, Conn.: Yale University Press, 1974.

Schutze, Jim. *The Accommodation: The Politics of Race in an American City.* Secaucus, N.J.: Citadel, 1986.

Schwartz, Bernard, ed. *Statutory History of the United States: Civil Rights.* New York: Chelsea House, 1970.

Shapiro, Martin. *Law and Politics in the Supreme Court.* New York: Free Press, 1964.

Shklar, Judith N. *Legalism.* Cambridge, Mass.: Harvard University Press, 1964.

———. *American Citizenship: The Quest for Inclusion.* Cambridge, Mass.: Harvard University Press, 1995.

Singh, Robert. *The Congressional Black Caucus: Racial Politics in the U.S. Congress.* Thousand Oaks, Calif.: Sage, 1998.

Singley, Bernestine, ed. *When Race Becomes Real: Black and White Writers Confront Their Personal Histories.* Chicago: Chicago Review Press, 2002.

Sonenshein, Raphael J. *Politics in Black and White: Race and Power in Los Angeles.* Princeton, N.J.: Princeton University Press, 1993.

Stark, Andrew. "Beyond Quid Pro Quo: What's Wrong with Private Gain from Public Office?" *American Political Science Review* (March 1997), 91:108–120.

Stillman, Richard J., II. *The Rise of the City Manager: A Public Professional in Local Government.* Albuquerque: University of New Mexico Press, 1974.

Stoker, Laura. "Interests and Ethics in Politics." *American Political Science Review* (June 1992), 86:369–380.

Stone, Clarence N. *Regime Politics: Governing Atlanta, 1946–1988.* Lawrence: University Press of Kansas, 1989.

Stone, Harold A., Don K. Price, and Kathryn Stone. *City Manager Government in Nine Cities.* Chicago: Public Administration Service, 1940.

Suk-Young Chwe, Michael. "Minority Voting Rights Can Maximize Majority Welfare." *American Political Science Review* (March 1999), 93:85–97.

Svara, James H. *Official Leadership in the City: Patterns of Conflict and Cooperation.* New York: Oxford University Press, 1990.

Swain, Carol M. *Black Faces, Black Interests: The Representation of African Americans in Congress.* Cambridge, Mass.: Harvard University Press, 1993.

Taebel, Delbert. "Minority Representation on City Councils: The Impact of Structure on Blacks and Hispanics." *Social Science Quarterly* (June 1978), 59:142–152.

Thernstrom, Abigail M. *Whose Votes Count? Affirmative Action and Minority Voting Rights.* Cambridge, Mass.: Harvard University Press, 1987.

Thometz, Carol Estes. *The Decision-Makers: The Power Structure of Dallas.* Dallas: Southern Methodist University Press, 1963.

Timpone, Richard J. "Mass Mobilization or Government Intervention? The Growth of Black Registration in the South." *Journal of Politics* (May 1995), 57:425–442.

U.S. Congress, House, Committee on the Judiciary, Subcommittee on Civil and Constitutional Rights, *Hearings on Extension of the Voting Rights Act,* 97th Cong., 1st Sess., May–July 1981, parts 1 and 2.

U.S. Congress, Senate, Judiciary Committee, 97th Cong., 2nd Sess., 1982, S. Rept. 97-417.

U.S. Department of Justice, United States Attorney, Northern District of Texas, Press Release, August 30, 2002.

Wasby, Stephen L. *Race Relations Litigation in an Age of Complexity.* Charlottesville: University Press of Virginia, 1995.

Weber, David J. *Foreigners in Their Native Land: Historical Roots of the Mexican Americans.* Albuquerque: University of New Mexico Press, 1973.

Weber, Max. "Politics as a Vocation." In H. H. Gerth and C. Wright Mills, trans. and ed., *Max Weber: Essays in Sociology,* 77–128. New York: Oxford University Press, 1958.

Welch, Susan. "The Impact of At-Large Elections on the Representation of Blacks and Hispanics." *Journal of Politics* (November 1990), 52:1050–1076.

Welch, Susan, and Timothy Bledsoe. *Urban Reform and Its Consequences: A Study in Representation.* Chicago: University of Chicago Press, 1988.

West, Richard. "The Forgotten City." *D* magazine (July 1984), 11:158–161, 171–172.

Wildgen, John K. "Social Alchemy in the Courtroom: The 'Double Regression' Hoax." *Social Science Quarterly* (September 1993), 74:471–479.

Williams, Roy H., and Kevin J. Shay. *Time Change: An Alternative View of the History of Dallas.* Dallas: To Be Publishing, 1991.

Wilson, William H. *Hamilton Park: A Planned Black Community in Dallas.* Baltimore, Md.: The Johns Hopkins University Press, 1998.

WPA Dallas Guide and History. Dallas: Dallas Public Library and University of North Texas Press, 1992.

Young, H. Peyton. *Equity: In Theory and Practice.* Princeton, N.J.: Princeton University Press, 1994.

Young, Iris Marion. *Justice and the Politics of Difference.* Princeton, N.J.: Princeton University Press, 1990.

Yut, Scott. "Using Candidate Race to Define Minority-Preferred Candidates under Section 2 of the Voting Rights Act." *The University of Chicago Legal Forum* (1995), 1995:571–599.

Zimmerman, Joseph F. "Election Systems and Representative Democracy." *National Civic Review* (fall–winter 1995), 84:287–310.

UNPUBLISHED DISSERTATIONS, THESES, AND PAPERS

Allyn, Robert. "How Dallas Switched Parties: Peter O'Donnell and the Dallas Republicans: 1950–1972." M.A. thesis, Southern Methodist University, 1983.

Anhalt, Bari E. "Minority Representation and the Substantive Representation of Interests." Paper prepared for the annual meeting of the American Political Science Association, San Francisco, 1996.

Austin, Rory A. "Measuring the Effects of Local Electoral Structures." Paper prepared for the annual meeting of the American Political Science Association, Boston, 1998.

Barta, Carolyn Jenkins. "The Dallas News and Council-Manager Government." M.A. thesis, University of Texas at Austin, 1970.

Davis, Michele A. "Beyond Redistricting: How the Voting Rights Act Has Transformed Democracy in Norfolk, Virginia." University of Virginia [dissertation in progress].
———. "The Evolution of the Voting Rights Act and Its Impact on Virginia Localities." M.A. thesis, University of Virginia, 2000.

King, Kimi Lynn, Jennifer Marie Morbitt, and John Francis Ryan. "Voting Rights and Wrongs: Federal District Court Decision-Making, 1965–1993." Paper prepared for the annual meeting of the American Political Science Association, San Francisco, 1996.

"Local Government Election Systems: Policy Research Project Report Number 62." Lyndon B. Johnson School of Public Affairs. Austin: University of Texas, 1984.

Luttbeg, Norman R. "The Origins of Competition in Municipal Elections: A Study of 118 Randomly Chosen Cities with Populations of at Least 25,000." Paper prepared for the annual meeting of the American Political Science Association, San Francisco, 1996.

Muncy, Analeslie. "Redistricting from Hell: The Dallas Experience." Paper prepared for the National Institute of Municipal Law Officers Annual Conference, San Diego, California, October 29, 1991.

Rush, Mark. "The Beginning of the End or the End of the Beginning? Voting Rights after *Shaw* v. *Reno* and *Miller* v. *Johnson.*" Paper prepared for the annual meeting of the American Political Science Association, Chicago, 1995.

Van Vechten, Renee Bukovchik. "Nonpartisan Elections in the United States." Paper prepared for the annual meeting of the American Political Science Association, San Francisco, 1996.

CITY OF DALLAS DOCUMENTS

Audience Research & Development, Dallas. "A Study of Dallas Citizen Attitudes: Management Summary," August 1999.

Bartholomew, Harland, & Associates. "A Master Plan for Dallas." St. Louis: H. Bartholomew & Associates, 1943–45.

Bartos, Jerry. "Newsletter to Constituents and Friends," May 26, 1993.

"Charter of City of Dallas, 1973"; including Charter Supplement, 1976.

"Charter of City of Dallas," 1991.

"Charter of City of Dallas," 1907; including Charter Amendments to 1952.

"Charter of the City of Dallas," 1931; as amended in 1968.

City of Dallas. "City Services Analysis Program" (File No. 92-1355). City Council Briefing Meeting, April 15, 1992.

————. "Goals for Dallas."

————. "Goals for Dallas Compared for Black Dallas and Mexican American Objectives," 1978.

————. "The Dallas Plan." 1994.

————. 2001 Redistricting Project; "Approved Minutes," 2001.

————. 2001 Redistricting Project: "Transcripts of Public Hearings," 2001.

Dallas Together Forum. "Dallas Working Together: Report of the Southern Sector Initiative," 1997.

Dallas Together Forum. "Final Report," January 1989.

Days, Drew S., III, Assistant Attorney General, Civil Rights Division, Letter to Lee E. Holt, Dallas City Attorney, November 19, 1979, published as Appendix to *City of Dallas* v. *United States,* 482 F.Supp. 183, 186–187 (1979).

Keheley, Clifford V. Memorandum to City Council, April 10, 1992. Briefing Meeting, Dallas City Council, April 15, 1992, 92–1355.

Kessler, George E. "A City Plan for Dallas: Report of Park Board," May 1911.

McCleary, Donald C. "Dallas' Form of Government: A Report to the Dallas Citizens Council," March 1994.

NEWSPAPERS AND PERIODICALS

Black Economic Times
Congressional Digest
Congressional Quarterly Weekly Report
D magazine
Dallas Business Journal
Dallas Morning News
Dallas Observer
Dallas Times Herald
The Economist
Emerge
Governing
National Journal
New York Times
St. Petersburg Times
Texas Monthly

AUTHOR INTERVIEWS, CONVERSATIONS, AND LETTERS (in Dallas unless otherwise indicated)

Allard, Jean. Director, Metropolitan Planning Commission, Chicago, September 2, 1995 in Chicago.

Aronson, Maxine. Telephone, September 6, 2001.

Barger, Carol. October 16, 1995.

Billingsley, Lucy. October 14, 1995.
Blumer, Donna. March 4, 1996.
Brice, Wanda. Telephone, February 23, 1998.
Caraway, Barbara Mallory. March 12, 1996.
Cullum, Charles. January 27, 1996.
Duncan, Larry. April 22, 1996.
Evans, Jack. March 26, 1996.
Fielding, Paul N. April 17, 1996.
Fitzgibbons, Ruth Miller. January 14, 1998; October 14, 1995.
Garrison, Steve. September 7, 1995.
Green, Cecil H. Letter, September 28, 1995.
Hall, Linda. Telephone, February 23, 1998.
Halstead, Donna D. February 15, 1996; Letter, April 1, 1999.
Harrison, Adlene. September 6, 1996.
Hart, Jan. July 2, 1996.
Hart, Linda. November 16, 1994; October 14, 1995.
Hicks, Donald W., Sr. April 4, 1996.
Hill, Patricia Evridge. Telephone, January 9, 1998.
Kirk, Ron. October 23, 1997.
Luna, Chris. September 26, 1996.
Marcus, Stanley. Letter, January 27, 1999.
Mayes, Charlotte. April 29, 1996.
McDaniel, Craig. February 21, 1996.
Miller, Laura. Telephone, July 5, 1996.
Miller, Robert. September 12, 1995.
Miller, Shirley. September 12, 1995.
Muncie, Analeslie. Telephone, January 2, 2002.
Palmer, Lori. October 2, 1995.
Pavey, Sarah Lee Cabell. February 22, 1996.
Perrine, Katherine. Telephone, October 1995.
Poss, Mary. January 23, 1996.
Rabin, Idelle. February 19, 1996.
Raggio, Louise. August 29, 1995.
Reagan, Sydney Chandler, Jr. September 4, 1995; Letter, September 4, 1995.
Salazar, Steve. September 9, 1996.
Sherouse, Mark A. August 8, 1995.
Sias, Mary. April 23, 1996.
Steakley, Marvin. October 5, 1995.
Stimson, Robert. April 8, 1996.
Strauss, Annette. January 19, 1998.
Thomas, Gail. August 18, 1995.
Tiller, Martha. August 11, 1995.
Ware, John. December 16, 1997.
Wells, Max W. March 5, 1996.
Werner, Joseph G., Jr. Telephone, June 27, 1997.
Wright, Curtis. Letter, December 26, 1997.

ARCHIVAL SOURCES, DALLAS PUBLIC LIBRARY

Juanita Craft Collection.
Robert Folsom Mayoral Papers.
Max Goldblatt Collection, 1965–1990.
Dan Weiser Collection, 1960–1988.
Wes Wise Mayoral Papers.

ORAL HISTORY RECORDS PROJECT, DALLAS PUBLIC LIBRARY

Interviews conducted in 1979–1982 with Bruce Alger, George Allen, Judy Bonner
Amps, James Aston, Alex Bickley, Emmett Conrad, Juanita Craft, Charles Cullum,
Robert Cullum, Jack Evans, Robert Folsom, Enid Gray, Bryghte Godbold, Max
Goldblatt, John Plath Green, A. C. Greene, Adlene Harrison, S. J. Hay, J. Erik Jons-
son, Avery Mays, W. Scott McDonald, Wallace Savage, George Schrader, John
Stemmons, R. L. Thornton Jr., Garry Weber, and Wes Wise.

PUBLIC REMARKS IN DALLAS

Adams, Lindalyn, Margaret McDermott, Hortense Sanger, and Ruth Collins Sharp.
"The Shaping of Dallas." Charter 100, April 9, 1985.
African-American Heritage Month Program. "Civil Rights in Dallas: A Reappraisal."
J. Erik Jonsson Central Library, February 11, 1997. Panelists: Joe L. Atkins, Eva
McMillan, Mamie McKnight, L. A. Bedford, and Jim Schutze.
Cattarulla, Kay, Cheryl Craigie, Lee Cullum, Juanita Miller, and Rena Pederson. Panel:
"Is Dallas a Great City Yet—Or Just a Midwestern Burg with Veneer?" Charter 100
of Dallas, March 17, 1999.
Greater Dallas Planning Council. "The Power of the Mayor: How Much and How?"
Panelists: Councilwoman Barbara Mallory-Caraway, Professor Royce Hanson, and
Dallas Morning News Columnist Hank Tatum. January 23, 1997.
Hoffman, Robert. Address on "The Dallas Plan," Charter 100 of Dallas and Interna-
tional Women's Forum, Dallas. April 25, 1996.
Hutchison, Ray, and David Laney, Remarks by chair of the 1989 Charter Advisory
Committee and chair of the 2002 Charter Review Commission. Dallas Assembly,
November 26, 2002.
Kirk, Ron. Annual remarks at the Mayor's Breakfast. The Dallas Summit, September
21, 1999.
Miller, Laura. Julia Sweeney's Talk Series. March 23, 1999.
Price, John Wiley. "Issues and Opportunities: A Look Ahead." Greater Dallas Plan-
ning Council, May 20, 1998.
Sanger, Hortense. Remarks to Charter 100 of Dallas, April 9, 1985.
Walz, Karen S. Remarks by Executive Director, Dallas City Plan, Inc. Charter 100,
April 25, 1996.
Ware, John. Address to Downtown Dallas Rotary Club, January 15, 1997.
Williams, J. McDonald. Remarks on the Southern Sector Initiative, Charter 100 of Dal-
las, February 11, 1998.

Cases

CITY OF DALLAS

City of Dallas v. *United States*, 482 F.Supp. 183 (1979).
Goldblatt v. *City of Dallas*, 279 F. Supp. 106 (1968).
Goldblatt v. *City of Dallas*, 391 U.S. 360 (1968).
Goldblatt v. *City of Dallas*, 414 F.2d 774 (5th Cir. 1969).
Heggins v. *City of Dallas*, 469 F.Supp. 739 (1979).
Lipscomb v. *Jonsson*, 459 F.2d 335 (5th Cir. 1972).
Lipscomb v. *Wise*, 399 F.Supp. 782 (1975).
Lipscomb v. *Wise*, 551 F.2d 1043 (5th Cir. 1977).
Lipscomb v. *Wise*, 583 F.2d 212 (1978).
Lipscomb v. *Wise*, 643 F.2d 319 (1981).
Williams v. *City of Dallas*, 734 F.Supp. 1317 (1990).
Williams v. *City of Dallas*, 1991 U.S. Dist. LEXIS 1669 (N.D. Tex. Feb. 4, 1991).
Wise v. *Lipscomb*, 434 U.S. 1008 (1978).
Wise v. *Lipscomb*, 434 U.S. 1329 (1977).
Wise v. *Lipscomb*, 437 U.S. 535 (1978).

OTHER CASE REFERENCES

Abrams v. *Johnson*, 521 U.S. 74 (1997).
Allen v. *State Board of Elections*, 393 U.S. 544 (1969).
Avery v. *Midland County*, 390 U.S. 474 (1968).
Baker v. *Carr*, 369 U.S. 186 (1962).
Beer v. *United States*, 425 U.S. 130 (1976).
Berry v. *Doles*, 438 U.S. 190 (1978).
Bradas v. *Rapides Parish Police Jury*, 508 F.2d 1109 (1975).
Briscoe v. *Bell*, 432 U.S. 404 (1977).
Brown v. *Board of Education*, 347 U.S. 483 (1954).
Burns v. *Richardson*, 384 U.S. 73 (1966).
Bush v. *Vera*, 517 U.S. 952 (1996).
Chapman v. *Meier*, 420 U.S. 1 (1975).
Chisom v. *Roemer*, 853 F.2d 1186 (5th Cir. 1988).
Chisom v. *Roemer*, 501 U.S. 380, 414-16 (1991).
City of Mobile v. *Bolden*, 446 U.S. 55 (1980).

City of Rome v. *United States,* 446 U.S. 156 (1980).

Colegrove v. *Green,* 328 U.S. 549 (1946).

Coleman v. *Miller,* 307 U.S. 433 (1939).

Connor v. *Finch,* 431 U.S. 407 (1977).

Connor v. *Johnson,* 402 U.S. 690 (1971).

Dallas County v. *Reese,* 421 U.S. 477 (1975).

Davis v. *Bandemer,* 478 U.S. 109 (1986).

Dusch v. *Davis,* 387 U.S. 112 (1967).

East Carroll Parish School Board v. *Marshall,* 424 U.S. 636 (1976).

Fortson v. *Dorsey,* 379 U.S. 433 (1965).

Gaffney v. *Cummings,* 412 U.S. 735 (1973).

Georgia v. *United States,* 411 U.S. 526 (1973).

Graves v. *Barnes,* 343 F.Supp. 704 (W.D. Tex. 1972). Consolidated cases, also referred to as the Texas Legislative Apportionment Cases.

Graves v. *Barnes,* 378 F.Supp. 640 (1974).

Grovey v. *Townsend,* 295 U.S. 45 (1935).

Holder v. *Hall,* 114 S.Ct. 2581 (1994).

Luther v. *Borden,* 7 Howard 1 (1849).

Mahan v. *Howell,* 410 U.S. 315 (1973).

Marbury v. *Madison,* 1 Cranch 137 (1803).

Miller v. *Johnson,* 515 U.S. 900 (1995).

Morris v. *Gressette,* 432 U.S. 491 (1977).

Nixon v. *Condon,* 286 U.S. 73 (1932).

Nixon v. *Herndon,* 273 U.S. 536 (1927).

Oregon v. *Mitchell,* 400 U.S. 112 (1970).

Perkins v. *Matthews,* 400 U.S. 379 (1971).

Port Arthur v. *United States,* 459 U.S. 159 (1982).

Presley v. *Etowah County Commission,* 478 U.S. 109 (1986).

Presley v. *Etowah County Commission,* 502 U.S. 491 (1992).

Reed v. *Mann,* 237 F.Supp. 22, 24-25 (1964).

Reese v. *Dallas County, Alabama,* 505 F.2d 879 (5th Cir. 1974).

Reynolds v. *Sims,* 377 U.S. 533 (1964).

Rimarcik v. *Johansen,* 310 F.Supp. 61 (1970).

Robinson v. *Commissioner's Court, Anderson County,* 505 F.2d 674 (1974).

Rogers v. *Lodge,* 458 U.S. 613 (1982).

Shaw v. *Hunt,* 517 U.S. 899 (1996) ("Shaw II").

Shaw v. *Reno,* 509 U.S. 630 (1993).

Smith v. *Allwright,* 321 U.S. 649 (1944).

South Carolina v. *Katzenbach,* 383 U.S. 301 (1966).

Terry v. *Adams,* 345 U.S. 461 (1953).

Thornburg v. *Gingles,* 478 U.S. 30 (1986).

Turner v. *McKeithen,* 490 F.2d 191 (5th Cir. 1973).

United Jewish Organizations v. *Carey* 430 U.S. 144 (1977).

United States v. *Board of Commissioners of Sheffield,* 435 U.S. 110 (1978).

United States v. *Classic,* 313 U.S. 299 (1944).

United States v. *Hays,* 515 U.S. 737 (1995).

Voinovich v. *Quilter,* 113 S.Ct. 1149 (1993).
Wesberry v. *Sanders,* 376 U.S. 1 (1964).
Westwego Citizens for Better Government v. *Westwego,* 872 F.2d 1201 (5th Cir. 1989).
Whitcomb v. *Chavis,* 403 U.S. 124 (1971).
White v. *Regester,* 412 U.S. 755 (1973).
Wright v. *Rockefeller,* 376 U.S. 52 (1964).
Zimmer v. *McKeithen,* 485 F.2d 1297 (5th cir.1973).

Index

Accommodation, The: The Politics of Race in an American City (Schutze), 73
ACI. *See* Austin Commercial Inc.
Adkins, Jack C., 121
Adoue, J. B., Jr., 80, 198(n2)
Affirmative action, 10, 36, 256–257, 266, 275
AFL-CIO. *See* American Federation of Labor-Congress of Industrial Organizations
Agenda, systemic, 230
Aguirre, Pedro, 164
Alabama
  and VRA, 10(n9), 16(n29), 18, 19, 124(n24)
Alaska
  and VRA, 18, 18–19(n38), 22–23(n51)
Alcorn, Lee, 214, 244
Aldermanic system, 89, 94
Alger, Bruce, 103
Allen, George, 129–130, 132, 147, 188, 201, 223, 247–248
Allen, James B., 19
Allen v. *State Board of Elections* (1969), 20, 57
Allyn, Rob, 239
Allyn & Co., 243
Almaguer, Manuel, 164
American Civil Liberties Union, 26
American Federation of Labor-Congress of Industrial Organizations (AFL-CIO), 101
Anderson, Charles, 202–203, 227, 234, 255, 256, 261
Anti-establishment mood (1960s), 112

Arizona
  voter registration, 23
  and VRA, 18, 21(n46), 22(n50), 22–23(n57)
Asian American Voters Coalition, 142
Asians, 141. *See also under* Dallas
Atlanta (Ga.)
  joint-venture plan, 263
  power politics, 114, 116
Atlanta Constitution, 29
At-large elections, 27, 28, 45, 47, 48, 52(n81), 58, 59, 71, 92–93, 95, 99–100, 101
  and minority representation, 100, 102, 120, 130, 179, 180, 269
  See also under Dallas City Council
Attorney general, 15, 18, 19, 20
  and VRA, 29 (*see also* Justice, Department of)
Austin, Rory A., 178
Austin (Texas)
  at-large system, 101
  council-manager system, 198
Austin Commercial Inc. (ACI), 239
Austin Industries, 239
Automatic coverage formula. *See* Trigger mechanisms
Avery v. *Midland* (1967), 45

Baker v. *Carr* (1962), 37, 43, 123
Balance of influence, 226
Banfield, Edward C., 100
Barber, James David, 69
Barta, Carolyn, 188, 200, 223
Bartholomew, Harland, 231, 232

Bartlett, Steve, 118, 186, 187, 209, 212, 215, 217, 218, 223, 224, 238, 240
Bartos, Jerry, 254
Bartos, Lorlee, 189
Bedford, L. A., 210
Benevides, Ted, 258
Bexar County (Texas), 50–51
Bickley, Alex, 126
Black, Hugo, 40, 56
Black codes, 13
Blackmun, Harry A., 62, 135
Blacks
  accommodationist protest of, 11, 15
  and economic rights, 14, 19
  in legislatures, 3, 19, 247
  and majority congressional district, 60
  minority-dominated districts, 52–53, 61, 131 (*see also under* Dallas)
  and "safe" seats, 52–53
  in U.S. population, 82
  and voter registration, 27(n70)
  and voting, 2, 10, 11, 13–15, 16, 21, 49, 57, 94, 133, 140
  and VRA, 23, 56, 57, 158, 165 (*see also* Dallas, and VRA)
  See also under Dallas; Texas
Blair, Fred, 138, 139, 171, 173, 200–201, 207, 257
Blair, William, Jr., 178
Blessing, Elizabeth, 108–109, 223
Blessing, William, 109
Bloom, Sam, 72
Blumer, Donna, 205, 209, 213, 221, 222, 224
Bolton, Terrell, 205, 258
Bond, Anthony, 207
Bonhoeffer, Dietrich, 1
Boone, Mike, 187(n56)
Booz-Allen & Hamilton (consultants), 126
Box, Glenn, 186, 201
Bradley, Tom, 167, 213(n64)
Breakfast Group (Dallas), 106, 227
Brennan, William J., Jr., 38, 43, 45, 59, 135
Briscoe v. *Bell* (1977), 18(n37)
Brown v. *Board of Education* (1954), 36–37, 43

Bryan, John Neely, 77
Buchmeyer, Jerry, 3, 143–144, 145, 146, 147, 148, 149, 150, 166–167, 253
Burger, Warren E., 135
Burke County (Ga.), 58
Burns v. *Richardson* (1966), 49
Burt, R. E., 97
Bush, George, 103
Button, James W., 259

Cabell, Earle, 108, 109, 186
Cain, Bruce, 63
Caldwell, Osborn, 162
California
  voter registration, 23
  and VRA, 21(n42), 22(n50), 22–23(n51)
Callejo, Adelfa B., 132, 251
Caraway, Barbara Mallory, 193, 209, 248(n59), 265
Caraway, Dwaine, 193, 209, 246
Cardozo, Benjamin, 119, 120
Catfish Club (Dallas), 101
CCA. *See* Citizens Charter Association
CDBG. *See* Community Development Block Grant Program
Census
  1980, 138, 139, 140, 145, 182
  1990, 142, 145, 150, 182, 198
  2000, 1, 18
Census Bureau, 169
Central Dallas Association, 237
Certiorari, 134
CGS. *See* Committee for Good Schools
Chambers, James, 114
Charter Government Committee (Phoenix), 104
Charter League, 108, 109
Childs, Richard S., 96–97
Chisholm, Shirley, 188
Cincinnati City Charter Committee, 104
Cisneros, Henry, 254
Citizens Charter Association (CCA) (Dallas), 98, 101, 102, 104, 105–107, 109, 110–111, 117, 118, 121, 122, 123, 126, 147, 157–159, 160(fig.), 162, 185, 187, 201, 227, 232–233, 272

and blacks, 107, 156, 163–164, 166, 176, 196, 271
and campaign contradictions, 156, 168
demise, 112–113
dominance (1935–1975), 158, 190
and Hispanics, 164, 196
and minorities, 156, 157
Citizens for Representative Government (CRG), 101, 109, 122
City of Mobile v. Bolden (1980), 23–24, 37(n15), 57–58, 140
Civil Rights Act
1957, 14, 15
1960, 14
1964, 15, 19
Civil Rights Commission, 17
Civil Rights Division (CRD) (DOJ), 29–30, 137
Voting Section, 29
Civil rights march (1965), 15
Civil rights movement (1960s), 14, 15, 103, 169, 268
Civil War Amendments, 13
Clark, Tom C., 37, 43
Clarke, Frank, 163
Clay, William, 188
Clements, William P., 103
Click, Ben, 223, 257
Clinton, Bill, 103
Coalition politics, 151–152, 165, 166, 272, 277
Cobb, Roger W., 230
Coggins, Paul, 203, 206
Colgrove v. Green (1946), 40
Colorado
voter registration, 23
and VRA, 22(n50), 22–23(n51)
Commission form of government, 89, 94–96
Committee for Good Schools (CGS), 112
Community Development Block Grant Program (CDBG), 260
Condorect, Marquis de, 271
Congress and member occupations, 187
Congressional Black Caucus, 188
Congressional district apportionment cases, 26

Congressional primary elections, 42
Congressional Quarterly, 187
Conley, R. T., 254
Connecticut, 21(n46)
Considérant, Victor Prosper, 77, 78
Constitution, U.S., 119
Article I, 39, 40, 42, 43
Article IV, 1(n2), 38–39
and Congress, 91
Tenth Amendment, 34, 56
Fourteenth Amendment, 11, 13, 23, 33, 42, 58, 60, 61, 121, 122, 127, 150, 268–269
Fifteenth Amendment, 11, 13, 15, 16, 17, 33, 42, 43, 56, 58, 107, 121, 127, 150–151, 268
Twenty-fourth Amendment, 13
Twenty-sixth Amendment, 13
and political parties, 157
and slaves, 12
and states, 89–90
and voting and states, 12–13, 14
Cottrell, Comer, 163(n11), 262
Cottrell, Isabell, 262
Council-manager form of government, 89, 91, 92, 94, 96–99, 197–201, 211
mayor elected by council, 97
See also under Dallas City Council
Court case decisions, 307–309. See also Dallas, cases
Court of Appeals (Fifth Circuit), 51, 123–124, 126–129, 132–133, 134, 135
Courts and electoral process, 276, 277
"Cracking," 144, 156
defined, 52
Craft, Juanita, 162, 169, 188, 247–248, 249
Foundation, 249
Home Location, 249–250
Crawford, John, 238
Crenshaw, Marvin, 140, 142, 143, 164, 165, 248
Crenshaw, Sandra, 210
CRG. See Citizens for Representative Government; Committee for Representative Government

Cronyism and corruption. *See under* Dallas
Crow, Trammell, 235
Curry, R. L., 252, 253

Dahl, Robert A., 116
Dallas (Texas)
    absentee ballots, 192–193
    Asians, 82, 83, 141, 142
    ballot access, 157–158, 176
    bank CEOs, 85, 108
    belief patterns, 68–70, 114
    black activists, 138
    black businesses, 261–262, 264
    black city managers, 214
    black city officials, 162(n9)
    black homeowners, 110
    black leaders, 106–107, 110–111, 163,
        169, 206
    black newspaper (*see Dallas Express*)
    black population, 150, 170, 199, 206
    black precincts, 157, 160(fig.), 244, 272
    blacks, 70–71, 79, 80, 82, 83, 86, 93, 99,
        101, 120, 124–125, 129, 132, 138,
        140, 141, 144, 149, 150, 152, 259 (*see
        also under* Citizens Charter
        Association)
    blacks and at-large elections, 180, 182
    blacks and districts, 170, 171–172, 174,
        180, 181(table), 240
    blacks and single-member districts,
        164–166, 182, 188, 259
    bond rating, 242
    budget and bond issues, 242–247, 274
    business leaders, 85, 108, 179, 186–187,
        188, 226–228, 231, 233, 237, 243,
        267, 274
    campaign contribution limits, 168
    campaign finance, 166–168, 177
    cases, 42, 99, 107, 111, 121–152, 307
    chronology, iii–xv
    Citizens Association, 95, 104
    citizens' attitude survey (1999), 244
    Citizens Council (DCC), 69, 70, 71–72,
        106, 107, 108, 115, 163(n11), 164,
        187, 212, 215, 226–227, 237, 242
    citizen voting age population, 184

city charter, 18, 59, 95, 98, 137, 157, 228
city government forms, 89, 94–99, 129
city manager, 231, 255–256, 273, 274
    (*see also* Anderson, Charles;
    Benevides, Ted; Hart, Jan; Knight,
    Richard; Schrader, George; Ware,
    John)
City Park Board, 249, 250
City Plan Commission, 235, 241
civil rights ordinance, 247
and Civil War, 78
"clean city," 71, 202
code of ethics, 207–211
Community Development Commission,
    260
council-manager government, 71, 98,
    104, 228
as county seat, 77
cronyism and corruption, 201–207,
    241–242, 272
Democratic conservatives, 105, 157
and Democratic Party, 102–103, 110,
    158, 160 (fig.)
director of planning (*see* Springer,
    Marvin)
distributive economic benefits, 242
economic development, 83–86,
    230–231, 237, 241, 275
Economic Development Planner (*see*
    Martinez, Dennis)
economics and environment, 70, 73
electoral competitiveness, 189–195, 272
electoral fraud, 192–193
environmental pollution, 250–255
exceptionalism myth, 68–70, 77, 87
and federal programs, 90, 246(n54),
    252–254, 260, 261
fire (1860), 77, 78
gambling, 69–70
General Bond Capital Improvement
    Program (1998), 242
geographical location, 76–79
Governing magazine ranking, 198(n4)
Hispanic businesses, 262, 264
Hispanic population, 170–171, 179, 184
Hispanics, 74, 79, 81, 82, 83, 86, 111,

120, 124–133, 138, 139, 141, 142,
143(n96), 144, 146, 149, 151–152,
164, 253, 258, 259 (*see also under*
Citizens Charter Association)
Hispanics and districts, 180, 181(table),
182, 240
Hispanics and single-member districts,
164, 165, 179, 180, 182
housing, 247, 250–251, 252–255
Housing Authority, 251, 252, 253
image, 70–71
intolerance of dissent, 71–73, 87, 93,
127, 157
Ku Klux Klan, 72, 97
labor, 101, 110, 118
liberals, 101, 109, 157, 252
low-income residents, 245, 250, 275
mayor, 98, 141, 187, 231, 274 (*see also*
Adoue, J. B., Jr.; Bartlett, Steve; Burt,
R. E.; Cabell, Earle; Evans, Jack;
Harrison, Adlene; Jonsson, J. Erik;
Kirk, Ron; Rodgers, Woodall; Strauss,
Annette; Taylor, Starke; Thornton,
Robert L.; Wise, Wes)
mayoral election (1995, 1999), 3
mayor-manager relations, 216–217
mayor-council relations, 211–216
and military, 83–84
minority contracting, 261–265, 267, 274
minority-dominant districts, 145, 148,
149, 156, 159, 160(fig.), 162, 163,
178, 189, 192, 270–271, 272
minority employment in city
government, 255–258, 259, 266, 270,
271, 275
and minority office holders, 31, 107,
125, 162(n9), 177, 201, 255–258
neighborhood groups, 235–237, 241,
275
newspapers, 231 (*see also individual
names*)
north, 234, 235, 240, 241, 243–244, 260
and oil, 84, 85
Office of Management Services, 138
Olympics 2012 bid, 247
partisan elections prohibited, 157

planning and zoning, 231–242, 274, 275
police department, 256–259
political minority, 101, 105, 144, 152,
156
politics, 88–113, 156, 157(ns3&4), 162,
274 (*see also* Dallas City Council)
population, 82–83, 170
population shift, 138
power structure, 114–117, 118, 230, 274
and presidential elections, 158, 159, 160
(fig.)
public sector services and goods
redistribution, 258–261, 266, 275
reapportionment plan, 139
Redistricting Commission, 184
Republican National Convention site
(1984), 227
Republicans, 101, 104, 106, 110, 157,
160 (fig.), 166, 234
size, 232–233
slating and minority access, 162–164,
180, 182, 271
slating groups, 102, 104–106, 111–113,
127–128, 157(n3), 162 (*see also*
Citizens Charter Association)
socioeconomic divide, 162
south, 70, 231, 233–234, 240, 241,
245–246, 259, 267
Spanish heritage, 74–76
sports arena, 233, 237, 238–240, 243,
247
Trades Assembly, 95
treasurer (*see* Florence, Fred F.)
as triracial city, 2–3, 82–83
and urban sprawl, 231
utopian experiments, 77, 250
voter turnout, 193–195, 244, 272, 273
voting population (1845), 76
and VRA, 67, 79, 111–113, 120,
121–152
VRA effects on, 155–196, 269, 270, 275
(*see also* Dallas *subentries*: ballot
access, campaign finance, electoral
competitiveness; Dallas City Council
subentries: redistricting, single-
member districts)

Dallas (Texas) (*continued*)
  wards, 95
  West, 250–251, 252, 253, 254, 255, 272
  See also Citizens Charter Association;
    Committee for Representative
    Government; Dallas City Council;
    Progressive Voters League
Dallas Alliance, 251
Dallas Area Rapid Transit (DART), 203,
  236, 239, 247, 264–265, 266
Dallas City Council, 94, 114
  at-large system, 3, 71, 97, 98, 99,
    100–102, 119–120, 121, 135, 136,
    140, 141, 148, 150, 156, 158,
    165–166, 168, 180, 181 (table), 191
    (table), 198, 248, 271, 273
  black at-large member (1995), 3
  black voting bloc, 107, 159
  black women candidates, 189
  blacks on, 107, 125, 129, 138, 141, 162,
    178, 189, 190(table), 195, 219, 243,
    244, 247, 266
  candidate requirements, 157(ns2&4)
  candidates by race, date of candidacy,
    and date of election (1967–1997), 99,
    108, 112, 121, 122, 125, 128, 129,
    158, 162, 164, 165, 279–287
  candidates racist literature, 178
  and CCA, 104, 105–107, 108, 109,
    110–111, 112–113, 157–159,
    160(fig.), 162
  charter advisory committee, 141
  committees, 220–221
  contested seats, 190
  council-manager government, 197–204,
    211
  council-manager government and single-
    member districts, 199, 200–201, 223
  district deference, 241, 274
  districts, 98, 99, 100–101, 122, 140, 144,
    148, 150, 156, 170(fig.), 171–177 (*see
    also* Dallas, minority-dominant
    districts; Race and representation)
  8-3 plan, 121, 129, 134, 135, 137, 138,
    140, 142, 143, 144, 167, 169, 170
    (fig.), 181 (table), 191 (table), 200,
    223, 242, 255, 273

  8-4-1 plan, 126, 139
  election (1975), 137
  election patterns, 106–111, 147–148
  11-0 plan, 143
  15.0 plan, 145, 212
  first female elected on, 108
  14-1 plan, 145, 146, 149–150, 165, 174,
    181 (table), 182, 184, 189, 191 (table),
    192, 193, 213, 223, 237, 242, 248,
    263, 264, 270, 271, 273, 275
  Hispanics on, 138, 141, 189, 190 (table),
    195, 219, 243, 244, 247, 248, 266
  identity politics, 247
  incumbency, 190–192
  mayoral term, 150
  mayor elected at-large, 141, 148, 198
    (*see also* Dallas, mayor)
  mayor elected by, 98
  member relations, 219–225, 249
  members (1967–2001), 71, 141(n90),
    185–189, 200, 201–205, 210, 247,
    254, 260, 265, 271–272, 288–289
  and minorities, 3–4, 85, 111, 120, 129,
    139, 140, 142, 144, 148, 149, 158,
    165, 190, 197, 247, 248, 267 (*see also
    subentry* policy and minority
    representation
  minorities and proportional
    representation, 182–184
  minorities and the courts, 165–166
  mixed system plan, 120, 121, 126, 129,
    143, 151, 156, 180, 191(table), 195,
    196, 197, 270, 273
  overlay districts, 141
  and patronage, 256, 275
  pay, 98, 141, 219(n83)
  and policy, 225–228, 229–230,
    236–237, 247–250, 261, 266–267,
    274
  policy and minority representation, 229,
    267
  politics, 4, 94–113, 229, 267
  redistricting, 135–140, 142, 144,
    145–146, 148–150, 168–177, 179,
    273
  "rule of 14," 245

single-member districts, 126, 129, 130,
132, 133, 139, 141, 142, 156, 162,
163, 165, 166, 177, 178, 180,
181(table), 189, 191(table), 234, 241,
266, 270, 271–272, 273
single-member districts and budget, 246,
266
single-member districts and co-
dependency, 246–247
single-member districts and
divisiveness, 200–201
single-members districts and minority
interests, 248, 255, 266–267, 270
single-member districts and
redistricting, 168–177
6-3 plan, 121, 123, 134
size, 99, 101, 131, 189, 274
special election, 137
10-4-1 plan, 141, 142, 145, 146, 174
10-1 plan, 139, 140, 145
term limits, 105, 150, 207(n43), 219
12-1 plan, 144, 145
Dallas Coalition of Mexican-American
Organizations, 111, 164
Dallas County, 50, 79–80, 94(n16),
103–104, 158, 192
Dallas County Democratic Association,
105
Dallas County Heritage Society, 249
Dallas Dispatch, 72
Dallas Express, 107
Dallas Homeowners Association (DHA),
110
Dallas Homeowners League (DHL),
109–110, 140, 236
Dallas Legal Services, 124, 163
Dallas Morning News, 31, 72, 97, 106, 109,
114, 115, 126, 143, 165, 167, 200,
203, 205, 206, 208, 211, 222, 226
(n105), 239, 246, 258
candidate endorsements, 161(table),
162, 245
and CCA candidates, 159
and planning, 232
poll, 210, 260
and Trinity project, 243

Dallas Observer, 203, 205, 210
Dallas Plan, 237–238, 242, 243
Dallas Times-Herald, 114–115, 200, 236
Dallas Together (commission), 140, 141,
142
Dallas Together Forum, 262
Dam, Phap, 141
DART. See Dallas Area Rapid Transit
David, Mattie, 240
Davidson, Chandler, 27
Davis, Levi, 255
Davis, Richard O., 261
Davis, Tony, 188
Davis Automotive (company), 261
DCC. See Dallas, Citizens Council
Dealy, Joe, 114
Dealey, George B., 72, 232
Declaration of Independence, 9
Democracy and information aggregation,
271
Democratic Party, 158
Chicago convention (1968), 11
See also under Dallas; Texas
Democratic Progressive Voters League,
107
Descriptive representation, 54, 55, 151
Detroit (Mich.) mayoral government, 198
Devany, Joseph A., 109
DHA. See Dallas Homeowners Association
DHL. See Dallas Homeowners League
Dickey, Tom, 204–205
D magazine, 85, 203, 206
DOJ. See Justice, Department of
Dorgan, Byron L., 239
Douglas, Frederick, 155
Douglas, William O., 40–41, 44, 46–47
Douglass, Frederick, Voting Council
(Dallas), 138
Du Bois, W. E. B., 14

East Carroll Parish School Board v.
Marshall (1976), 51, 133
Ecological fallacy problem, 155, 159(n6)
Economic growth engine, 116
EDS. See Electronic Data Systems
Effective (VRA definition), 17
Eisenhower, Dwight D., 103, 113

Elder, Charles D., 230
Election law, 2. *See also* Voting Rights Act
Electronic Data Systems (EDS), 241
El Fenix Corporation, 262
Ellis-Kirk, Matrice, 208
Elites, 113, 114–116, 230. *See also* Dallas, business leaders
Elkin, Stephen L., 116–117
Elliott, Claude, 78
Enforcement Acts, First and Second (1870, 1871), 13
Environmental Protection Agency (EPA), 244, 250, 253–254
EPA. *See* Environmental Protection Agency
"Equal protection of the laws" clause (Fourteenth Amendment), 43–45, 47, 61, 122, 123, 151, 166, 174, 269
"Essential theory," 123
Estes, Joe Ewing, 123
Euchner, Charles C., 239
Evans, Jack, 138, 256

Fairbanks, Robert B., 118
Fair Park Museum (Dallas), 249
Fantroy, James, 210
FBI. *See* Federal Bureau of Investigation
Federal Bureau of Investigation (FBI), 203, 263
Federalism, 34, 56
Federalist no. 51, 10
Federal Register, 18
Feeney, Susan, 31
Fielding, Don, 109
Fielding, Paul, 71, 203–204, 213, 221, 224, 241, 248(n61), 263, 264
Fifteenth Amendment. *See under* Constitution, U.S.; Voting Rights Act
Finkelman, Lois, 260
Florence, Fred F., 69
Florida
   and VRA, 22–23(n51)
Folsom, Robert, 178, 185, 200, 207, 223
Ford, Charles B., 198(n2)
Fortas, Abe, 45
Fortson v. *Dorsey* (1964), 45, 49
Fort Worth (Texas), 69

Forward Dallas Association, 107
Fourier, Charles, 77
Fourteenth Amendment. *See under* Constitution, U.S.; Voting Rights Act
Frankfurter, Felix, 40, 44, 63, 119
Freeland, Gene G., 101
Freire, Paulo, 88

Gahl, Robert, 202
Galveston (Texas), 89, 95
Garcia, Domingo, 219, 224, 248(n59), 256, 263, 264
Garrow, David, 206
Gatlin, Larry, 119
Georgia
   and VRA, 18, 29
Gerry, Joe, 108
Gerrymander, 27, 46, 169, 211, 273
   racial, 41, 46, 52, 60–61, 132, 174–176, 182
"Ghetto Area," discrimination, 127, 128, 132
Ghetto residents, 49
Ginsburg, Ruth Bader, 62
Goals for Dallas, 101, 233
Goldblatt, Max B., 99, 121–124, 138, 164, 165 (N15)
Goldblatt v. *City of Dallas* (1968), 122–124, 126, 128
Goldstein, Joseph, 62
Gomillion v. *Lightfoot* (1960), 46
Good Government League (San Antonio), 104, 118
Governing magazine, 198
Government Performance Project, 198 (n4)
Graves v. *Barnes* and consolidated cases. *See Texas Legislative Apportionment Cases*
Green, Cecil H., 84
Greyson, Sandy, 260
Grofman, Bernard, 48
Guinier, Lani, 24, 52, 53, 54, 55

Halstead, Donna, 186, 220, 224
Handy Andy (company), 241
Hanson, Royce, 118, 206
Harlan, John M., 44, 45, 57

Harrison, Adlene, 219, 243, 244
Hart, Jan, 201, 217, 218, 223, 224
Harvard Law Review, 36
Hasidic Jews, 61
Hatch, Orrin, 25
Hawaii
  and VRA, 18
Hayes, Bobby, 163
Heggins, Elsie Faye, 135, 138, 139, 162,
    171, 173, 188, 200, 223, 248 (n59)
Heggins v. *City of Dallas* (1979),
    135–136(ns72&74)
Heilig, Peggy, 201
Hernandez, Frank, 164, 165
Hicks, Don, 138, 139, 209, 218, 223, 240,
    241–245, 248(n59), 257, 263
Hicks, Tom, 208
Hill, Don, 209
Hill, Patricia Evridge, 117
Hill, Robert M., 136–137
Hispanics
  immigration, 82
  majority districts, 61, 131
  and mixed systems, 180(n48)
  organizations, 30, 116
  in U.S. population, 82
  voter registration, 23, 130
  and voting rights, 50–51
  and VRA, 158
  See also Minorities, language; *under*
    Dallas; Texas
Hispanic Women's Network of Texas, 142
Hoblitzelle, Karl, 107–108
Holder v. *Hall* (1994), 61–62, 131(n60)
Holmes, Zan, 206
Home rule, 94
"Honest graft," 202, 272. *See also* Dallas,
    cronyism and corruption
House Judiciary Committee, 24, 25, 26
House Subcommittee on Criminal Justice,
    258
Housewright, Ed, 143
Housing and Urban Development,
    Department of (HUD), 252, 253, 254,
    255
Houston, Sam, 78

HUD. *See* Housing and Urban
    Development, Department of
Hunt, Ray, 236, 238
Hunter, David, 31
Hunter, Floyd, 114
Hutchison, Ray, 140, 141
Hyde, Henry, 25

Idaho
  and VRA, 18
Illiteracy, defined, 22
"Influence" districts, 52, 107
"Intent" standard, 140, 150, 177–178
Interdenominational Minister's Alliance,
    164
International City Managers Association,
    101
Interest representation, 53
Irving (Texas), 233

Jackson, Alpnonso, 248(n61), 254
Jackson, Maynard H., 106
Jay, John, 32
Jaybird Democratic Association (Texas),
    42
Jews, 61, 80
Johnson, Lyndon B., 9, 15, 19
Johnson, Peter, 142
Jones, Gerald, 29
Jones, Harry, 253
Jones, Jesse, 166
Jonsson, J. Erik, 84, 101, 106, 108, 109,
    115, 125–126, 158, 217, 223, 233
Jordan, Darrell, 164
Judicial activism, 34(n3), 36
Judicial restraint, 276
Judicial review, 12, 38
Judiciary and politics, 63
Justice, Department of (DOJ), 1, 27,
    29–31, 173, 270
  preclearance rulings, 4, 29, 30, 142, 145,
    149, 174
  Voting Section, 54
  See also Civil Rights Division

Karr, Alphonse, 197
Keheley, Cliff, 238

Kemp, Jack, 252, 253, 254
Kendall, Joe, 204
Kennedy, Anthony M., 54
Kennedy, John F., 11, 21, 67, 73, 115
Kessler, George E., 232, 237
Kilby, Jack, 85
King, Gary, 155
King, Martin Luther, Jr., 206
Kingdon, John, 230
Kirk, Ron, 155, 162, 164, 167, 186, 187,
    200, 202, 204, 206, 208, 209,
    213–215, 217, 220, 221–222,
    224–225, 239, 240, 243, 245, 270
Kirven, Joe, 164
Knight, Richard, 240, 256
Kolb, Cay, 235, 236
Kousser, J. Morgan, 28
Krane, Dale, 29–30
Krebs, Timothy B., 220
Krueger, Bob, 30
Ku Klux Klan, 72
Kull, Andrew, 19

La Raza Unida, 111
La Reunion Colony, 77, 78
Lasswell, Harold D., 88, 113
Lawrence, D. H., 67
LEAD. See League for Educational
    Advancement in Dallas
League for Educational Advancement in
    Dallas (LEAD), 112
League of United Latin American Citizens
    LULAC), 30
Ledbetter Neighborhood Association
    (Dallas), 143
Leslie, Warren, 114–115
Lill, Veletta, 265
Lincoln, Abraham, 278
Lippmann, Walter, 203
Lipscomb, Albert, 71, 124–125, 128,
    129–130, 141, 143, 159, 160(fig.),
    162, 164, 165, 167, 188, 200, 209,
    210, 215, 219, 221, 223, 248(ns59&
    60), 258, 269, 264
  corruption charges, 203–208, 241–242,
    263

Lipscomb v. Jonsson (1972), 111,
    124–127), 128
Lipscomb v. Wise (1975), 129, 132, 159
Los Angeles (Calif.) black mayor. See
    Bradley, Tom
Louisiana
  and VRA, 10(n9), 16 (n29), 18
Loza, John, 205, 209
LULAC. See League of United Latin
    American Citizens
Luna, Chris, 209, 219, 221, 224, 239, 246,
    256, 263, 264
Luther v. Borden (1849), 38

Madison, James, 10
Mahon, Eldon, 126, 129, 130–131,
    147–148, 165, 169, 270
Maine
  and VRA, 21(n46)
Majority rule and protection of minority,
    34, 269, 270
Majority votes, 27, 55, 91
MALDEF. See Mexican American Legal
    Defense and Educational Fund
    League of United Latin American
    Citizens
Mallory, Barbara, 162
Marbury v. Madison (1803), 12, 39
Marcus, Stanley, 72–73, 208
Marshall, John, 39
Marshall, Thurgood, 135
Martinez, Dennis, 238
Martinez, René,
Martinez family business, 262
Massachusetts
  and VRA, 21 (n46)
Mayes, Charlotte, 188, 219, 220, 221, 246
Mayor-alderman. See Aldermanic system
Mayor-council government, 94
Mays, Avery, 108, 110, 158, 160(fig.)
Mays, Richard, 193(n68)
McCullough, David, 229
McDermott, Eugene, 84
McDermott, Margaret, 216
McFarland, Clay, 109
McGonigle, Steve, 31

McGovern, George, 159
McKool, Mike, Jr., 149
Medrano, Pancho, 124
Medrano, Ricardo, 138, 139, 164, 172, 200
Melton, Robert, 265
Mexican American Legal Defense and
    Educational Fund League of United
    Latin American Citizens (MALDEF),
    30, 139
Mexican-Americans. *See* Hispanics
Mexican Revolution (1910), 81
Mexican War (1846–1848), 74, 75
Mexico, 74–76
Michigan
    and VRA, 22–23(n51)
Miller, Jack, 251
Miller, Laura, 203, 205, 208, 209, 213,
    222, 225, 260
Miller v. *Johnson* (1995), 60–61
Mills, C. Wright, 113
Mills, Glenn, Jr., 162
Minorities
    candidates, 24, 28, 30, 59
    and elected officials influence, 54–56
    electoral influence, 52
    language, 11–12, 152
    in legislatures, 2, 3–4
    and political participation, 32, 37
    urban, 43–44
    and voting, 2, 10, 11, 16, 22, 41, 50, 63,
        155
    and VRA, 23, 56
    See also Asians; Blacks; Hispanics; Jews
Minority- and Women-owned Business
    Enterprise, 262
Minority-dominant districts, 52–53, 60, 61.
    See also under Dallas
Minority-preferred candidates, 162–163,
    164, 165
Minton, Sherman, 43
"Mirror-the-constituency" view, 274
Mississippi
    and VRA, 10(n9), 16(n29), 18
Mobile (Ala.), 58
Model City Charter, 99–100, 197, 198, 273

Molotch, Harvey, 116
Montemayor, Joe, 164
Moody, Joe, 108
Moreno, Samuel A., 255
Multimember districts, 48, 50, 59, 134
Muncy, Analeslie, 207
Mundt, Robert J., 201
Murph, D. H., 251
Murphy, Frank, 41
Murphy, Lonnie, 159, 162
Murr, L. A., 122

NAACP. *See* National Association for the
    Advancement of Colored People
Nash, John M., 209
Nash, Mattie, 162, 252, 253, 254
National Association for the Advancement
    of Colored People (NAACP), 30, 169,
    207, 214, 244
National Municipal League, 96, 197, 198,
    273
Nealy, Kathy, 167, 243
Negro Day (Dallas), 249
New Deal (1930s), 103
New Hampshire
    and VRA, 21(n46)
New Haven (Conn.), 116
New Mexico
    voter registration, 23
    and VRA, 22(n50)
New York
    and redistricting, 61
    and VRA, 21(n46)
New York Times, 73
New Orleans (La.) strong mayor
    government, 198
Nichols, Ken, 210
Nixon, Richard M., 159
Noah, Ray, 264
Norfolk (Va.), 52(n87)
Nrman, Pettis, 163
North Carolina
    districting, 53, 60
    and VRA, 18, 22–23(n23)

Oakley, Ed, 178, 193
O'Connor, Sandra Day, 38, 59, 60

O'Donnell, Peter, Jr., 103–104(n45)
Oklahoma
    and VRA, 22(n50)
Olind, Rebecca, 251
Olmsted, Frederick Law, 81
"One person, one vote," 26, 44–45, 98,
    122, 123, 124, 182
Owens, George, 107

"Packing," 144, 156
    defined, 52
Palmer, Lori, 141
Participatory democracy, 112
Patterson, Lucy, 186, 207
Peacock, Henry Bates, 84
Pelissero, John P., 220
Perot, Ross, Jr., 103, 238, 239, 240
Peterson, Paul E., 268
Peterson, William, 26
Phillips, Wendell, 19
Phoenix (Ariz.)
    Charter Government Committee, 104
    council-manager government, 198–199
Pitkin, Hanna, 278
Plunkitt, George Washington, 202
Pluralist theory, 115–116, 225
Plurality voting, 55, 91
Political parties, 42, 55–56, 63, 102, 157
Political subdivision (VRA definition),
    17–18
Politics, cooperative deliberative, 278
Politics: Who Gets What, When, How
    (Lasswell), 113
Populism, 88, 159
Poss, Mary, 215
Powell, Adam Clayton, Jr., 19
Powell, Lewis F., Jr., 134
Power elites, 113
Power structure, 113–118
PR. *See* Proportional representation
Precedent. *See* Stare decisis
Presidential elections, 103, 158–159, 160
    (fig.)
    and voter turnout, 22, 193, 195
Presley v. *Etowah County Commission*
    (1986), 31–32 (n89), 54
Price, Jesse, 121

Price, John Wiley, 206, 214, 256, 257, 258
Pricer, Glenn, 72
Progressive reform, 95, 96, 197, 201–202
Progressive Voters League (PVL),
    106–107, 122, 166
Pro-Line Corporation, 261–262
Proportional representation (PR), 28, 53,
    92–92, 93(n8), 178, 182, 185, 199,
    277
PVL. *See* Progressive Voters League
Pylon Salesmanship Club, 188

Qualitative research and analysis, 2, 4

Race and representation, 1–2, 9, 14, 21, 28,
    32, 41, 46–47, 60–61, 94, 107, 127,
    129, 138, 144, 148, 150, 151, 156,
    177–179, 182–184, 199, 256, 276
    See also Minorities, candidates; Voting
        Rights Act; Voting rights case law
Racial bloc voting, 150
Racial integration, 103
Ragsdale, Diane, 141, 188, 200, 248
    (ns59&61), 257, 259
Reagan, Ronald, 26
Reconstruction Era, 103
    civil rights laws and repeal, 13–14
Redistricting, 1, 58, 135–140
    by race, 53
    and seats-in-proportion-to-population,
        178
    See also under Dallas City Council
Reese, Margie, 265
Reese v. *Dallas County, Alabama* (1974),
    124(n24)
Regime theory. *See* Pluralist theory
Rehnquist, William H., 48, 135
Representative democracy, 112
Republican Party/Republicans. *See under*
    Dallas; Texas
"Responsiveness" standard. *See*
    Substantive representation
"Results" standard, 150, 178
Reynolds v. *Sims* (1964), 26, 44–45
Richards, Ann, 186
Richards, Floyd, 204
Rizos, Nick, 205
Robinson, Hugh G., 236

Robinson, Marvin, 148, 166
Rodgers, Woodall, 232
Rogers v. *Lodge* (1982), 58(n121)
RSR Corporation, 252
Rucker, Jerry, 141(n90), 166
Rudwick, Eliot, 14
Rush, Mark, 12
Russell, H. J. & Co., 239
Ryden, David K., 55

"Safe" districts, 52, 53, 107, 131(n60),
    138, 156, 177, 179, 184–185, 271
"Safe" seats, 3-4, 52–53, 61, 99, 177, 277
    65% rule, 53, 61
San Antonio (Texas), 104, 117–118
San Diego (Calif.), 101–102
"Save the Trinity" campaign, 243
Scalia, Antonin, 27, 61
Schoelen, Cindy, 205
Schoellkopf, John, 110
Schoop, Jack, 233
Schrader, George, 200, 217, 236, 255
Schroeder, James, 233
Schutze, Jim, 73, 260
Schwartz, Bernard, 33
Scotch, Richard, 254
Scott, William L., 29
Self-interest, enlightened, 277
Senate Judiciary Committee, 27
Senate Subcommittee on the Constitution,
    26
Separation of powers, 34
Sepulveda, Luis, 254
Shafer, George, 242
Shaw v. *Hunt* (1996), 60
Shaw v. *Reno* (1993), 59–60 (n128), 60,
    61, 174
Shivers, Allan, 103–104 (n45)
Singer, Hortense, 72
Single-member districts, 3, 5, 27, 47, 49,
    52, 55, 91, 92, 93, 1-1–102, 106, 118,
    120, 134
  in Norfolk (Va.), 52(n87)
  and VRA, 155, 269 (*see also under*
    Dallas City Council)
  See also under Dallas City Council
Sixty-five percent rule, 53, 61

Slating groups. *See under* Dallas
Sloan, Robert, 138, 148, 171
Smith, Antonio Maceo, 106
Smith, Forrest, 164
Smith v. *Allwright* (1944), 107, 156
Smothers, Clay, 192
Solon, Rita, 164
Souter, David H., 62
South Carolina
  and VRA, 18, 56
  environmental injustices study, 251
South Carolina v. *Katzenbach* (1966), 56,
    57
South Dakota
  and VRA, 22–23(n51)
South Dallas Cultural Center, 249
South Dallas/Fair Park Advisory Board,
    246
South Dallas/Fair Park Trust Fund,
    245–246
Southern Christian Leadership Conference,
    142
Southland Corporation, 236
Southwest Voter Registration Project, 23
Spain, 74
Springer, Marvin, 232
Stare decisis, 35
State and federal power, 56, 89–90
States' rights, 89–90, 276
Stevens, John Paul, 62, 135
Stewart, Jerry, 202
Stewart, Potter, 45, 135
Stimson, Bob, 242, 248
Stokes, Louis, 188
Stone, Clarence N., 116
Strauss, Annette, 140, 142, 145, 209
Substantive representation, 54–55, 150
Suk-Young Chwe, Michael, 271
Sullivan, John, 205
Supreme Court, 36–39, 40–41, 42–53,
    119, 127
  activism, 34(n3), 36
  plurality decisions, 36
  and Texas law, 42–43
  and VRA, 56–62, 134–135, 269
Swain, Carol M., 55, 247

Tammany Hall, 202
Tandy, Charles, 254
Tatum, Henry, 212
Taylor, Starke, 139, 240, 251
Taylor Publishing (Dallas), 73
Tejanos, 75
Tennessee
  voting rights, 37
Tenth Amendment. *See under* Constitution,
  U. S.
Terrell, Charles, 111, 164
Terrell Election Law (1903, 1905) (Texas),
  94
Terry v. *Adams* (1953), 42
Test or devices (VRA definition), 18(n36),
  21, 22, 24, 56–57
Texas
  and American Indians, 78–79
  Asians, 82
  ballot access, 156–157
  blacks, 75, 80, 94
  Centennial Celebration (1936), 68, 69
  Colonization Law (1824), 75
  conservatism, 89, 103
  Constitution (1876), 93, 94
  counties, 76
  Democratic Party, 42, 93, 94, 102–103
  denial of black voting and participation,
    14, 42, 50, 94
  districting, 46, 53
  and DOJ, 30–31
  and electoral process, 18(n34), 35, 50,
    94
  empresario grants (1821), 76
  European migration, 82
  "Freedman Town," 80
  as frontier state, 78,
  general law cities, 94(n14)
  government units, 76
  Hispanics, 50, 74, 76, 80
  independence (1836), 74–75
  individualism, 89
  Jews, 80
  land settlement, 76
  liberals, 103
  minority freeholder, 31

Open Meetings Act (1967), 222
  and political parties law, 157
  poll tax, 93, 94
  primaries, 42, 94, 102, 128, 156
  and racial integration, 103
  Republican Party, 103–104
  Revolution (1845), 75, 76
  slavery, 75, 81
  statehood (1845), 75, 76
  and voter registration, 23, 94
  and VRA, 19, 22–23(ns50&51), 30–31,
    74, 76
  white primaries, 94, 156
Texas Instruments (TI), 84–85
Texas Legislative Apportionment Cases
  (1972), 127
Texas Mexicans (Tejanos), 75
Thernstrom, Abigail M., 53
Thomas, Clarence, 61–62
Thometz, Carol Estes, 114, 115
Thornburg v. *Gingles* (1986), 48(n70),
  59–60, 111, 162(n10), 178
Thornton, Robert L. (Bob), 69, 71–72, 108,
  115
Thornton-Reese, Maxine, 178, 193, 209,
  265
Thruston, W. Bryan, 202
TI. *See* Texas Instruments
Tocqueville, Alexis de, 277
Tower, John G., 103
Treaty of Guadalupe-Hidalgo (1848), 75
Trigger mechanism (VRA), 18–19, 21,
  22–23(n51)
Trinity River Corridor Project, 242–243,
  247
Trinity River Development Plan (Dallas),
  70
Troy, Robert, 265
Twenty-fourth Amendment. *See under*
  Constitution, U.S.
Twenty-sixth Amendment. *See under*
  Constitution, U.S.

Unis, Tom, 112–113, 163
United Jewish Organizations v. *Carey*
  (1997), 53, 61
U.S. District Court, 3

for the District of Columbia, 1, 15, 18, 20, 135, 136, 138
Unity, 278
Utah
  voter registration, 23

Vaughan, Chandler, 249
Virginia
  and VRA, 18, 29
"Vote No," (on 10-4-1), 142
Vote/voting (VRA definition), 17
Voting dilution, 26–29, 32, 46, 47–48, 52, 58, 59, 62, 127, 128, 130, 155
  "cluster," 13
  "effects" and "intent" standards, 140, 150, 177–178
  See also Voting Rights Act, amendment (1982) *and* voting discrimination *subentries*
Voting participation, 2, 10, 52
Voting Rights Act (VRA) (1965), 1, 4, 11
  administrative enforcement, 29–31, 61
  amendment (1970), 10, 21–22, 268
  amendment (1975), 10, 22–23, 74, 76, 134, 268
  amendment (1982), 10, 23–26, 58–59, 120, 140, 155, 177, 178, 268
  case law, 56–62, 270
  critics of, 10
  effects of, 11, 15–16, 20–21, 23, 26–29, 31, 62–63, 67, 120, 135, 268, 275 (*see also* Dallas, and VRA effects on)
  and election practices changes, 29–32, 56–57
  evolution of, 12–15
  and fair representation, 5, 9, 20, 27, 34, 63, 120, 151, 178, 276
  and Fourteenth or Fifteenth Amendments, 23
  Benjamin Hooks on, 9
  individual and group political standing, 4–5, 55, 60, 62, 155, 268, 269 (*see also* Voting rights case law)
  intent to discriminate criterion, 177
  and Lyndon B. Johnson, 9
  language, 17–18
  preclearance provisions, 20–21, 26, 29,

56, 57, 76, 120, 136, 275 (*see also* Justice, Department of, preclearance rulings)
  proposed changes, 275–278
  protected groups, 158, 177, 277
  registration and voting impact, 10, 21–22, 23, 27(n70)
  section 2, 16–18, 20, 20(n43), 23, 24, 26, 28, 57–59, 60, 61, 140, 144, 158, 176, 177, 178
  section 4, 16, 18–19, 20, 23
  section 4b, 16(n27)
  section 5 (temporal and preclearance provisions), 1, 3, 16, 20–21, 22, 23, 54, 56–57, 60, 76, 120, 121, 134, 137, 139, 174, 275, 276
  and three-judge district courts, 136(n73)
  uniform standards, 22, 32
  and voting discrimination, 24, 26–29, 32, 58, 133, 155 (*see also* Voting dilution; Amendment (1982) *subentry*)
  See also Voting rights case law; *under* Dallas; Texas
Voting rights case law, 33–63, 269
  and apportionment and districting, 38, 39–41, 43–47, 53, 60 (n132)
  and Constitution, 33–39, 40
  political question doctrine, 38–39
  representation equity phase, 46–56
  right to an effective voice phase, 54–56
  right to vote phase, 41–43
  vote equality phase, 43–47
  and VRA, 33, 38, 54, 56–62
  See also Dallas, cases
VRA. *See* Voting Rights Act

Walne, Alan, 260
Ware, John, 162(n9), 208, 211, 214, 216, 218, 229, 238, 239, 240–241, 245, 256
Warren, Earl, 45, 56, 57
Washington, Booker T., 14, 19
Weber, Gary, 106, 168, 178
Weber, Max, 185
Welch, Susan, 179–180
Wells, Max, 201, 220

"We Love Dallas" campaign, 243
Wesbury v. *Saunders* (1964), 13, 41
West Dallas Coalition for Environmental Justice, 254
Whitcomb v. *Chavis* (1971), 49, 51, 127
White, Byron R., 38, 59, 60
White, Mabel, 162
White v. *Regester* (1973), 23, 49–50, 51, 52, 58
Whose Votes Count? Affirmative Action and Minority Voting Rights (Thernstrom), 53
Williams, Roy, 140, 141, 142, 143, 164, 165
Williams v. *City of Dallas* (1990), 142–144, 146–148, 150, 166–167, 172 (n32), 196
Wilson, James Q., 100

Wisdom, John Minor, 127
Wise, Wes, 108, 110, 139, 158, 159, 160 (fig.), 168, 186, 200, 219
Woodford, Suzie, 208
WPA Dallas Guide and History (Federal Writer's Project), 117
Wright, S. M., 164
Wright v. *Rockefeller* (1964), 41, 45
Wynne, Buck, 253–254
Wyoming
    and VRA, 21 (n46)

Young, Iris Marion, 55
Yut, Scott, 59

Zeder, Fred, 106
Zimmer v. *McKeithen* (1973), 51, 52, 58
Zoning, cumulative, 234